LECTURES
INTRODUCTORY TO THE
THEORY OF FUNCTIONS
OF TWO
COMPLEX VARIABLES

CAMBRIDGE UNIVERSITY PRESS
C. F. CLAY, Manager
London: FETTER LANE, E.C.
Edinburgh: 100, PRINCES STREET

Berlin: A. ASHER AND CO.
Leipzig: F. A. BROCKHAUS
New York: G. P. PUTNAM'S SONS
Bombay and Calcutta: MACMILLAN AND CO., Ltd.
Toronto: J. M. DENT AND SONS, Ltd.
Tokyo: THE MARUZEN-KABUSHIKI-KAISHA

All rights reserved

LECTURES

INTRODUCTORY TO THE

THEORY OF FUNCTIONS

OF TWO

COMPLEX VARIABLES

DELIVERED TO THE UNIVERSITY OF CALCUTTA
DURING JANUARY AND FEBRUARY 1913

BY

A. R. FORSYTH,

Sc.D., LL.D., Math.D., F.R.S.
CHIEF PROFESSOR OF MATHEMATICS IN THE
IMPERIAL COLLEGE OF SCIENCE AND TECHNOLOGY, LONDON

Cambridge:
at the University Press
1914

Cambridge:
PRINTED BY JOHN CLAY, M.A.
AT THE UNIVERSITY PRESS.

PREFACE

THE present volume consists substantially of a course of lectures which, by special invitation of the authorities, I delivered in the University of Calcutta during parts of January and February, 1913. The invitation was accompanied by a stipulation that the lectures should be published.

As regards choice of subject for the course, I was allowed complete freedom. It was intimated that the class would be mainly or entirely of a post-graduate standing. What was desired, above all, was an exposition of some subject that, later on, might suggest openings to those who had the will and the skill to pursue research.

Accordingly I selected a subject, which may be regarded as being still in not very advanced stages of development, and into the exposition of which I could incorporate some results of my own which had been in my possession for some time. Owing to the limitations of the period over which the course should extend, it was not practicable to make the lectures a systematic discussion of the whole subject; and I therefore had to choose portions, in order to discuss a variety of topics and to indicate some paths along which further progress might be possible. Thus, instead of concentrating upon one particular issue, I preferred to deal with several distinct lines of investigation, even though their treatment had to be relatively brief.

Wherever it was possible to refer to books or to memoirs, I duly referred my students to the authorities. In particular, I urged them to prepare themselves so that they could proceed to the study of algebraic functions of two variables; because happily, in that region, there is the treatise by Picard and Simart, *Fonctions algébriques de deux variables indépendantes*, which includes an account of the researches made by Picard and others in the last thirty years. As this treatise is so full, I made no attempt to give to my students what could only have been a truncated account of the elements of that theory; but, as will be seen, what I did was to restate some of its problems from a different (and, as I think, a more general) point of view.

At several stages in my lectures, I deviated from the almost usual practice of dealing with only a single uniform function of two complex variables. I thought it preferable to deal with two dependent variables as functions of two independent variables. Characteristic properties of the variation of uniform analytic functions of two variables are brought into fuller discussion, when two such functions are regarded simultaneously. The combination of at least two such functions is necessary when the general theory of quadruply-periodic functions is under review. The same combination of two functions seems to me desirable in the general discussion of the theory of algebraic functions of two variables whether these occur, or do not occur, in connection with quadruply-periodic functions; the consideration of relations between independent variables and dependent variables is thereby made more complete, and illustrations will be found in the course of the book. Even in the simplest case that has any significance, when these algebraic relations are nothing more than the expression of the lineo-linear substitutions, it is of course necessary to have two new variables expressible in terms of the variables already adopted.

PREFACE vii

The following is a summary outline of the whole course of lectures.

The first Chapter deals with the various suggestions that have been made for the geometrical representation of two complex variables. The intuitive usefulness of the Argand representation, when we are concerned with functions of a single independent complex variable, is universally recognised; but there seems to be a deficiency in the usefulness of each of the geometrical representations when more than a single independent complex variable occurs.

The second Chapter is devoted to the consideration of the analytical properties of the lineo-linear substitution, defining two variables in terms of two others, each uniquely by means of the others. It is a generalisation of the homographic substitution for a single variable; some of the properties of the latter are extended to the case when there are two variables. In particular, insistence is laid upon certain invariantive properties of such substitutions.

The third Chapter is concerned with the expressibility of uniform analytic functions in power-series. The limitation of the range of convergence of such series leads to the notion of the various kinds of singularity which, under the classification made by Weierstrass, uniform analytic functions can possess.

The fourth Chapter is devoted to the consideration of the form of a uniform analytic function in the immediate vicinity of any assigned place in the field of variation. The central theorem is due to Weierstrass, and was established by him for functions of n variables; I have developed it in some detail when there are only two variables; and it is applied to the description of the behaviour of a function in the vicinity of any one of its various classes of places, whether ordinary or singular.

The fifth Chapter is occupied with two constructive theorems, both of them originally enunciated (without proof) by Weierstrass, as to the character of functions either entirely devoid or almost devoid of essential singularities. A function, entirely devoid of essential singularities, is expressible as a rational function of the variables; the proof given is a modification of the proof first given by Hurwitz. A function, which has essential singularities only in the infinite parts of the field of variation, is expressible as the quotient of two functions which are regular in all finite parts of the field; the proof, which is given, follows Cousin's investigations for the general case of n variables.

The next Chapter is devoted to integrals. The earlier paragraphs are concerned with double integrals of quantities which are uniform functions of two variables; after an exposition of Poincaré's extension of Cauchy's main integral theorem, these paragraphs are mainly occupied with simple examples of a subject which awaits further development. The later paragraphs are concerned with integrals, whether single or double, of algebraic functions, a theory to which Picard's investigations have made substantial contributions. In restating the problems for the sake of students, I took the line of introducing a couple of algebraic functions, instead of only a single algebraic function, of two variables, so that there may be complete liberty of selection of two independent variables. The geometry of surfaces has led to valuable results connected with integrals of algebraic functions of two variables, just as the geometry of curves led to valuable results connected with integrals of algebraic functions of one variable. But my own view is that the development of the theory, however much it has been helped by the geometry, must (under present methods) ultimately be made to depend completely upon analysis. This will be more complicated when two algebraic equations are propounded than when there is only a single equation; but its character will be unaltered. And so I have stated the problem for what seems to me the more general case.

In Chapter VII I have discussed the behaviour of two uniform analytic functions considered simultaneously. In particular, when the functions are independent and free (in the sense that they have no common factor), it is shewn that their level places are isolated; and the investigations in Chapter IV are used to obtain an expression for the multiplicity of occurrence of such a level place, when it is not simple.

The last Chapter is devoted to the foundations of the theory of uniform periodic functions of two variables. In the early part of the chapter, I have worked out the various kinds of cases that can occur. The method may be deemed tedious; it certainly could not be used for the functions of n variables with not more than $2n$ sets of periods; but it brings into relief the discrimination between the cases which, stated initially only from the point of view of periodicity, are degenerate or resoluble or impossible or actual. The theta-functions are then introduced on the basis of a result in Chapter V; and the discrimination between functions with three period-pairs and those with four period-pairs is indicated. Later, some theorems enunciated (but not proved) by Weierstrass are established for functions of two variables, together with some extensions, all these being concerned with algebraic relations between homoperiodic uniform functions devoid of essential singularities in the finite part of the field of variation. The Chapter concludes with some simple examples belonging to the simplest class of hyperelliptic functions. But I have not attempted, in these lectures, to expound the details of the theory of quadruply-periodic functions of two variables; it can be found in specific treatises to which references are given in the text.

My whole purpose, in the Calcutta course, was to deal with a selection of principles and of generalities that belong to the initial stages of the theory of functions of two complex variables.

Often before, I have had to thank the Staff of the Cambridge University Press for their efficient help during the progress of proof-sheets of my books. This volume has made special demands upon their patience; throughout, as is their custom within my experience, they have met my wishes with readiness and skill. To all of them, once again, I tender my grateful thanks.

A. R. FORSYTH.

IMPERIAL COLLEGE OF SCIENCE
AND TECHNOLOGY, LONDON, S.W.
February, 1914.

TABLE OF CONTENTS

CHAPTER I.

GEOMETRICAL REPRESENTATION OF THE VARIABLES.

§§		PAGE
1.	General introductory remarks	1
2.	Functions of two variables; reason for occasionally considering two such functions, independent of one another	2
3, 4.	Geometrical representation of the variables; three methods . .	4
5.	Representation in four-dimensional space	5
6.	Representation by lines in ordinary space	7
7–9.	Limitations upon the use of the line	7
10–13.	Other methods of using lines in space for the geometrical representation	12
14.	Representation by points in two planes, or by two independent points in the same plane	13
15.	Inferences from the two-plane representation of the variables . .	14
16.	Extension of Riemann's definition of a function of a single variable to functions of two variables	16
17.	Extension of the property of conformal representation, when there are two independent variables	18
18.	But it belongs to any place in the field, and does not extend to loci or to areas	19
19, 20.	Analytical expression of frontiers of a doubly infinite region in the field, with examples	20

CHAPTER II.

LINEO-LINEAR TRANSFORMATIONS; INVARIANTS AND COVARIANTS.

21.	Lineo-linear transformations in two variables	25
22, 23.	Canonical form of the transformation, in the alternatives from the characteristic equation, with expressions for its powers . .	26
24.	Invariant-centres of transformations	29
25.	Curves conserved, in character, under homographic substitutions in one variable	32
26.	Frontiers conserved, in character, under lineo-linear transformations in two variables	32
27.	Simplest conserved equations: quadratic frontiers	34

CONTENTS

§§		PAGE
28.	When the axes of real quantities are conserved	35
29.	Another method of constructing the equations of some conserved frontiers	35
30.	Invariants and covariants of quadratic frontiers	39
31.	Introduction of homogeneous variables and umbral forms; use of Lie's theory of continuous groups	39
32.	Simple examples of invariants and covariants	41
33.	The infinitesimal transformations	42
34.	The partial differential equations of the first order characteristic of the infinitesimal transformations	44
35.	Number of algebraically independent integrals	46
36, 37.	Method of determining the integrals, in general	46
38.	Determination of the four invariants	48
39.	Contragredient variables	49
40.	Suggested canonical form of equations for a quadratic frontier	50
41.	Periodic lineo-linear transformations	52
42.	Equation for the multipliers; conditions for periodicity; with examples	52

CHAPTER III.

UNIFORM ANALYTIC FUNCTIONS.

43.	Preliminary definitions; *field, domain, vicinity,* for the variables	57
44.	*Uniform, multiform,* for functions, with an example	58
45.	*Continuous, analytic, regular, integral, transcendental, algebraic, meromorphic,* for functions	59
46.	Property of function establishing its regularity	61
47, 48.	Upper limits for the moduli of derivatives of a regular function; some double integrals	64
49.	A theorem expressing, by means of a double integral, any number of terms in the expansion of a regular function	67
50.	Dominant functions, associated with a regular function	70
51.	Absolute convergence of a double power-series	72
52.	A regular function must acquire infinite values somewhere in the whole z, z' field; identity of two regular functions under a condition; when the regular function reduces to a polynomial	72
53.	A regular function must acquire a zero value somewhere in the whole z, z' field	75
54.	The investigations of Picard, Borel, and others, in regard to the same property for a regular function of one variable	77
55.	Extension of Picard's theorem concerning functions of one variable	78
56.	Weierstrass's process of analytical continuation of a function; the region of continuity	79
57.	*Singularities, unessential, essential,* of uniform functions	82
58.	Two kinds of unessential singularity for a uniform function of two variables; discriminated, in name, by *pole* and (the other type of) *unessential singularity*	84
59.	Extension, to functions of two variables, of Laurent's theorem for functions of one variable	86

CHAPTER IV.

UNIFORM FUNCTIONS IN RESTRICTED DOMAINS.

§§		PAGE
60.	Expression of a regular function $f(z, z') - f(0, 0)$ in the immediate vicinity of 0, 0, the function $f(z, z')$ being regular	92
61–63.	Weierstrass's theorem for the case when $f(z, 0) - f(0, 0)$ is not an identical zero; likewise for the case when $f(0, z') - f(0, 0)$ is not an identical zero, together with a corollary from the theorem as to an expression for $f(z, z') \div f(0, 0)$ in these cases	93
64.	New expression (distinct from Weierstrass's expression) for $f(z, z') - f(0, 0)$ when either $f(z, 0) - f(0, 0)$, or $f(0, z') - f(0, 0)$, or both expressions, may be an identical zero, with summary of results, and a general example	98
65.	Weierstrass's method of proceeding, adapted to two variables, for the cases of § 64, with examples	105
66, 67.	On the *level* values of functions in the immediate vicinity of the value $f(0, 0)$ at 0, 0, with examples	108
68.	The *order* of the zero-value of $f(z, z') - f(a, a')$	111
69.	*Divisibility* of one function by another	112
70.	Analytical tests of divisibility, when both $f(0, 0)$ and $g(0, 0)$ are zero	113
71.	Analytical tests that the two functions $f(z, z')$ and $g(z, z')$ in the latter case should possess a common factor $h(z, z')$ such that $h(0, 0)$ is zero; reducibility of functions	115
72.	Expression of a uniform function in the immediate vicinity of a pole; it has an infinitude of poles near a pole	119
73.	Expression of a uniform function near an unessential singularity; when the expression is irreducible, the unessential singularity is isolated .	121
74.	Expression of a uniform function near an essential singularity; references to authorities	122

CHAPTER V.

FUNCTIONS WITHOUT ESSENTIAL SINGULARITIES IN THE FINITE PART OF THE FIELD OF VARIATION.

75.	Two theorems on the expression of a uniform function of two variables .	124
76.	Properties of a polynomial function of z and z' as regards singularities .	124
77.	Properties of a rational function of z and z' as regards singularities . .	125
78.	Proof (based on Hurwitz's proof) of Weierstrass's theorem that a uniform function, which has no essential singularity anywhere in the whole field of variation, is rational	125
79.	A possible expression for a function which has no essential singularity in an assigned finite part of the field	129
80.	Weierstrass's theorem (as adumbrated) on functions having essential singularities only in the infinite part of the field	130

§§		PAGE
81.	Cousin's proof of the theorem; his preliminary lemmas	131
82.	Division of a domain into regions with which functions are associated; functions *equivalent* in a region or at a point	133
83, 84.	Construction of a function $F(z, z')$, equivalent to the assigned functions associated with each region	135
85.	Cousin's extended theorem, so as to lead to an ultimate product-theorem	138
86.	The general theorem as to the expression of a function of two variables having no essential singularities in the finite part of the field	141
87–90.	Establishment of the theorem that such a function is expressible as the quotient of two regular functions	143
91, 92.	Appell's sum-theorem, with an example	147
93.	Example of a product-theorem for a special class of functions	150

CHAPTER VI.

INTEGRALS; IN PARTICULAR, DOUBLE INTEGRALS.

94.	Two kinds of double integrals; the class arising from repeated simple integration	152
95.	Definition of a double integral with complex variables	153
96.	Theorem on double integrals with real variables	156
97–99.	Application to the double integral $\iint f(z, z')\,dz\,dz'$, taken through a limited four-dimensional space, when $f(z, z')$ is regular; Poincaré's extension of Cauchy's Theorem	158
100.	Several examples of double integrals when $f(z, z')$ is not regular within the region, deduced by means of the inferences in §§ 97–99	161
101.	Some remarks on algebraic functions of two variables; the most general form of function	170
102.	Similarly as to the form of the most general function involving two algebraic functions	172
103.	Single integrals of algebraic functions; preliminary condition if they are to have no infinities	178
104, 105.	Equivalent forms of a single integral	180
106, 107.	For two quite general algebraic equations in two dependent variables, integrals of the first kind do not exist	185
108.	Double integrals, in equivalent forms	187
109, 110.	Some conditions that a double integral should be of the first kind	190
111.	Partial extension of Abel's theorem	193

CHAPTER VII.

LEVEL PLACES OF TWO SIMULTANEOUS FUNCTIONS.

112.	Theorem as to the possession, somewhere in the whole field of variation, of common zeros by two functions which are regular for finite values	198
113.	Lemma as to the march of the gradual diminution of $|f(z, z')|$ and $|g(z, z')|$	199

CONTENTS

§§		PAGE
114.	Application of the lemma to establish the theorem enunciated in § 112	202
115.	Extension of the theorem to a couple of functions devoid of essential singularities in the finite part of the plane	203
116.	Order of the common zero, when isolated: the condition for isolation	204
117.	A common zero may happen not to be isolated; conditions	205
118.	Summary of results as to the possession of common zeros	206
119.	But the two functions must be *independent*, and must be *free*, if the common zero is isolated	208
120.	Determination of the order of a common isolated zero	209
121, 122.	Common level-places of two functions, independent and free	210

CHAPTER VIII.

UNIFORM PERIODIC FUNCTIONS.

123.	Definition of periodicity, and periods	213
124.	Why infinitesimal periods for functions of two variables are excluded from consideration; Weierstrass's theorem	213
125.	A uniform analytic function cannot possess more than four pairs of linearly independent periods	216
126.	Preliminary lemma	217
127–130.	Jacobi's theorem: one pair of periods: two pairs of periods	222
131–133.	Three pairs of periods: canonical form of period-tableau	226
134.	Complete field of variation for variables of triply periodic functions	231
135–137.	Four pairs of periods	232
138.	Representation of variation for variables of quadruply periodic functions	236
139.	Uniform triply periodic functions: a general expression	238
140.	Triple theta-functions	240
141, 142.	Law of coefficients in a double Fourier-series, in order that it may be a triple theta-function	241
143.	Periodicity of double Fourier-series in general	243
144.	Special forms of coefficients leading to special functions	244
145.	Remark on the addition-theorem for theta-functions	246
146.	The sixteen triple theta-functions	246
147, 148.	Limitation on coefficients so as to secure oddness or evenness	248
149.	Interchange of triple theta-functions for half-period increments of the variables, (i) in general, (ii) when each of the functions is either even or odd, (iii) when the coefficients are specialised so as to give double theta-functions	250
150.	Table of the interchanges in § 149	253
151.	Some selected zero places of the theta-functions	253
152–154.	Two uniform quadruply periodic functions considered simultaneously: their common irreducible level places are isolated and are finite in number, when there are no essential singularities for finite values of the variables	255

CONTENTS

§§		PAGE
155.	The number of irreducible level places of two uniform quadruply periodic functions is independent of the level values: *grade* of two functions	259
156.	Algebraic relations between three uniform quadruply periodic functions, having the same periods	260
157.	Any uniform quadruply periodic function satisfies a partial differential equation of the first order	262
158.	Expressibility of a quadruply periodic function, (i) in terms of three given homoperiodic functions; (ii) in terms of a homoperiodic function and its first derivatives	262
159.	Algebraic equation between two homoperiodic functions and their Jacobian	264
160.	Expressibility of a quadruply periodic function in terms of two homoperiodic functions and their Jacobian	265
161, 162.	The double theta-functions, and the hyperelliptic functions of order two	266
163–166.	Illustrations of the theorems of §§ 156–160	271
	INDEX	278

CHAPTER I

GEOMETRICAL REPRESENTATION OF THE VARIABLES

In regard to functions of a single complex variable, reference may generally be made, for statements of results and for quoted theorems, to the author's *Theory of Functions*. No reference is made to the ultimate foundations of the theory of functions of a single real variable; a full discussion will be found in Hobson's *Functions of a real variable*.

For a large part of the contents of the first two chapters, reference may be made to two papers by the author[*]; and particular references to memoirs will be made from time to time as they are quoted.

But in addition, reference should be made to a paper[†] by Poincaré, who discusses groups, classes of invariants, and conformation of space, when the representation of the two complex variables is made by means of four-dimensional space.

1. This course of lectures is devoted to the theory of functions of two or more complex variables. It will be assumed that the substantial results of the theory of functions of a single complex variable are known; so that references to such results may be made briefly or even only indirectly, and suggestions, especially in regard to the extensions of ideas furnished by that theory, can be discussed in their wider aspect without any delay over preliminary explanations.

My intention is to deal with some of the principles and the generalities of the selected subject. Special illustrations and developments will be given from time to time; but limitations forbid the possibility of attempting an exposition of the whole range of knowledge already attained. Moreover, my hope is to establish some new results, and suggest some problems; in order to make that hope a reality within this course, some developments must be sacrificed. The sacrifice, however, need only be temporary, in one sense; because references to the important authorities will be given, and their work can be consulted and studied in amplification of these lectures.

[*] "Simultaneous complex variables and their geometrical representation," *Messenger of Math.*, vol. xl (1910), pp. 113—134; "Lineo-linear transformations of two complex variables," *Quart. Journ. Math.*, vol. xliii (1912), pp. 178—207.

[†] "Les fonctions analytiques de deux variables et la représentation conforme," *Rend. Circ. Mat. Palermo*, t. xxiii (1907), pp. 185—220.

Usually, it will be assumed that the number of independent variables is two. In making this restriction, a double purpose is proposed.

Not a few of the propositions for two variables, with appropriate changes, can justly be enunciated for n variables; and sometimes they will be enunciated explicitly. In such cases, they usually are true for functions of a single variable also; and they become generalisations of the last-mentioned and simplest form of the corresponding proposition. Results of this type have their importance in the body of the theory. But it is desirable to have other results also, which may be called characteristic of the theory for more than a single variable, in the sense that they have no corresponding counterpart in the theory for a single variable.

Again, it is desirable, wherever possible, to obtain results equally characteristic of the theory in another direction, that is to say, results which are not mere specialisations of results for the case of three or more variables. Such a result is provided in the case of the quadruply-periodic functions of two variables and their association with single integrals involving the quadratic radical of a quintic or sextic polynomial. The case might be taken as the appropriate specialisation of $2n$-ply periodic functions of n variables and their proper association with single integrals involving the quadratic radical of a polynomial of order $2n+1$ or $2n+2$. These latter functions, however, are notoriously not the most general multiply-periodic functions for values of n from 3, inclusive and upwards. Consequently, it is sufficient to develop the association with quadratic radicals of a quintic or sextic polynomial; the formal generalisations of the results so obtained are only limited and restricted forms of the results belonging to the wider, but not most completely general, theory.

These combined considerations constitute my reason for dealing mainly with the theory of functions of two independent complex variables.

The two variables will be denoted by z and z'.

2. One illustration of real generalisation from the theory of functions of a single variable arises as follows. In that theory, when a variable w is connected with a variable z by a relation $f(w, z) = 0$ of any form, we frequently consider that w is defined as a function of z by the relation. But frequently also there is a necessity for regarding z as a function of w; and important results, especially in connection with periodic functions, are obtained by using this dual notion of inversion. A question naturally suggests itself:—what is the general form of this notion of inversion when there are two independent variables?

A function w of z and z' can be regarded as given by a relation $f(w, z, z') = 0$, any precision as to the form of f being irrelevant to the immediate discussion. A limited use of the notion of inversion can be applied at once to the relation. Just as in the Cartesian equation of a surface in ordinary space it is often a matter of indifference which of the three coordinates is to be regarded as expressed by the equation in terms of the other two, so now we may regard the relation $f(w, z, z') = 0$ as defining any one of the three variables w, z, z' in terms of the other two. Such an interpretation of the relation does not imply the complete process of inversion in the simpler case, whereby the quantity initially regarded as independent is expressed in terms of the quantity initially regarded as dependent. In the present case, the initially independent variables z and z' are not expressible in terms of the single initially dependent variable w.

The limitation in the use of the notion, however, disappears when two functionally distinct quantities w and w' occur. This occurrence might arise through the existence of two functional relations
$$f(w, z, z') = 0, \quad g(w', z, z') = 0,$$
or of two apparently more general functional relations
$$F(w, w', z, z') = 0, \quad G(w, w', z, z') = 0.$$
We assume that the equations $F = 0$, $G = 0$, do actually define distinct functions w and w' in the sense that they are independent equations; that is, we assume that their Jacobian
$$J\left(\frac{F, G}{w, w'}\right)$$
does not vanish identically. Moreover, for our purpose, w and w' are not merely to be distinct from one another; they are to be independent functions of z and z', so that the Jacobian
$$J\left(\frac{w, w'}{z, z'}\right)$$
does not vanish identically. Now
$$J\left(\frac{w, w'}{z, z'}\right) J\left(\frac{z, z'}{w, w'}\right) = 1,$$
$$J\left(\frac{F, G}{w, w'}\right) J\left(\frac{w, w'}{z, z'}\right) = J\left(\frac{F, G}{z, z'}\right),$$
always; hence neither of the Jacobians
$$J\left(\frac{z, z'}{w, w'}\right), \quad J\left(\frac{F, G}{z, z'}\right)$$
can vanish identically. In other words, we can interpret the two relations $F = 0$ and $G = 0$ in a new way; they define z and z' as two distinct and independent functions of the two independent variables w and w'.

Ex. Thus the equations
$$w^2 + w'^2 + z^2 + z'^2 = a, \quad w^3 - w'^3 + z^3 - z'^3 = b,$$
satisfy both conditions; the quantities w and w' are independent functions of z and z'. And conversely for z and z' as independent functions of w and w'.

On the other hand, the equations
$$ww' - z - z' = 0, \quad w^2 - w' - 1 = 0,$$
being independent equations, determine w and w' as distinct functions of the variables, for $J\left(\dfrac{F,\ G}{w,\ w'}\right)$ does not vanish identically. But these distinct functions are not independent functions of z and z', for $J\left(\dfrac{w,\ w'}{z,\ z'}\right)$ vanishes identically. As a matter of fact, both w and w' are functions solely of the combination $z + z'$ of the variables, and therefore w and w' are expressible in terms of each other alone; the actual relation of expression is the second of the two equations.

Thus, by the introduction of a second and independent function w', we are in a position to adopt completely the notion of inversion, as distinct from any precise expression of inversion, for the case of two complex independent variables[*]. The inversion will be equally possible from any two relations, which are the exact and complete equivalent of $F = 0$ and $G = 0$ in whatever form these relations may be given. In particular, if F and G are algebraical in w and w', they have an exact equivalent in relations of the type $f = 0$ and $g = 0$, obtained by eliminating w' and w in turn between $F = 0$ and $G = 0$.

Finally, we could regard any two of the four variables z, z', w, w' as independent and the remaining two as dependent. The necessary and sufficient condition is that no Jacobian of F and G with regard to any two of the variables shall vanish identically.

Accordingly, for many purposes, we shall find it desirable to consider simultaneously two independent functions w and w' of the two independent variables z and z'.

Geometrical Representation of the Variables.

3. Next, it proves both convenient and useful in the theory of functions of one variable to associate a geometrical representation of the variables with the analysis. It happens that this representation is simple and complete while full of intuitive suggestions; and though[†] the notion of geometrical interpretation has not been adopted by all investigators and has occasionally been deliberately avoided by the sterner analytical schools, it has acquired importance because of the character of the results to which it has led. The representation, initiated by Argand, is obtained by the customary association of a point upon a plane with one variable, and of a point upon

---

[*] When there are n independent variables $z_1, \ldots, z_n$, then n functions $w_1, \ldots, w_n$ are required for the corresponding complete use of inversion.

[†] There is a wide diversity of practice, in regard to the extent of the adoption of geometrical notions in the development of the analysis of the theory of functions. As an indication of this variety, it is sufficient to note the different relations to the subject as borne in the work of Cauchy, Hermite, Kronecker, Poincaré, Riemann, and Weierstrass.

another plane with the other variable; and the functional relation between the two variables is exhibited as a conformal representation of either plane upon the other.

An adequate geometrical representation of two independent complex variables is a more difficult problem than the representation of a single complex variable; at any rate, there is as yet no unique solution of the problem which has been found quite so satisfactory as the Argand solution of the problem for a single variable.

In order to let the full variation appear, we resolve each of the complex variables into its real and its imaginary parts; so we write
$$z = x + iy, \quad z' = x' + iy'.$$
Here x, y, x', y' are real; when z and z' are independent in every respect, each of these four real quantities admits of independent variation through the range of reality between $-\infty$ and $+\infty$. Thus a four-fold set of variations is required for the purpose; and such a set cannot be secured simply among the facilities offered by the ordinary space of experience.

4. Several methods have been proposed. No method has been adopted universally. The respective measures of success are attained through some greater or smaller amount of elaboration; but each increase of elaboration causes a decrease of simplicity, and therefore also a decrease of intuitive suggestiveness, in the geometrical representation.

Among the methods, there are three which require special mention. In one of them, four-dimensional space is chosen as the field of variation. In the second, a line (straight or curved) is taken as the geometrical entity representing the two variables simultaneously. In the third, each of the variables is represented by a point in a plane (the planes being the same or different), so that two points are taken as the geometrical entity representing the two variables simultaneously.

5. Of these methods, the simplest (in a formal analytical bearing) is based upon the use of four-dimensional space; and applications to the theory of functions of two complex variables have been made by Poincaré[*], Picard[†], and others. The four real variables x, y, x', y' are associated with four axes of reference. Sometimes they are taken as the ultimate variables; sometimes they are made real functions of other ultimate real variables, from one to three in number according to the dimensions of the continuum

---

[*] "Sur les fonctions de deux variables," *Acta Math.*, t. ii (1883), pp. 97—113; "Sur les résidus des intégrales doubles," *Acta Math.*, t. ix (1887), pp. 321—380; "Analysis situs," *Journ. de l'École Polyt.*, Sér. 2, t. i (1895), pp. 1—123; "Analysis situs," *Rend. Circ. Mat. Palermo*, t. xiii (1899), pp. 285—345, t. xviii (1904), pp. 45—110, and elsewhere.

[†] *Traité d'Analyse*, t. ii, ch. ix; *Théorie des fonctions algébriques de deux variables indépendantes*, t. i, ch. ii, in the course of which other references are given.

to be represented. Thus a single relation between x, y, x', y' provides a hypersurface (or an ordinary space) in the quadruple space; and, along the hypersurface, each of the four variables can be conceived as expressible in terms of three variable parameters. Two such relations provide a surface in the quadruple space; along the surface, each of the variables can be conceived as expressible in terms of two variable parameters. Similarly, three such relations provide a curve along which each of the variables can be conceived as expressible in terms of a single variable parameter. Lastly, four such relations provide a point or a number of points. The intersection of a hypersurface and a surface is made up of a curve or a number of curves. Two surfaces intersect in points; two hypersurfaces intersect in a surface or surfaces. We consider only real surfaces, curves, and points, in such intersections; because what is desired is a representation of the four real variables, from which the complex variables are composed.

The representation, by itself, does not seem sufficiently definite and restricted. There is no preferential combination in geometry among the four coordinate axes, which compels a combination of x and y for one of the complex variables, while x' and y' must be combined for the other. But this original lack of restriction is supplied, so far as concerns functions of z and z', by retaining the partial differential equations of the first order, which are satisfied by the real and the imaginary parts of any function w. Writing $w = u + iv = f(z, z')$, where u and v are real, we have

$$\frac{\partial u}{\partial x} = \frac{\partial v}{\partial y}, \quad \frac{\partial u}{\partial y} = -\frac{\partial v}{\partial x}, \quad \frac{\partial u}{\partial x'} = \frac{\partial v}{\partial y'}, \quad \frac{\partial u}{\partial y'} = -\frac{\partial v}{\partial x'},$$

so that u satisfies (as does v also) the equations

$$\frac{\partial^2 u}{\partial x^2} + \frac{\partial^2 u}{\partial y^2} = 0, \quad \frac{\partial^2 u}{\partial x \partial x'} + \frac{\partial^2 u}{\partial y \partial y'} = 0, \quad \frac{\partial^2 u}{\partial x'^2} + \frac{\partial^2 u}{\partial y'^2} = 0,$$

$$\frac{\partial^2 u}{\partial x \partial y'} - \frac{\partial^2 u}{\partial y \partial x'} = 0.$$

From a value of u, satisfying these equations, the value of v to be associated with it in the value of w can be obtained by quadratures. Thus we have a geometry, tempered implicitly by differential equations.

The comparative difficulty of dealing with the ideas of four-dimensional geometry tends to prevent this mode of representation from being intuitively useful, at least to those minds who regard the stated results to be analytical relations merely disguised in a geometrical vocabulary. In particular, the method fails to provide (as the other methods equally fail to provide) a representation of quadruple periodicity which serves the same kind of purpose as is served by the plane representation of double periodicity; and *a fortiori* there is an even graver lack, when divisions of multiple space are required in connection with functions of two variables that are automorphic under lineo-linear transformations. Still, it is the fact that certain results have been obtained through the use of this method in the extension of one of Cauchy's integral-theorems, in the formation of the residues of double integrals, in the topology of multiple space, and in the conformation of spaces.

6. The second of the indicated methods of representation of the four variable elements in two complex variables is based upon the fact that four independent coordinates are necessary and sufficient for the complete specification of a straight line in ordinary space. Such a line would be determined uniquely by the two points (and, reciprocally, would uniquely determine the two points) at which it meets a couple of parallel planes; and therefore, if one variable z is represented by a variable point in one plane and the other variable z' is represented by a variable point in the other plane, we might regard the line joining the points z and z' in the respective planes as a geometrical representation of the two variables z and z' conjointly. (It can also be determined by a point, and a direction through the point; again, the determination requires four real variables in all.)

We must, however, bear in mind that the two points on the line are the ultimate representation of the two variables. When the whole line* (with the assistance of the two invariable parallel planes of reference) is taken to represent the two variables, a question at once arises as to the geometrical relations between a line z, z' and a line w, w', which correspond to two analytical relations between the variables. Does the whole line z, z', under any transforming relation, become the whole line w, w'?

7. It is only a *specially restricted set of transforming relations, which admit such a transformation of a whole line.* The result can be established as follows.

For simplicity, we assume that the planes for z and z' are at unit distance apart, and likewise that the planes for w and w' are at unit distance apart; and we write
$$w = u + iv, \quad w' = u' + iv'.$$
The Cartesian coordinates of any point on the z, z' line are
$$\sigma x + (1 - \sigma) x', \quad \sigma y + (1 - \sigma) y', \quad 1 - \sigma,$$
and those of any point on the w, w' line are
$$\rho u + (1 - \rho) u', \quad \rho v + (1 - \rho) v', \quad 1 - \rho,$$
where ρ and σ are real quantities, each parametric along its line. Let two relations
$$F(w, w', z, z') = 0, \quad G(w, w', z, z') = 0,$$
be such as to give a birational correspondence between w, w' and z, z'. If,

---

* For the following investigation reference may be made to the first of the author's two papers quoted on p. 1.

then, in connection with these relations, the whole z, z' line is transformed uniquely into the whole w, w' line, and vice-versa, some birational correspondence between the current points upon the lines must exist; and so the coordinates of the current point upon one line must be connected, by functional relations, with the coordinates of the current point upon the other line.

Because of the independent equations $F = 0$, $G = 0$, the quantities u, v, u', v' are functions of x, y, x', y' alone; and these functions do not involve σ. Similarly x, y, x', y' are functions of u, v, u', v' alone; and these functions do not involve ρ. Hence ρ is a function of σ only, such as to take the values 0 and 1 (in either order) when σ has the values 0 and 1; and, for the current points, we must have

$$\rho u + (1 - \rho) u' = f(\xi, \eta, 1 - \sigma),$$
$$\rho v + (1 - \rho) v' = g(\xi, \eta, 1 - \sigma),$$

where f and g are appropriate functions of their arguments, and

$$\xi = \sigma x + (1 - \sigma) x', \quad \eta = \sigma y + (1 - \sigma) y'.$$

As ρ is some function of σ alone, the former relation gives

$$\left. \begin{array}{l} \rho \dfrac{\partial u}{\partial x} + (1-\rho) \dfrac{\partial u'}{\partial x} = \sigma \dfrac{\partial f}{\partial \xi}, \quad \rho \dfrac{\partial u}{\partial x'} + (1-\rho) \dfrac{\partial u'}{\partial x'} = (1-\sigma) \dfrac{\partial f}{\partial \xi} \\[6pt] \rho \dfrac{\partial u}{\partial y} + (1-\rho) \dfrac{\partial u'}{\partial y} = \sigma \dfrac{\partial f}{\partial \eta}, \quad \rho \dfrac{\partial u}{\partial y'} + (1-\rho) \dfrac{\partial u'}{\partial y'} = (1-\sigma) \dfrac{\partial f}{\partial \eta} \end{array} \right\},$$

and therefore

$$\left\{ \rho \frac{\partial u}{\partial x} + (1-\rho) \frac{\partial u'}{\partial x} \right\} \left\{ \rho \frac{\partial u}{\partial y'} + (1-\rho) \frac{\partial u'}{\partial y'} \right\}$$
$$= \left\{ \rho \frac{\partial u}{\partial y} + (1-\rho) \frac{\partial u'}{\partial y} \right\} \left\{ \rho \frac{\partial u}{\partial x'} + (1-\rho) \frac{\partial u'}{\partial x'} \right\}.$$

The relation holds for all values of ρ, and the quantities u and u' do not involve ρ; hence

$$\frac{\partial u}{\partial x} \frac{\partial u}{\partial y'} = \frac{\partial u}{\partial y} \frac{\partial u}{\partial x'},$$

$$\frac{\partial u}{\partial x} \frac{\partial u'}{\partial y'} + \frac{\partial u'}{\partial x} \frac{\partial u}{\partial y'} = \frac{\partial u}{\partial y} \frac{\partial u'}{\partial x'} + \frac{\partial u'}{\partial y} \frac{\partial u}{\partial x'},$$

$$\frac{\partial u'}{\partial x} \frac{\partial u'}{\partial y'} = \frac{\partial u'}{\partial y} \frac{\partial u'}{\partial x'}.$$

Similarly, the second relation requires the conditions

$$\frac{\partial v}{\partial x} \frac{\partial v}{\partial y'} = \frac{\partial v}{\partial y} \frac{\partial v}{\partial x'},$$

$$\frac{\partial v}{\partial x} \frac{\partial v'}{\partial y'} + \frac{\partial v'}{\partial x} \frac{\partial v}{\partial y'} = \frac{\partial v}{\partial y} \frac{\partial v'}{\partial x'} + \frac{\partial v'}{\partial y} \frac{\partial v}{\partial x'},$$

$$\frac{\partial v'}{\partial x} \frac{\partial v'}{\partial y'} = \frac{\partial v'}{\partial y} \frac{\partial v'}{\partial x'}.$$

Moreover, because both $u + iv$ and $u' + iv'$ are functions of z and z', we have the permanent relations

$$\frac{\partial u}{\partial x} = \frac{\partial v}{\partial y}, \quad \frac{\partial u}{\partial y} = -\frac{\partial v}{\partial x}, \quad \frac{\partial u}{\partial x'} = \frac{\partial v}{\partial y'}, \quad \frac{\partial u}{\partial y'} = -\frac{\partial v}{\partial x'},$$

$$\frac{\partial u'}{\partial x} = \frac{\partial v'}{\partial y}, \quad \frac{\partial u'}{\partial y} = -\frac{\partial v'}{\partial x}, \quad \frac{\partial u'}{\partial x'} = \frac{\partial v'}{\partial y'}, \quad \frac{\partial u'}{\partial y'} = -\frac{\partial v'}{\partial x'}.$$

By using these relations, the three equations involving the derivatives of v and v' can be transformed into the three equations involving the derivatives of u and u'; and therefore, as the permanent relations exist for all functional relations, we need retain only the three equations involving the derivatives of u and u' as the essential independent equations for our problem.

8. The complete integral of the first of these three retained equations—it involves u only—is

$$u = \alpha x - \beta y + \alpha' x' - \beta' y' + \kappa,$$

where $\alpha, \beta, \alpha', \beta', \kappa$ are any real constants, provided the condition

$$\alpha \beta' - \alpha' \beta = 0$$

is satisfied. The permanent relations then give

$$v = \beta x + \alpha y + \beta' x' + \alpha' y' + \kappa',$$

where κ' is any real constant; and so

$$w = u + iv$$
$$= (\alpha + i\beta) z + (\alpha' + i\beta') z' + \kappa + i\kappa'.$$

The presence of the term $\kappa + i\kappa'$ in w merely means a change of origin in the w-plane; neglecting this temporarily, we have

$$w = (\alpha + i\beta) z + (\alpha' + i\beta') z'.$$

Now let

$$\alpha + i\beta = A e^{\mu i}, \quad \alpha' + i\beta' = A' e^{\mu' i},$$

where A, A', μ, μ' are real; then the condition $\alpha\beta' - \alpha'\beta = 0$ becomes

$$AA' \sin(\mu - \mu') = 0,$$

so that either $A = 0$, or $A' = 0$, or $\mu = \mu'$, giving three possibilities.

Similarly, the complete integral of the third of the retained equations—it involves u' only—is

$$u' = \gamma x - \delta y + \gamma' x' - \delta' y' + \lambda,$$

where $\gamma, \delta, \gamma', \delta', \lambda$ are any real constants, provided the condition

$$\gamma \delta' - \gamma' \delta = 0$$

is satisfied. The permanent relations then give

$$v' = \delta x + \gamma y + \delta' x' + \gamma' y' + \lambda',$$

where λ' is any real constant; and so
$$w' = u' + iv'$$
$$= (\gamma + i\delta) z + (\gamma' + i\delta') z' + \lambda + i\lambda'.$$

The presence of the term $\lambda + i\lambda'$ in w' merely means a change of origin in the w'-plane; neglecting this temporarily, as before for w, we have
$$w' = (\gamma + i\delta) z + (\gamma' + i\delta') z'.$$
Now let
$$\gamma + i\delta = Ce^{\nu i}, \quad \gamma' + i\delta' = C'e^{\nu' i},$$
where C, C', ν, ν' are real; then the condition $\gamma\delta' - \gamma'\delta = 0$ becomes
$$CC' \sin(\nu - \nu') = 0,$$
so that either $C = 0$, or $C' = 0$, or $\nu = \nu'$, giving three possibilities.

The second of the three retained equations still has to be satisfied; it involves derivatives of u and of u', and it is satisfied identically by the foregoing values of u and u', provided
$$\alpha\delta' - \alpha'\delta = \beta\gamma' - \beta'\gamma,$$
or (what is the equivalent condition) provided
$$AC' \sin(\mu - \nu') = A'C \sin(\mu' - \nu).$$

9. Nine cases arise for consideration, because the three possibilities from the first of the retained equations must be combined with the three possibilities from the third of the retained equations. Each combination is governed by the last condition; and the expressions obtained must satisfy the conditions holding between ρ and σ. Moreover, in the end, w and w' are to be independent functions of the variables; and, for the present purpose of geometrical representation by a line, we manifestly may interchange z with z', and w with w'.

Of the nine combinations, two are impossible under these requirements, viz. $A = 0$, $C = 0$; and $A' = 0$, $C' = 0$. Four of them are equivalent to one another under these requirements, viz. $A = 0$, $\nu = \nu'$; $A' = 0$, $\nu = \nu'$; $\mu = \mu'$, $C = 0$; $\mu = \mu'$, $C' = 0$; and they lead to the expressions
$$w = (Az + A'z') e^{\mu i}, \quad w' = C'z'e^{\mu i}.$$
Two of them are equivalent to one another under these requirements, viz. $A = 0$, $C' = 0$; and $A' = 0$, $C = 0$; and they lead to the expressions
$$w = Aze^{\mu i}, \quad w' = C'z'e^{\mu i}.$$
The remaining combination, viz. $\mu = \mu'$, $\nu = \nu'$, under the requirements leads to the expressions
$$w = (Az + A'z') e^{\mu i}, \quad w' = (Cz + C'z') e^{\mu i}.$$
All these expressions must still satisfy the terminal condition applying to ρ and σ, viz. that ρ must be 0 or 1 when σ is 0 or 1. When these expressions

are inserted for the functions f and g in the earliest equations in § 7, the latter lead to the relations

$$\frac{\rho\alpha + (1-\rho)\gamma}{\sigma} = \frac{\rho\alpha' + (1-\rho)\gamma'}{1-\sigma},$$

$$\frac{\rho\beta + (1-\rho)\delta}{\sigma} = \frac{\rho\beta' + (1-\rho)\delta'}{1-\sigma},$$

and therefore

$$\frac{\rho A e^{\mu i} + (1-\rho) C e^{\nu i}}{\sigma} = \frac{\rho A' e^{\mu' i} + (1-\rho) C' e^{\nu' i}}{1-\sigma}.$$

For the first of the expressions, this becomes

$$\frac{\rho A}{\sigma} = \frac{\rho A' + (1-\rho) C'}{1-\sigma}.$$

In order that ρ may be 1 when σ is 1, we must have $A' = 0$ and the necessity, that then ρ must be 0 when σ is 0, imposes no further condition; the expression becomes

$$w = Aze^{\mu i}, \quad w' = C'z'e^{\mu i},$$

which is the same as the second.

For the second of the expressions, the relation is satisfied without any further condition.

For the third of the expressions, the relation becomes

$$\frac{\rho A + (1-\rho) C}{\rho A' + (1-\rho) C'} = \frac{\sigma}{1-\sigma}.$$

In order that ρ may be 1 when σ is 1, we must have $A' = 0$; and in order that ρ may be 0 when σ is 0, we must have $C = 0$; the expression becomes

$$w = Aze^{\mu i}, \quad w' = C'z'e^{\mu i},$$

the same as before.

In obtaining this result, we neglected temporarily an arbitrary change of origin in each of the planes; and we assumed that z can be interchanged with z', and w with w'. Thus we have the result:—

The only relations which give a birational transformation of the straight line, joining z and z' in two parallel planes, into a straight line, joining w and w' also in two parallel planes, either are

$$w = aze^{\alpha i} + be^{\beta i}, \quad w' = a'ze^{\alpha i} + ce^{\gamma i},$$

where a, a', b, c, α, β, γ are real constants, or can be changed into this form by interchanging z and z', or w and w', or both.

These relations, as equations in a general theory, are so trivial as to be negligible; and so we can assert generally that two functional relations $F(w, w', z, z') = 0$ and $G(w, w', z, z') = 0$, which transform the variables z

and z' in their respective parallel planes into the variables w and w' likewise in their respective parallel planes, do not (save in the foregoing trivial cases) admit a birational transformation of the whole straight line joining z and z' into the whole straight line joining w and w'.

10. Manifestly, therefore, we need not retain the suggested geometrical representation of two variables by the whole straight line joining the two points z and z', because the only effective part of the representation is provided by the two points in which the line cuts the planes.

Nor would any other method of selecting the four real variables for the specification of the straight line be more effective. For example, the line would be uniquely selected by assigning a point where it cuts a given plane and assigning its direction relative to fixed axes in space; and then we could take

$$z = x + iy, \quad z' = e^{i\phi} \tan \theta,$$

with the usual significance for x, y, θ, ϕ. It is easy to see that, when we take a plane at unit distance from the given plane, and we write $z'' = z + z'$, the former representation by the straight line arises for z and z''. As before, the whole straight line is not an effective representation of the two complex variables; the only effective part of the representation is the point in the given plane and the direction relative to fixed axes.

11. Another method of constructing a straight line to represent two complex variables z and z' has been propounded by Vivanti[*], whereby it is given as the intersection of the two planes

$$xX + yZ = 1, \quad x'Y + y'Z = 1,$$

where X, Y, Z are current coordinates in space. The immediate vicinity of a line z_0, z_0' is assumed to be the aggregate of all lines such that

$$(x - x_0)^2 + (y - y_0)^2 \leqslant r^2, \quad (x' - x_0')^2 + (y' - y_0')^2 \leqslant r'^2,$$

where r and r' are arbitrary small quantities; and the boundary of the vicinity is made up of the lines

$$(x - x_0)^2 + (y - y_0)^2 = r^2, \quad (x' - x_0')^2 + (y' - y_0')^2 = r'^2.$$

It is easy to see that, as before, the whole straight line as a single geometrical entity is not an effective representation of the two complex variables z and z'; the only effective part of the representation depends upon the coordinates of the two points in which the line cuts the planes of reference $Y = 0$, $X = 0$ (or any two of the coordinate planes).

[*] *Rend. Circ. Mat. Palermo*, t. ix (1895), pp. 108—124.

12. The preceding investigation suggests cognate questions which will only be propounded. Two functional relations, $F(w, w', z, z') = 0$ and $G(w, w', z, z') = 0$, transform a pair of points z and z', in parallel planes, into a pair (or into several pairs) of points w and w', also in parallel planes. Let z and z' be connected by any analytical curve; let a corresponding pair of points w and w' also be connected by any analytical curve; and suppose that the two analytical curves have a birational correspondence with one another. Then

(i) How are the equations of this correspondence connected, if at all, with the original functional relations? and what are these equations when the two analytical curves are assigned?

(ii) What functional relations are possible if, under them, the whole z, z' curve is to be transformed into the whole w, w' curve?

(iii) When functional relations are given and an analytical z, z' curve is assigned, what are the equations of the w, w' curve, if and when the whole curves are transformed into one another?

13. One warning must be given before we pass away from the consideration of a line, straight or curved, as a geometrical representation of a couple of complex variables. The preceding remarks refer to the possibility of this geometrical representation; they do not refer to functions of two complex variables which are functions of a line. Functions of a real line occur in mathematical physics; thus the energy of a closed wire, conveying a current in a magnetic field, is a function of the shape of the wire. This notion has been extended by Volterra* on the basis of Poincaré's generalisation of one of Cauchy's integral-theorems. In the case of the integral of a uniform function of one complex variable, we know that the value is zero round any contour, which does not enclose a singularity of the function, and that the integral between two assigned points is (subject to the usual proviso as to singularities) independent of the path between the points; that is, the integral can be regarded as a function of the final point. So also (as we shall see) the integral of a function of two complex variables over a closed surface in four-dimensional space is zero if the surface encloses no singularity of the function; and when the surface is not closed, the integral (subject to a similar proviso as to singularities) depends upon the boundary of the surface; that is, the integral can be regarded as a function of the boundary-line.

This property has nothing in common with the line-representation of two complex variables which has been discussed.

14. The third of the indicated methods of representation of two complex variables is the effective relic of the discarded line-representation. It is the simple, but not very suggestive, method of representing the two variables z

---

* Acta Math., t. xii (1889), pp. 233—286.

and z' by two points, either in the same plane or in different planes, the two points always being unrelated. It is the method usually adopted by Picard and others. For quite simple purposes, it proves useful; thus it is employed by Picard* in dealing with the residues of the double integrals of rational functions, and it is important in his theory of the periods of double integrals of algebraic functions.

Let me say at once that the point-representation of z and z' is not completely satisfactory, in the sense that it does not provide a representation which gives a powerful geometrical equivalent for analytical needs. One illustration will suffice for the moment. It is a known theorem†, due originally to Jacobi in a simpler form, that a uniform function of two variables cannot possess more than four pairs of periods. The point-representation of two variables admits of an effective presentation of simple periodicity for either variable or for both variables, of double periodicity for either variable or for both variables separately, of triple periodicity for both variables in combination; but (as will be seen later in these lectures) it does not lend itself to a presentation of quadruple periodicity for both variables in combination, a presentation which is much needed for functions so fundamental as the quotients of the double theta-functions. An attempt to circumvent the latter difficulty will be made later for one class of quadruply-periodic functions. But the general difficulty remains. There are other limitations also upon the effectiveness of the method of representation by points; they need not be emphasised at this stage.

New ideas, or some uniquely effective new idea, can alone supply our needs. In the meanwhile, we possess only two fairly useful methods, viz., the method of four-dimensional space, and the method of two-plane representation.

Properties of the two-plane representation.

15. As the principal use of the representation of two variables in four-dimensional space occurs in connection with double integrals, illustrations can be deferred until that subject arises for discussion. We proceed now to make a few simple inferences from the two-plane representation of two variables‡.

We shall use the word *place* to denote, collectively, the two points in the z-plane and the z'-plane respectively which represent the values of z and

---

* See the reference to the second treatise by Picard, quoted on p. 5.

† The general theorem is that a uniform function of n independent variables cannot possess more than $2n$ independent sets of periods. The simplest case, when $n=1$, was originally established by Jacobi, *Ges. Werke*, t. ii, pp. 27—32. For the general theorem, see the author's *Theory of Functions*, § 110, § 239, where some references are given.

‡ For much of the investigation that follows, reference may be made to the author's paper, quoted on p. 7.

of z'. Let w and w' be two independent functions of z and z', so that their Jacobian J, where

$$J = J\left(\frac{w, w'}{z, z'}\right),$$

does not vanish identically; and let the places z, z' and w, w' be associated by functional relations. Any small variation from the former place, represented by dz and dz', determines a small variation from the latter place, which may be represented by dw and dw'; the analytical relations between these small variations are of the form

$$dw = A\,dz + B\,dz', \quad dw' = C\,dz + D\,dz',$$

where A, B, C, D are free from differential elements, and $AD - BC = J$.

Next, let d_1z and d_1z', d_2z and d_2z' denote any two small variations from the z, z' place; and let d_1w and d_1w', d_2w and d_2w' denote the consequent small variations from the w, w' place. Then

$$\begin{vmatrix} d_1w, & d_1w' \\ d_2w, & d_2w' \end{vmatrix} = \begin{vmatrix} A\,d_1z + B\,d_1z', & C\,d_1z + D\,d_1z' \\ A\,d_2z + B\,d_2z', & C\,d_2z + D\,d_2z' \end{vmatrix}$$

$$= J \begin{vmatrix} d_1z, & d_1z' \\ d_2z, & d_2z' \end{vmatrix}.$$

Manifestly, if $d_1z\,d_2z' - d_2z\,d_1z'$ vanishes, then $d_1w\,d_2w' - d_2w\,d_1w'$ also vanishes; and the converse holds, because J is not zero. Hence if, at the place z, z', two similar infinitesimal triangles are taken in the planes of z and of z' respectively, the corresponding infinitesimal triangles at the place w, w' in the planes of w and of w' respectively also are similar; and conversely.

This property holds for all pairs of similar infinitesimal triangles; and therefore, when the z-plane and the z'-plane are put into conformal relation with one another, the w-plane and the w'-plane are also put into conformal relation with one another. This result is the geometrical form of the analytical result that, when the two equations

$$F(w, w', z, z') = 0, \quad G(w, w', z, z') = 0,$$

determine w and w' as independent functions of z and z', a relation $\phi(z, z') = 0$, involving z and z' only, leads to some relation $\psi(w, w') = 0$, involving w and w' only.

Another interpretation of the relation

$$\begin{vmatrix} d_1w, & d_1w' \\ d_2w, & d_2w' \end{vmatrix} = J \begin{vmatrix} d_1z, & d_1z' \\ d_2z, & d_2z' \end{vmatrix}$$

is as follows:—When w and w' are two independent functions of two independent complex variables z and z', and when d_1z, d_1z', d_1w, d_1w' are any one set of simultaneous small variations, while d_2z, d_2z', d_2w, d_2w' are any other set of simultaneous small variations, the quantity

$$\begin{vmatrix} d_1w, & d_1w' \\ d_2w, & d_2w' \end{vmatrix} \div \begin{vmatrix} d_1z, & d_1z' \\ d_2z, & d_2z' \end{vmatrix}$$

is independent of differential elements and depends only upon the places z, z' and w, w'.

16. The converse also is true, viz.:—

Let z and z' be two complex variables, such that
$$z = x + iy, \quad z' = x' + iy',$$
where x, y, x', y' are four real independent variables; and let w and w' be other two complex variables, such that
$$w = u + iv, \quad w' = u' + iv',$$
where u, v, u', v' are four real independent quantities, being functions of x, y, x', y'; then, if the magnitude

$$\begin{vmatrix} d_1w, & d_1w' \\ d_2w, & d_2w' \end{vmatrix} \div \begin{vmatrix} d_1z, & d_1z' \\ d_2z, & d_2z' \end{vmatrix},$$

for all infinitesimal variations, is independent of these variations, w and w' are independent functions of z and z' alone.

This property, which for two independent complex variables corresponds to Riemann's definition-property[*] for functionality in the case of a single complex variable, can be established as follows. Let

$$\frac{\partial w}{\partial x} = \alpha, \quad \frac{\partial w}{\partial y} = \beta, \quad \frac{\partial w}{\partial x'} = \gamma, \quad \frac{\partial w}{\partial y'} = \delta,$$

$$\frac{\partial w'}{\partial x} = \alpha', \quad \frac{\partial w'}{\partial y} = \beta', \quad \frac{\partial w'}{\partial x'} = \gamma', \quad \frac{\partial w'}{\partial y'} = \delta',$$

so that
$$\left. \begin{array}{l} dw = \alpha\, dx + \beta\, dy + \gamma\, dx' + \delta\, dy' \\ dw' = \alpha'dx + \beta'dy + \gamma'dx' + \delta'dy' \end{array} \right\}.$$

Then
$$\begin{vmatrix} d_1w, & d_1w' \\ d_2w, & d_2w' \end{vmatrix}$$

$$= \begin{vmatrix} \alpha d_1x + \beta d_1y + \gamma d_1x' + \delta d_1y', & \alpha'd_1x + \beta'd_1y + \gamma'd_1x' + \delta'd_1y' \\ \alpha d_2x + \beta d_2y + \gamma d_2x' + \delta d_2y', & \alpha'd_2x + \beta'd_2y + \gamma'd_2x' + \delta'd_2y' \end{vmatrix}$$

$$= \begin{vmatrix} \alpha, & \alpha' \\ \beta, & \beta' \end{vmatrix} \begin{vmatrix} d_1x, & d_1y \\ d_2x, & d_2y \end{vmatrix} + \begin{vmatrix} \alpha, & \alpha' \\ \gamma, & \gamma' \end{vmatrix} \begin{vmatrix} d_1x, & d_1x' \\ d_2x, & d_2x' \end{vmatrix} + \begin{vmatrix} \alpha, & \alpha' \\ \delta, & \delta' \end{vmatrix} \begin{vmatrix} d_1x, & d_1y' \\ d_2x, & d_2y' \end{vmatrix}$$

$$+ \begin{vmatrix} \beta, & \beta' \\ \gamma, & \gamma' \end{vmatrix} \begin{vmatrix} d_1y, & d_1x' \\ d_2y, & d_2x' \end{vmatrix} + \begin{vmatrix} \beta, & \beta' \\ \delta, & \delta' \end{vmatrix} \begin{vmatrix} d_1y, & d_1y' \\ d_2y, & d_2y' \end{vmatrix} + \begin{vmatrix} \gamma, & \gamma' \\ \delta, & \delta' \end{vmatrix} \begin{vmatrix} d_1x', & d_1y' \\ d_2x', & d_2y' \end{vmatrix}.$$

[*] Riemann's *Ges. Werke*, p. 5.

Also
$$\begin{vmatrix} d_1z, & d_1z' \\ d_2z, & d_2z' \end{vmatrix}$$
$$= \begin{vmatrix} d_1x + id_1y, & d_1x' + id_1y' \\ d_2x + id_2y, & d_2x' + id_2y' \end{vmatrix}$$
$$= \begin{vmatrix} d_1x, & d_1x' \\ d_2x, & d_2x' \end{vmatrix} + i \begin{vmatrix} d_1y, & d_1x' \\ d_2y, & d_2x' \end{vmatrix} + i \begin{vmatrix} d_1x, & d_1y' \\ d_2x, & d_2y' \end{vmatrix} - \begin{vmatrix} d_1y, & d_1y' \\ d_2y, & d_2y' \end{vmatrix}.$$

These two quantities are to stand to one another in a non-vanishing ratio, which is independent of the arbitrarily chosen differential elements that occur in them. Consequently, when we denote this ratio by J, we must have

$$\alpha\beta' - \alpha'\beta = 0,$$
$$\alpha\gamma' - \alpha'\gamma = J,$$
$$\alpha\delta' - \alpha'\delta = iJ,$$
$$\beta\gamma' - \beta'\gamma = iJ,$$
$$\beta\delta' - \beta'\delta = -J,$$
$$\gamma\delta' - \gamma'\delta = 0;$$

and these necessary conditions also suffice to secure the property.

The first of these conditions shews that a quantity m exists such that
$$\beta = m\alpha, \quad \beta' = m\alpha';$$
and the sixth shews that a quantity n exists such that
$$\delta = n\gamma, \quad \delta' = n\gamma'.$$
The third condition then gives
$$iJ = \alpha\delta' - \alpha'\delta = n(\alpha\gamma' - \alpha'\gamma) = nJ;$$
the fourth and the fifth conditions similarly give
$$iJ = mJ, \quad -J = mnJ;$$
and the second condition gives the value of J. Thus all the conditions are satisfied if
$$m = i, \quad n = i, \quad J = \alpha\gamma' - \alpha'\gamma.$$
But now
$$\frac{\partial w}{\partial y} = \beta = i\alpha = i\frac{\partial w}{\partial x}, \quad \frac{\partial w}{\partial y'} = \delta = i\gamma = i\frac{\partial w}{\partial x'},$$
and these are the only equations affecting w alone. The theory of partial differential equations of the first order shews that their most general integral is any function of $x + iy$ and of $x' + iy'$ alone, that is, w is a function of z and z' alone. Similarly
$$\frac{\partial w'}{\partial y} = i\frac{\partial w'}{\partial x}, \quad \frac{\partial w'}{\partial y'} = i\frac{\partial w'}{\partial x'},$$

F.

18   GEOMETRICAL   [CH. I

and these are the only equations affecting w' alone; hence, as before, w' also is a function of z and z' alone. Moreover, we now have

$$\frac{\partial w}{\partial z} = \frac{\partial w}{\partial x} = \alpha, \quad \frac{\partial w}{\partial z'} = \frac{\partial w}{\partial x'} = \gamma,$$

$$\frac{\partial w'}{\partial z} = \frac{\partial w'}{\partial x} = \alpha', \quad \frac{\partial w'}{\partial z'} = \frac{\partial w'}{\partial x'} = \gamma';$$

and therefore

$$J = \alpha\gamma' - \alpha'\gamma = \frac{\partial w}{\partial z}\frac{\partial w'}{\partial z'} - \frac{\partial w}{\partial z'}\frac{\partial w'}{\partial z}.$$

Also J is a non-vanishing quantity. Hence w and w' are independent functions of z and z' alone—which is the result to be established.

17. The Riemann definition-property for a function of a single complex variable leads to a relation

$$\frac{\delta w}{\delta' w} = \frac{\delta z}{\delta' z};$$

this relation, when interpreted geometrically, gives the conformal representation of the w-plane and the z-plane upon one another. The property just established in connection with the quantity

$$d_1 z \cdot d_2 z' - d_2 z \cdot d_1 z'$$

has a corresponding geometrical interpretation.

For simplicity, let z and z' be represented in the same plane. At any point O in the plane, take OA, OB, OC, OD to represent $d_1 z$, $d_1 z'$, $d_2 z$, $d_2 z'$. Along the internal bisector of the angle between OA and OD, take OP a mean proportional between the lengths OA and OD; and along the internal bisector of the angle between OB and OC, take OQ a mean proportional between the lengths OB and OC. Complete the parallelogram of which OP and OQ are adjacent sides; let M denote the product of the lengths of its diagonals, and let θ denote the sum of the inclinations of those diagonals to the positive direction of the axis of real quantities; then

$$d_1 z \cdot d_2 z' - d_2 z \cdot d_1 z' = Me^{\theta i}.$$

Constructing a similar parallelogram in connection with the variations of w and w', we should have

$$d_1 w \cdot d_2 w' - d_2 w \cdot d_1 w' = Ne^{\phi i}.$$

Consequently

$$Ne^{\phi i} = JMe^{\theta i}.$$

Now let two sets of pairs of small variations of z and z' be taken, one of them leading to a quantity $Me^{\theta i}$, the other of them leading to a quantity $M'e^{\theta' i}$; and let the corresponding quantities, arising out of the

two sets of pairs of the consequent small variations of w and w', be $Ne^{\phi i}$ and $N'e^{\phi' i}$. Then
$$Ne^{\phi i} = JMe^{\theta i}, \quad N'e^{\phi' i} = JM'e^{\theta' i},$$
and therefore
$$\frac{N'}{N} = \frac{M'}{M}, \quad \phi' - \phi = \theta' - \theta,$$
which is the extension, to two functions of two variables, of the conformation property for a function of one variable. Moreover, the extension is determinate; for the parallelogram, constructed to give the representation of $d_1 z \cdot d_2 z' - d_2 z \cdot d_1 z'$, is unique in magnitude and orientation.

18. While a geometrical interpretation of functionality can thus be provided at any place in the two planes of the independent variables, a limitation upon the general utility of the method is found at once when we proceed to the transformation of equations. It does not, in fact, provide any natural extension of the transformation of loci and of areas which occurs when there is only one complex variable.

Thus consider the periodic substitution
$$z\sqrt{2} = w + w', \quad z'\sqrt{2} = w - w',$$
which gives
$$w\sqrt{2} = z + z', \quad w'\sqrt{2} = z - z'.$$

Corresponding to any z, z' place, there exists a unique w, w' place. But the combination, of a definite locus in the z plane unaffected by variations of z' with a definite locus in the z' plane unaffected by variations of z, does not lead to similar loci in the planes of w and of w'. Thus suppose that z and z' describe the circles
$$z = ae^{\theta i}, \quad z' = a'e^{\theta' i},$$
in their respective planes; the corresponding ranges in the w and w' planes are given by the equations
$$(u + u')^2 + (v + v')^2 = 2a^2, \quad (u - u')^2 + (v - v')^2 = 2a'^2,$$
neither of which gives a locus in the w plane alone or in the w' plane alone. The z circle and the z' circle, which can be described by the respective variables independently of each other, determine ∞^2 places in the w and w' planes combined, but there is no locus either in the w plane alone or in the w' plane alone corresponding to the two circles.

Again, the content of the field of variation represented by
$$|z| \leqslant a, \quad |z'| \leqslant a',$$
can be described very simply; it consists of the ∞^4 places given by combining any point within or upon the z circle with any point within or

upon the z' circle. When this field of variation is transformed by the periodic substitution, the new field of variation is represented by
$$|w + w'| \leqslant a\sqrt{2}, \quad |w - w'| \leqslant a'\sqrt{2};$$
it consists of ∞^4 places in the w and w' planes, each corresponding uniquely to the appropriate one of the ∞^4 places in the z and z' planes; but there is no verbal description of the w, w' field so simple as the verbal description of the z, z' field which has been transformed.

Analytical expression of frontiers of two-plane regions.

19. One consequence emerges from even the foregoing simple illustration, and it is confirmed by other considerations.

When we have a four-fold field of variation such that places in it are represented by a couple of relations
$$\phi(x, y, x', y') \leqslant 0, \quad \psi(x, y, x', y') \leqslant 0,$$
the three-fold boundary of the field consists of two portions, viz. the range represented by
$$\phi(x, y, x', y') = 0, \quad \psi(x, y, x', y') \leqslant 0,$$
and the range represented by
$$\phi(x, y, x', y') \leqslant 0, \quad \psi(x, y, x', y') = 0.$$
These two portions of the three-fold boundary themselves have a common frontier represented by the equations
$$\phi(x, y, x', y') = 0, \quad \psi(x, y, x', y') = 0,$$
which give a two-fold range of variation. This last range is a secondary or subsidiary boundary for the original four-fold field; to distinguish it from the proper boundary, we shall call it the *frontier* of the field.

Accordingly, we may regard the frontier of a field of the suggested kind as given by two equations
$$\phi(x, y, x', y') = 0, \quad \psi(x, y, x', y') = 0.$$
(The simpler case of unrelated loci in the planes of z and of z' arises when ϕ does not contain x' or y', and ψ does not contain x or y; and, at least when ϕ and ψ are algebraic functions of their arguments, the foregoing relations can be modified into relations of the type
$$\theta(x, y, x') = 0, \quad \bar{\theta}(x, y, y') = 0,$$
or into relations of the type
$$\chi(x, x', y') = 0, \quad \bar{\chi}(y, x', y') = 0,$$
which are equivalent to them.) Now this form of the equations of the frontier of the field possesses the analytical advantage that, when the variables are changed from z and z' to w and w' by equations
$$F(w, w', z, z') = 0, \quad G(w, w', z, z') = 0,$$

the equations of the frontier of the w, w' field are of the same type as before, being of the form

$$\Phi(u, v, u', v') = 0, \quad \Psi(u, v, u', v') = 0.$$

It is necessary to find some analytical expression of the doubly-infinite content of these equations. In the special example arising out of the periodic substitution in § 18, we at once have the expressions

$$u\sqrt{2} = a\cos\theta + a'\cos\theta', \quad u'\sqrt{2} = a\cos\theta - a'\cos\theta',$$
$$v\sqrt{2} = a\sin\theta + a'\sin\theta', \quad v'\sqrt{2} = a\sin\theta - a'\sin\theta',$$

giving the doubly-infinite range of variation for u, v, u', v', when θ and θ' vary independently. But when the equations of the frontier do not lead, by mere inspection, to the needed expressions, we can proceed as follows.

Let $x, y, x', y' = a, b, a', b'$ be an ordinary place on the frontier given by the equations $\phi = 0$ and $\psi = 0$, in the sense that no one of the first derivatives of ϕ and of ψ vanishes there; and in its vicinity let

$$x = a + \xi, \quad y = b + \eta, \quad x' = a' + \xi', \quad y' = b' + \eta'.$$

Then we have

$$0 = \xi \frac{\partial \phi}{\partial a} + \eta \frac{\partial \phi}{\partial b} + \xi' \frac{\partial \phi}{\partial a'} + \eta' \frac{\partial \phi}{\partial b'} + [\xi, \eta, \xi', \eta']_2 + \ldots,$$

$$0 = \xi \frac{\partial \psi}{\partial a} + \eta \frac{\partial \psi}{\partial b} + \xi' \frac{\partial \psi}{\partial a'} + \eta' \frac{\partial \psi}{\partial b'} + [\xi, \eta, \xi', \eta']_2 + \ldots,$$

there being only a finite number of terms when ϕ and ψ are algebraic in form. Introduce two new parameters s and t, and take

$$s = \xi\alpha + \eta\beta + \xi'\gamma + \eta'\delta,$$
$$t = \xi\alpha' + \eta\beta' + \xi'\gamma' + \eta'\delta',$$

where $\alpha, \beta, \gamma, \delta, \alpha', \beta', \gamma', \delta'$ are constants such that the determinant

$$\begin{vmatrix} \frac{\partial \phi}{\partial a}, & \frac{\partial \phi}{\partial b}, & \frac{\partial \phi}{\partial a'}, & \frac{\partial \phi}{\partial b'} \\ \frac{\partial \psi}{\partial a}, & \frac{\partial \psi}{\partial b}, & \frac{\partial \psi}{\partial a'}, & \frac{\partial \psi}{\partial b'} \\ \alpha, & \beta, & \gamma, & \delta \\ \alpha', & \beta', & \gamma', & \delta' \end{vmatrix}$$

does not vanish. Then the four equations can be resolved so as to express ξ, η, ξ', η' in terms of s and t; owing to the limitations imposed, the deduced expressions are regular functions of s and t, vanishing with them; and so we have each of the variables x, y, x', y', expressed as functions of two real variables s and t, regular at least in some non-infinitesimal range.

In order to indicate the two-fold variation in the content of the frontier, it now is sufficient to consider regions of variation in the plane of the real variables s and t. Thus, corresponding to a region in that plane included within a curve $k(s, t) = 0$, there are frontier ranges of variation in the z and the z' planes, determined respectively by the equations

$$\left.\begin{aligned} x - a &= p(s, t) \\ y - b &= q(s, t) \\ 0 &\geq k(s, t) \end{aligned}\right\}, \qquad \left.\begin{aligned} x' - a' &= p'(s, t) \\ y' - b' &= q'(s, t) \\ 0 &\geq k(s, t) \end{aligned}\right\},$$

that is, by the interiors of curves

$$f(x - a, y - b) = 0, \quad g(x' - a', y' - b') = 0,$$

the current descriptions of these interiors being related.

Moreover, the equations $F = 0$ and $G = 0$ potentially express u, v, u', v' in terms of x, y, x', y'; and so the frontier range of variation in the w and w' planes would be given by substituting the obtained values of x, y, x', y', as regular functions of s and t, in the expressions for u, v, u', v', that is, the frontier range of variation is defined by equations of the form

$$u, v, u', v' = \text{functions of two real variables } s \text{ and } t.$$

But, in dealing with the geometrical content of the frontier, whether with the variables z and z' or with the variables w and w', care must be exercised as to what is justly included. We are not, for instance, to include every point within the curve $f(x - a, y - b) = 0$ conjointly with every point within the curve $g(x' - a', y' - b') = 0$, even if both curves are closed; we are to include every point within either curve conjointly with the point within the other curve that is appropriately associable with it through the values of s and t.

Ex. 1. The method just given for the expression of x, y, x', y' is general in form; but there is no necessity to adopt it when simpler processes of expression can be adopted. Thus in the case of the equations

$$x^2 + y^2 + x'^2 = 1, \quad x^2 - y^2 = y',$$

a complete representation of the variables is given by

$$x = \sin s \cos t, \quad y = \sin s \sin t, \quad x' = \cos s, \quad y' = \sin^2 s \cos 2t.$$

A full range of variation in the plane of s and t is

$$0 \leqslant s \leqslant \pi, \quad 0 \leqslant t \leqslant 2\pi.$$

When we select, as a portion of this range, the area of the triangle bounded by the lines

$$s - t = 0, \quad s + t = \tfrac{1}{2}\pi, \quad t = 0,$$

the limiting curves corresponding to $f=0$ and $g=0$ are a curvilinear figure made up of a straight line and two quarter-circles in the z-plane, and another curvilinear figure in the z'-plane made up of a parabola and arcs of the two curves

$$y' = (1-x'^2)(2x'^2-1), \quad y' = -(1-x'^2)(2x'^2-1).$$

Ex. 2. For the periodic substitution

$$w\sqrt{2} = z+z', \quad w'\sqrt{2} = z-z',$$

a z, z' frontier defined by the equations

$$x^2 + x'^2 = 1, \quad y^2 + y'^2 = 1,$$

is transformed into a w, w' frontier defined by the equations

$$u^2 + u'^2 = 1, \quad v^2 + v'^2 = 1;$$

that is, the frontier is conserved unchanged.

Ex. 3. To shew how a field of variation can be limited, consider the four-fold field represented by the equations

$$x^2 + y^2 + x'^2 \leqslant 1, \quad 2x^2 + 3y^2 + y'^2 \leqslant 1.$$

As regards the z-plane, the first equation allows the whole of the interior of the circle $x^2 + y^2 = 1$. The second equation allows the whole of the interior of the ellipse $2x^2 + 3y^2 = 1$. The region common to these areas is the interior of the ellipse; hence the content in the z-plane is the interior of the ellipse $2x^2 + 3y^2 = 1$, so that x^2 ranges from 0 to $\frac{1}{2}$, and y^2 ranges from 0 to $\frac{1}{3}$.

As regards the z'-plane, we have

$$3x'^2 - y'^2 = 2 - x^2, \quad 2x'^2 - y'^2 = 1 + y^2.$$

Because of the range of x^2, the first of these equations gives the region between the two hyperbolas

$$3x'^2 - y'^2 = 2, \quad 3x'^2 - y'^2 = \tfrac{3}{2}.$$

Because of the range of y^2, the second of these equations gives the region between the two hyperbolas

$$2x'^2 - y'^2 = \tfrac{4}{3}, \quad 2x'^2 - y'^2 = 1.$$

The required content in the z'-plane is the area common to these two regions; that is, it is the interior of two crescent-shaped areas between the hyperbolas

$$2x'^2 - y'^2 = 1, \quad 3x'^2 - y'^2 = 2.$$

The whole field of four-fold variation of the variables z and z' is made by combining any point within or upon the first ellipse with any point within or upon the contour of each of the crescent-shaped areas.

Ex. 4. Discuss the four-fold field of variation represented by the equations

$$x^2 + y^2 + 2a(xx' + yy') \leqslant k^2,$$
$$x'^2 + y'^2 + 2c(xy' - yx') \leqslant l^2.$$

20. The last two examples will give some hint as to the process of estimating the field of variation when it is limited by a couple of frontier equations in the form

$$\theta(x, y, x') = 0, \quad \Theta(x, y, y') = 0,$$

or in the equivalent form

$$\chi(x, x', y') = 0, \quad \mathrm{X}(y, x', y') = 0.$$

We draw the family of curves represented by $\theta = 0$ for parametric values of x'; for limited forms of θ, there will be a limited range of variation for x and y, bounded by some curve or curves. Similarly, we draw the family of curves represented by $\Theta = 0$ for parametric values of y'; as for θ, so for Θ, there will be a limited range of variation for x and y, bounded by some other curve or other curves. Further, the equations $\chi = 0$ and $X = 0$ may impose restrictions upon the range of x' and the range of y', which are parametric for the preceding curves. In the net result for the z-range, when subject to the equations $\theta = 0$ and $\Theta = 0$, we can take the internal region common to all the interiors of these closed curves.

The same kind of consideration would be applied to the equations $\chi = 0$ and $X = 0$, so as to obtain the range in the z'-plane as dominated by these equations.

And the four-fold field of variation for z and z' is obtained by combining every point in the admissible region of the z-plane with every point in the admissible region of the z'-plane.

Note. In the preceding discussion, a special selection is made of the four-fold fields of variation which are determined by a couple of relations $\phi \leqslant 0$, $\psi \leqslant 0$.

It is of course possible to have a four-fold field of variation, determined by a single relation $\phi \leqslant 0$. The boundary of such a field is given by the single equation $\phi = 0$; there is no question of a frontier.

It is equally possible to have a four-fold field of variation, determined by more than two relations, say by $\phi \leqslant 0$, $\psi \leqslant 0$, $\chi \leqslant 0$. The boundary then consists of three portions, given by $\phi = 0$, $\psi \leqslant 0$, $\chi \leqslant 0$; $\phi \leqslant 0$, $\psi = 0$, $\chi \leqslant 0$; $\phi \leqslant 0$, $\psi \leqslant 0$, $\chi = 0$. The frontier consists of three portions, given by $\phi \leqslant 0$, $\psi = 0$, $\chi = 0$; $\phi = 0$, $\psi \leqslant 0$, $\chi = 0$; $\phi = 0$, $\psi = 0$, $\chi \leqslant 0$. And there could arise the consideration of what may be called an edge, defined by the three equations $\phi = 0$, $\psi = 0$, $\chi = 0$.

Sufficient illustration of what is desired, for ulterior purposes in these lectures, is provided by the consideration of four-fold fields determined by two relations.

CHAPTER II

LINEO-LINEAR TRANSFORMATIONS: INVARIANTS AND COVARIANTS

Lineo-linear transformations.

21. WHATEVER measure of success may be attained, great or small, with the geometrical representation, the analytical work persists; the geometry is desired only as ancillary to the analysis. So we shall leave the actual geometrical interpretation at its present stage.

The fundamental importance of the lineo-linear transformations of the type

$$w = \frac{az + b}{cz + d}$$

in the theory of automorphic functions of a single variable is well-known. We proceed to a brief, and completely analytical, consideration of lineo-linear transformations of two complex variables*, shewing the type of equations that play in the analytical theory the same kind of invariantive part as does a circle or an arc of a circle in the geometry connected with a single complex variable.

These lineo-linear transformations between two sets of non-homogeneous variables have arisen as a subject of investigation in several regions of research. Naturally, their most obvious analytical occurrence is in the theory of groups. When the groups are finite, they have been discussed for real variables by Valentiner†, Gordan‡, and others; they are of special importance for algebraic functions of two variables and for ordinary linear equations of the third order which are algebraically integrable§. Again, and with real variables, they arise in the plane geometry connected with Lie's theory of continuous groups‖. They have been discussed, with complex

---

* For much of the following investigation, as far as the end of this chapter, reference may be made to the second of the author's papers quoted on p. 1.

† *Vidensk. Selsk. Skr.*, 6 Række, *naturvid. og math. Afd.*, v., 2 (1889).

‡ *Math. Ann.*, t. lxi (1905), pp. 453—526.

§ See the author's *Theory of Differential Equations*, vol. iv, ch. v.

‖ Lie-Scheffers, *Vorl. ü. cont. Gruppen*, (1893), pp. 13—82.

variables, by Picard* in connection with the possible extension, to two independent variables, of the theory of automorphic functions. And a memoir by Poincaré has already been mentioned†.

22. We take the general lineo-linear transformation (or substitution) between two sets of complex variables in the form

$$\frac{w}{az + bz' + c} = \frac{w'}{a'z + b'z' + c'} = \frac{1}{a''z + b''z' + c''},$$

where all the quantities $a, b, c, a', b', c', a'', b'', c''$ are constants, real or complex. The first step in the generalisation of the theory for a single variable is the construction of the canonical form; and this can be achieved simply by using known results‡ in the linear transformations of homogeneous variables. For our purpose, these are

$$y_1 = ax_1 + bx_2 + cx_3,$$
$$y_2 = a'x_1 + b'x_2 + c'x_3,$$
$$y_3 = a''x_1 + b''x_2 + c''x_3,$$

so that we have

$$\frac{z}{x_1} = \frac{z'}{x_2} = \frac{1}{x_3}, \qquad \frac{w}{y_1} = \frac{w'}{y_2} = \frac{1}{y_3}.$$

The quantities w and w' are independent functions of z and z'; and therefore the determinant

$$\begin{vmatrix} a, & b, & c \\ a', & b', & c' \\ a'', & b'', & c'' \end{vmatrix},$$

denoted by Δ, is not zero. As a matter of fact,

$$J\left(\frac{w, w'}{z, z'}\right) = \frac{\Delta}{(a''z + b''z' + c'')^3}.$$

The equation

$$\begin{vmatrix} a - \theta, & b, & c \\ a', & b' - \theta, & c' \\ a'', & b'', & c'' - \theta \end{vmatrix} = 0$$

is called the characteristic equation of the substitution. This characteristic equation is invariantive when the two sets of variables are subjected to the same transformation; that is to say, if we take

$$\frac{W}{\alpha w + \beta w' + \gamma} = \frac{W'}{\alpha' w + \beta' w' + \gamma'} = \frac{1}{\alpha'' w + \beta'' w' + \gamma''},$$

$$\frac{Z}{\alpha z + \beta z' + \gamma} = \frac{Z'}{\alpha' z + \beta' z' + \gamma'} = \frac{1}{\alpha'' z + \beta'' z' + \gamma''},$$

---

* *Acta Math.*, t. i (1882), pp. 297—320; *ib.*, t. ii (1883), pp. 114—135.
† See the reference on p. 1.
‡ Jordan, *Traité des substitutions*, Book ii, ch. ii, § v; Burnside, *Theory of groups*, (2nd ed., 1911), ch. xiii.

and express W and W' in terms of Z and Z', the characteristic equation of the concluding substitution between W, W', Z, Z' is the same as the above characteristic equation of our initial substitution between w, w', z, z'.

There are three cases to be discussed, according as the characteristic equation, which is of the form
$$\theta^3 - \Delta_1 \theta^2 + \Delta_2 \theta - \Delta = 0,$$
has three simple roots, or a double root and a simple root, or a triple root.

Case I. Let all the roots of the characteristic equation be simple; and denote them by $\theta_1, \theta_2, \theta_3$. Then quantities $\alpha_r : \beta_r : \gamma_r$, determined as to their ratios by the equations
$$a\alpha_r + a'\beta_r + a''\gamma_r = \theta_r \alpha_r,$$
$$b\alpha_r + b'\beta_r + b''\gamma_r = \theta_r \beta_r,$$
$$c\alpha_r + c'\beta_r + c''\gamma_r = \theta_r \gamma_r,$$
are such that, if
$$Y_r = \alpha_r y_1 + \beta_r y_2 + \gamma_r y_3, \quad X_r = \alpha_r x_1 + \beta_r x_2 + \gamma_r x_3,$$
we have
$$Y_r = \theta_r X_r.$$

The canonical form of the homogeneous substitution is
$$Y_1 = \theta_1 X_1, \quad Y_2 = \theta_2 X_2, \quad Y_3 = \theta_3 X_3;$$
and so the canonical form of the lineo-linear transformation is
$$\left. \begin{array}{l} \dfrac{\alpha_1 w + \beta_1 w' + \gamma_1}{\alpha_3 w + \beta_3 w' + \gamma_3} = \lambda \dfrac{\alpha_1 z + \beta_1 z' + \gamma_1}{\alpha_3 z + \beta_3 z' + \gamma_3} \\[2mm] \dfrac{\alpha_2 w + \beta_2 w' + \gamma_2}{\alpha_3 w + \beta_3 w' + \gamma_3} = \mu \dfrac{\alpha_2 z + \beta_2 z' + \gamma_2}{\alpha_3 z + \beta_3 z' + \gamma_3} \end{array} \right\},$$
where the quantities λ and μ, called the multipliers of the transformation, are
$$\lambda = \frac{\theta_1}{\theta_3}, \quad \mu = \frac{\theta_2}{\theta_3},$$
being the quotients of roots of the characteristic equation. The multipliers are unequal to one another, and neither of them is equal to unity.

This canonical form can be expressed by the equations
$$W = \lambda Z, \quad W' = \mu Z'.$$

Case II. Let one root of the characteristic equation be double and the other simple; and denote the roots by $\theta_1, \theta_1, \theta_3$. The canonical form of the homogeneous substitution is
$$Y_1 = \theta_1 X_1, \quad Y_2 = \kappa X_1 + \theta_1 X_2, \quad Y_3 = \theta_3 X_3,$$
where the forms of the variables X and Y are the same as in the first case; and the constant κ, in general, is not zero.

The canonical form of the lineo-linear transformation is of the type
$$W = \lambda Z, \quad W' = \lambda Z' + \sigma Z,$$
where
$$\lambda = \frac{\theta_1}{\theta_3},$$
and the constant σ, in general, is not zero. The repeated multiplier λ is not equal to unity.

Case III. Let the characteristic equation have a triple root θ. The canonical form of the homogeneous substitution is
$$Y_1 = \theta X_1, \quad Y_2 = \alpha X_1 + \theta X_2, \quad Y_3 = \beta X_1 + \gamma X_2 + \theta X_3;$$
and the canonical form of the lineo-linear transformation is of the type
$$W = Z + \rho, \quad W' = Z' + \sigma Z + \tau,$$
where the repeated multiplier is unity, and the constants ρ, σ, τ, in general, do not vanish.

23. Any power of the transformation can at once be derived from its canonical form. Let the transformation be applied m times in succession, and let the resulting variables be denoted by w_m and w_m'; then
$$\frac{\alpha_1 w_m + \beta_1 w_m' + \gamma_1}{\alpha_3 w_m + \beta_3 w_m' + \gamma_3} = \lambda^m \frac{\alpha_1 z + \beta_1 z' + \gamma_1}{\alpha_3 z + \beta_3 z' + \gamma_3},$$
$$\frac{\alpha_2 w_m + \beta_2 w_m' + \gamma_2}{\alpha_3 w_m + \beta_3 w_m' + \gamma_3} = \mu^m \frac{\alpha_2 z + \beta_2 z' + \gamma_2}{\alpha_3 z + \beta_3 z' + \gamma_3},$$
expressing w_m and w_m' in terms of z and z'.

When $\lambda^m = 1$ and $\mu^m = 1$, the mth power of the transformation gives an identical substitution. For then
$$\frac{\alpha_1 w_m + \beta_1 w_m' + \gamma_1}{\alpha_1 z + \beta_1 z' + \gamma_1} = \frac{\alpha_2 w_m + \beta_2 w_m' + \gamma_2}{\alpha_2 z + \beta_2 z' + \gamma_2} = \frac{\alpha_3 w_m + \beta_3 w_m' + \gamma_3}{\alpha_3 z + \beta_3 z' + \gamma_3}.$$
When each of these three equal fractions is denoted by ρ, we have
$$\alpha_1 (w_m - \rho z) + \beta_1 (w_m' - \rho z') + \gamma_1 (1 - \rho) = 0,$$
$$\alpha_2 (w_m - \rho z) + \beta_2 (w_m' - \rho z') + \gamma_2 (1 - \rho) = 0,$$
$$\alpha_3 (w_m - \rho z) + \beta_3 (w_m' - \rho z') + \gamma_3 (1 - \rho) = 0.$$
The determinant of the coefficients α, β, γ is not zero, because otherwise the canonical form of the original transformation would contain only one independent equation; hence
$$w_m - \rho z = 0, \quad w_m' - \rho z' = 0, \quad 1 - \rho = 0,$$
that is,
$$w_m = z, \quad w_m' = z',$$
shewing that the mth power of the original transformation gives an identical substitution, if $\lambda^m = 1$ and $\mu^m = 1$.

Invariant centres.

24. Certain places are left unaltered by the lineo-linear transformation between the z, z' field and the w, w' field. On the analogy with the corresponding points in the homographic transformation $w(cz+d) = az+b$, these unaltered places may be called double places or (because repetitions of the transformation still leave them unaltered) they will be called the *invariant centres* of the transformation.

Returning to the initial form of the transformation, and denoting any invariant centre by ζ and ζ', we have

$$a\zeta + b\zeta' + c = \theta\zeta,$$
$$a'\zeta + b'\zeta' + c' = \theta\zeta',$$
$$a''\zeta + b''\zeta' + c'' = \theta \ ;$$

with our preceding assumptions, θ manifestly is a root of the characteristic equation. Hence when all the roots of this equation are simple, we generally have three invariant centres, say ζ_1 and ζ_1', ζ_2 and ζ_2', ζ_3 and ζ_3', associated with θ_1, θ_2, θ_3 respectively. It is easy to verify that

$$\theta_1(\alpha_2\zeta_1 + \beta_2\zeta_1' + \gamma_2)$$
$$= (a\alpha_2 + a'\beta_2 + a''\gamma_2)\zeta_1 + (b\alpha_2 + b'\beta_2 + b''\gamma_2)\zeta_1' + c\alpha_2 + c'\beta_2 + c''\gamma_2$$
$$= \theta_2(\alpha_2\zeta_1 + \beta_2\zeta_1' + \gamma_2),$$

so that, as θ_1 and θ_2 are unequal, we must have

$$\alpha_2\zeta_1 + \beta_2\zeta_1' + \gamma_2 = 0.$$

Similarly
$$\alpha_3\zeta_1 + \beta_3\zeta_1' + \gamma_3 = 0,$$
while
$$\alpha_1\zeta_1 + \beta_1\zeta_1' + \gamma_1 \neq 0.$$

Thus the invariant centres are given by the equations

$$\left.\begin{array}{r}\alpha_2\zeta_1 + \beta_2\zeta_1' + \gamma_2 = 0\\ \alpha_3\zeta_1 + \beta_3\zeta_1' + \gamma_3 = 0\end{array}\right\},$$
$$\left.\begin{array}{r}\alpha_3\zeta_2 + \beta_3\zeta_2' + \gamma_3 = 0\\ \alpha_1\zeta_2 + \beta_1\zeta_2' + \gamma_1 = 0\end{array}\right\},$$
$$\left.\begin{array}{r}\alpha_1\zeta_3 + \beta_1\zeta_3' + \gamma_1 = 0\\ \alpha_2\zeta_3 + \beta_2\zeta_3' + \gamma_2 = 0\end{array}\right\},$$

a result which can be inferred also from the canonical form of the transformation.

In deducing this result, certain tacit assumptions have been made as to the exclusion of critical relations. It will easily be seen that the transformation

$$w\sqrt{2} = z+z', \quad w'\sqrt{2} = z-z',$$

is not an example (for the present purpose) of the general transformation.

Manifestly, we can take

$$\begin{vmatrix} w, & w', & 1 \\ \zeta_2, & \zeta_2', & 1 \\ \zeta_3, & \zeta_3', & 1 \end{vmatrix} \div \begin{vmatrix} w, & w', & 1 \\ \zeta_1, & \zeta_1', & 1 \\ \zeta_2, & \zeta_2', & 1 \end{vmatrix} = \lambda \begin{vmatrix} z, & z', & 1 \\ \zeta_2, & \zeta_2', & 1 \\ \zeta_3, & \zeta_3', & 1 \end{vmatrix} \div \begin{vmatrix} z, & z', & 1 \\ \zeta_1, & \zeta_1', & 1 \\ \zeta_2, & \zeta_2', & 1 \end{vmatrix},$$

$$\begin{vmatrix} w, & w', & 1 \\ \zeta_3, & \zeta_3', & 1 \\ \zeta_1, & \zeta_1', & 1 \end{vmatrix} \div \begin{vmatrix} w, & w', & 1 \\ \zeta_1, & \zeta_1', & 1 \\ \zeta_2, & \zeta_2', & 1 \end{vmatrix} = \mu \begin{vmatrix} z, & z', & 1 \\ \zeta_3, & \zeta_3', & 1 \\ \zeta_1, & \zeta_1', & 1 \end{vmatrix} \div \begin{vmatrix} z, & z', & 1 \\ \zeta_1, & \zeta_1', & 1 \\ \zeta_2, & \zeta_2', & 1 \end{vmatrix},$$

as a canonical form of the lineo-linear transformation.

This canonical form leads at once to an expression of the relations between the two sets of variables in the immediate vicinity of the invariant centres. Near ζ_1 and ζ_1', we have

$$z = \zeta_1 + \delta_1 z, \quad z' = \zeta_1' + \delta_1 z', \quad w = \zeta_1 + \delta_1 w, \quad w' = \zeta_1' + \delta_1 w',$$

where

$$\frac{\delta_1 w}{\zeta_2 - \zeta_1} - \frac{\delta_1 w'}{\zeta_2' - \zeta_1'} = \frac{1}{\lambda} \left\{ \frac{\delta_1 z}{\zeta_2 - \zeta_1} - \frac{\delta_1 z'}{\zeta_2' - \zeta_1'} \right\},$$

$$\frac{\delta_1 w}{\zeta_3 - \zeta_1} - \frac{\delta_1 w'}{\zeta_3' - \zeta_1'} = \frac{\mu}{\lambda} \left\{ \frac{\delta_1 z}{\zeta_3 - \zeta_1} - \frac{\delta_1 z'}{\zeta_3' - \zeta_1'} \right\}.$$

Near ζ_2 and ζ_2', we have

$$z = \zeta_2 + \delta_2 z, \quad z' = \zeta_2' + \delta_2 z', \quad w = \zeta_2 + \delta_2 w, \quad w' = \zeta_2' + \delta_2 w',$$

where

$$\frac{\delta_2 w}{\zeta_3 - \zeta_2} - \frac{\delta_2 w'}{\zeta_3' - \zeta_2'} = \frac{\lambda}{\mu} \left\{ \frac{\delta_2 z}{\zeta_3 - \zeta_2} - \frac{\delta_2 z'}{\zeta_3' - \zeta_2'} \right\},$$

$$\frac{\delta_2 w}{\zeta_1 - \zeta_2} - \frac{\delta_2 w'}{\zeta_1' - \zeta_2'} = \frac{1}{\mu} \left\{ \frac{\delta_2 z}{\zeta_1 - \zeta_2} - \frac{\delta_2 z'}{\zeta_1' - \zeta_2'} \right\}.$$

Near ζ_3 and ζ_3', we have

$$z = \zeta_3 + \delta_3 z, \quad z' = \zeta_3' + \delta_3 z', \quad w = \zeta_3 + \delta_3 w, \quad w' = \zeta_3' + \delta_3 w',$$

where

$$\frac{\delta_3 w}{\zeta_1 - \zeta_3} - \frac{\delta_3 w'}{\zeta_1' - \zeta_3'} = \mu \left\{ \frac{\delta_3 z}{\zeta_1 - \zeta_3} - \frac{\delta_3 z'}{\zeta_1' - \zeta_3'} \right\},$$

$$\frac{\delta_3 w}{\zeta_2 - \zeta_3} - \frac{\delta_3 w'}{\zeta_2' - \zeta_3'} = \lambda \left\{ \frac{\delta_3 z}{\zeta_2 - \zeta_3} - \frac{\delta_3 z'}{\zeta_2' - \zeta_3'} \right\}.$$

Moreover this new canonical form, involving explicitly the places of the invariant centres in their expressions, shews that the assignment of three invariant centres and two multipliers is generally sufficient for the construction of a canonical form of a lineo-linear transformation of the first type.

Ex. 1. Some very special assignments of invariant centres may lead to equations that do not characterise lineo-linear transformations. The resulting equations, in that event, belong to the range of exceptions.

Thus, if we take
$$\left.\begin{matrix}\zeta_1=1\\ \zeta_1'=-1\end{matrix}\right\}, \quad \left.\begin{matrix}\zeta_2=a\\ \zeta_2'=-a\end{matrix}\right\}, \quad \left.\begin{matrix}\zeta_3=a^2\\ \zeta_3'=-a^2\end{matrix}\right\},$$
where a is neither zero nor unity, and if we assign arbitrary multipliers λ and μ different from unity and different from one another, the canonical equations can be satisfied only by
$$w+w'=0, \quad z+z'=0,$$
which is not a lineo-linear transformation of the z, z' field into the w, w' field.

Other special examples of this exceptional class can easily be recognised. One inclusive example is given by the relations

$$\frac{\zeta_2'-\zeta_3'}{A}=\frac{\zeta_2-\zeta_3}{B}=\frac{\zeta_2\zeta_3'-\zeta_3\zeta_2'}{C}, \quad \begin{vmatrix}\zeta_1, & \zeta_1', & 1\\ \zeta_2, & \zeta_2', & 1\\ \zeta_3, & \zeta_3', & 1\end{vmatrix}=0;$$

$$\frac{\zeta_3'-\zeta_1'}{A}=\frac{\zeta_3-\zeta_1}{B}=\frac{\zeta_3\zeta_1'-\zeta_1\zeta_3'}{C},$$

and then the equations acquire the unsuitable form
$$Aw-Bw'+C=0, \quad Az-Bz'+C=0.$$

Ex. 2. When neither point in any one of the three invariant centres is at infinity, we can (by unessential changes of all the variables that amount to change of origin, rotation of axes, and magnification, in each of the planes independently of one another) give a simplified expression to the canonical form.

Suppose that no one of the quantities ζ_1, ζ_1', ζ_2, ζ_2', ζ_3, ζ_3' then is zero; alternative forms, when this supposition is not justified, are left as an exercise. We then transform the z-plane and the w-plane by the congruent relations
$$z-\zeta_1=(\zeta_2-\zeta_1)Z, \quad w-\zeta_1=(\zeta_2-\zeta_1)W;$$
and we transform the z'-plane and the w'-plane by the congruent relations
$$z'-\zeta_1'=(\zeta_2'-\zeta_1')Z', \quad w'-\zeta_1'=(\zeta_2'-\zeta_1')W'.$$
All of these are of the type just described; they require the same change of origin, the same magnification, and the same rotation, for the z-plane and the w-plane; and likewise for the z'-plane and the w'-plane. The effect of the transformation is to place, in the Z, Z' field and the W, W' field, two of the invariant centres at 0, 0 and 1, 1.

The third invariant centre then becomes a, a', where
$$a=\frac{\zeta_3-\zeta_1}{\zeta_2-\zeta_1}, \quad a'=\frac{\zeta_3'-\zeta_1'}{\zeta_2'-\zeta_1'}.$$
The equations, in a canonical form, of the lineo-linear transformations of the Z, Z' field into the W, W' field, having 0, 0; 1, 1; a, a'; for the invariant centres, are

$$\frac{\begin{vmatrix}W, & W', & 1\\ 1, & 1, & 1\\ a, & a', & 1\end{vmatrix}}{W-W'}=\lambda\frac{\begin{vmatrix}Z, & Z', & 1\\ 1, & 1, & 1\\ a, & a', & 1\end{vmatrix}}{Z-Z'}$$

$$\frac{Wa'-W'a}{W-W'}=\mu\frac{Za'-Z'a}{Z-Z'},$$

where λ and μ are different from one another and where (so far as present explanations extend) neither λ nor μ is equal to unity.

But it must be remembered, in taking these equations as the canonical form, that definite (if special) identical modifications of the z-plane and the w-plane have been made simultaneously, and likewise for the z'-plane and the w'-plane. The result of these modifications, in so far as they affect the original lineo-linear transformation, is left for consideration as an exercise.

Invariantive Frontiers.

25. In the theory of automorphic functions of a single complex variable, it proves important to have bounded regions of variation of the independent variable which are changed by the homographic substitutions into regions that are similarly bounded. Thus we have the customary period-parallelogram for the doubly-periodic functions; any parallelogram, under the transformations

$$w = z + \omega_1, \quad w = z + \omega_2,$$

remains a parallelogram and—with an appropriate limitation that the real part of ω_2/ω_1 is not zero—the opposite sides of the parallelogram correspond to one another. Similarly a circle or a straight line, under a transformation or a set of transformations of the type

$$(cz + d)\, w = az + b,$$

remains a circle or sometimes becomes a straight line; and so we can construct a curvilinear polygon, suited for the discussion of automorphic functions. These boundary curves—straight lines and circles—are the simplest which conserve their general character throughout the transformations indicated; they are the only algebraic curves of order not higher than the second which have this property. They are not the only algebraic curves, which have this property, when we proceed to orders higher than the second; thus bicircular quartics are homographically transformed into bicircular quartics.

For the appropriate division of the plane of the variable, when automorphic functions of a single complex variable are under consideration so as to secure an arrangement of polygons in each of which the complete variation of the functions can take place, other limitations—such as relations between constants so as to secure conterminous polygons—are necessary. They need not concern us for the moment. What is of importance is the conservation of general character in the curve or, what is the same thing, conservation of general character in the equation of the curve, under the operation of a homographic transformation.

26. Corresponding questions arise in the theory of functions of two complex variables. We have already seen that, when a z, z' field is determined by two relations, its frontier is represented by a couple of equations between the real and the imaginary parts of both variables; and therefore what is desired, for our immediate illustration, is a determination of the general character of a couple of equations which, giving the frontier of a z, z' field, are changed by the lineo-linear transformation into a couple of equations which, giving the frontier of a corresponding w, w' field, are of the same general character for the two fields. The invariance of form of such equations, at any rate for the most simple cases, must therefore be investigated.

We shall limit ourselves to the determination of only the simplest of those frontiers of a field of variation which are invariantive in character under a lineo-linear translation. Also, we shall consider only quite general transformations; special and more obvious forms may occur for special transformations, such as those contained in the simplest finite groups. Accordingly, in the equations

$$\frac{w}{az + bz' + c} = \frac{w'}{a'z + b'z' + c'} = \frac{1}{a''z + b''z' + c''},$$

we resolve the variables into their real and imaginary parts, viz.

$$z = x + iy, \quad z' = x' + iy', \quad w = u + iv, \quad w' = u' + iv';$$

and we require the simplest equations of the form

$$\phi(x, y, x', y') = 0, \quad \psi(x, y, x', y') = 0,$$

which, under the foregoing transformation, become

$$\Phi(u, v, u', v') = 0, \quad \Psi(u, v, u', v') = 0,$$

where Φ and Ψ are of the same character, in degree and combinations of the variables, as ϕ and ψ. Moreover, the constants in the transformation may be complex; so we write

$$a = a_1 + ia_2, \quad b = b_1 + ib_2, \quad c = c_1 + ic_2,$$
$$a' = a_1' + ia_2', \quad b' = b_1' + ib_2', \quad c' = c_1' + ic_2',$$
$$a'' = a_1'' + ia_2'', \quad b'' = b_1'' + ib_2'', \quad c'' = c_1'' + ic_2'',$$

in order to have the real and imaginary parts. Lastly, let

$$N_1 = a_1 x + b_1 x' - a_2 y - b_2 y' + c_1, \quad N_2 = a_2 x + b_2 x' + a_1 y + b_1 y' + c_2,$$
$$N_1' = a_1' x + b_1' x' - a_2' y - b_2' y' + c_1', \quad N_2' = a_2' x + b_2' x' + a_1' y + b_1' y' + c_2',$$
$$N_1'' = a_1'' x + b_1'' x' - a_2'' y - b_2'' y' + c_1'', \quad N_2'' = a_2'' x + b_2'' x' + a_1'' y + b_1'' y' + c_2'',$$
$$D = N_1''^2 + N_2''^2;$$

then the real equations of transformation are

$$Du = N_1 N_1'' + N_2 N_2'',$$
$$Dv = N_2 N_1'' - N_1 N_2'',$$
$$Du' = N_1' N_1'' + N_2' N_2'',$$
$$Dv' = N_2' N_1'' - N_1' N_2''.$$

Further, we have
$$D(u^2 + v^2) = N_1^2 + N_2^2,$$
$$D(uu' + vv') = N_1 N_1' + N_2 N_2',$$
$$D(uv' - u'v) = N_1 N_2' - N_2 N_1',$$
$$D(u'^2 + v'^2) = N_1'^2 + N_2'^2.$$

These equations express each of the quantities u, v, u', v', $u^2 + v^2$, $uu' + vv'$, $uv' - u'v$, $u'^2 + v'^2$, in the form of a rational fraction that has D for its denominator. The denominator D and each of the numerators in the eight fractions are linear combinations (with constant coefficients) of the quantities 1, x, y, x', y', $x^2 + y^2$, $xx' + yy'$, $xy' - x'y$, $x'^2 + y'^2$.

The same form of result holds when we express x, y, x', y' in terms of u, v, u', v'; any quantity, that is a linear combination of 1, x, y, x', y', $x^2 + y^2$, $xx' + yy'$, $xy' - x'y$, $x'^2 + y'^2$, comes to be a rational fraction the numerator of which is a linear combination of 1, u, v, u', v', $u^2 + v^2$, $uu' + vv'$, $uv' - u'v$, $u'^2 + v'^2$; the denominator is a linear combination of the same quantities, and is the same for all the fractions that represent the values of x, y, x', y', $x^2 + y^2$, $xx' + yy'$, $xy' - yx'$, $x'^2 + y'^2$. Consequently, any equation
$$A(x^2 + y^2) + C(xx' + yy') + D(xy' - yx') + B(x'^2 + y'^2)$$
$$+ Ex + Fy + Gx' + Hy' = K$$
is transformed into an equation
$$A'(u^2 + v^2) + C'(uu' + vv') + D'(uv' - u'v) + B'(u'^2 + v'^2)$$
$$+ E'u + F'v + G'u' + H'v' = K',$$
where all the quantities $A, \ldots, K$ are constants, as also are $A', \ldots, K'$, each member of either set being expressible linearly and homogeneously in terms of the members of the other set.

27. Thus the transformed equation is of the same general character, concerning combinations and degree in the variables, as the original equation; and there is little difficulty in seeing that it is the equation of lowest degree which has this general character of invariance. Further, two such simultaneous equations are transformed into two such simultaneous equations of the same character.

This is the generalisation of the property that the equation of a circle is transformed into the equation of another circle by a homographic substitution in a single complex variable.

Accordingly, when a z, z' field having a frontier given by two equations of the foregoing character is transformed by a lineo-linear transformation into a w, w' field, the frontier of the new field is given by two similar equations. We define such a frontier as quadratic, when it is given by equations of the second degree in the variables; and therefore we can sum up the whole investigation by declaring that *a z, z' field, which has a quadratic frontier, is transformed by a lineo-linear transformation into a w, w' field, which also has a quadratic frontier.*

28. One special inference can be made, which has its counterpart in homographic substitutions for a single variable, viz., when all the coefficients in a lineo-linear transformation are real, the axes of real parts of the complex variables in their respective planes are conserved. For when all the constants are real, we have

$$vD = (a''b - ab'')(xy' - x'y) + (ac'' - a''c)y + (bc'' - b''c)y',$$
$$v'D = (a''b' - a'b'')(xy' - x'y) + (a'c'' - a''c')y + (b'c'' - b''c')y';$$

and therefore the configuration given by $y = 0$ and $y' = 0$ becomes the configuration given by $v = 0$ and $v' = 0$. The converse also holds, owing to the lineo-linear character of the transformation.

These axes of real quantities in the planes of the complex variables are, of course, an exceedingly special case of the general quadratic frontier, which can be regarded as given by the two equations

$$A_1(x^2 + y^2) + B_1(x'^2 + y'^2) + C_1(xx' + yy') + D_1(xy' - x'y)$$
$$+ E_1 x + F_1 y + G_1 x + H_1 y = K_1,$$
$$A_2(x^2 + y^2) + B_2(x'^2 + y'^2) + C_2(xx' + yy') + D_2(xy' - x'y)$$
$$+ E_2 x + F_2 y + G_2 x + H_2 y = K_2.$$

Let $\bar{z}$ and $\bar{z}'$ be the conjugates of z and z' respectively, so that

$$\bar{z} = x - iy, \quad \bar{z}' = x' - iy';$$

then the general quadratic frontier can also be regarded as given by the equations

$$A_1 z\bar{z} + B_1 z'\bar{z}' + C_1' z\bar{z}' + D_1' z'\bar{z} + E_1' z + F_1' \bar{z} + G_1' z + H_1' \bar{z} = K_1,$$
$$A_2 z\bar{z} + B_2 z'\bar{z}' + C_2' z\bar{z}' + D_2' z'\bar{z} + E_2' z + F_2' \bar{z} + G_2' z + H_2' \bar{z} = K_2,$$

where A_1, B_1, K_1, A_2, B_2, K_2 are real constants, while C_1' and D_1', C_2' and D_2', E_1' and F_1', E_2' and F_2', G_1' and H_1', G_2' and H_2', are pairs of conjugate constants.

Manifestly any equation of this latest form is transformable by the lineo-linear substitution into another equation of the same form.

29. Another mode of discussing the frontier of a z, z' field, which is represented by two equations that have an invariantive character under a lineo-linear transformation, is provided by the generalisation of a special mode of dealing with the same question for a single complex variable.

The general homographic substitution affecting a single complex variable has the canonical form

$$\frac{w - \alpha}{w - \beta} = K \frac{z - \alpha}{z - \beta},$$

3—2

where α and β are the double points of the substitution, and K is the multiplier. Let

$$w = u + iv, \quad z = x + iy, \quad \alpha = a + ia', \quad \beta = b + ib', \quad K = \kappa e^{ki},$$

where $u, v, x, y, a, a', b, b', \kappa, k$ are real; then

$$\frac{u - a + i(v - a')}{u - b + i(v - b')} = \kappa e^{ki} \frac{x - a + i(y - a')}{x - b + i(y - b')},$$

and therefore

$$\tan^{-1} \frac{(u - b)(v - a') - (u - a)(v - b')}{(u - a)(u - b) + (v - a')(v - b')}$$
$$- \tan^{-1} \frac{(x - b)(y - a') - (x - a)(y - b')}{(x - a)(x - b) + (y - a')(y - b')} = k.$$

Hence the circle

$$(x - a)(x - b) + (y - a')(y - b') = m\{(x - b)(y - a') - (x - a)(y - b')\},$$

which passes through the double points (a, a') and (b, b') of the substitution, is transformed into the circle

$$(u - a)(u - b) + (v - a')(v - b') = M\{(u - b)(v - a') - (u - a)(v - b')\},$$

which also passes through those common points. The constants m and M are connected by the relation

$$m - M = (1 + mM) \tan k.$$

At a common point, the two circles cut at an angle k, which depends only upon the multiplier; thus when an arbitrary circle is taken through the common points, it is transformed by the homographic substitution into another circle through those points cutting it at an angle that depends only upon the constants of the substitution.

This process admits of immediate generalisation to the case of two complex variables. Let the lineo-linear transformation in two variables be taken in its canonical form; and write

$$\alpha_1 z + \beta_1 z' + \gamma_1 = l_1' + i l_1'', \quad \alpha_1 w + \beta_1 w' + \gamma_1 = L_1' + i L_1'',$$
$$\alpha_2 z + \beta_2 z' + \gamma_2 = l_2' + i l_2'', \quad \alpha_2 w + \beta_2 w' + \gamma_2 = L_2' + i L_2'',$$
$$\alpha_3 z + \beta_3 z' + \gamma_3 = l_3' + i l_3'', \quad \alpha_3 w + \beta_3 w' + \gamma_3 = L_3' + i L_3'',$$

where $l_1', l_1'', l_2', l_2'', l_3', l_3''$ are real linear functions of x, y, x', y' and $L_1', L_1'', L_2', L_2'', L_3', L_3''$ are respectively the same real linear functions of u, v, u', v'. The three invariant centres are the places given by the equations

$$\left. \begin{array}{c} l_2' = 0 \\ l_2'' = 0 \\ l_3' = 0 \\ l_3'' = 0 \end{array} \right\}, \quad \left. \begin{array}{c} l_3' = 0 \\ l_3'' = 0 \\ l_1' = 0 \\ l_1'' = 0 \end{array} \right\}, \quad \left. \begin{array}{c} l_1' = 0 \\ l_1'' = 0 \\ l_2' = 0 \\ l_2'' = 0 \end{array} \right\};$$

and they are also the same places given by what are effectively the same equations

$$\left.\begin{aligned}L_2' &= 0\\ L_2'' &= 0\\ L_3' &= 0\\ L_3'' &= 0\end{aligned}\right\}, \quad \left.\begin{aligned}L_3' &= 0\\ L_3'' &= 0\\ L_1' &= 0\\ L_1'' &= 0\end{aligned}\right\}, \quad \left.\begin{aligned}L_1' &= 0\\ L_1'' &= 0\\ L_2' &= 0\\ L_2'' &= 0\end{aligned}\right\}.$$

The canonical form of the lineo-linear transformation now is

$$\frac{L_1' + iL_1''}{L_3' + iL_3''} = \lambda \frac{l_1' + il_1''}{l_3' + il_3''},$$

$$\frac{L_2' + iL_2''}{L_3' + iL_3''} = \mu \frac{l_2' + il_2''}{l_3' + il_3''};$$

and therefore, among other inferences, we have

$$\tan^{-1}\frac{L_1'L_3'' - L_3'L_1''}{L_1'L_3' + L_1''L_3''} - \tan^{-1}\frac{l_1'l_3'' - l_3'l_1''}{l_1'l_3' + l_1''l_3''} = -\arg \lambda,$$

$$\tan^{-1}\frac{L_3'L_2'' - L_2'L_3''}{L_3'L_2' + L_3''L_2''} - \tan^{-1}\frac{l_3'l_2'' - l_2'l_3''}{l_3'l_2' + l_3''l_2''} = \quad \arg \mu,$$

$$\tan^{-1}\frac{L_2'L_1'' - L_1'L_2''}{L_2'L_1' + L_2''L_1''} - \tan^{-1}\frac{l_2'l_1'' - l_1'l_2''}{l_2'l_1' + l_2''l_1''} = \quad \arg \lambda - \arg \mu.$$

Accordingly, the frontier configuration, represented by any two of the three equations

$$l_3'l_2'' - l_2'l_3'' = p\,(l_3'l_2' + l_3''l_2''),$$
$$l_1'l_3'' - l_3'l_1'' = q\,(l_1'l_3' + l_1''l_3''),$$
$$l_2'l_1'' - l_1'l_2'' = r\,(l_2'l_1' + l_2''l_1''),$$

where the three constants p, q, r are subject to the relation

$$p + q + r = pqr,$$

so that the three equations are really equivalent to only two independent equations, is changed by the transformation into the frontier configuration represented by any two of the three equations

$$L_3'L_2'' - L_2'L_3'' = P\,(L_3'L_2' + L_3''L_2''),$$
$$L_1'L_3'' - L_3'L_1'' = Q\,(L_1'L_3' + L_1''L_3''),$$
$$L_2'L_1'' - L_1'L_2'' = R\,(L_2'L_1' + L_2''L_1''),$$

where the three constants P, Q, R are subject to the relation

$$P + Q + R = PQR,$$

so that these three equations are really equivalent to only two independent equations. Moreover, if

$$\mu = Ge^{gi}, \quad \lambda = He^{hi},$$

where g, h, G, H are real constants while G and H are positive, we have
$$P - p = (1 + Pp) \tan g,$$
$$Q - q = -(1 + Qq) \tan h,$$
$$R - r = (1 + Rr) \tan (h - g).$$
It is easy to verify that, if either of the relations
$$P + Q + R = PQR, \quad p + q + r = pqr,$$
is satisfied, the other also is satisfied in virtue of these last equations.

The quadratic frontier of the z, z' field and the quadratic frontier of the transformed w, w' field both pass through the three invariant centres of the lineo-linear transformation.

Ex. 1. In connection with the homographic substitution in a single variable
$$\frac{w - a}{w - \beta} = K \frac{z - a}{z - \beta}$$
(in the preceding notation), shew that the constant m in the equation of the circle
$$(x - a)(x - b) + (y - a')(y - b') = m\{(x - b)(y - a') - (x - a)(y - b')\}$$
is the tangent of the angle at which the circle cuts the straight line joining the double points of the substitution.

Prove also that, if $2d$ is the distance between the double points, r is the radius of the foregoing circle, and R the radius of the circle into which it is transformed,
$$\frac{1}{R^2} - \frac{2 \cos k}{rR} + \frac{1}{r^2} = \frac{\sin^2 k}{d^2}.$$

Ex. 2. Shew that the circle
$$(x - a)^2 + (y - b)^2 = n^2\{(x - a')^2 + (y - b')^2\}$$
is transformed, by the homographic substitution, into the circle
$$(u - a)^2 + (v - b)^2 = N^2\{(u - a')^2 + (v - b')^2\},$$
where
$$N = \kappa n.$$
Interpret the result geometrically.

Ex. 3. Construct a lineo-linear transformation which has $0, 0$; $1, 1$; $i, -i$ for its invariant centres; and shew that there are quadratic frontiers of the z, z' field, which pass through these invariant centres and are represented by any two of the three equations
$$x^2 + y^2 + x'^2 + y'^2 - 2(xx' + yy') - 2(xy' - x'y) - 2(y - y')$$
$$= a\{x^2 + y^2 - (x'^2 + y'^2) + 2(x - x')\},$$
$$x^2 + y^2 + x'^2 + y'^2 + 2(xx' + yy') - 2(xy' - x'y) - 2(x + x')$$
$$= \beta\{x^2 + y^2 - (x'^2 + y'^2) - 2(y + y')\},$$
$$x^2 + y^2 - (x'^2 + y'^2) = \gamma(xy' - x'y),$$
provided the constants a, β, γ satisfy the relation
$$\gamma(a + \beta) = 2a + 2\beta - \gamma.$$

Verify that the lineo-linear transformation changes these equations into equations in u, v, u', v' of the same form but with different constants a', β', γ' satisfying the relation

$$\gamma'(a'+\beta') = 2a' + 2\beta' - \gamma'.$$

Shew that, at the invariant centre 0, 0, small variations dz and dz' cause small variations dw and dw' such that

$$dw - dw' = \frac{1}{\lambda}(dz - dz'),$$

$$dw + dw' = i\frac{\mu}{\lambda}(dz + dz');$$

and obtain the relations between the small variations at each of the other two invariant centres.

Invariants and Covariants of quadratic frontiers.

30. Owing to the importance of the quadratic frontier, because it is given by two equations of the second order that are invariantive in general character under any lineo-linear transformation, we shall briefly consider those combinations of the coefficients which are actually invariantive under all such transformations. The proper discussion of the invariants and covariants, which belong to two equations of any order that are invariantive in general character under the transformations, requires an elaboration of analysis that will take us far from the main purpose into what really is the full theory of invariants and covariants. It will be sufficient to give the elements of that theory as connected with the fundamental procedure. Moreover, we shall take a general quadratic frontier and not merely the special class which pass through the invariant centres of an assigned transformation; and we require the quantities which are invariantive under all lineo-linear transformations and not merely under one particular transformation. We further shall only deal with such invariantive quantities as are algebraically independent of one another.

31. There are several modes of procedure; in all of them, it is convenient to use homogeneous variables, as was done in establishing the canonical form of the lineo-linear substitution. So we take

$$\frac{z}{x_1} = \frac{z'}{x_2} = \frac{1}{x_3}, \qquad \frac{w}{y_1} = \frac{w'}{y_2} = \frac{1}{y_3}.$$

Also, as the variables respectively conjugate to z, z', w, w' have been introduced, we shall require variables respectively conjugate to $x_1, x_2, x_3, y_1, y_2, y_3$; denoting these by $\bar{x}_1, \bar{x}_2, \bar{x}_3, \bar{y}_1, \bar{y}_2, \bar{y}_3$, we take

$$\frac{\bar{z}}{\bar{x}_1} = \frac{\bar{z}'}{\bar{x}_2} = \frac{1}{\bar{x}_3}, \qquad \frac{\bar{w}}{\bar{y}_1} = \frac{\bar{w}'}{\bar{y}_2} = \frac{1}{\bar{y}_3}.$$

For the present purpose, we take a z, z' field determined by two relations $Q \leqslant 0$, $Q' \leqslant 0$, where

$$Q = Ay_1\bar{y}_1 + By_1\bar{y}_2 + Cy_1\bar{y}_3 + Dy_2\bar{y}_1 + Ey_2\bar{y}_2 + Fy_2\bar{y}_3$$
$$+ Gy_3\bar{y}_1 + Hy_3\bar{y}_2 + Ky_3\bar{y}_3,$$
$$Q' = A'y_1\bar{y}_1 + B'y_1\bar{y}_2 + C'y_1\bar{y}_3 + D'y_2\bar{y}_1 + E'y_2\bar{y}_2 + F'y_2\bar{y}_3$$
$$+ G'y_3\bar{y}_1 + H'y_3\bar{y}_2 + K'y_3\bar{y}_3;$$

its quadratic frontier is given by the equations

$$Q = 0, \quad Q' = 0,$$

which, on division by the non-vanishing quantity $y_3\bar{y}_3$, acquire the form of our earlier equations. In Q the coefficients A, E, K are real, while B and D, C and G, F and H, are conjugates in the stated pairs; and similarly for the coefficients in Q'.

The method of procedure that we shall use is based upon an application of Lie's theory of continuous groups to these quantities Q and Q'; and the application proves fairly simple in detail when we use umbral forms simultaneously with the expressed forms. Accordingly, we introduce umbral coefficients $\sigma_1, \sigma_2, \sigma_3, \sigma_1', \sigma_2', \sigma_3'$, with their conjugates $\bar{\sigma}_1, \bar{\sigma}_2, \bar{\sigma}_3$, $\bar{\sigma}_1', \bar{\sigma}_2', \bar{\sigma}_3'$; we take

$$\left. \begin{array}{l} \Pi = \sigma_1 y_1 + \sigma_2 y_2 + \sigma_3 y_3 \\ \bar{\Pi} = \bar{\sigma}_1 \bar{y}_1 + \bar{\sigma}_2 \bar{y}_2 + \bar{\sigma}_3 \bar{y}_3 \end{array} \right\}, \quad \left. \begin{array}{l} \Pi' = \sigma_1' y_1 + \sigma_2' y_2 + \sigma_3' y_3 \\ \bar{\Pi}' = \bar{\sigma}_1' \bar{y}_1 + \bar{\sigma}_2' \bar{y}_2 + \bar{\sigma}_3' \bar{y}_3 \end{array} \right\},$$

and we write

$$Q = \Pi\bar{\Pi}, \quad Q' = \Pi'\bar{\Pi}'.$$

We then both define and secure the umbral character of these new coefficients by imposing the customary condition that the only combinations of the umbral constants which have significance are those leading to the expressed coefficients in the form

$$A = \sigma_1\bar{\sigma}_1, \quad D = \sigma_2\bar{\sigma}_1, \quad G = \sigma_3\bar{\sigma}_1,$$
$$B = \sigma_1\bar{\sigma}_2, \quad E = \sigma_2\bar{\sigma}_2, \quad H = \sigma_3\bar{\sigma}_2,$$
$$C = \sigma_1\bar{\sigma}_3, \quad F = \sigma_2\bar{\sigma}_3, \quad K = \sigma_3\bar{\sigma}_3;$$

and likewise for the coefficients of Q'.

When the lineo-linear transformation, in the form

$$\left. \begin{array}{l} y_1 = ax_1 + bx_2 + cx_3 \\ y_2 = a'x_1 + b'x_2 + c'x_3 \\ y_3 = a''x_1 + b''x_2 + c''x_3 \end{array} \right\},$$

and its conjugate, in the form

$$\left. \begin{array}{l} \bar{y}_1 = \bar{a}\bar{x}_1 + \bar{b}\bar{x}_2 + \bar{c}\bar{x}_3 \\ \bar{y}_2 = \bar{a}'\bar{x}_1 + \bar{b}'\bar{x}_2 + \bar{c}'\bar{x}_3 \\ \bar{y}_3 = \bar{a}''\bar{x}_1 + \bar{b}''\bar{x}_2 + \bar{c}''\bar{x}_3 \end{array} \right\},$$

are applied to Q and Q', these become P and P' respectively, so that we take
$$Q = P, \quad Q' = P',$$
and then
$$P = A_1 x_1 \bar{x}_1 + B_1 x_1 \bar{x}_2 + C_1 x_1 \bar{x}_3 + D_1 x_2 \bar{x}_1 + E_1 x_2 \bar{x}_2 + F_1 x_2 \bar{x}_3$$
$$+ G_1 x_3 \bar{x}_1 + H_1 x_3 \bar{x}_2 + K_1 x_3 \bar{x}_3,$$
$$P' = A_1' x_1 \bar{x}_1 + B_1' x_1 \bar{x}_2 + C_1' x_1 \bar{x}_3 + D_1' x_2 \bar{x}_1 + E_1' x_2 \bar{x}_2 + F_1' x_2 \bar{x}_3$$
$$+ G_1' x_3 \bar{x}_1 + H_1' x_3 \bar{x}_2 + K_1' x_3 \bar{x}_3.$$

We take
$$S = s_1 x_1 + s_2 x_2 + s_3 x_3, \quad S' = s_1' x_1 + s_2' x_2 + s_3' x_3,$$
$$\bar{S} = \bar{s}_1 \bar{x}_1 + \bar{s}_2 \bar{x}_2 + \bar{s}_3 \bar{x}_3, \quad \bar{S}' = \bar{s}_1' \bar{x}_1 + \bar{s}_2' \bar{x}_2 + \bar{s}_3' \bar{x}_3,$$
where $s_1, s_2, s_3, s_1', s_2', s_3'$ are new umbral coefficients, while $\bar{s}_1, \bar{s}_2, \bar{s}_3, \bar{s}_1', \bar{s}_2', \bar{s}_3'$ are their conjugates; and we write
$$P = S\bar{S}, \quad Q = S'\bar{S}',$$
regarding Π as transformed into S, $\bar{\Pi}$ into $\bar{S}$, Π' into S', and $\bar{\Pi}'$ into $\bar{S}'$. Then the laws of relation between the umbral coefficients in Π and S, and in $\bar{\Pi}$ and $\bar{S}$, are
$$\left.\begin{array}{l} s_1 = a\sigma_1 + a'\sigma_2 + a''\sigma_3 \\ s_2 = b\sigma_1 + b'\sigma_2 + b''\sigma_3 \\ s_3 = c\sigma_1 + c'\sigma_2 + c''\sigma_3 \end{array}\right\}, \quad \left.\begin{array}{l} \bar{s}_1 = \bar{a}\bar{\sigma}_1 + \bar{a}'\bar{\sigma}_2 + \bar{a}''\bar{\sigma}_3 \\ \bar{s}_2 = \bar{b}\bar{\sigma}_1 + \bar{b}'\bar{\sigma}_2 + \bar{b}''\bar{\sigma}_3 \\ \bar{s}_3 = \bar{c}\bar{\sigma}_1 + \bar{c}'\bar{\sigma}_2 + \bar{c}''\bar{\sigma}_3 \end{array}\right\};$$
and the same laws of relation hold between the umbral coefficients in Π' and S', and in $\bar{\Pi}'$ and $\bar{S}'$. Finally, in connection with our transformation, we write
$$\Delta = \begin{vmatrix} a, & b, & c \\ a', & b', & c' \\ a'', & b'', & c'' \end{vmatrix}, \quad \bar{\Delta} = \begin{vmatrix} \bar{a}, & \bar{b}, & \bar{c} \\ \bar{a}', & \bar{b}', & \bar{c}' \\ \bar{a}'', & \bar{b}'', & \bar{c}'' \end{vmatrix},$$
where Δ has the same significance as before, $\bar{\Delta}$ is its conjugate, and neither Δ nor $\bar{\Delta}$ vanishes.

32. As an example of an invariant, consider the quantity
$$I = \begin{vmatrix} A_1, & B_1, & C_1 \\ D_1, & E_1, & F_1 \\ G_1, & H_1, & K_1 \end{vmatrix}.$$
To express it in umbral symbols, three sets of these are required because it is of degree three in the non-umbral coefficients. Denoting these by $s_1, s_2, s_3, t_1, t_2, t_3, u_1, u_2, u_3$, with their conjugates, we easily find that I is equal to
$$\tfrac{1}{6} \begin{vmatrix} s_1, & s_2, & s_3 \\ t_1, & t_2, & t_3 \\ u_1, & u_2, & u_3 \end{vmatrix} \begin{vmatrix} \bar{s}_1, & \bar{s}_2, & \bar{s}_3 \\ \bar{t}_1, & \bar{t}_2, & \bar{t}_3 \\ \bar{u}_1, & \bar{u}_2, & \bar{u}_3 \end{vmatrix},$$

that is, to

$$\tfrac{1}{6} \begin{vmatrix} \sigma_1, & \sigma_2, & \sigma_3 \\ \tau_1, & \tau_2, & \tau_3 \\ \upsilon_1, & \upsilon_2, & \upsilon_3 \end{vmatrix} \begin{vmatrix} a, & b, & c \\ a', & b', & c' \\ a'', & b'', & c'' \end{vmatrix} \begin{vmatrix} \bar{\sigma}_1, & \bar{\sigma}_2, & \bar{\sigma}_3 \\ \bar{\tau}_1, & \bar{\tau}_2, & \bar{\tau}_3 \\ \bar{\upsilon}_1, & \bar{\upsilon}_2, & \bar{\upsilon}_3 \end{vmatrix} \begin{vmatrix} \bar{a}, & \bar{b}, & \bar{c} \\ \bar{a}', & \bar{b}', & \bar{c}' \\ \bar{a}'', & \bar{b}'', & \bar{c}'' \end{vmatrix},$$

that is, to

$$\tfrac{1}{6} \Delta\bar{\Delta} \begin{vmatrix} \sigma_1, & \sigma_2, & \sigma_3 \\ \tau_1, & \tau_2, & \tau_3 \\ \upsilon_1, & \upsilon_2, & \upsilon_3 \end{vmatrix} \begin{vmatrix} \bar{\sigma}_1, & \bar{\sigma}_2, & \bar{\sigma}_3 \\ \bar{\tau}_1, & \bar{\tau}_2, & \bar{\tau}_3 \\ \bar{\upsilon}_1, & \bar{\upsilon}_2, & \bar{\upsilon}_3 \end{vmatrix};$$

and therefore

$$\begin{vmatrix} A_1, & B_1, & C_1 \\ D_1, & E_1, & F_1 \\ G_1, & H_1, & K_1 \end{vmatrix} = \Delta\bar{\Delta} \begin{vmatrix} A, & B, & C \\ D, & E, & F \\ G, & H, & K \end{vmatrix},$$

a relation which establishes the invariantive property of the quantity I which is a function of the non-umbral coefficients of P alone.

The same combination of the coefficients of P' alone is easily seen to be an invariant. The simplest covariants are P and P'; for we have

$$Q = P, \quad Q' = P'.$$

33. Passing now to the consideration of invariants and of covariants that belong to the general quadratic frontier, we define any quantity

$$\phi(y_1, y_2, y_3, \bar{y}_1, \bar{y}_2, \bar{y}_3, A, \dots, K, A', \dots, K')$$

to be such a function if it satisfies a relation

$$\Phi = \Delta^\rho \bar{\Delta}^\rho \phi,$$

where Φ is the same function of $x_1, x_2, x_3, \bar{x}_1, \bar{x}_2, \bar{x}_3, A_1, \dots, K_1, A_1', \dots, K_1'$ as ϕ is of its own arguments. We shall deal only with integral (not with fractional) homogeneous combinations of the variables and the coefficients; and we assume that, in the foregoing relation which defines an invariant or a covariant, the index of $\bar{\Delta}$ is the same as that of Δ because we are limiting ourselves to the properties of real frontiers as defined by two real equations. And we retain the customary discrimination, by the occurrence or the non-occurrence of variables, between a covariant and an invariant.

By Lie's theory of continuous groups[*], it is sufficient to retain the aggregate of the most general infinitesimal transformations of a continuous transformation in order to construct the full effect of the finite continuous

---

[*] For proofs of this fundamental theorem, see Campbell, *Theory of continuous groups*, chap. iii.

transformation. Accordingly, for our immediate purpose, it is sufficient to obtain an algebraically complete aggregate of integrals of the set of partial differential equations which characterise the full tale of the infinitesimal transformations in question. To obtain these, we take

$$\left. \begin{array}{lll} a = 1 + \epsilon_1, & b = \epsilon_2, & c = \epsilon_3 \\ a' = \epsilon_4, & b' = 1 + \epsilon_5, & c' = \epsilon_6 \\ a'' = \epsilon_7, & b'' = \epsilon_8, & c'' = 1 + \epsilon_9 \end{array} \right\},$$

$$\left. \begin{array}{lll} \bar{a} = 1 + \bar{\epsilon}_1, & \bar{b} = \bar{\epsilon}_2, & \bar{c} = \bar{\epsilon}_3 \\ \bar{a}' = \bar{\epsilon}_4, & \bar{b}' = 1 + \bar{\epsilon}_5, & \bar{c}' = \bar{\epsilon}_6 \\ \bar{a}'' = \bar{\epsilon}_7, & \bar{b}'' = \bar{\epsilon}_8, & \bar{c}'' = 1 + \bar{\epsilon}_9 \end{array} \right\}.$$

For the most general infinitesimal transformation, all the quantities ϵ and $\bar{\epsilon}$ are small, arbitrary, and independent of one another, subject to the condition that ϵ_n and $\bar{\epsilon}_n$, for the nine values of n, are conjugate to one another.

The laws of relation among the umbral coefficients now are

$$\left. \begin{array}{l} s_1 - \sigma_1 = \epsilon_1 \sigma_1 + \epsilon_4 \sigma_2 + \epsilon_7 \sigma_3 \\ s_2 - \sigma_2 = \epsilon_2 \sigma_1 + \epsilon_5 \sigma_2 + \epsilon_8 \sigma_3 \\ s_3 - \sigma_3 = \epsilon_3 \sigma_1 + \epsilon_6 \sigma_2 + \epsilon_9 \sigma_3 \end{array} \right\}, \quad \left. \begin{array}{l} \bar{s}_1 - \bar{\sigma}_1 = \bar{\epsilon}_1 \bar{\sigma}_1 + \bar{\epsilon}_4 \bar{\sigma}_2 + \bar{\epsilon}_7 \bar{\sigma}_3 \\ \bar{s}_2 - \bar{\sigma}_2 = \bar{\epsilon}_2 \bar{\sigma}_1 + \bar{\epsilon}_5 \bar{\sigma}_2 + \bar{\epsilon}_8 \bar{\sigma}_3 \\ \bar{s}_3 - \bar{\sigma}_3 = \bar{\epsilon}_3 \bar{\sigma}_1 + \bar{\epsilon}_6 \bar{\sigma}_2 + \bar{\epsilon}_9 \bar{\sigma}_3 \end{array} \right\}.$$

Consequently the infinitesimal variations of the coefficients in the equations of the quadratic frontier are given by the equations

$$\left. \begin{array}{l} \delta A = A_1 - A = \epsilon_1 A + \epsilon_4 D + \epsilon_7 G + \bar{\epsilon}_1 A + \bar{\epsilon}_4 B + \bar{\epsilon}_7 C \\ \delta B = B_1 - B = \epsilon_1 B + \epsilon_4 E + \epsilon_7 H + \bar{\epsilon}_2 A + \bar{\epsilon}_5 B + \bar{\epsilon}_8 C \\ \delta C = C_1 - C = \epsilon_1 C + \epsilon_4 F + \epsilon_7 K + \bar{\epsilon}_3 A + \bar{\epsilon}_6 B + \bar{\epsilon}_9 C \\ \delta D = D_1 - D = \epsilon_2 A + \epsilon_5 D + \epsilon_8 G + \bar{\epsilon}_1 D + \bar{\epsilon}_4 E + \bar{\epsilon}_7 F \\ \delta E = E_1 - E = \epsilon_2 B + \epsilon_5 E + \epsilon_8 H + \bar{\epsilon}_2 D + \bar{\epsilon}_5 E + \bar{\epsilon}_8 F \\ \delta F = F_1 - F = \epsilon_2 C + \epsilon_5 F + \epsilon_8 K + \bar{\epsilon}_3 D + \bar{\epsilon}_6 E + \bar{\epsilon}_9 F \\ \delta G = G_1 - G = \epsilon_3 A + \epsilon_6 D + \epsilon_9 G + \bar{\epsilon}_1 G + \bar{\epsilon}_4 H + \bar{\epsilon}_7 K \\ \delta H = H_1 - H = \epsilon_3 B + \epsilon_6 E + \epsilon_9 H + \bar{\epsilon}_2 G + \bar{\epsilon}_5 H + \bar{\epsilon}_8 K \\ \delta K = K_1 - K = \epsilon_3 C + \epsilon_6 F + \epsilon_9 K + \bar{\epsilon}_3 G + \bar{\epsilon}_6 H + \bar{\epsilon}_9 K \end{array} \right\};$$

with a corresponding set of nine expressions for the infinitesimal variations of the coefficients $A', \ldots, K'$.

The infinitesimal variations of the variables are given by the relations

$$\left. \begin{array}{l} y_1 - x_1 = \epsilon_1 x_1 + \epsilon_2 x_2 + \epsilon_3 x_3 \\ y_2 - x_2 = \epsilon_4 x_1 + \epsilon_5 x_2 + \epsilon_6 x_3 \\ y_3 - x_3 = \epsilon_7 x_1 + \epsilon_8 x_2 + \epsilon_9 x_3 \end{array} \right\}, \quad \left. \begin{array}{l} \bar{y}_1 - \bar{x}_1 = \bar{\epsilon}_1 \bar{x}_1 + \bar{\epsilon}_2 \bar{x}_2 + \bar{\epsilon}_3 \bar{x}_3 \\ \bar{y}_2 - \bar{x}_2 = \bar{\epsilon}_4 \bar{x}_1 + \bar{\epsilon}_5 \bar{x}_2 + \bar{\epsilon}_6 \bar{x}_3 \\ \bar{y}_3 - \bar{x}_3 = \bar{\epsilon}_7 \bar{x}_1 + \bar{\epsilon}_8 \bar{x}_2 + \bar{\epsilon}_9 \bar{x}_3 \end{array} \right\};$$

and therefore, so far as small quantities up to the first order are concerned, we have

$$\left.\begin{aligned}x_1 - y_1 &= -\epsilon_1 y_1 - \epsilon_2 y_2 - \epsilon_3 y_3 \\ x_2 - y_2 &= -\epsilon_4 y_1 - \epsilon_5 y_2 - \epsilon_6 y_3 \\ x_3 - y_3 &= -\epsilon_7 y_1 - \epsilon_8 y_2 - \epsilon_9 y_3\end{aligned}\right\}, \quad \left.\begin{aligned}\bar{x}_1 - \bar{y}_1 &= -\bar{\epsilon}_1 \bar{y}_1 - \bar{\epsilon}_2 \bar{y}_2 - \bar{\epsilon}_3 \bar{y}_3 \\ \bar{x}_2 - \bar{y}_2 &= -\bar{\epsilon}_4 \bar{y}_1 - \bar{\epsilon}_5 \bar{y}_2 - \bar{\epsilon}_6 \bar{y}_3 \\ \bar{x}_3 - \bar{y}_3 &= -\bar{\epsilon}_7 \bar{y}_1 - \bar{\epsilon}_8 \bar{y}_2 - \bar{\epsilon}_9 \bar{y}_3\end{aligned}\right\}.$$

And, lastly, we have

$$\Delta \bar{\Delta} = 1 + \epsilon_1 + \epsilon_5 + \epsilon_9 + \bar{\epsilon}_1 + \bar{\epsilon}_5 + \bar{\epsilon}_9.$$

34. Now any covariant or invariant satisfies the equation

$$\phi(x_1, x_2, x_3, \bar{x}_1, \bar{x}_2, \bar{x}_3, A_1, \ldots, K_1, A_1', \ldots, K_1')$$
$$= (\Delta \bar{\Delta})^\rho \, \phi(y_1, y_2, y_3, \bar{y}_1, \bar{y}_2, \bar{y}_3, A, \ldots, K, A', \ldots, K').$$

Substitute in this defining equation the values of $A_1, \ldots, K_1, A_1', \ldots, K_1'$, $y_1, y_2, y_3, \Delta \bar{\Delta}$; write

$$\left.\begin{aligned}\theta_1 &= A \frac{\partial}{\partial A} + B \frac{\partial}{\partial B} + C \frac{\partial}{\partial C} + A' \frac{\partial}{\partial A'} + B' \frac{\partial}{\partial B'} + C' \frac{\partial}{\partial C'} \\ \theta_5 &= D \frac{\partial}{\partial D} + E \frac{\partial}{\partial E} + F \frac{\partial}{\partial F} + D' \frac{\partial}{\partial D'} + E' \frac{\partial}{\partial E'} + F' \frac{\partial}{\partial F'} \\ \theta_9 &= G \frac{\partial}{\partial G} + H \frac{\partial}{\partial H} + K \frac{\partial}{\partial K} + G' \frac{\partial}{\partial G'} + H' \frac{\partial}{\partial H'} + K' \frac{\partial}{\partial K'}\end{aligned}\right\},$$

$$\left.\begin{aligned}\bar{\theta}_1 &= A \frac{\partial}{\partial A} + D \frac{\partial}{\partial D} + G \frac{\partial}{\partial G} + A' \frac{\partial}{\partial A'} + D' \frac{\partial}{\partial D'} + G' \frac{\partial}{\partial G'} \\ \bar{\theta}_5 &= B \frac{\partial}{\partial B} + E \frac{\partial}{\partial E} + H \frac{\partial}{\partial H} + B' \frac{\partial}{\partial B'} + E' \frac{\partial}{\partial E'} + H' \frac{\partial}{\partial H'} \\ \bar{\theta}_9 &= C \frac{\partial}{\partial C} + F \frac{\partial}{\partial F} + K \frac{\partial}{\partial K} + C' \frac{\partial}{\partial C'} + F' \frac{\partial}{\partial F'} + K' \frac{\partial}{\partial K'}\end{aligned}\right\},$$

$$\left.\begin{aligned}\theta_2 &= A \frac{\partial}{\partial D} + B \frac{\partial}{\partial E} + C \frac{\partial}{\partial F} + A' \frac{\partial}{\partial D'} + B' \frac{\partial}{\partial E'} + C' \frac{\partial}{\partial F'} \\ \bar{\theta}_2 &= A \frac{\partial}{\partial B} + D \frac{\partial}{\partial E} + G \frac{\partial}{\partial H} + A' \frac{\partial}{\partial B'} + D' \frac{\partial}{\partial E'} + G' \frac{\partial}{\partial H'}\end{aligned}\right\},$$

$$\left.\begin{aligned}\theta_3 &= A \frac{\partial}{\partial G} + B \frac{\partial}{\partial H} + C \frac{\partial}{\partial K} + A' \frac{\partial}{\partial G'} + B' \frac{\partial}{\partial H'} + C' \frac{\partial}{\partial K'} \\ \bar{\theta}_3 &= A \frac{\partial}{\partial C} + D \frac{\partial}{\partial F} + G \frac{\partial}{\partial K} + A' \frac{\partial}{\partial C'} + D' \frac{\partial}{\partial F'} + G' \frac{\partial}{\partial K'}\end{aligned}\right\},$$

$$\left.\begin{aligned}\theta_4 &= D \frac{\partial}{\partial A} + E \frac{\partial}{\partial B} + F \frac{\partial}{\partial C} + D' \frac{\partial}{\partial A'} + E' \frac{\partial}{\partial B'} + F' \frac{\partial}{\partial C'} \\ \bar{\theta}_4 &= B \frac{\partial}{\partial A} + E \frac{\partial}{\partial D} + H \frac{\partial}{\partial G} + B' \frac{\partial}{\partial A'} + E' \frac{\partial}{\partial D'} + H' \frac{\partial}{\partial G'}\end{aligned}\right\},$$

$$\theta_6 = D\frac{\partial}{\partial G} + E\frac{\partial}{\partial H} + F\frac{\partial}{\partial K} + D'\frac{\partial}{\partial G'} + E'\frac{\partial}{\partial H'} + F'\frac{\partial}{\partial K'} \Bigg\},$$

$$\bar{\theta}_6 = B\frac{\partial}{\partial C} + E\frac{\partial}{\partial F} + H\frac{\partial}{\partial K} + B'\frac{\partial}{\partial C'} + E'\frac{\partial}{\partial F'} + H'\frac{\partial}{\partial K'}$$

$$\theta_7 = G\frac{\partial}{\partial A} + H\frac{\partial}{\partial B} + K\frac{\partial}{\partial C} + G'\frac{\partial}{\partial A'} + H'\frac{\partial}{\partial B'} + K'\frac{\partial}{\partial C'} \Bigg\},$$

$$\bar{\theta}_7 = C\frac{\partial}{\partial A} + F\frac{\partial}{\partial D} + K\frac{\partial}{\partial G} + C'\frac{\partial}{\partial A'} + F'\frac{\partial}{\partial D'} + K'\frac{\partial}{\partial G'}$$

$$\theta_8 = G\frac{\partial}{\partial D} + H\frac{\partial}{\partial E} + K\frac{\partial}{\partial F} + G'\frac{\partial}{\partial D'} + H'\frac{\partial}{\partial E'} + K'\frac{\partial}{\partial F'} \Bigg\};$$

$$\bar{\theta}_8 = C\frac{\partial}{\partial B} + F\frac{\partial}{\partial E} + K\frac{\partial}{\partial H} + C'\frac{\partial}{\partial B'} + F'\frac{\partial}{\partial E'} + K'\frac{\partial}{\partial H'}$$

and expand both sides of the equation in powers of the small quantities ϵ and $\bar{\epsilon}$. Equating the coefficients of these small quantities on the two sides, and denoting our covariantive function

$$\phi(y_1, y_2, y_3, \bar{y}_1, \bar{y}_2, \bar{y}_3, A, ..., K, A', ..., K')$$

by ϕ, we have the partial differential equations

$$\left.\begin{aligned}\theta_1\phi - y_1\frac{\partial\phi}{\partial y_1} = \rho\phi, &\quad \bar{\theta}_1\phi - \bar{y}_1\frac{\partial\phi}{\partial \bar{y}_1} = \rho\phi \\ \theta_5\phi - y_2\frac{\partial\phi}{\partial y_2} = \rho\phi, &\quad \bar{\theta}_5\phi - \bar{y}_2\frac{\partial\phi}{\partial \bar{y}_2} = \rho\phi \\ \theta_9\phi - y_3\frac{\partial\phi}{\partial y_3} = \rho\phi, &\quad \bar{\theta}_9\phi - \bar{y}_3\frac{\partial\phi}{\partial \bar{y}_3} = \rho\phi\end{aligned}\right\},$$

$$\left.\begin{aligned}\theta_2\phi - y_2\frac{\partial\phi}{\partial y_1} = 0, &\quad \bar{\theta}_2\phi - \bar{y}_2\frac{\partial\phi}{\partial \bar{y}_1} = 0 \\ \theta_3\phi - y_3\frac{\partial\phi}{\partial y_1} = 0, &\quad \bar{\theta}_3\phi - \bar{y}_3\frac{\partial\phi}{\partial \bar{y}_1} = 0 \\ \theta_4\phi - y_1\frac{\partial\phi}{\partial y_2} = 0, &\quad \bar{\theta}_4\phi - \bar{y}_1\frac{\partial\phi}{\partial \bar{y}_2} = 0 \\ \theta_6\phi - y_3\frac{\partial\phi}{\partial y_2} = 0, &\quad \bar{\theta}_6\phi - \bar{y}_3\frac{\partial\phi}{\partial \bar{y}_2} = 0 \\ \theta_7\phi - y_1\frac{\partial\phi}{\partial y_3} = 0, &\quad \bar{\theta}_7\phi - \bar{y}_1\frac{\partial\phi}{\partial \bar{y}_3} = 0 \\ \theta_8\phi - y_2\frac{\partial\phi}{\partial y_3} = 0, &\quad \bar{\theta}_8\phi - \bar{y}_2\frac{\partial\phi}{\partial \bar{y}_3} = 0\end{aligned}\right\},$$

as equations satisfied by the function ϕ. Moreover, by Lie's theory, any function ϕ, which satisfies all these equations, is a covariant (or invariant) of the required type.

35. Having regard to the fact that ultimately we are dealing with quadratic frontiers and with transformations between w, w' and z, z', we shall consider only those integral functions ϕ, which are homogeneous (say of order m) in y_1, y_2, y_3 and homogeneous (also then of order m) in $\bar{y}_1$, $\bar{y}_2$, $\bar{y}_3$. We also shall consider only such functions ϕ as are homogeneous (say of degree n) in the coefficients $A, \ldots, K$ and homogeneous (say of degree n') in the coefficients $A', \ldots, K'$. Then, from the first set of equations and by means of Euler's theorem on homogeneous functions, we have

$$n + n' - m = 3\rho.$$

It follows that every integral invariant of a quadratic frontier has its degree in the coefficients of the boundary a multiple of 3.

When the index ρ is taken as equal to the foregoing value, and when we note the equality between the indices of Δ and $\bar{\Delta}$ in the relation which defines the covariants, the first six equations can be replaced by the four

$$\left.\begin{array}{l}\theta_1\phi - y_1\dfrac{\partial\phi}{\partial y_1} = \theta_5\phi - y_2\dfrac{\partial\phi}{\partial y_2} = \theta_9\phi - y_3\dfrac{\partial\phi}{\partial y_3} \\[2mm] \bar{\theta}_1\phi - \bar{y}_1\dfrac{\partial\phi}{\partial\bar{y}_1} = \bar{\theta}_5\phi - \bar{y}_2\dfrac{\partial\phi}{\partial\bar{y}_2} = \bar{\theta}_9\phi - \bar{y}_3\dfrac{\partial\phi}{\partial\bar{y}_3}\end{array}\right\};$$

and we then retain the other twelve equations, so that we have a set of sixteen partial equations of the first order.

It is easy to verify that the conditions of co-existence of these sixteen equations are satisfied, either identically or in virtue of the equations in the set. Hence the set of equations constitutes a complete Jacobian system of partial equations of the first order. The possible arguments in any solution ϕ are twenty-four in number, viz., the nine coefficients $A, \ldots, K$, the nine coefficients $A', \ldots, K'$, and the six variables y_1, y_2, y_3, $\bar{y}_1$, $\bar{y}_2$, $\bar{y}_3$; consequently, by the customary theory of such systems*, the number of algebraically independent integrals is eight, the excess of the number of possible arguments over the number of equations in the complete system.

36. After the limitations that have been imposed, every integral ϕ of the system is homogeneous of degree m in y_1, y_2, y_3, and also homogeneous of degree m in $\bar{y}_1$, $\bar{y}_2$, $\bar{y}_3$. Let it be represented by

$$\Sigma U_{p,q,p',q'} y_1^{m-p-q} y_2^p y_3^q \bar{y}_1^{m-p'-q'} \bar{y}_2^{p'} \bar{y}_3^{q'};$$

* See my *Theory of Differential Equations*, vol. v, chap. iii.

then, in order that it may satisfy the equations, we must have the relations (among others)

$$\theta_4 . U_{p,q,p',q'} - (p+1) U_{p+1,q,p',q'} = 0$$
$$\bar{\theta}_4 . U_{p,q,p',q'} - (p'+1) U_{p,q,p'+1,q'} = 0$$
$$\theta_7 . U_{p,q,p',q'} - (q+1) U_{p,q+1,p',q'} = 0$$
$$\bar{\theta}_7 . U_{p,q,p',q'} - (q'+1) U_{p,q,p',q'+1} = 0$$

By the continued use of these equations, all the coefficients $U_{p,q,p',q'}$ can be obtained when once $U_{0,0,0,0}$ (say U) is known; and therefore, as usual in the theory of homogeneous forms, the whole covariant can be regarded as known when its leading term $U y_1^m y_1^{-m}$ is known.

Again, and just as in the ordinary theory, the leading coefficient U of the covariant satisfies the equations

$$\theta_2 U = 0, \quad \theta_3 U = 0, \quad \theta_6 U = 0, \quad \theta_8 U = 0,$$
$$\bar{\theta}_2 U = 0, \quad \bar{\theta}_3 U = 0, \quad \bar{\theta}_6 U = 0, \quad \bar{\theta}_8 U = 0,$$
$$\theta_5 U - \theta_9 U = 0, \quad \bar{\theta}_5 U - \bar{\theta}_9 U = 0.$$

These ten equations also are a complete Jacobian system of partial differential equations of the first order. Each integral can involve the eighteen possible arguments, constituted by the constants in the two equations of the quadratic frontier; and therefore the system of equations possesses eight algebraically independent integrals which are the leading coefficients of the eight covariants constituting the algebraically complete set of integrals of the full system of equations. It follows that, in this method of proceeding, we have to obtain eight algebraically independent integrals of the preceding set of ten equations in the second complete Jacobian system.

37. The actual process of solving the equations is the customary process that applies to complete Jacobian systems that are linear and homogeneous. The algebra required in the manipulation is long and tedious for the present set of equations; so the results will merely be stated, especially as they can be obtained by another method (or combination of methods) applicable to the equations of the quadratic frontier. The summary of the final integration of the ten equations, which are to possess eight algebraically independent integrals, is as follows:—

Every integral of the system is expressible algebraically in terms of the eight independent integrals $A, A', I, J, J', I', T, T'$, where I is the invariant of Q, I' the similar invariant of Q',

$$J = \Sigma A' \frac{\partial I}{\partial A}, \qquad J' = \Sigma A \frac{\partial I'}{\partial A'},$$

(the summation being extended over all the coefficients of Q and Q'), and where T and T' are the coefficients of λ and μ respectively in the expression

$$(\lambda A + \mu A') \begin{vmatrix} B, & C \\ B', & C' \end{vmatrix} \begin{vmatrix} G, & D \\ G', & D' \end{vmatrix}$$

$$+ (\lambda E + \mu E') \begin{vmatrix} A, & C \\ A', & C' \end{vmatrix} \begin{vmatrix} A, & G \\ A', & G' \end{vmatrix}$$

$$+ (\lambda K + \mu K') \begin{vmatrix} A, & B \\ A', & B' \end{vmatrix} \begin{vmatrix} A, & D \\ A', & D' \end{vmatrix}$$

$$+ (\lambda F + \mu F') \begin{vmatrix} A, & B \\ A', & B' \end{vmatrix} \begin{vmatrix} G, & A \\ G', & A' \end{vmatrix}$$

$$+ (\lambda H + \mu H') \begin{vmatrix} A, & D \\ A', & D' \end{vmatrix} \begin{vmatrix} C, & A \\ C', & A' \end{vmatrix}.$$

Moreover, A determines a covariant $Ay_1\bar{y}_1 + ...$, that is, Q; A' determines a covariant $A'y_1\bar{y}_1 + ...$, that is, Q'; T determines a covariant $Ty_1^2\bar{y}_1^2 + ...$, say R; T'' determines a covariant $T''y_1^2\bar{y}_1^2 + ...$, say R'; and I, J, J', I' are invariants. Finally, any quantity connected with the quadratic frontier that is invariantive under the lineo-linear transformation is expressible in terms of Q, Q', R, R', I, J, J', I'.

38. Had our quest been for invariants alone, the preceding analysis shews that they must satisfy the equations

$$\theta_1 - \theta_5 = 0, \quad \theta_5 - \theta_9 = 0, \quad \bar{\theta}_1 - \bar{\theta}_5 = 0, \quad \bar{\theta}_5 - \bar{\theta}_9 = 0,$$

$$\theta_2 = 0, \quad \theta_3 = 0, \quad \theta_4 = 0, \quad \theta_6 = 0, \quad \theta_7 = 0, \quad \theta_8 = 0,$$

$$\bar{\theta}_2 = 0, \quad \bar{\theta}_3 = 0, \quad \bar{\theta}_4 = 0, \quad \bar{\theta}_6 = 0, \quad \bar{\theta}_7 = 0, \quad \bar{\theta}_8 = 0.$$

But always
$$\theta_1 + \theta_5 + \theta_9 = \bar{\theta}_1 + \bar{\theta}_5 + \bar{\theta}_9,$$
so that, in virtue of the first four we have
$$\theta_1 = \bar{\theta}_1,$$
and therefore $\theta_5 = \bar{\theta}_5$, $\theta_9 = \bar{\theta}_9$. The two equations
$$\bar{\theta}_1 - \bar{\theta}_5 = 0 \quad \text{and} \quad \bar{\theta}_5 - \bar{\theta}_9 = 0$$
are therefore satisfied in virtue of
$$\theta_1 - \theta_5 = 0, \quad \theta_5 - \theta_9 = 0;$$
and so the system for the invariants contains fourteen independent equations. They are a complete Jacobian system, and involve the eighteen arguments constituted by the coefficients of Q and Q'; hence there are four algebraically independent invariants.

They can be obtained simply as follows. We have seen that

$$\begin{vmatrix} A, & B, & C \\ D, & E, & F \\ G, & H, & K \end{vmatrix}$$

is an invariant of Q; the same function for $\alpha Q + \beta Q'$, where α and β are arbitrary parameters, also is an invariant of the system. Let

$$\begin{vmatrix} \alpha A + \beta A', & \alpha B + \beta B', & \alpha C + \beta C' \\ \alpha D + \beta D', & \alpha E + \beta E', & \alpha F + \beta F' \\ \alpha G + \beta G', & \alpha H + \beta H', & \alpha K + \beta K' \end{vmatrix} = \alpha^3 I + \alpha^2 \beta J + \alpha \beta^2 J' + \beta^3 I';$$

then I, J, J', I' are four invariants, independent of one another, and therefore suitable for the aggregate of the four algebraically independent invariants. They manifestly agree with the four invariants in the earlier aggregate of invariants and covariants.

Ex. Prove that the complete system for a single equation $Q=0$ is composed of Q and I.

39. The detailed consideration of the invariantive forms will not be considered further. What has actually been done should suffice to shew the march of a general method of proceeding for the particular problem.

But one warning must be given if this general method is to be applied to a wider problem, viz. the determination of all the covariantive concomitants of all kinds whatever that are to be associated with any single form or with any couple of forms that are integral and homogeneous in y_1, y_2, y_3, and also integral and homogeneous of the same order in $\bar{y}_1, \bar{y}_2, \bar{y}_3$, where we still assume the lineo-linear transformation for y_1, y_2, y_3 and its conjugate for $\bar{y}_1, \bar{y}_2, \bar{y}_3$ as the transformations under which the concomitants are to be invariantive. For this problem, it is necessary to introduce variables contragredient to the variables x_1, x_2, x_3 and y_1, y_2, y_3, according to the customary law of variation in the theory of forms; that is, if we denote these further variables by ξ_1, ξ_2, ξ_3, η_1, η_2, η_3, and their conjugates, they are subject to the lineo-linear transformations

$$\left.\begin{aligned} \xi_1 &= a\eta_1 + a'\eta_2 + a''\eta_3 \\ \xi_2 &= b\eta_1 + b'\eta_2 + b''\eta_3 \\ \xi_3 &= c\eta_1 + c'\eta_2 + c''\eta_3 \end{aligned}\right\}, \quad \left.\begin{aligned} \bar{\xi}_1 &= \bar{a}\bar{\eta}_1 + \bar{a}'\bar{\eta}_2 + \bar{a}''\bar{\eta}_3 \\ \bar{\xi}_2 &= \bar{b}\bar{\eta}_1 + \bar{b}'\bar{\eta}_2 + \bar{b}''\bar{\eta}_3 \\ \bar{\xi}_3 &= \bar{c}\bar{\eta}_1 + \bar{c}'\bar{\eta}_2 + \bar{c}''\bar{\eta}_3 \end{aligned}\right\}.$$

It will be noticed (as is to be expected) that the umbral coefficients, used to express a given homogeneous form symbolically, are themselves contragredient to the variables. Manifestly we have

$$y_1\eta_1 + y_2\eta_2 + y_3\eta_3 = x_1\xi_1 + x_2\xi_2 + x_3\xi_3,$$
$$\bar{y}_1\bar{\eta}_1 + \bar{y}_2\bar{\eta}_2 + \bar{y}_3\bar{\eta}_3 = \bar{x}_1\bar{\xi}_1 + \bar{x}_2\bar{\xi}_2 + \bar{x}_3\bar{\xi}_3.$$

It need hardly be pointed out that, while the complex variables x_1, x_2, x_3 correspond to the point-variables in the ordinary theory of ternary forms, the complex variables ξ_1, ξ_2, ξ_3 correspond to the line-variables in that theory.

In order to obtain the most general concomitant of any kind, we should apply the preceding method to a function of the type

$$\phi(y_1, y_2, y_3, \bar{y}_1, \bar{y}_2, \bar{y}_3, \eta_1, \eta_2, \eta_3, \bar{\eta}_1, \bar{\eta}_2, \bar{\eta}_3, A, \ldots),$$

F.

involving all the variables and the coefficients of any or all of the initial given system of forms whose aggregate of concomitants is wanted. There is plenty of room and opportunity for research; but the investigations would take us into the wider pure algebra of the theory of homogeneous forms, and they will not be pursued in these lectures.

Ex. 1. Let U and V be any two covariants that belong to a form or to a system of homogeneous forms; and let

$$\left.\begin{aligned} Y_1 &= \frac{\partial U}{\partial y_2}\frac{\partial V}{\partial y_3} - \frac{\partial U}{\partial y_3}\frac{\partial V}{\partial y_2} \\ Y_2 &= \frac{\partial U}{\partial y_3}\frac{\partial V}{\partial y_1} - \frac{\partial U}{\partial y_1}\frac{\partial V}{\partial y_3} \\ Y_3 &= \frac{\partial U}{\partial y_1}\frac{\partial V}{\partial y_2} - \frac{\partial U}{\partial y_2}\frac{\partial V}{\partial y_1} \end{aligned}\right\},$$

$$\left.\begin{aligned} \overline{Y}_1 &= \frac{\partial U}{\partial \overline{y}_2}\frac{\partial V}{\partial \overline{y}_3} - \frac{\partial U}{\partial \overline{y}_3}\frac{\partial V}{\partial \overline{y}_2} \\ \overline{Y}_2 &= \frac{\partial U}{\partial \overline{y}_3}\frac{\partial V}{\partial \overline{y}_1} - \frac{\partial U}{\partial \overline{y}_1}\frac{\partial V}{\partial \overline{y}_3} \\ \overline{Y}_3 &= \frac{\partial U}{\partial \overline{y}_1}\frac{\partial V}{\partial \overline{y}_2} - \frac{\partial U}{\partial \overline{y}_2}\frac{\partial V}{\partial \overline{y}_1} \end{aligned}\right\}.$$

Prove that Y_1, Y_2, Y_3 are cogredient with y_1, y_2, y_3, and that $\overline{Y}_1$, $\overline{Y}_2$, $\overline{Y}_3$ are cogredient with $\overline{y}_1$, $\overline{y}_2$, $\overline{y}_3$; and shew that

$$U(Y_1, Y_2, Y_3, \overline{Y}_1, \overline{Y}_2, \overline{Y}_3) \quad \text{and} \quad V(Y_1, Y_2, Y_3, \overline{Y}_1, \overline{Y}_2, \overline{Y}_3)$$

are covariants of the system.

In particular, when U and V are the two initial quantities Q and Q' belonging to a quadratic frontier, determine the two covariants which are thus constructed.

Ex. 2. Shew that when a quartic frontier, generally covariantive under a lineo-linear transformation, is given by equations $Q=0$ and $Q'=0$, where symbolically

$$Q = \Pi^2 \overline{\Pi}^2 \quad \text{and} \quad Q' = \Pi'^2 \overline{\Pi}'^2,$$

the algebraically complete set of invariants and pure covariants belonging to the system consists, in addition to Q and Q', of sixty functions.

40. One other matter is left for investigation outside the range of these lectures. We have already dealt with the canonical form to which the expression of a lineo-linear transformation can be reduced. Also we have seen that there are quadratic frontiers, represented by the two equations of lowest degree, which keep a general invariantive character under such a transformation. It remains to consider what is the simplest canonical form to which two simultaneous equations representing such a quadratic frontier can be reduced, where there no longer is a question of invariance under a single transformation only*. This more general problem has some analogy with the problem of reducing to canonical forms the equations of two conics.

---

* The simplest examples of forms, invariant under a single given transformation, have already been given; they are the equations of the frontier which passes through the three invariant centres of the transformation.

In that solved problem, certain invariants of the system are necessarily conserved; in this propounded problem, the four invariants of the system of two equations, which already have been obtained, must also be conserved.

One appropriate form is suggested almost at once by the known result in the case of two conics referred to their common self-conjugate triangle. It is natural to enquire whether two forms

$$P = Ax_1\bar{x}_1 + Bx_1\bar{x}_2 + Cx_1\bar{x}_3 + Dx_2\bar{x}_1 + Ex_2\bar{x}_2 + Fx_2\bar{x}_3 + Gx_3\bar{x}_1 + Hx_3\bar{x}_2 + Kx_3\bar{x}_3,$$
$$P' = A'x_1\bar{x}_1 + B'x_1\bar{x}_2 + C'x_1\bar{x}_3 + D'x_2\bar{x}_1 + E'x_2\bar{x}_2 + F'x_2\bar{x}_3 + G'x_3\bar{x}_1 + H'x_3\bar{x}_2 + K'x_3\bar{x}_3,$$

can simultaneously, by homogeneous linear transformation of the variables, be changed to forms

$$P = X_1\bar{X}_1 + X_2\bar{X}_2 + X_3\bar{X}_3,$$
$$P' = A''X_1\bar{X}_1 + B''X_2\bar{X}_2 + C''X_3\bar{X}_3,$$

where no two of the three quantities A'', B'', C'' are equal to one another, and no one of them is equal to unity. With these last restrictions, we have

$$I + \alpha J + \alpha^2 J' + \alpha^3 I' = (1 + \alpha A'')(1 + \alpha B'')(1 + \alpha C''),$$

for arbitrary values of α; consequently, the three invariants J/I, J'/I, I'/I (which are absolute invariants) are independent of one another, and no one of them vanishes. Thus the general condition as regards conservation of invariants is satisfied.

Now all the quantities A, E, K, A', E', K' are real; hence a requirement that they shall respectively acquire the values 1, 1, 1, A'', B'', C'', where A'', B'', C'' are real, imposes six conditions. Also B and D, B' and D', C and G, C' and G', F and H, F' and H', are (in each combination) conjugate constants; hence a requirement that all these coefficients shall vanish imposes twelve conditions. In order, therefore, that the suggested canonical forms shall be possible, eighteen conditions of the specified kind must be satisfied.

Suppose, then, that the variables are transformed by the relations

$$x_1 = \theta X_1 + \phi X_2 + \psi X_3,$$
$$x_2 = \theta' X_1 + \phi' X_2 + \psi' X_3,$$
$$x_3 = \theta'' X_1 + \phi'' X_2 + \psi'' X_3,$$

where the complex constants are at our disposal. Let

$$\nabla = \begin{vmatrix} \theta, & \phi, & \psi \\ \theta', & \phi', & \psi' \\ \theta'', & \phi'', & \psi'' \end{vmatrix}, \quad \bar{\nabla} = \begin{vmatrix} \bar{\theta}, & \bar{\phi}, & \bar{\psi} \\ \bar{\theta}', & \bar{\phi}', & \bar{\psi}' \\ \bar{\theta}'', & \bar{\phi}'', & \bar{\psi}'' \end{vmatrix};$$

then
$$1 = \nabla \bar{\nabla} I,$$
$$A'' + B'' + C'' = \nabla \bar{\nabla} J,$$
$$B''C'' + C''A'' + A''B'' = \nabla \bar{\nabla} J',$$
$$A''B''C'' = \nabla \bar{\nabla} I',$$

so that the values of A'', B'', C'' are given by means of the quantities J/I, J'/I, I'/I, three real quantities. Also, as each of the nine arbitrary constants $\theta, \ldots, \psi''$ is complex, we have effectively eighteen constants at our disposal, formally sufficient to satisfy the eighteen conditions which take the form of linear equations.

It therefore may be inferred that a couple of general forms P and P' can be transformed so that they acquire forms of the suggested type.

Periodic transformations.

41. These results, as regards lineo-linear transformations, are general. Simple forms occur when the transformations are periodic, that is, are such that after a finite number of repetitions in succession we return to the initial variables; and these provide the generalisation of finite groups of homographic transformations in a single variable.

The requirement of periodicity will impose conditions upon the unequal multipliers λ and μ in the first type (§ 22).

The second type cannot be periodic unless σ vanishes. But if σ does vanish, the type can be periodic when an appropriate condition is imposed upon the repeated multiplier λ.

The third type cannot be periodic unless all the constants ρ, σ, τ vanish. But if all these constants vanish, we have merely the identical transformation at once. There is no modification of the variables, and consequently there is no question of periodicity.

When therefore we deal with periodic substitutions, we have to consider only the first type of transformation which has unequal multipliers λ and μ, and a limited form of the second type which has a repeated multiplier λ.

42. A multiplier is the quotient of two roots of the characteristic equation; hence the equation, which is satisfied by a multiplier, is the eliminant of

$$\theta^3 - \Delta_1 \theta^2 + \Delta_2 \theta - \Delta = 0,$$
$$t^3 \theta^3 - \Delta_1 t^2 \theta^2 + \Delta_2 t \theta - \Delta = 0.$$

The eliminant is of degree nine in t; but there is a factor $(t-1)^3$, which is irrelevant to the present issue and must therefore be rejected. One of the simplest ways of obtaining the residual equation is to proceed by the method of Bezout and Cayley for constructing the eliminant; it leads to the result

$$\begin{vmatrix} 1+t+t^2, & \Delta_1(1+t), & \Delta_2 \\ \Delta_2 t(1+t), & \Delta(1+t+t^2) + \Delta_1 \Delta_2 t, & \Delta_1 \Delta(1+t) \\ \Delta_1 t^2, & \Delta_2 t(1+t), & \Delta(1+t+t^2) \end{vmatrix} = 0,$$

which, when the determinant is expanded, becomes

$$\Delta^2(t^6 + 1) + (3\Delta^2 - \Delta_1\Delta_2\Delta)(t^5 + t)$$
$$+ (6\Delta^2 - 5\Delta_1\Delta_2\Delta + \Delta_1^3\Delta + \Delta_2^3)(t^4 + t^2)$$
$$+ (7\Delta^2 - 6\Delta_1\Delta_2\Delta - \Delta_1^2\Delta_2^2 + 2\Delta_1^3\Delta + 2\Delta_2^3)t^3 = 0.$$

This is a reciprocal equation, as is to be expected from the mode of occurrence of the multipliers in the canonical form of the transformation.

For the first type of transformation, the six roots of this multiplier equation are

$$\lambda, \quad \mu, \quad \frac{1}{\lambda}, \quad \frac{1}{\mu}, \quad \frac{\lambda}{\mu}, \quad \frac{\mu}{\lambda};$$

and the solution of the equation effectively involves the two quantities $\Delta_1\Delta^{-\frac{1}{3}}$ and $\Delta_2\Delta^{-\frac{2}{3}}$, which are homogeneous (of order zero) in the coefficients of the original transformation.

For the second type, the six roots of the multiplier equation are

$$\lambda, \quad \lambda, \quad \frac{1}{\lambda}, \quad \frac{1}{\lambda}, \quad 1, \quad 1;$$

and we must have

$$27\Delta^2 - 18\Delta_1\Delta_2\Delta - \Delta_1^2\Delta_2^2 + 4\Delta_1^3\Delta + 4\Delta_2^3 = 0,$$

being the discriminant condition for the equality of two roots of the characteristic equation.

When the lineo-linear transformation is periodic of order n, then

$$\lambda^n = 1, \quad \mu^n = 1;$$

and n must be the lowest integer for which both the conditions are satisfied. Thus, for the first type,

$$\lambda = e^{2\pi i r/n}, \quad \mu = e^{2\pi i s/n},$$

where r and s are unequal positive integers, greater than zero, less than n, and such that r, s, n have no common factor other than unity. Then

$$\Delta_1 = \theta_3(1 + e^{2\pi i r/n} + e^{2\pi i s/n}),$$
$$\Delta_2 = \theta_3^2 \{e^{2\pi i r/n} + e^{2\pi i s/n} + e^{2\pi i (r+s)/n}\},$$
$$\Delta = \theta_3^3 e^{2\pi i (r+s)/n};$$

and the conditions for periodicity of order n are

$$\Delta_1^2 \{1 + e^{2\pi i r/n} + e^{2\pi i s/n}\}^{-2} = \Delta_2 \{e^{2\pi i r/n} + e^{2\pi i s/n} + e^{2\pi i (r+s)/n}\}^{-1},$$
$$\Delta_1^3 \{1 + e^{2\pi i r/n} + e^{2\pi i s/n}\}^{-3} = \Delta e^{-2\pi i (r+s)/n}.$$

The conditions thus imposed upon r and s require that n should be greater than 2; and so lineo-linear transformations, of which the characteristic equation has three unequal roots, cannot possess quadratic periodicity.

As a matter of mere algebra, it is easy to verify that the original transformation

$$\frac{w}{az+bz'+c} = \frac{w'}{a'z+b'z'+c'} = \frac{1}{a''z+b''z'+c''}$$

is of quadratic periodicity in the two cases settled by the relations

$$\left.\begin{aligned}\frac{b'-1}{b} &= \frac{c'}{c} = \frac{a'}{a-1} \\ \frac{a''}{a-1} &= \frac{b''}{b'} = \frac{c''-1}{c} = \frac{1-a^2-a'b}{c(a-1)}\end{aligned}\right\},$$

$$\left.\begin{aligned}\frac{b'+1}{b} &= \frac{c'}{c} = \frac{a'}{a+1} \\ \frac{a''}{a+1} &= \frac{b''}{b'} = \frac{c''+1}{c} = \frac{1-a^2-a'b}{c(a+1)}\end{aligned}\right\}.$$

In each case four parametric constants, which may be taken to be a, b, c, a', are left unrestricted by the limitation of quadratic periodicity.

For the second type of transformation, the characteristic equation of which has a double root and a simple root, the discriminant condition has to be satisfied by all forms. If the transformation is to be periodic, another condition (the vanishing of the quantity σ) must also be satisfied whatever the order; and then the order of periodicity is the lowest value of λ such that

$$\lambda^n = 1,$$

so that we can take

$$\lambda = e^{2\pi i r/n},$$

where r is any integer between 0 and n, which is prime to n.

Ex. 1. The simplest example of such a transformation is

$$w = \lambda z, \quad w' = \lambda z'.$$

The z plane can be divided into n triangular wedges, bounded by lines through the origin inclined at successive angles $2\pi/n$ to one another; and similarly for the z' plane. The whole z, z' configuration is then transformed into itself by a double rotation of each plane through an angle $2\pi r/n$ about an axis through the origins perpendicular to the planes; and the z, z' field, made up of two such wedges in the z and z' planes, is transformed into the w, w' field, made up of two similar wedges in the w and w' planes.

Ex. 2. When the original transformation is linear and has the form

$$w = az + bz' + c, \quad w' = a'z + b'z' + c',$$

a factor $\theta - 1$ can be dropped from the characteristic equation which then becomes

$$\theta^2 - (a+b')\theta + ab' - a'b = 0.$$

Let the roots of this equation be ν and ν'; the canonical form of the substitution is

$$\alpha w + \beta w' + \gamma = \nu (\alpha z + \beta z' + \gamma),$$
$$\alpha' w + \beta' w' + \gamma' = \nu'(\alpha' z + \beta' z' + \gamma'),$$

where

$$a\alpha + a'\beta = \nu\alpha, \quad b\alpha + b'\beta = \nu\beta, \quad c\alpha + c'\beta = (\nu-1)\gamma,$$
$$a\alpha' + a'\beta' = \nu'\alpha', \quad b\alpha' + b'\beta' = \nu'\beta', \quad c\alpha' + c'\beta' = (\nu'-1)\gamma'.$$

Ex. 3. Find a canonical form of the periodic transformation
$$w\sqrt{2}=z+z', \quad w'\sqrt{2}=z-z'.$$

Ex. 4. Prove that all transformations of the linear type, which have quadratic periodicity, belong either to the form
$$w=-z+c, \quad w'=-z'+c',$$
or to the form
$$w=az+bz'+c, \quad w'=\frac{1-a^2}{b}z-az'-\frac{1+a}{b}c,$$
where a, b, c, c' are arbitrary constants.

Ex. 5. Prove that all cubic linear transformations have either the form
$$w=\theta z+c, \quad w'=\theta'z'+c';$$
or the form $w=az+bz'+c$, with either
$$w'=-\frac{1}{b}(a^2+a\theta^2+\theta)z-(a+\theta^2)z'-\frac{c}{b}(a-\theta),$$
or
$$w'=-\frac{1}{b}(a^2+a+1)z-(a+1)z'+c',$$
where θ and θ' are imaginary cube-roots of unity, and a, b, c, c' are unrestricted constants.

Ex. 6. Shew that, if
$$\frac{w}{az+bz'+c}=\frac{w'}{a'z+b'z'+c'}=\frac{1}{a''z+b''z'+c''},$$
then
$$\frac{z}{Aw+A'w'+A''}=\frac{z'}{Bw+B'w'+B''}=\frac{1}{Cw+C'w'+C''},$$
where A, A', A'', ..., C, C', C'' are the respective minors of a, a', a'', ..., c, c', c'' in the non-vanishing determinant Δ, where
$$\Delta=\begin{vmatrix} a, & b, & c \\ a', & b', & c' \\ a'', & b'', & c'' \end{vmatrix};$$
and prove that
$$(a''z+b''z'+c'')^3 J\left(\frac{w,w'}{z,z'}\right)=\Delta.$$

Prove that the roots of the characteristic equation for this inverse transformation, expressing z and z' in terms of w and w', viz.
$$\begin{vmatrix} A-\phi, & A', & A'' \\ B, & B'-\phi, & B'' \\ C, & C', & C''-\phi \end{vmatrix}=0,$$
are connected with the roots of the characteristic equation of the original transformation by the relation
$$\theta\phi=\Delta;$$
and verify that the invariant centres for the inverse transformation are the same as those for the original transformation.

Ex. 7. Obtain for a lineo-linear transformation, between two sets of n variables, results corresponding to those in the preceding example.

Ex. 8. Prove that the invariant centre ζ_1 and ζ_1' of the general lineo-linear transformation is given by the equations

$$\frac{\zeta_1}{A''+c\theta_1} = \frac{\zeta_1'}{B''+c'\theta_1} = \frac{1}{C''-(a+b')\theta_1+\theta_1^2},$$

the denominator in the third fraction being distinct from zero. Prove also that, for the quantities $a_1 : \beta_1 : \gamma_1$,

$$a_1\zeta_1 + \beta_1\zeta_1' + \gamma_1 = \gamma_1 \frac{(\theta_2-\theta_1)(\theta_3-\theta_1)}{C''-(a+b')\theta_1+\theta_1^2}.$$

Ex. 9. Shew that, when n is a prime number, all the periodic substitutions

$$\left.\begin{aligned}w &= az + bz' + c \\ w' &= -\frac{a-1}{b}(a - e^{s\pi i/n})z - (a - 1 - e^{s\pi i/n})z' - \frac{c}{b}(a - e^{s\pi i/n})\end{aligned}\right\}$$

for $s = 2, \ldots, n-1$, are powers of the same periodic substitution for $s = 1$.

Shew that all the substitutions

$$w = az + c, \quad w' = a'z' + c',$$

where a and a' are primitive nth roots of unity, are periodic.

Do the two preceding classes contain all the purely linear substitutions which are periodic?

CHAPTER III

Uniform Analytic Functions

43. We now proceed to the more immediate and direct consideration of the properties and the characteristics of functions of two independent complex variables, beginning with the simplest fundamental propositions. Not a few of these can be considered as well known; they are included for the sake of completeness, and also for the sake of reference. Some among them are expressed in forms that appear more comprehensive than the customary enunciations. Others of them appear to be new, such as those which deal with the characteristic relations and the properties of two functions of a couple of variables considered simultaneously; and these, as being more novel than the others, are expounded at fuller length (Chaps. VII and VIII).

Though the exposition is restricted to the case when there are only two independent complex variables, it should be noted that many of the theorems belong, *mutatis mutandis*, also to functions of n independent variables. For others, however, further ideas are needed before a corresponding extension can similarly be effected.

We begin with definitions and explanations of the more frequent terms adopted, many of which are obvious extensions of the corresponding usages for functions of one complex variable.

The whole range of the variables z and z' is often called the *field* of variation. The extent of the field sometimes depends upon the properties of the functions concerned; otherwise, it implies the four-fold range of variation between $-\infty$ and $+\infty$.

A restricted portion of a field of variation is called a *domain*, the range of a domain being usually indicated by analytical relations. Thus we may have the domain of a place a, a', given by relations

$$|z-a| \leqslant r, \quad |z'-a'| \leqslant r';$$

we may have a domain given by relations

$$\phi(x-\alpha, y-\beta, x'-\alpha', y'-\beta') \leqslant c, \quad \psi(x-\alpha, y-\beta, x'-\alpha', y'-\beta') \leqslant c',$$

where $a = \alpha + i\beta$, $a' = \alpha' + i\beta'$, the equations being such as to secure a finite range of values of z and a finite range of values of z'. When r and r' (or c and c', in the alternative case) are small, the domain of a and a' is sometimes called the *vicinity*, or the *immediate vicinity*, of the place a, a'.

In these definitions we substitute $\frac{1}{|z|}$ for $|z-a|$ when a is at infinity, and $\frac{1}{|z'|}$ for $|z'-a'|$ when a' is at infinity.

44. A function of z and z', say $w = f(z, z')$, is said to be *uniform*, when every assigned pair of values of z and z' gives one (and only one) value of w. Through familiarity with properties subsequently established, the notion that z and z' may attain their assigned values in any manner whatever sometimes comes to be associated with the definition; but the notion is not part of the definition.

The function w is said to be *multiform*, when every assigned pair of values of z and z' gives a finite number of values of w, the finite number being the same for all z, z' places where the function exists. Sometimes it is convenient to specify the number in the definition; when there are m values, and no more than m values, w is sometimes called m-valued.

A function w may have an infinite number of values for given values of z and z'. Among such functions, each class can be specified by its own general property. Thus one simple class of this kind arises from integrals of functions that have additive periods.

Just as with uniform functions, so with multiform and other functions, familiarity with properties subsequently established leads to the notion that a specification of the path or range by which z and z' attain their values will lead to the acquisition of some definite one among the m values; again, the notion is not part of the definition.

Even in this matter of the description of the range of z and of z', care must be exercised; it may become necessary to take account, not merely of the actual range of z and of z', but also of the mode of description of those actual ranges. Consider, for example*, the function
$$w = (z^2 - z' + 1)^{\frac{1}{2}}.$$
Take $z = 0$ and $z' = 0$ as the initial place; and consider the branch of w which has the value $+1$ at that place.

We make z vary from 0 to $+1$ by describing (in the direction indicated by the arrow) a simple curve OAB which, when combined with the axis OB of real quantities, encloses the point $\frac{1}{2}i$ and does not enclose the point i.

---

* The example was suggested to me by Prof. W. Burnside. Another example, viz.
$$w = (z - z' + 1)^{\frac{1}{2}},$$
is given by Sauvage, *Ann. de Marseille*, t. xiv (1904), section I, a particular path being specified. Obviously any number of special examples of the same type can be constructed.

We make z' vary from 0 to $+1$ by describing the straight line $O'C'$ in the direction indicated by the arrow; the point D' on that line is given by $z' = \frac{3}{4}$.

Consider two different descriptions of these paths.

In the first description, keep z' at O', while z describes the whole path OAB; and then keep z at B, while z' describes its whole path $O'C'$. For this description, the final value of w is manifestly $+1$.

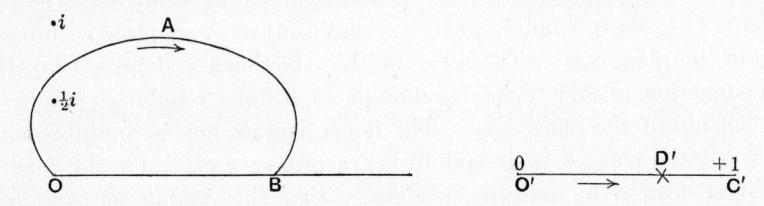

In the second description, keep z at O, while z' describes the part $O'D'$ of its whole path; then keep z' at D', thus making $w = (z^2 + \frac{1}{4})^{\frac{1}{2}}$ for that value of z', and now make z describe its whole path OAB. When z arrives at B by this path, the value of w is $-(\frac{5}{4})^{\frac{1}{2}}$, that is, when z is at B and z' at D' by this description of paths, the value of $(z^2 - z' + 1)^{\frac{1}{2}}$ has become $-(\frac{5}{4})^{\frac{1}{2}}$. Now keep z at B, and let z' describe $D'C'$, the remainder of its path; the final value of w is manifestly -1.

It thus appears in the case of the special function that, even when the range for each variable is perfectly precise, the final value can depend upon the mode of description of the precise ranges. The matter belongs, in its simplest form, to the theory of algebraic functions.

45. A function $f(z, z')$ is said to be *continuous* if, when the real and imaginary parts of z and of z' are substituted and the function is expressed in its real and imaginary parts $u + vi$, both the functions u and v of x, y, x', y' are continuous.

Let the function $f(z, z')$ be uniform and continuous, everywhere within a field of z, z' variation. It is said to be *analytic*, when it possesses derivatives of all orders with regard to both variables

$$\frac{\partial f(z, z')}{\partial z}, \quad \frac{\partial f(z, z')}{\partial z'}, \ldots,$$

which are uniform and continuous everywhere within that field; or what is equivalent, it is said to be analytic if $f(z, z')$ is an analytic function of z when any arbitrary fixed value is assigned to z' and is also an analytic function of z' when any arbitrary fixed value is assigned to z. But it need hardly be pointed out that, while $f(z, z')$ is—under this definition—expressible as a power-series of z alone having functions of the parametric z' for coefficients, and also as a power-series of z' alone having functions of the parametric z for coefficients, an expansion in powers of z and z' simultaneously is a matter of proof, to be considered later.

It is a known proposition that an absolutely converging double series can be rearranged in any manner and can be summed in any order, the sum being the same in all arrangements and for all orders of summation. Suppose, then, that the double power-series

$$\Sigma\Sigma c_{m,m'}(z-a)^m(z'-a')^{m'},$$

where m and m' are positive whole numbers (including zero), and where the coefficients $c_{m,m'}$ are constants, converges absolutely at every place within some domain of the place a, a'. The series, within the domain, defines a function; and the function is said to be *regular*, or to behave regularly, everywhere in the domain of the place a, a'. The domain must not be infinitesimal in extent; and the place a, a' is said to be an *ordinary* place for the function. When it is desired to indicate specifically that the double series contains only positive powers of $z-a$ and $z'-a'$ in accordance with the definition, we call the series *integral*, or *whole*, or *holomorphic*; and sometimes the function is called integral or holomorphic within the domain of the place a, a'.

When the power-series is finite in both sequences of indices, the function is a polynomial in z and z'. When it is infinite in either sequence or in both sequences, the function represented is usually called *transcendental*, unless it can be represented by algebraic forms.

When the function is transcendental, the question arises as to the range of the domain over which the power-series converges. When the domain is limited, a question arises as to whether the power-series, representing the function within the domain, can be continued analytically beyond the limits of the domain.

Perhaps the simplest example of a multiform function w of z and z' occurs, when the three variables are connected by an algebraic equation

$$A(w, z, z') = 0,$$

where A is a polynomial in each of its arguments. As already explained, it sometimes proves desirable in this connection to consider two multiform functions w and w', defined by algebraic equations

$$C(w, w', z, z') = 0, \quad D(w, w', z, z') = 0,$$

where C and D are polynomial in each of their arguments. In this event, the ordinary processes of elimination enable us to substitute equations

$$A(w, z, z') = 0, \quad B(w', z, z') = 0,$$

for the equations $C = 0$, $D = 0$; but care must be exercised to secure that the separate roots of $A = 0$ and of $B = 0$ must be grouped so as to give the simultaneous roots of $C = 0$, $D = 0$.

For example, we shall have (Chap. VI) to consider an expression

$$\Sigma\Sigma \frac{R(w, w', z, z')}{J\left(\dfrac{C, D}{w, w'}\right)},$$

where $R(w, w', z, z')$ denotes an integral polynomial in w and w', and where the double finite summation extends over the simultaneous roots of $C=0$, $D=0$. In the method adopted for its evaluation, we are led to introduce terms which arise from combinations of the roots of $A=0$, $B=0$, that do not provide simultaneous roots of $C=0$, $D=0$.

In the first case, to the function w: and, in the second case, to the functions w and w': the epithet *algebraic* is assigned. Manifestly, among the four variables w, w', z, z', any two can be described as algebraic functions of the other two, unless (in limited cases) elimination should lead to a single relation between two variables alone.

In this initial stage, it is not necessary to state the definitions of terms *pole, accidental* (or *non-essential*) *singularity, essential singularity*. New and modified definitions are required, because functions of two variables possess properties which have no simple analogue in the properties of functions of a single variable. These definitions will be given later (§§ 57, 58), when the properties are under actual consideration. As will be seen, a discrimination between functions of two variables and functions of more than two variables can be made, so as to give a classification proper to functions of two variables. We may, however, mention in passing that, in the vicinity of any non-essential singularity a, a', a uniform analytic function is expressible in a form

$$\frac{Q(z-a, z'-a')}{P(z-a, z'-a')},$$

where Q and P are functions, which are regular in a domain of a and a'. Such a function is sometimes called *meromorphic* in the vicinity of the place a, a'.

The simplest example of a meromorphic function occurs when both Q and P are polynomial functions of their arguments; in that case, the function is called *rational*.

Some properties of regular functions.

46. Consider functions that are regular everywhere in some finite domain of an assigned place a, a'. By writing $z - a = \zeta$ or $\dfrac{1}{\zeta}$, according as $|a|$ is finite or infinite, and by writing $z' - a' = \zeta'$ or $\dfrac{1}{\zeta'}$, according as $|a'|$ is finite or is infinite, we can take the assigned place as $0, 0$, without any loss of generality.

We then have a theorem* connected with the definition of the analytic property, as follows:—

When a function $f(z, z')$, for values of $|z| \leqslant r$ and of $|z'| \leqslant r'$, is a regular function of z everywhere within the assigned z-circle for every value of z' within its assigned circle, and also is a regular function of z' everywhere within the assigned z'-circle for every value of z within its assigned circle, it is a regular function of z and z' everywhere within the indicated field of z, z' variation.

Let the function $f(z, z')$ be represented by a series

$$f(z, z') = \sum_{m=0}^{\infty} g_m(z') z^m,$$

as is possible under the first hypothesis. If M_0' denote the greatest value of $|f(z, z')|$ for any assigned value z_0' of z' within the z'-circle, and for all the values of z within its circle, our series gives

$$f(z, z_0') = \sum_{m=0}^{\infty} g_m(z_0') z^m;$$

and then by a well-known theorem†, we have

$$|g_m(z_0')| < \frac{M_0'}{r^m}.$$

Consequently, if M denote the greatest value of $|f(z, z')|$ within the whole z, z' field considered, we have

$$M_0' \leqslant M,$$

and therefore

$$|g_m(z_0')| < \frac{M}{r^m},$$

for all values of m, for any value of z_0' such that $|z_0'| \leqslant r'$. Consequently, for all values of z' in question, we have

$$|g_m(z')| < \frac{M}{r^m}.$$

Now $f(z, z')$ is a regular function of z' for every value of z for which $|z| \leqslant r$; hence $g_0(z')$, being the value of $f(z, z')$ when $z = 0$, and

$$g_m(z') = \frac{1}{m!} \left[\frac{\partial^m}{\partial z^m} f(z, z') \right]_{z=0},$$

for all values of m, are regular functions of z'. Accordingly, we can write

$$g_m(z') = \sum_{n=0}^{\infty} c_{m,n} z'^n,$$

---

* The theorem is true under even less restricted conditions. See two papers by Osgood, *Math. Ann.*, t. lii (1899), pp. 462—464, *ib.*, t. liii (1900), pp. 461—464; and a paper by Hartogs, *ib.*, t. lxii (1906), pp. 1—88.

† *Theory of Functions*, § 22.

where the series represents a regular function of z'; and as $|g_m(z')|$ throughout the whole range of variation of z' is less than M/r^m, we have, again by the theorem already quoted,
$$|c_{m,n}| < \frac{M}{r^m} \cdot \frac{1}{r'^n}.$$

On these results, consider the double series
$$F(z, z') = \sum_{m=0}^{\infty} \sum_{n=0}^{\infty} c_{m,n} z^m z'^n;$$
if it converges absolutely, we can take it in the form
$$\sum_{n=0}^{\infty} \left\{ \sum_{m=0}^{\infty} c_{m,n} z'^n \right\} z^m,$$
that is,
$$\sum_{n=0}^{\infty} g_m(z') z^m,$$
and so we shall have
$$F(z, z') = f(z, z')$$
for the field of variation within which $F(z, z')$ converges absolutely. But we have just proved that
$$|c_{m,n}| < \frac{M}{r^m r'^n};$$
and therefore we have
$$|F(z, z')| = \left| \sum_{m=0}^{\infty} \sum_{n=0}^{\infty} c_{m,n} z^m z'^n \right|$$
$$\leqslant \sum_{m=0}^{\infty} \sum_{n=0}^{\infty} |c_{m,n}| |z|^m |z'|^n$$
$$< \sum_{m=0}^{\infty} \sum_{n=0}^{\infty} \frac{M}{r^m r'^n} |z|^m |z'|^n$$
$$< \frac{M}{\left\{1 - \frac{|z|}{r}\right\}\left\{1 - \frac{|z'|}{r'}\right\}},$$
for all values of $|z| < r$ and all values of $|z'| < r'$.

This result establishes the absolute convergence of $F(z, z')$; and so we have
$$f(z, z') = \sum_{m=0}^{\infty} \sum_{n=0}^{\infty} c_{m,n} z^m z'^n,$$
where the double series converges absolutely in a field $|z| \leqslant k < r$, $|z'| \leqslant k' < r'$, while k and k' are not infinitesimal.

Consequently the function $f(z, z')$, under the postulated conditions, is a regular function of the variables z and z'.

47. Now let $f(z, z')$ be a regular function of z and z' everywhere in the domain
$$|z-a| \leqslant r, \quad |z'-a'| \leqslant r',$$
and within this domain let M be the greatest value of $|f(z, z')|$. Then, if the power-series for $f(z, z')$ is
$$f(z, z') = \sum_{m=0} \sum_{n=0} c_{m,n} (z-a)^m (z'-a')^n,$$
we have
$$c_{m,n} = \frac{1}{m!\, n!} \left\{ \frac{\partial^{m+n} f(z, z')}{\partial z^m \partial z'^n} \right\}_{z=a, z'=a'},$$
and also
$$|c_{m,n}| \leqslant \frac{M}{r^m r'^n},$$
shewing that
$$\left| \left\{ \frac{\partial^{m+n} f(z, z')}{\partial z^m \partial z'^n} \right\}_{z=a, z'=a'} \right| \leqslant m!\, n!\, \frac{M}{r^m r'^n}.$$

Another expression for $c_{m,n}$ can be obtained by a simple extension of Cauchy's well-known integral-theorems for a single variable. Denoting by $g(z)$ a function that is uniform, continuous, and analytic, within a range $|z-a| \leqslant r$, we have
$$g(a) = \frac{1}{2\pi i} \int \frac{g(z)}{z-a} dz,$$
$$\left\{ \frac{d^n g(z)}{dz^n} \right\}_{z=a} = \frac{n!}{2\pi i} \int \frac{g(z)}{(z-a)^{n+1}} dz,$$
for all values of n, the integrals being taken positively round any simple closed curve which lies entirely within the region and encloses the point a. The extension indicated can be established in exactly the same way as these theorems just quoted; the analysis and the reasoning are so similar to those for the simple case that they can be stated very briefly.

For our function $f(z, z')$ which is uniform, continuous, and analytic, and therefore regular, everywhere in the domain
$$|z-a| \leqslant r, \quad |z'-a'| \leqslant r',$$
we have
$$f(a, z') = \frac{1}{2\pi i} \int \frac{f(z, z')}{z-a} dz,$$
$$\left\{ \frac{\partial^m f(z, z')}{\partial z^m} \right\}_{z=a} = \frac{m!}{2\pi i} \int \frac{f(z, z')}{(z-a)^{m+1}} dz,$$
the integrals being taken positively round any simple closed curve which lies entirely within the region bounded by $|z-a| = r$ and encloses the point a, and holding for every value of z' for which $f(z, z')$ is defined. Again, $f(a, z')$ and $\left\{ \frac{\partial^m f(z, z')}{\partial z^m} \right\}_{z=a}$, owing to the character of $f(z, z')$ within the z, z' field of variation, are regular functions of z' throughout the z'-region bounded by

$|z'-a'|=r'$; hence, by a repeated application of Cauchy's integral-theorems, we have

$$f(a, a') = \frac{1}{2\pi i} \int \frac{f(a, z')}{z'-a'} dz',$$

$$\left[\frac{\partial^n}{\partial z'^n} f(a, z')\right]_{z'=a'} = \frac{n!}{2\pi i} \int \frac{f(a, z')}{(z'-a')^{n+1}} dz',$$

the integrals being taken positively round any simple closed curve which lies entirely within the region bounded by $|z'-a'|=r'$ and encloses the point a'. The variations of z and z' are independent of one another, as also are the integrations in the two planes of the variables; combining the results, we have

$$f(a, a') = \frac{1}{(2\pi i)^2} \iint \frac{f(z, z')}{(z-a)(z'-a')} dz dz'$$

$$= -\frac{1}{4\pi^2} \iint \frac{f(z, z')}{(z-a)(z'-a')} dz dz',$$

$$\left\{\frac{\partial^{m+n} f(z, z')}{\partial z^m \partial z'^n}\right\}_{z=a, z'=a'} = -\frac{m! n!}{4\pi^2} \iint \frac{f(z, z')}{(z-a)^{m+1}(z'-a')^{n+1}} dz dz',$$

the integrals being taken round simple closed curves in the z-plane and the z'-plane, the z-curve lying entirely within the region $|z-a|=r$ and enclosing the point a, and the z'-curve lying entirely within the region $|z'-a'|=r'$ and enclosing the point a'.

We thus have expressions, in the form of double contour integrals, for the value of $f(z, z')$ and of every derivative of $f(z, z')$ at the place a, a'.

Again, let M denote the greatest value of $|f(z, z')|$ for places within the whole z, z' domain of variation represented by $|z-a| \leqslant r, |z'-a'| \leqslant r'$; then at every place on the double contour integral we have

$$|f(z, z')| \leqslant M.$$

Proceeding exactly as in the case of a single variable, we can shew that

$$\left|\iint \frac{f(z, z')}{(z-a)(z'-a')} dz dz'\right| \leqslant 4\pi^2 M,$$

and therefore

$$|f(a, a')| \leqslant M,$$

which is merely a statement that the value of $|f(z, z')|$ at a particular place in the field is not greater than its greatest value in the field; and we can also shew that

$$\left|\iint \frac{f(z, z')}{(z-a)^{m+1}(z'-a')^{n+1}} dz dz'\right| \leqslant \frac{4\pi^2}{r^m r'^n} M,$$

and therefore

$$\left|\left\{\frac{\partial^{m+n} f(z, z')}{\partial z^m \partial z'^n}\right\}_{z=a, z'=a'}\right| \leqslant m! n! \frac{M}{r^m r'^n},$$

which is the former result.

Another method of stating these results is as follows. Let z, z' be any place within the field of variation where $f(z, z')$ is regular; in the z-plane, take any simple closed curve lying within the field and enclosing the point z, say a circle of centre z, and let t denote the complex variable of a current point on this curve; and in the z'-plane, take any simple closed curve lying within the field and enclosing the point z', say a circle of centre z', and let t' denote the complex variable of a current point on this curve. Then

$$f(z, z') = -\frac{1}{4\pi^2} \iint \frac{f(t, t')}{(t-z)(t'-z')} dt dt',$$

$$\frac{\partial^{m+n} f(z, z')}{\partial z^m \partial z'^n} = -\frac{m! \, n!}{4\pi^2} \iint \frac{f(t, t')}{(t-z)^{m+1}(t'-z')^{n+1}} dt dt'.$$

Ex. Prove that, for the foregoing function $f(z, z')$ and with the foregoing curves of integration, the value of each of the integrals

$$-\frac{1}{4\pi^2} \iint \frac{f(t, t')}{(t-z)^{m+1}} dt dt', \quad -\frac{1}{4\pi^2} \iint \frac{f(t, t')}{(t'-z')^{n+1}} dt dt',$$

for all positive integer values (including zero) of m and n, is zero.

48. We shall come later (Chap. VI) to a fuller discussion of double integrals involving complex variables; meanwhile, it will be sufficient to state that integrals of the foregoing type, in which the integrations with regard to z and to z' are completely independent of one another, belong to a very special and limited class of double integrals. They may even be regarded as merely iterated simple integrals; and many of their properties can be deduced as mere extensions of corresponding properties for simple integrals.

Thus we know that the value of the integral

$$\frac{1}{2\pi i} \int f(z) dz,$$

taken positively round the whole boundary of any region within which $f(z)$ is uniform, continuous, and analytic, is zero, even if the region is multiply connected; and it follows, as a corollary, that the value of the integral taken round any simple closed curve is unaltered if the curve is deformed without crossing any point where $f(z)$ ceases to have any one of the three specified qualities. This result can at once be generalised, merely through a double use of the result, into the following theorems:—

I. Let $F(z, z')$ denote a function which, over a limited region in the z-plane with a complete boundary unaffected by variations of z', and over a limited region in the z'-plane with a complete boundary unaffected by variations of z, is uniform, continuous, and analytic. Then* zero is the value of the integral

$$-\frac{1}{4\pi^2} \iint F(z, z') dz dz',$$

---

* The constant $-1/4\pi^2$ is inserted here merely for the purpose of formal expression.

taken positively round all parts of the complete boundary* of the z-region, and positively over all parts of the complete boundary of the z'-region, when these boundaries are entirely unrelated to each other.

II. For the same type of function, and with the same type of range of integration, the value of an integral

$$-\frac{1}{4\pi^2}\iint F(z, z')\,dz\,dz'$$

is unaltered when the z-boundary and the z'-boundary are deformed separately or together in any continuous manner which, while leaving them unrelated, does not cross a place where the function $F(z, z')$ does not possess each of the three specified qualities.

It is to be noted that the theorems are exclusive and not inclusive. The function $F(z, z')$ might cease to possess the property of being continuous (thus it might be $z^{-2}z'^{-2}$ in a region round 0, 0), without causing the integral

$$-\frac{1}{4\pi^2}\iint F(z, z')\,dz\,dz'$$

to be different from zero as in the first theorem, and without preventing the deformation contemplated in the second theorem. For the moment, we are concerned with the theorems as enunciated.

49. As an illustration of the use of all the preceding theorems, we shall establish the following proposition:—

Let $f(z, z')$ denote a function which is regular everywhere in a z, z' field represented by the relations

$$|z| \leqslant r, \quad |z'| \leqslant r';$$

and let t and t' be current variables in that field. Then the magnitude

$$f(z, z') + \frac{1}{4\pi^2}\iint \frac{f(t, t')}{(t-z)(t'-z')}\left\{\frac{z^{m+1}}{t^{m+1}} + \frac{z'^{n+1}}{t'^{n+1}} - \frac{z^{m+1}z'^{n+1}}{t^{m+1}t'^{n+1}}\right\}dt\,dt',$$

when the double integral is taken positively round a simple closed curve enclosing the z-origin and the point z in the z-plane, and positively round a simple closed curve enclosing the z'-origin and the point z' in the z'-plane, is a polynomial $P(z, z')$ of order m in z and of order n in z', such that

$$\left\{\frac{\partial^{r+s}P(z, z')}{\partial z^r \partial z'^s}\right\}_{z=0, z'=0} = \left\{\frac{\partial^{r+s}f(z, z')}{\partial z^r \partial z'^s}\right\}_{z=0, z'=0}$$

for the values $r = 0, ..., m$ and $s = 0, ..., n$ in all simultaneous combinations, the descriptions of the two curves being unrelated.

---

* That is, with the customary convention as to the positive direction of any portion of the boundary when the included area is multiply connected; see my *Theory of Functions*, § 2.

The result can also be stated in the form

$$P(z, z') = -\frac{1}{4\pi^2} \iint \frac{f(t, t')}{(t-z)(t'-z')} \left\{1 - \left(\frac{z}{t}\right)^{m+1}\right\} \left\{1 - \left(\frac{z'}{t'}\right)^{n+1}\right\} dt dt',$$

and can easily be established from this form by inserting the values of $\left\{1 - \left(\frac{z}{t}\right)^{m+1}\right\} \div \left(1 - \frac{z}{t}\right)$ and $\left\{1 - \left(\frac{z'}{t'}\right)^{n+1}\right\} \div \left(1 - \frac{z'}{t'}\right)$ and using the preceding theorems as they stand.

The derivation of the result from the first form requires a different use of the theorems: it is set out as an exercise in integrals, as follows.

As our function $f(z, z')$ is everywhere regular within the specified field, the only places where the subject of integration ceases to be regular within the selected domain are

(i) at $t = z$, $t' = z'$;   (ii) at $t = z$, $t' = 0$;

(iii) at $t = 0$, $t' = z'$;   and   (iv) at $t = 0$, $t' = 0$.

After the preceding theorems, it is sufficient to take the double integral positively along small curves round these places.

For a double integral, taken positively round small circles, one in the z-plane round the point z and one in the z'-plane round the point z', so that we should have

$$t - z = \rho e^{\theta i}, \quad t' - z' = \rho' e^{\theta' i},$$

where ρ and ρ' are small, while θ and θ' vary independently each from 0 to 2π, the value of the integral

$$-\frac{1}{4\pi^2} \iint f(t, t') \left\{\frac{z^{m+1}}{t^{m+1}} + \frac{z'^{n+1}}{t'^{n+1}} - \frac{z^{m+1} z'^{n+1}}{t^{m+1} t'^{n+1}}\right\} \frac{dt dt'}{(t-z)(t'-z')}$$

is the value of

$$f(t, t') \left\{\frac{z^{m+1}}{t^{m+1}} + \frac{z'^{n+1}}{t'^{n+1}} - \frac{z^{m+1} z'^{n+1}}{t^{m+1} t'^{n+1}}\right\}$$

when $t = z$, $t' = z'$; that is, the value of the integral for the double small contour round z and z' is $f(z, z')$.

For a double integral, taken positively round small circles, one in the z-plane round the point z, and one in the z'-plane round the origin, we have

$$t - z = \rho e^{\theta i}, \quad t' = \rho' e^{\phi' i},$$

where ρ and ρ' are small. We then expand $(t' - z')^{-1}$ in ascending powers of t'/z', and obtain the subject of integration in the form

$$-\frac{f(t, t')}{t - z} \left\{\frac{z^{m+1}}{t^{m+1}} + \frac{z'^{n+1}}{t'^{n+1}} - \frac{z^{m+1} z'^{n+1}}{t^{m+1} t'^{n+1}}\right\} \sum_{s=0} \frac{t'^s}{z'^{s+1}}.$$

Let integration be effected first along the path in the z-plane; on the completion of the path, the value of the integral is

$$-\frac{1}{2\pi i} \int f(z, t') \left(1 + \frac{z'^{n+1}}{t'^{n+1}} - \frac{z'^{n+1}}{t'^{n+1}}\right) \left(\sum \frac{t'^s}{z'^{s+1}}\right) dt',$$

that is,
$$-\frac{1}{2\pi i}\int f(z, t')\left(\Sigma \frac{t'^s}{z'^{s+1}}\right) dt'.$$

This integral is to be taken along a small closed path in the z'-plane round $t' = 0$, and $f(z, t')$ is regular; hence the value of the integral is zero. Thus the double integral, taken round the place $t = z$, $t' = 0$, contributes zero to the value of the general double integral.

Similarly the double integral, taken round the place $t = 0, t' = z'$, contributes zero to the value of the general double integral.

For a double integral, taken positively round small circles, one in the z-plane round the z-origin and one in the z'-plane round the z'-origin, we have
$$t = \rho e^{\phi i}, \quad t' = \rho' e^{\phi' i},$$
where ρ and ρ' are small. We then expand $\{(t-z)(t'-z')\}^{-1}$ in ascending powers of t/z and t'/z', the expansion being
$$\sum_{\mu=0}\sum_{\nu=0} t^\mu t'^\nu z^{-\mu-1} z'^{-\nu-1};$$
and so the subject of integration becomes
$$f(t, t')\left\{\frac{z^{m+1}}{t^{m+1}} + \frac{z'^{n+1}}{t'^{n+1}} - \frac{z^{m+1}z'^{n+1}}{t^{m+1}t'^{n+1}}\right\}\sum_{\mu=0}\sum_{\nu=0} \frac{t^\mu t'^\nu}{z^{\mu+1}z'^{\nu+1}}.$$

The value of the part
$$-\frac{1}{4\pi^2}\iint f(t, t')\frac{z^{m+1}}{t^{m+1}}\sum_{\mu=0}\sum_{\nu=0} \frac{t^\mu t'^\nu}{z^{\mu+1}z'^{\nu+1}} dt dt',$$
taken round the contour as indicated, is zero (Ex., § 47), because there are no negative powers of t'. Similarly the value of the part
$$-\frac{1}{4\pi^2}\iint f(t, t')\frac{z'^{n+1}}{t'^{n+1}}\sum_{\mu=0}\sum_{\nu=0} \frac{t^\mu t'^\nu}{z^{\mu+1}z'^{\nu+1}} dt dt'$$
is zero. Again, the value of the integral
$$-\frac{1}{4\pi^2}\iint f(t, t')\frac{dt dt'}{t^{r+1}t'^{s+1}}$$
is
$$\left\{\frac{1}{r!\,s!}\frac{\partial^{r+s}f(t, t')}{\partial t^r \partial t'^s}\right\}_{t=0, t'=0},$$
for all integers $r = 0, 1, \ldots$, and all integers $s = 0, 1, \ldots$. When either of the integers r and s is negative, and when both of the integers are negative, the value of the integral is zero. Hence, taken positively along the small contour that encloses the z-origin in the z-plane and the z'-origin in the z'-plane, we have
$$\frac{1}{4\pi^2}\iint \frac{f(t, t')}{(t-z)(t'-z')}\frac{z^{m+1}z'^{n+1}}{t^{m+1}t'^{n+1}} dt dt'$$
$$= -\sum_{r=0}^{m}\sum_{s=0}^{n}\left[\frac{z^r z'^s}{r!\,s!}\left\{\frac{\partial^{r+s}f(t, t')}{\partial t^r \partial t'^s}\right\}_{t=0, t'=0}\right].$$

We thus have the full value of the integral

$$-\frac{1}{4\pi^2}\iint \frac{f(t, t')}{(t-z)(t'-z')}\left\{\frac{z^{m+1}}{t^{m+1}} + \frac{z'^{n+1}}{t'^{n+1}} - \frac{z^{m+1}z'^{n+1}}{t^{m+1}t'^{n+1}}\right\} dt dt',$$

taken positively round our contour in the z-plane enclosing the z-origin and the point z, and our contour in the z'-plane enclosing the z'-origin and the point z'; it is

$$f(z, z') - \sum_{r=0}^{m}\sum_{s=0}^{n}\left[\frac{z^r z'^s}{r!\, s!}\left\{\frac{\partial^{r+s} f(t, t')}{\partial t^r \partial t'^s}\right\}_{t=0,\, t'=0}\right].$$

Consequently our magnitude

$$f(z, z') + \frac{1}{4\pi^2}\iint \frac{f(t, t')}{(t-z)(t'-z')}\left\{\frac{z^{m+1}}{t^{m+1}} + \frac{z'^{n+1}}{t'^{n+1}} - \frac{z^{m+1}z'^{n+1}}{t^{m+1}t'^{n+1}}\right\} dt dt'$$

is equal to the polynomial

$$\sum_{r=0}^{m}\sum_{s=0}^{n}\left[\frac{z^r z'^s}{r!\, s!}\left\{\frac{\partial^{r+s} f(t, t')}{\partial t^r \partial t'^s}\right\}_{t=0,\, t'=0}\right];$$

and when this polynomial is denoted by $P(z, z')$, we manifestly have

$$\left\{\frac{\partial^{r+s} P(z, z')}{\partial z^r \partial z'^s}\right\}_{z=0,\, z'=0} = \left\{\frac{\partial^{r+s} f(t, t')}{\partial t^r \partial t'^s}\right\}_{t=0,\, t'=0}.$$

The proposition is thus established.

The result, in either form, shews that it is possible to construct an expression the value of which shall be a polynomial approximation to the value of a function $f(z, z')$ in a field where it is a regular function of its arguments.

Ex. Evaluate the integral

$$-\frac{1}{4\pi^2}\iint \frac{f(t, t')}{(t-z)^{p+1}(t'-z')^{q+1}}\frac{z^{m+1}z'^{n+1}}{t^{m+1}t'^{n+1}} dt\, dt',$$

with the same suppositions as to the function $f(z, z')$ and the range of integration.

50. In connection with the function $f(z, z')$, which is regular within the field $|z-a| \leqslant r$ and $|z'-a'| \leqslant r'$, and for which $|f(z, z')|$ is never greater than M for places in the field, consider a function $\phi(z, z')$ defined by the relation

$$\phi(z, z') = \frac{M}{\left(1 - \dfrac{z-a}{r}\right)\left(1 - \dfrac{z'-a'}{r'}\right)}.$$

Evidently $\phi(z, z')$ can be expanded in a double power-series in $z - a$ and $z' - a'$, which converges absolutely for values of z and z' such that

$$|z - a| \leqslant \rho < r, \quad |z' - a'| \leqslant \rho' < r';$$

and it has the form

$$\phi(z, z') = M \sum_{m=0}\sum_{n=0} \frac{(z-a)^m (z'-a')^n}{r^m\, r'^n}.$$

Hence
$$\frac{\partial^{m+n}\phi(z, z')}{\partial z^m \partial z'^n} = \frac{m!\, n!}{r^m r'^n} M \sum_{p=0} \sum_{q=0} \frac{(p+m)!\,(q+n)!}{m!\, p!\, n!\, q!} \frac{(z-a)^p}{r^p} \frac{(z'-a')^q}{r'^q};$$

and therefore
$$\left\{\frac{\partial^{m+n}\phi(z, z')}{\partial z^m \partial z'^n}\right\}_{z=a,\, z'=a'} = \frac{m!\, n!}{r^m r'^n} M,$$

for all values of m and n. It therefore follows that
$$|f(a, a')| \leqslant \phi(a, a'),$$

$$\left|\left\{\frac{\partial^{m+n} f(z, z')}{\partial z^m \partial z'^n}\right\}_{z=a,\, z'=a'}\right| \leqslant \left\{\frac{\partial^{m+n}\phi(z, z')}{\partial z^m \partial z'^n}\right\}_{z=a,\, z'=a'}.$$

The function $\phi(z, z')$, related in this manner to a function $f(z, z')$ from some characteristics of which it is constructed, is called a *dominant* function. Manifestly the result can be extended to any number of independent complex variables by a precisely similar process.

These dominant functions prove to be of great importance in various regions of analysis; thus, for example, they are of general use in the present methods of establishing many theorems concerning the actual existence of integrals of whole classes of differential equations, particularly in connection with certain broad external assigned conditions under which those integrals exist.

A dominant function $\phi(z, z')$ is not necessarily unique. In the same circumstances as before, consider a function $\psi(z, z')$ defined by the relation

$$\psi(z, z') = \frac{M}{1 - \dfrac{z-a}{r} - \dfrac{z'-a'}{r'}}$$

which also is expressible as a double power-series in $z-a$ and $z'-a'$, converging absolutely for the region $\dfrac{|z-a|}{r} + \dfrac{|z'-a'|}{r'} \leqslant k < 1$. Proceeding as for $\phi(z, z')$, we find, for all integer values of m and n,

$$\left\{\frac{\partial^{m+n}\psi(z, z')}{\partial z^m \partial z'^n}\right\}_{z=a,\, z'=a'} = \frac{(m+n)!}{r^m r'^n} M.$$

Now $(m+n)! \geqslant m!\, n!$; hence

$$\left\{\frac{\partial^{m+n}\psi(z, z')}{\partial z^m \partial z'^n}\right\}_{z=a,\, z'=a'} \geqslant \left\{\frac{\partial^{m+n}\phi(z, z')}{\partial z^m \partial z'^n}\right\}_{z=a,\, z'=a'}$$
$$\geqslant \left|\left\{\frac{\partial^{m+n} f(z, z')}{\partial z^m \partial z'^n}\right\}_{z=a,\, z'=a'}\right|,$$

so that $\psi(z, z')$ also is a dominant function*.

---

* Poincaré uses the term *majorante*.

51. During the foregoing investigations, particular series in suitable circumstances have been declared to converge; and it will be noted that, in such series as have occurred, the convergence has been absolute. We do not propose to consider, in detail, the general theory of convergence of double series. When convergence is absolute, no other kind of convergence need be considered specially; and such series, as will be discussed in these lectures, will be discussed with a view to absolute convergence. What is wanted here is a knowledge of some non-infinitesimal region of variation of the variables in which the respective series converge absolutely*.

In this regard, one warning must be given. Both in what precedes and in what will follow, a region of variation, in which a double series converges absolutely, is usually defined by a couple of relations of the form $|z| \leqslant \rho < r$, $|z'| \leqslant \rho' < r'$, where ρ, ρ', r, r' are positive constants, while r and r' are not infinitesimal. It must not therefore be assumed—and it is not the case in fact—that the whole region, within which a double series converges absolutely, must be determined by two (and only two) relations of the preceding form; thus the whole region of absolute convergence of the double series, that represents the dominant function $\psi(z, z')$ of § 50, is determined by the single relation

$$\frac{|z-a|}{r} + \frac{|z'-a'|}{r'} \leqslant k < 1,$$

as there stated†.

To repeat the substance of what has just been said, what is mainly wanted at the initial stage is a knowledge of some non-infinitesimal region of absolute convergence of the series, not necessarily a knowledge (however desirable) of the whole region of convergence.

52. Three simple propositions relating to uniform analytic functions can be established at once.

I. *A uniform analytic function must acquire infinite values somewhere in the whole z, z' field, unless it reduces to a mere constant.*

Suppose that a uniform analytic function $f(z, z')$ does not acquire infinite values anywhere in the z, z' field. In that event, there must be some greatest value for $|f(z, z')|$ in the field, say M, where M is finite; and no matter how the field is extended, this value of M for $|f(z, z')|$ cannot be exceeded.

Accordingly, we take a domain in the field, determined by the relations

$$|z| \leqslant R, \quad |z'| \leqslant R';$$

---

* For the theory of absolute convergence of double series, readers may consult Bromwich, *An introduction to the theory of infinite series.*

† Other examples of the same type are given by Bromwich, p. 504 of his treatise just quoted.

and, under the hypothesis, we can make R and R' as large as we please. We still shall have, over this domain, M as the greatest value of $|f(z, z')|$.

In the domain thus chosen, let $f(z, z')$ be represented by a double power-series, as in §47; and let the series be
$$\sum_{m=0}\sum_{n=0} c_{m,n} z^m z'^n.$$
By our preceding results, we have
$$|c_{m,n}| \leqslant \frac{M}{R^m R'^n},$$
for all values of m and of n, independently of one another. We can increase the domain of the field to any extent; so that, by increasing R and R' sufficiently, we can make
$$|c_{m,n}| = 0,$$
for all values of m and n except simultaneous zero values. Hence, under the hypothesis that $f(z, z')$ does not acquire infinite values, every term in the series vanishes except the first, which is a constant; the proposition therefore is established.

Note. It is obvious that the place, where a function acquires an infinite value, does not lie within the domain over which the function is regular nor (to anticipate the explanations connected with the continuation of series representing regular functions) does such a place lie within the region of continuity of the function. Every such place lies on the boundary of the region of continuity of the function.

Thus consider the function
$$\frac{z+z'}{z-z'}.$$
For all places other than $z = 0$, $z' = 0$, which lie in the field and are given by $z = z'$, the function is infinite; such places do not lie within the region of continuity of the function. At the place $z = 0$, $z' = 0$, the value of the function is indeterminate; near $z = 0$, $z' = 0$, say such that
$$z = re^{\theta i}, \quad z' = r'e^{\theta' i},$$
where r and r' are small, we have
$$\left|\frac{z+z'}{z-z'}\right| = \left\{\frac{r^2 + r'^2 + 2rr' \cos(\theta - \theta')}{r^2 + r'^2 - 2rr' \cos(\theta - \theta')}\right\}^{\frac{1}{2}},$$
which as r and r' tend to zero independently of one another can be made to acquire any value. Thus at $z = 0$, $z' = 0$, the function is not regular; the place does not lie within the region of continuity of the function.

II. If two functions, both of them regular within one and the same domain, acquire the same value at every place within any region of that domain, they acquire the same value at every place within the whole domain, the region (like the domain) being one of four-fold variation.

Firstly, suppose that the origin of the domain lies within the region considered; and round that origin, take a smaller domain given by $|z| \leqslant k < \rho$ and $|z'| \leqslant k' < \rho'$, lying entirely within the region.

Let the two regular functions be $f(z, z')$ and $g(z, z')$; and suppose that the double power-series representing them in the whole domain are

$$f(z, z') = \sum_{m=0}^{\infty} \sum_{n=0}^{\infty} c_{m,n} z^m z'^n,$$

$$g(z, z') = \sum_{m=0}^{\infty} \sum_{n=0}^{\infty} k_{m,n} z^m z'^n,$$

both series converging absolutely within that domain. Then the difference of the functions $f(z, z') - g(z, z')$ is represented by the absolutely converging double series

$$\sum_{m=0}^{\infty} \sum_{n=0}^{\infty} (c_{m,n} - k_{m,n}) z^m z'^n.$$

Now this function is everywhere zero within the smaller domain, so that its (greatest) modulus M_0 never differs from zero; accordingly we have

$$|c_{m,n} - k_{m,n}| \leqslant \frac{M_0}{\rho^m \rho'^n}$$
$$= 0,$$

so that

$$c_{m,n} = k_{m,n},$$

for all values of m and n. Consequently, the coefficients in the power-series representing the functions are the same; and so the two functions are the same within the whole domain.

Secondly, when the origin of the domain does not lie within the region considered, we take an origin within that region; and proceed as before. The coefficients in the power-series, representing the two functions in the smaller domain round the new origin, are the same. There, these coefficients determine the functions uniquely; and so, when the process of analytical continuation (§ 56) is adopted in exactly the same way for the two functions so as to cover the whole of the original domain in which they are regular, the two functions remain everywhere the same within the whole of that domain.

III. If $f(z, z')$ is a regular function of z and z' for all finite values of the variables, and if there exists a finite positive quantity M such that, no matter how $|z|$ and $|z'|$ are increased, there exist integers m and n for which

$$\left| \frac{f(z, z')}{z^m z'^n} \right| \leqslant M,$$

then $f(z, z')$ is a polynomial in z and z', of degree m in z and of degree n in z', when m and n are the smallest integers satisfying the condition.

Let $f(z, z')$ be expressed as a double power-series

$$f(z, z') = \sum_{p=0}^{\infty} \sum_{q=0}^{\infty} c_{p,q} z^p z'^q;$$

then
$$c_{p,q} = \frac{1}{p!}\frac{1}{q!}\left\{\frac{\partial^{p+q} f(z, z')}{\partial z^p \, \partial z'^q}\right\}_{z=0, z'=0}$$
$$= -\frac{1}{4\pi^2}\iint \frac{f(t, t')}{t^{p+1} t'^{q+1}}\, dt\, dt',$$

where the double integral is taken round any simple closed contour (say a circle) enclosing the origin in the z-plane, and any simple closed contour (also say a circle) enclosing the origin in the z'-plane. Let the former circle be of radius R and the latter of radius R', so that we can take
$$t = Re^{\theta i}, \quad t' = R'e^{\theta' i};$$
then
$$|c_{p,q}| \leqslant \frac{1}{4\pi^2}\iint \left|\frac{f(t, t')}{t^p \, t'^q}\right| d\theta \, d\theta'.$$

Now no matter how $|t|$ and $|t'|$ increase, we have
$$\left|\frac{f(t, t')}{t^m \, t'^n}\right| < M,$$
and therefore
$$\left|\frac{f(t, t')}{t^p \, t'^q}\right| \leqslant \frac{M}{|t^{p-m} \, t'^{q-n}|} < \frac{M}{R^{p-m} \, R'^{q-n}}.$$
Consequently
$$|c_{p,q}| < \frac{1}{4\pi^2}\frac{M}{R^{p-m} \, R'^{q-n}}\iint d\theta \, d\theta'$$
$$< \frac{M}{R^{p-m} \, R'^{q-n}}.$$

By hypothesis, we can increase R and R' without limit; hence, for all values of p that are greater than m, or for all values of q that are greater than n, and for both sets of values simultaneously, we have
$$|c_{p,q}| = 0,$$
and therefore
$$c_{p,q} = 0,$$
for those values. Accordingly, when we remove from the series those terms which have vanishing coefficients, the modified expression for $f(z, z')$ becomes
$$\sum_{p=0}^{m} \sum_{q=0}^{n} c_{p,q} z^p z'^q,$$
shewing that $f(z, z')$ is a polynomial in z and z', of degree m in z alone and of degree n in z' alone.

53. It follows, from the first investigation in § 52, that a uniform analytic function must acquire infinite values. In particular, a general polynomial in z and z' acquires infinite values, when $|z|$ is infinite while $|z'|$ is not zero, or when $|z'|$ is infinite while $|z|$ is not zero, or when both $|z|$ and $|z'|$ are infinite, though in the last event conditions may have to be satisfied*.

* For example, the function $1 + z + z'$ does not become infinite when $|z|$ is infinite and $|z'|$ is infinite unless $|z + z'|$ also is infinite.

The questions then arise:—Must a uniform analytic function of z and z' acquire a zero value within the whole field of variation? And, what is a subsidiary question governed by the answer to this preceding question, must a uniform analytic function of z and z' acquire any assigned value within the whole field of variation? Naturally, in considering the questions, we assume that we are dealing with functions that do not reduce to a mere constant.

First, a brief proof will justify the answer that a uniform analytic function of z and z' must acquire a zero value somewhere within the whole field of variation. Let $f(z, z')$ be a function of z and z', which is uniform; consequently, if

$$\phi(z, z') = \frac{1}{f(z, z')},$$

the function $\phi(z, z')$ is uniform. Further, $\phi(z, z')$ is continuous, unless $f(z, z')$ has zero values. Let $f(z, z')$ be analytic; then $\phi(z, z')$ also is analytic. Thus, assuming that $f(z, z')$ is a regular function, that has no zero within the whole field of variation, its reciprocal $\phi(z, z')$ is uniform, continuous, and analytic throughout the domain where $f(z, z')$ is regular. Consequently, $\phi(z, z')$ is a function that is regular throughout the whole field.

Now we have seen that a uniform analytic function must acquire an infinite value or infinite values somewhere in the field of variation of the variables; hence our function $\phi(z, z')$ must acquire an infinite value somewhere, that is, the regular function $f(z, z')$ must acquire a zero value somewhere and therefore the hypothesis, that $f(z, z')$ has no zero, is untenable. But as was the case with the place where the function acquires an infinite value, so that the function is not regular there and the place does not belong to the region of continuity of the function, so it may happen that a place where a function acquires a zero value does not belong to the region of continuity of the function.

Thus the function $e^{z+z'}$ is regular over a domain given by finite values of $|z|$ and finite values of $|z'|$; it is not regular for infinite values of $|z|$ alone and of $|z'|$ alone, because it cannot be expanded in powers of $\frac{1}{z}$ and $\frac{1}{z'}$. When z is real, infinite, and negative, while $|z'|$ is finite, the function $e^{z+z'} = 0$; and so for other places. No one of these places belongs to the region of continuity of the regular function $e^{z+z'}$.

The corresponding question, as to the acquisition of an assigned value α, would similarly be answered in the affirmative after a consideration of the function $f(z, z') - \alpha$ which, under the foregoing argument, would have to acquire a zero value; so $f(z, z')$ would have to acquire an assigned value.

The difficulty, that the zero of the function perhaps will not occur in the domain of regularity, may be illustrated by returning to the corresponding question in the theory of functions of a single complex variable; indeed, it would be raised directly, for example, by taking $z' = 0$, in the case of a regular function.

54. It is a result, in Weierstrass's theory of uniform functions of a single variable*, that, in the vicinity z_0 of an essential singularity of a uniform function $f(z)$, there always is at least one point within a circle $|z - z_0| = \epsilon$, where ϵ is any assigned small quantity, such that
$$|f(z) - \alpha| < \epsilon,$$
where α is any assigned quantity. But the specified point does not need to be distinct from the point z_0.

Picard† discriminates between essential singularities according as the value α is, or is not, actually acquired at a point inside the circle $|z - z_0| = \epsilon$ which is not its centre, the centre being the essential singularity. As examples, illustrating the discrimination, he adduces the two functions
$$\frac{1}{\sin \frac{1}{z}}, \quad e^{\frac{1}{z}},$$
considering both of them in the vicinity of their essential singularity at the z-origin.

The function‡ $1 \big/ \sin \left(\frac{1}{z}\right)$ has any number of poles in the immediate vicinity of the origin; they are given by $z = \frac{1}{k\pi}$, where k is any integer sufficiently large to keep z within the suggested vicinity. The function does not vanish for any value of z (other than $z = 0$) within that vicinity‡. But consider a range of z near $z = 0$ along the positive part of the axis of y, so that we can write
$$z = ir,$$
where the small positive quantity r is at our disposal; we have
$$\frac{1}{\sin \frac{1}{z}} = \frac{2i}{e^{-\frac{1}{r}} - e^{\frac{1}{r}}}.$$

The denominator can be made as large as we please by making r as small as we please; my own view is that, when r is made zero, so that z approaches the origin along the axis of y and falls into the origin, the function in question does actually acquire the value zero at the origin. But the value is acquired only at the essential singularity $z = 0$, and at no point in the vicinity of $z = 0$, other than the centre itself.

Similarly for the other function.

---

* Weierstrass, *Ges. Werke*, t. ii, p. 124; see my *Theory of Functions*, § 33.

† His valuable, and far-reaching, ideas were expounded in some memoirs to which reference is given in his *Traité d'Analyse*, t. ii, ch. v. See also, for further investigations, Borel, *Leçons sur les fonctions entières*, (1900), ch. i; *ib.*, ch. v; *ib.*, Note i.

‡ Picard, *l. c.*, p. 126, p. 128; in the second sentence, I have added the words "other than $z = 0$."

The difference between Picard's statement and my own is obvious. Picard considers the vicinity of $z_0 = 0$, and does not include the actual point $z_0 = 0$, not regarding it as a point where the value or a value of the function can be stated. I do include the actual point $z_0 = 0$ and do regard it as a point where, if the function nowhere else acquires some assigned value, it must there acquire that assigned value; and that assigned value can then be stated as a value that can be acquired there. But the point $z_0 = 0$ is actually merged in the essential singularity.

And, it need hardly be added, all the valuable investigations* of Picard, Hadamard, Borel, and others, are unaffected by these considerations. The discrimination is between functions, that acquire an assigned value in the vicinity of the essential singularity at a point which does not coincide with the singularity, and functions that acquire the assigned value only at the essential singularity.

The whole discussion thus suggests, even for functions of a single variable, the idea of places where our function, regular within a domain, ceases (at the boundary of the domain, or elsewhere) to maintain its character of regularity. To the consideration of these possibilities we now proceed.

55. First, however, in connection with the earlier remarks, a reference to a theorem by Picard must be made.

It may happen that an integral function $f(z)$ cannot acquire a finite value a for a finite value of z, so that the equation $f(z) = a$ then has no finite root; thus $e^z = 0$ has no finite root. Picard shews that an integral function $f(z)$, which for finite values of z cannot acquire a finite value a and cannot acquire another distinct finite value b, reduces to a constant†.

The similar question would then arise for an integral function $G(z, z')$ of two variables. Suppose that there are no values of z and z', which are simultaneously finite, such that $G(z, z')$ can acquire a special finite value a; and similarly suppose that there are no values, also restricted to be simultaneously finite, such that $G(z, z')$ can acquire another special finite value b, where b is different from a. To z' assign a finite value c'; as $G(z, z')$ is an integral function of z and z', being regular for finite values of z and z', then $G(z, c')$ is an integral function of z. By the suggested postulate about $G(z, z')$, the integral function $G(z, c')$ cannot acquire for finite values of z either the finite value a or the different finite value b; accordingly, by Picard's theorem, $G(z, c')$ can only be a constant, which must necessarily be a finite constant because $|G(z, z')|$ is finite for finite values of z. As this holds for any assigned value c' of z', it follows that $G(z, z')$ is constant

---

* See the lectures by Borel, already cited.

† Picard's proof depends upon the theory of modular functions (*Traité d'Analyse*, t. ii, 2nd ed., pp. 251—254). Borel, (*Leçons sur les fonctions entières*, Note i, pp. 103—106) gives a direct proof of this theorem without the intervention of any theory of special functions.

for each assigned finite value of z'; but the constant values of $G(z, z')$ are not necessarily one and the same. Now $G(z, z')$ is an integral function of z', because it is an integral function of z and z'; hence all the requirements will so far be met by taking
$$G(z, z') = g(z'),$$
an integral function of z' alone.

Again, by the suggested postulate about $G(z, z')$, there is no finite value of z'—simultaneously with a finite value of z—for which $G(z, z')$ can acquire the finite value a or the different finite value b; and therefore there is no finite value of z' for which the integral function $g(z')$ can acquire the finite value a or the different finite value b. By a repeated application of Picard's theorem, it follows that $g(z')$ can only be a constant, and therefore $G(z, z')$ can only be a constant.

It therefore follows that, *if an integral function $G(z, z')$ cannot, for any finite value of z and any finite value of z' taken simultaneously, acquire a finite value a; and also cannot, for any finite value of z and any finite value of z' taken simultaneously, acquire a finite value b different from a; then $G(z, z')$ is a constant.*

The result is manifestly the merest generalisation of Picard's theorem. It is specially important to note that the limitation about the non-acquisition of the finite values a and b is confined to finite values of z and of z'. A variable function may be unable to acquire a finite value a for finite values of z and z', but could acquire that value for infinite values of z and finite values of z', or for finite values of z and infinite values of z', or for infinite values of z and of z'; such is the case, for the value zero, of the variable integral function
$$e^{P(z, z')},$$
where $P(z, z')$ is a polynomial in z and z'.

Analytical Continuation.

56. Now let us consider a function $f(z, z')$, which is regular everywhere in a domain round a place a, a' determined by
$$|z - a| \leqslant r, \quad |z' - a'| \leqslant r';$$
it can be represented by a double series of powers of $z - a$ and $z' - a'$, the series converging absolutely for values of z and z' such that
$$|z - a| \leqslant \rho < r, \quad |z' - a'| \leqslant \rho' < r'.$$
Denoting the series by $P(z - a, z' - a')$, we have
$$f(z, z') = P(z - a, z' - a')$$
for values of z and z' thus defined. The values of the constant coefficients in the double series are determined by the values, at the place a, a', of the derivatives of the function $f(z, z')$ of the appropriate orders.

Such a series* may be capable of the process called *analytical continuation* outside a given domain within which the series represents a regular function. Let $z = b$ and $z' = b'$ be any place within the domain; at this place b, b', the values of the function $f(z, z')$ and of its derivatives are unique and finite, and they can depend upon the origin a, a' of the domain.

Because the place b, b' lies within the domain of a, a', where $f(z, z')$ is regular, there is a definite domain, actually lying within the domain of a, a', appertaining to the place b, b', and providing a region over which $f(z, z')$ is regular; this domain is given by the relations
$$|z - b| \leqslant r - |b - a|, \quad |z' - b'| \leqslant r' - |b' - a'|.$$
Let the double power-series be constructed to represent $f(z, z')$ within this definite domain. The coefficients in this new double series are determined by the values, at the place b, b', of the function $f(z, z')$ and of its derivatives; and these may depend for their expression upon the initial double series $P(z - a, z' - a')$. Denote this new double series by
$$Q(z - b, z' - b'; a, a').$$
Within the specified domain round b, b', which belongs also to the domain round a, a', we have two power-series representing one and the same regular function $f(z, z')$; accordingly, (II, § 52) for all places z, z' within that specified limited domain, the new series Q provides no expression for the function $f(z, z')$ which, in significance, is additional to the expression for the function $f(z, z')$ provided by the old series P.

But now consider the range of absolute convergence of the double series Q, which will be the general domain of the place b, b'. It certainly includes the preceding specified domain, which lies within the general domain of the place a, a' in connection with the absolute convergence of the series P. It may extend beyond the boundary of that preceding specified domain; if it does, then it includes places z, z' not included within the domain of a, a'. For all such places, the series Q converges absolutely and therefore has a unique significance whereas, for them, the series P has no significance.

Accordingly, when some of the general domain of b, b' as connected with the absolute convergence of the series Q lies outside the general domain of a, a' as connected with the absolute convergence of the series P, our new series Q provides an expression for a regular function of z and z' which is not provided by the old series P, while over the region common to the two general domains the series Q represents the regular function which is represented by

---

* For many of the investigations which are given at this stage, reference can be made to the memoir by Weierstrass, "Einige auf die Theorie der analytischen Functionen mehrerer Veränderlichen sich beziehende Sätze," *Ges. Werke*, t. ii, pp. 135—188. A doctor's thesis by Dautheville, "Étude sur les séries entières par rapport à plusieurs variables imaginaires indépendantes," Gauthier-Villars (1885), may also be consulted.

the series P over the domain of a, a'. Using the term adopted for the corresponding result in the similar event for functions of a single variable, we say that (in the supposed circumstance of the more extensive character of the general domain of b, b') the series Q is a *continuation*, sometimes an analytical continuation, of the series P; and we call each of the two series an *element* of the regular function which they help to represent.

The process may be repeated by selecting a new place c, c', lying within the general domain of b, b' and not within the general domain of a, a'. When a definite domain of c, c' is constructed lying within the domain of b, b', and when we form a new double series for the function represented by $Q(z-b, z'-b'; a, a')$ by taking the value of the function and of its derivatives at c, c' as determining the coefficients for this new series, we can denote this series by

$$R(z-c, z'-c'; a, a'; b, b').$$

Within the specified domain round c, c', the new series R represents the same regular function as is represented by Q within that domain.

Again, now consider the range of convergence of the double series R, which range will be the general domain of c, c'. It certainly includes the specified domain round c, c'. It may extend beyond the boundary of that specified domain; and then it includes places z, z' not included in the general domain of b, b' and, when c, c' is properly chosen, not included in the general domain of a, a'. For all such places z, z', within the general domain of c, c' and outside the general domains of b, b' and of a, a', the series R provides a regular representation of the function which is not provided either by the series Q or by the series P, while over the part of the domain of c, c' that belongs to the domain of b, b' it represents the same function as is represented by the series Q. In this event, the series R provides a continuation of the series Q and it is another element of the function, now represented by the series P, Q, R.

And so on, from domain to domain. The ultimate aggregate of all the series, each providing a new element, is the combined analytical expression of a function. The ultimate aggregate of the z, z' field, provided by all the domains, is called the *region of continuity* of that function.

It is clear, after earlier explanations, that one of the simplest instances is provided by an integral function, that is, a double series converging for all finite values of z and z'; and its region of continuity consists of the part of the z, z' field given by finite values of z and z'.

Ex. Consider the double series

$$f = \sum_{r=0} \sum_{s=0} z^r z'^s$$

which converges for values of $|z| \leqslant k < 1$ and $|z'| \leqslant k' < 1$. At the place $z = -\frac{1}{2}$, $z' = -\frac{1}{2}$, we have

$$f_{0,0} = \frac{1}{\left(1+\frac{1}{2}\right)\left(1+\frac{1}{2}\right)} = \left(\frac{2}{3}\right)^2,$$

$$\frac{f_{m,n}}{m!\,n!} = \frac{1}{\left(1+\frac{1}{2}\right)^{m+1}\left(1+\frac{1}{2}\right)^{n+1}} = \left(\frac{2}{3}\right)^{m+n+2}.$$

When we form a series in powers of $z+\frac{1}{2}$ and $z'+\frac{1}{2}$, so that $-\frac{1}{2}$ and $-\frac{1}{2}$ is the new origin for a new domain, the series converges for values of z and z' such that

$$\left|z+\frac{1}{2}\right| \leqslant l < \frac{3}{2}, \quad \left|z'+\frac{1}{2}\right| \leqslant l' < \frac{3}{2}.$$

The series is

$$\Sigma\Sigma \frac{f_{m,n}}{m!\,n!}\left(z+\frac{1}{2}\right)^m\left(z'+\frac{1}{2}\right)^n,$$

that is, it is

$$\sum_{m=0}\sum_{n=0}\left(\frac{2}{3}\right)^{m+n+2}\left(z+\frac{1}{2}\right)^m\left(z'+\frac{1}{2}\right)^n.$$

For values of $|z| \leqslant k < 1$ and $|z'| \leqslant k' < 1$, the series gives no representation of f which is not given by the first series. For values of $|z| \geqslant 1$ such that $\left|z+\frac{1}{2}\right| \leqslant l < \frac{3}{2}$, and values of $|z'| \geqslant 1$ such that $\left|z'+\frac{1}{2}\right| \leqslant l' < \frac{3}{2}$, the second series does give a representation of f which is not given by the first series.

The first series is the expansion, within a domain round 0, 0, of the function

$$\frac{1}{(1-z)(1-z')}.$$

When we sum the second series, we have, as the sum,

$$\frac{\left(\frac{2}{3}\right)^2}{\left\{1-\frac{2}{3}\left(z+\frac{1}{2}\right)\right\}\left\{1-\frac{2}{3}\left(z'+\frac{1}{2}\right)\right\}},$$

that is,

$$\frac{1}{(1-z)(1-z')},$$

verifying the property that the two series, within their respective domains, are elements of one and the same function.

Singularities of uniform functions.

57. Any region of continuity of a function that is uniform, continuous, and analytic has for its *boundary* a place or an aggregate of places (whether these are given by values of the variables that are continuous in succession or are given by discrete sets of variables) where the function ceases to be regular. Such a place is called *singular* by Weierstrass[*].

Let k, k' be a singular place for a uniform function $f(z, z')$; then in the immediate vicinity of k, k', the function cannot be expanded as a converging

---

[*] See the memoir cited (§ 56) above, p. 156.

series of powers of $z-k$ and $z'-k'$. Two alternative possibilities present themselves as to the behaviour of functions in the vicinity of such a place.

Under the first of these alternatives, it can happen that a power-series $P_0(z-k, z'-k')$, representing some function regular at k, k' and vanishing there, exists such that the product
$$P_0(z-k, z'-k')f(z, z')$$
is regular in the immediate vicinity of k and k'. Denote this product by $F(z, z')$. Then $F(z, z')$, being a regular function of z and z' in the immediate vicinity of k and k', can be expanded in a double series of powers of $z-k$ and $z'-k'$ which converges absolutely within non-infinitesimal regions round k and k'. Denote this new series by $P_1(z-k, z'-k')$; then we have
$$f(z, z') = \frac{P_1(z-k, z'-k')}{P_0(z-k, z'-k')}.$$
Following Weierstrass*, we call such a place an *unessential singularity* of the function.

Under the second of the alternatives indicated, it can happen that no power-series $P_0(z-k, z'-k')$, representing some function of z and z' regular in the immediate vicinity of k, k', exists such that the product
$$P_0(z-k, z'-k')f(z, z')$$
is regular in the immediate vicinity of k, k'. Following Weierstrass*, we call such a place k, k' an *essential singularity* of the function $f(z, z')$.

It is to be noted, in passing, that, for the occurrence of an unessential singularity, it is sufficient to have a single power-series P_0 such that the product $P_0 f$ is regular in the immediate vicinity of the place. But there is no assumption (and it is not universally the fact) that only a single power-series exists having this property or that all such power-series, as exist having this property, are expressible in terms of P_0 alone. When two different expressions for the uniform function $f(z, z')$ are obtained in the vicinity of the place k, k', they must be equivalent; and we should then have a relation
$$\frac{Q_1(z-k, z'-k')}{Q_0(z-k, z'-k')} = \frac{P_1(z-k, z'-k')}{P_0(z-k, z'-k')}.$$
We shall assume that, while $P_1(0, 0)$ and $P_0(0, 0)$ vanish, the power-series P_1 and P_0 possess† no common factor vanishing at k, k', whether it takes the form of a regular power-series or a mere polynomial which is a special case of a regular power-series. Similarly, we shall assume that Q_1 and Q_0 possess no common factor vanishing at k, k'. Now
$$Q_1(z-k, z'-k') = \frac{P_1(z-k, z'-k')}{P_0(z-k, z'-k')} Q_0(z-k, z'-k').$$

* *l. c.*, p. 156.

† This matter will be considered later, so as to obtain the conditions necessary and sufficient to justify the assumption.

Here Q_1 is regular in the immediate vicinity of k, k', while P_1 and P_0 have no common factor vanishing at k, k'; hence Q_0 must contain P_0 as a factor. Let F denote the quotient of Q_0 by P_0, so that F is regular at k, k'; then
$$Q_0 = P_0 F, \quad Q_1 = P_1 F.$$
Again,
$$P_1(z-k, z'-k') = \frac{Q_1(z-k, z'-k')}{Q_0(z-k, z'-k')} P_0(z-k, z'-k').$$
Here P_1 is regular in the immediate vicinity of k, k', while Q_1 and Q_0 have no common factor vanishing at k, k'; hence P_0 must contain Q_0 as a factor. But
$$P_0 = Q_0 \cdot \frac{1}{F};$$
and therefore $1/F$ is regular at k, k'. Consequently both F and $1/F$ are regular at k, k'; and therefore F does not vanish at k, k'. It is not difficult to see that we then may choose a domain round k, k', which may be small but is not infinitesimal, such that F does not vanish in that domain; and then the behaviour of Q_0 in the immediate vicinity of the place k, k' is effectively the same as the behaviour of P_0 in that immediate vicinity.

Likewise for P_1 and Q_1 if they vanish at k, k'. When either does not vanish, the other will not vanish; they are different from zero at k, k' together.

It follows that, in discussing the behaviour of $f(z, z')$ in the immediate vicinity of k, k', any representation of $f(z, z')$ by a quotient P_1/P_0 can be used, if P_1 and P_0 have no common factor*.

58. In the case of functions of a single variable, it is known that there are different types of essential singularities, whether these occur at isolated points, or along lines, or over continuous areas. Special kinds of essential singularities are considered in that theory, and they furnish partial characteristics of some classes of functions; for example, not a few definite results have been achieved when the essential singularities in question can be approached as the limits of groups of particular points of a function; but the theory is far from easy or complete. *A fortiori*, it is to be expected that even greater difficulties will arise in the consideration of the types of essential singularities of uniform functions of a couple of variables.

But when we deal with unessential singularities of uniform functions, there is a real divergence between the theory of functions of a single variable, and the theory of functions of two variables or more than two variables. In the case of functions of one variable, there is only one type of unessential singularities, the only variation in the type being the variety of the order; such a point a is said to be an unessential singularity (or a

---

* The relation between two such functions as P_0 and Q_0 will be considered fully in Chapter IV: in particular, see § 64.

pole) of a function $f(z)$, and of order n for the function, when there is a positive integer n such that
$$(z-a)^n f(z)$$
is finite and not zero at the point.

In the case of uniform functions of two variables, we arrange the unessential singularities in two distinct types or classes. After the explanatory definition we know that, in the immediate vicinity of k, k', the function $f(z, z')$ can be expressed in the form
$$f(z, z') = \frac{P_1(z-k, z'-k')}{P_0(z-k, z'-k')},$$
where P_0 and P_1 are converging double series in powers of $z-k$ and $z'-k'$, of which P_0 vanishes at k, k'.

Two different cases then can occur as alternatives, discriminated according to the value acquired by P_1 at k, k'.

In the one case, leading to one of the two types of unessential singularities, it is the fact that P_1 does not vanish at k, k'. It then follows that, no matter how z tends to the value k and z' to the value k', the quantity $|f(z, z')|$ can, for sufficiently small values of $|z-k|$ and $|z'-k'|$, be made larger than any assigned magnitude, however large: that is to say, this large magnitude is assigned at will, and the appropriate small values of $|z-k|$ and $|z'-k'|$ are determined subsequently to the assignment. We therefore can take infinity as the limit for the assignment; and the place k, k' then gives a definite and unique value to $f(z, z')$, this value being infinite.

This type of unessential singularity is one of the two kinds of unessential singularity considered by Weierstrass. It is convenient to use for functions of two variables, the same name as is used, for functions of on variable, when the place gives a definite and unique infinity of the function. Accordingly we shall call this type of unessential singularity the polar type; and a place k, k', being an unessential singularity of the polar type for the uniform function, will be called a *pole* of the function $f(z, z')$.

In the other case, leading to the other of the two types of unessential singularities, it is the fact that P_1 does vanish at k, k'. The place k, k' then does not give a definite and unique infinite value for the function $f(z, z')$. Subsequent explanations may so far be anticipated here as to declare that particular modes of approach of z to k and of z' to k' can be selected, so as to make $f(z, z')$ tend towards any assigned value near k, k' and acquire that assigned value at k, k'; thus the function $f(z, z')$ does not acquire a definite unique value at the place.

This type of unessential singularity is the other of the two kinds of unessential singularity considered by Weierstrass. We have given a definite name to the other type of unessential singularity that can belong to uniform functions of two variables; to the type just indicated, we shall give simply the general name *unessential singularity* and, so far as concerns functions of two variables, there need be no confusion in taking this unrestricted name*.

Thus, for the function
$$\frac{z+z'}{z-z'}$$
the place $z=1$, $z'=1$ is a pole; the place $z=0$, $z'=0$ is an unessential singularity.

For the function
$$\frac{z+z'}{z-z'}e^{\frac{1}{z}+\frac{1}{z'}},$$
the place $z=1$, $z'=-1$ is a zero; the place $z=1$, $z'=1$ is a pole; the place $z=0$, $z'=0$ is an essential singularity.

For a function
$$\frac{P(z, z')}{Q(z, z')},$$
where $P(z, z')$ and $Q(z, z')$ are polynomials in z and z' having no common factor, all places satisfying the equation
$$Q(z, z')=0$$
are poles unless they also satisfy the equation
$$P(z, z')=0;$$
and all places satisfying the two equations
$$Q(z, z')=0, \quad P(z, z')=0,$$
are unessential singularities.

As a summary conclusion, we see that there are four kinds of places for a uniform analytic function of two variables, viz. ordinary places, poles, unessential singularities, essential singularities. The first set of these constitute the region of continuity of the function; the remainder constitute the boundary of the region of continuity of the function.

Extension of Laurent's Theorem.

59. As a last theorem for the present, we proceed to an extension of Laurent's theorem on functions of a single variable; in order to make the establishment simpler, we shall restate Cauchy's theorem concerning the

---

* Corresponding considerations arise for functions of n variables. Weierstrass arranges their unessential singularities in two kinds. One kind includes places that, as in the text, may be called poles; at such a place, the function definitely and uniquely acquires an infinite value. The other kind includes all unessential singularities which are not poles. Now it is conceivable that an unessential singularity of this second kind for a uniform function of n variables might be ranged in one or other of $n-1$ classes, according as there are m, ∞^1, ∞^2, ..., ∞^{n-2} ways (where m is finite) in which $z_1, z_2, ..., z_n$ could be made to approach the unessential singularity $a_1, a_2, ..., a_n$ so as to make the function
$$\frac{P_1(z_1-a_1, z_2-a_2, ..., z_n-a_n)}{P_0(z_1-a_1, z_2-a_2, ..., z_n-a_n)}$$
acquire an assigned value at the place.

The question manifestly does not arise when there are only two independent variables; hence the adoption of the names *pole* and *unessential singularity* in the text.

expansion of a function in a double series of positive powers. Consider a function $f(z, z')$ within a region where it is continuous, uniform, and analytic. Within that region (assumed to include 0, 0) consider the domain defined by

$$|z| \leqslant \rho < r, \quad |z'| \leqslant \rho' < r'.$$

Then we have the result

$$f(z, z') = \frac{1}{(2\pi i)^2} \iint \frac{f(t, t')}{(t-z)(t'-z')} \, dt \, dt',$$

when the double integral is taken round circles in the domain such that

$$|z| < |t| \leqslant \rho < r, \quad |z'| < |t'| \leqslant \rho' < r'.$$

Moreover, taking

$$\frac{1}{t-z} = \frac{1}{t} + \frac{z}{t^2} + \frac{z^2}{t^3} + \ldots + \frac{z^m}{t^n} + \frac{\left(\frac{z}{t}\right)^{m+1}}{1 - \frac{z}{t}},$$

$$\frac{1}{t'-z'} = \frac{1}{t'} + \frac{z'}{t'^2} + \frac{z'^2}{t'^3} + \ldots + \frac{z'^n}{t'^n} + \frac{\left(\frac{z'}{t'}\right)^{n+1}}{1 - \frac{z'}{t'}},$$

we obtain an expression for $f(z, z')$ in the form

$$f(z, z') = \sum_{p=0} \sum_{q=0} c_{p,q} z^p z'^q.$$

The forms for the coefficients $c_{p,q}$ have already been given; the upper values of the limits of $|c_{p,q}|$ for all positive integer values of p and q have already been given also, when the function $f(z, z')$ has the assigned properties; the series can be continued to infinity for both sets of indices, and it converges absolutely within the z, z' domain*.

Now consider a corresponding extension of Laurent's theorem, which may be enunciated as follows:—

Let $f(z, z')$ denote a function, which is uniform, continuous, and analytic, within a region in the field of variation defined by relations

$$R_0 > R \geqslant |z - a| \geqslant r > r_0, \quad R_0' > R' \geqslant |z' - a'| \geqslant r' > r_0'.$$

Denote by t and by s current variables (or points) on the circumferences of the outer circle of radius R_0 and the inner circle of radius r_0 in the z-plane; and similarly for t' and for s' on the circumferences of the outer circle of radius R_0' and the inner circle of radius r_0' in the z'-plane. Then the function $f(z, z')$ can be expressed as a series of integral powers of $z - a$ and $z' - a'$; the indices of those powers can range from $-\infty$ to $+\infty$ for each of the

---

* The analytical work, needed to establish the result, is so similar to the corresponding analysis for functions of a single variable (see my *Theory of Functions*, § 28) that it need not be set out in detail.

variables; and the double series converges absolutely for values of z and z' given by
$$R \geq |z-a| \geq r, \quad R' \geq |z'-a'| \geq r'.$$

By the generalisation of the first part of Cauchy's theorem, we have
$$f(z, z') = \frac{1}{(2\pi i)^2} \iint \frac{f(t, t')}{(t-z)(t'-z')} dt dt'$$
$$- \frac{1}{(2\pi i)^2} \iint \frac{f(s, t')}{(s-z)(t'-z')} ds dt' - \frac{1}{(2\pi i)^2} \iint \frac{f(t, s')}{(t-z)(s'-z')} dt ds'$$
$$+ \frac{1}{(2\pi i)^2} \iint \frac{f(s, s')}{(s-z)(s'-z')} ds ds'.$$

Now, for our values of a, a', z, z', t, t', we have
$$\frac{t-a}{t-z} = 1 + \frac{z-a}{t-a} + \ldots + \left(\frac{z-a}{t-a}\right)^m + \frac{t-a}{t-z}\left(\frac{z-a}{t-a}\right)^{m+1},$$
$$\frac{t'-a'}{t'-z'} = 1 + \frac{z'-a'}{t'-a'} + \ldots + \left(\frac{z'-a'}{t'-a'}\right)^n + \frac{t'-a'}{t'-z'}\left(\frac{z'-a'}{t'-a'}\right)^{n+1};$$
and so the integral
$$\frac{1}{(2\pi i)^2} \iint \frac{f(t, t')}{(t-z)(t'-z')} dt dt'$$
is expressible as a double series of terms
$$\Sigma\Sigma \, c_{p,q}(z-a)^p (z'-a')^q$$
for $p = 0, 1, \ldots, m$ and $q = 0, 1, \ldots, n$, where
$$c_{p,q} = \frac{1}{(2\pi i)^2} \iint \frac{f(t, t')}{(t-a)^{p+1}(t'-a')^{q+1}} dt dt';$$
together with a single series of terms
$$\sum_q \frac{1}{(2\pi i)^2} \iint \frac{f(t, t')}{t-z} \left(\frac{z-a}{t-a}\right)^{m+1} \left(\frac{z'-a'}{t'-a'}\right)^q dt dt',$$
for $q = 0, 1, \ldots, n$; and a single series of terms
$$\sum_p \frac{1}{(2\pi i)^2} \iint \frac{f(t, t')}{t'-z'} \left(\frac{z'-a'}{t'-a'}\right)^{n+1} \left(\frac{z-a}{t-a}\right)^p dt dt',$$
for $p = 0, 1, \ldots, m$; and a term
$$\frac{1}{(2\pi i)^2} \iint \frac{f(t, t')}{(t-z)(t'-z')} \left(\frac{z-a}{t-a}\right)^{m+1} \left(\frac{z'-a'}{t'-a'}\right)^{n+1} dt dt'.$$

To consider the coefficients in the double series, let M denote the greatest value of $|f(z, z')|$ within the whole region considered; then, as before,
$$|c_{p,q}| \leq \frac{M}{R_0^p R_0'^q},$$
though nothing can be declared as to a relation between $c_{p,q}$ and the derivative $\dfrac{\partial^{p+q} f(z, z')}{\partial z^p \partial z'^q}$ at a, a', for our function is not defined within the domain $|z-a| < r_0$, $|z'-a'| < r_0'$.

As regards the second series of terms, say S, we have
$$|S| \leqslant \sum_{q=0}^{n} \frac{|f(t, t')|}{R_0 - R} \left(\frac{R}{R_0}\right)^{m+1} \left(\frac{R'}{R_0'}\right)^{q+1} R_0 R_0'$$
$$\leqslant \sum_{q=0}^{n} \frac{M R_0 R_0'}{R_0 - R} \left(\frac{R}{R_0}\right)^{m+1} \left(\frac{R'}{R_0'}\right)^{q+1} ;$$

as $R < R_0$, indefinite increase of m makes each term in the series on the right-hand side as small as we please; and $R' < R_0'$: that is, by taking m indefinitely large, we can make $S = 0$.

Next, as regards the third series of terms, say S', we have
$$|S'| \leqslant \sum_{p=0}^{m} \frac{|f(t, t')|}{R_0' - R'} \left(\frac{R'}{R_0'}\right)^{n+1} \left(\frac{R}{R_0}\right)^{p+1} R_0 R_0'$$
$$\leqslant \sum_{p=0}^{m} \frac{M}{R_0' - R'} \left(\frac{R'}{R_0'}\right)^{n+1} \left(\frac{R}{R_0}\right)^{p+1} R_0 R_0' ;$$

as $R' < R_0'$, indefinite increase of n makes each term in the series on the right-hand side as small as we please; and $R < R_0$; that is, by taking n indefinitely large, we can make $S' = 0$.

Lastly, as regards the modulus of the single term, it is
$$\leqslant \frac{M R_0 R_0'}{(R_0 - R)(R_0' - R')} \left(\frac{R}{R_0}\right)^{m+1} \left(\frac{R'}{R_0'}\right)^{n+1},$$

which, with the assumptions made concerning m and n, can be made less than any assigned quantity, however small; that is, we can make the term zero.

In these circumstances, the expression for the first of the four integrals becomes
$$\sum_{p=0}^{m} \sum_{q=0}^{n} c_{p,q} (z-a)^p (z'-a')^q.$$

As $|z-a| \leqslant R < R_0$, $|z'-a'| \leqslant R' < R_0'$, and as $|c_{p,q}| \leqslant \frac{M}{R_0^p R_0'^q}$, this double series converges absolutely when m and n increase indefinitely and independently of one another. Thus the first integral is expressible as an absolutely converging series of positive powers of $z - a$ and $z' - a'$.

To obtain an expression for the second integral, which is
$$-\frac{1}{(2\pi i)^2} \iint \frac{f(s, t')}{(s-z)(t'-z')} ds dt',$$

we note that $|z - a| \geqslant r > r_0 > |s - a|$, while $|t' - z'| < |t' - a'|$; so we take
$$-\frac{z-a}{s-z} = 1 + \frac{s-a}{z-a} + \ldots + \left(\frac{s-a}{z-a}\right)^\mu + \frac{z-a}{z-s} \left(\frac{s-a}{z-a}\right)^{\mu+1},$$
$$\frac{t'-a'}{t'-z'} = 1 + \frac{z'-a'}{t'-a'} + \ldots + \left(\frac{z'-a'}{t'-a'}\right)^n + \frac{t'-a'}{t'-z'} \left(\frac{z'-a'}{t'-a'}\right)^{n+1}.$$

We proceed as in the last case. It is possible to increase μ without limit and n without limit; and we obtain, as the expression for the integral,
$$\sum_{p=0}\sum_{q=0} c_{\mu,n}(z-a)^{-\mu}(z'-a')^n,$$
where
$$c_{p,q} = \frac{1}{(2\pi i)^2}\iint \frac{f(s,t')}{(t'-a')^{q+1}}(s-a)^{p-1}ds\,dt'.$$
Also
$$|c_{p,q}| \leqslant M r_0^p R_0'^{-q};$$
and the double series converges absolutely for the retained range of values for z and z'.

Similarly, as the expression for the third of our double integrals, which is
$$-\frac{1}{(2\pi i)^2}\iint \frac{f(t,s')}{(t-z)(s'-z')}dt\,ds',$$
we obtain
$$\sum_{p=0}\sum_{q=0} c_{p,q}(z-a)^p(z'-a')^{-q},$$
where
$$c_{p,q} = \frac{1}{(2\pi i)^2}\iint \frac{f(t,s')}{(t-a)^{p+1}}(s'-a')^{q-1}dt\,ds'.$$
Also
$$|c_{p,q}| \leqslant M R_0^{-p} r_0'^q;$$
and this double series converges absolutely for the retained range of values for z and z'.

Lastly, as the expression for the fourth of our double integrals, which is
$$\frac{1}{(2\pi i)^2}\iint \frac{f(s,s')}{(s-z)(s'-z')}ds\,ds',$$
we obtain
$$\sum_{p=0}\sum_{q=0} c_{p,q}(z-a)^{-p}(z'-a')^{-q},$$
where
$$c_{p,q} = \frac{1}{(2\pi i)^2}\iint f(s,s')(s-a)^{p-1}(s'-a')^{q-1}ds\,ds'.$$
Also
$$|c_{p,q}| \leqslant M r_0^p r_0'^q;$$
and this double series converges absolutely for the retained range of values for z and z'.

Gathering these results together, we see that, in the circumstances as stated in the extended Laurent's theorem, the function $f(z, z')$ is expressible in the form
$$f(z,z') = \sum_{-\infty}^{\infty}\sum_{-\infty}^{\infty} c_{m,n}(z-a)^m(z'-a')^n,$$
the summation being for all integer values of m and of n between ∞ and $-\infty$; also

$|c_{m,n}| \leqslant MR_0^{-m}R_0'^{-n}$, when m is positive and n is positive,

$|c_{m,n}| \leqslant MR_0^{-m}r_0'^{n}$, ... positive .... negative,

$|c_{m,n}| \leqslant Mr_0^{m}R_0'^{-n}$, ... negative .... positive,

$|c_{m,n}| \leqslant Mr_0^{m}r_0'^{n}$, ... negative .... negative;

and the double series converges absolutely for values of z and z' given by

$$R_0 > R \geqslant |z-a| \geqslant r > r_0, \quad R_0' > R' \geqslant |z'-a'| \geqslant r' > r_0'.$$

It follows as an immediate corollary that *when a function $\phi(z, z')$ is uniform, continuous, and analytic for all the z, z' region of variation represented by the relations*

$$|z-a| \geqslant r > r_0, \quad |z'-a'| \geqslant r' > r_0',$$

it is expressible as a double series of negative powers in the form

$$\phi(z, z') = \sum_0 \sum_0 c_{m,n}(z-a)^{-m}(z'-a')^{-n},$$

where $|c_{m,n}| \leqslant Mr_0^{m}r_0'^{n}$,

M being the greatest value of $|\phi(z, z')|$ within the foregoing region; and the series converges absolutely for the specified range of values for z and z'.

The result is at once derivable from the extension of Laurent's theorem by making R_0 and R_0' increase without limit; and it can of course be established independently in the same manner as the general theorem.

Ex. 1. The function
$$e^{P\left(z, \frac{1}{z}, z', \frac{1}{z'}\right)},$$
where $P\left(z, \frac{1}{z}, z', \frac{1}{z'}\right)$ is a polynomial in $z, \frac{1}{z}, z', \frac{1}{z'}$, can be expanded in a series

$$\sum_{-\infty}^{\infty} \sum_{-\infty}^{\infty} c_{m,n} z^m z'^n,$$

for finite values of $|z|$ and $|z'|$ such that

$$|z| \geqslant r > \epsilon, \quad |z'| \geqslant r' > \epsilon',$$

where ϵ and ϵ' are positive non-zero quantities.

Ex. 2. Shew that the coefficient of $z^m z'^n$ (where m and n are positive) in the Laurent expansion of

$$e^{\frac{1}{2}\xi\left(z-\frac{1}{z}\right)+\frac{1}{2}\eta\left(z'-\frac{1}{z'}\right)},$$

$|\xi|$ and $|\eta|$ being finite and independent of z and of z', is

$$J_m(\xi) J_n(\eta),$$

where J_m and J_n are Bessel's functions of order m and n; and obtain the coefficient of $z^m z'^n$ in the same expansion (i) when either m or n is negative, (ii) when both m and n are negative.

CHAPTER IV

Uniform Functions in Restricted Domains

A theorem due to Weierstrass.

60. AFTER these preliminary results relating to expansions of a uniform function, which converge absolutely and are valid over the appropriate domains, it is important to take account of the detailed behaviour of the function in the immediate vicinity of each of its several kinds of places.

Accordingly, let a, a' be an ordinary place for a uniform, continuous, analytic function $f(z, z')$; the preceding investigations shew that $f(z, z')$, regular in some domain of that place, can be represented within the domain by a double series of positive powers of $z - a$ and $z' - a'$ which there converges absolutely. No generality, for our present purpose, is lost by assuming that $a = 0$ and $a' = 0$, for the assumption can be secured by taking $z - a = Z$, $z' - a' = Z'$. Hence we write

$$F(z, z') = f(z, z') - f(0, 0) = \Sigma\Sigma c_{m,n} z^m z'^n,$$

where the summation is for positive integer values of m and of n save only simultaneous zero values. Also, $|f(0, 0)|$ is finite and may be zero.

The detailed behaviour of the function $F(z, z')$ in the immediate vicinity of the place 0, 0 is governed by an important theorem, originally due to Weierstrass. After the analysis has been given, the principal results will be enunciated in a form that differs from Weierstrass's, because the limitation to two variables renders greater detail possible[*] than when n is the number of variables.

---

[*] The theorem is proved by Weierstrass for functions of n variables, *Ges. Werke*, t. ii, pp. 135—142. Another proof, due to Simart, is given by Picard, *Traité d'Analyse*, t. ii, pp. 243—245.

The theorem is discussed here for the special case when there are only two variables. For this case, a proof (which follows Weierstrass's proof for the general case) is given in my *Theory of Functions*, § 297; it is modified in the proof given in the text, because the theorem is not regarded from the point of view of establishing the existence of implicit functions of a single variable.

Our function $F(z, z')$, which is regular in a domain round 0, 0, can be expressed in a form
$$F(z, z') = \phi_0(z) + z'\phi_1(z) + z'^2\phi_2(z) + \ldots.$$
Two cases arise according as $F(z, 0)$ does not vanish, or does vanish, identically for all values of z within the domain.

61. First, suppose that $F(z, 0)$ does not vanish for all values of z. Denoting $F(z, 0)$ by $F_0(z)$, which is equal to $\phi_0(z)$, and introducing a new function $F_1(z, z')$ defined by the equation
$$F(z, z') = F_0(z) - F_1(z, z'),$$
we have a function $F_1(z, z')$ which, when $z' = 0$, vanishes for all values of z. Now $F_0(z)$ is independent of z' and does not vanish for all values of z; hence we can choose places z, z' in the vicinity of 0, 0, which lie within the region of convergence of $F(z, z')$ and are such that
$$|F_0| > |F_1|.$$
It is to be remembered that F_0 vanishes when $z = 0$; and so there may be some lower limit for $|z|$ below which this inequality is not satisfied. As $|z|$ increases, a zero of F_0 may be attained, and then the inequality would not be satisfied. Also as $|z'|$ increases, the value of $|F(z, z')|$ may increase; and so there may be some upper limit for $|z'|$ above which the inequality is not satisfied. Accordingly, we suppose that, for places satisfying the relations
$$\rho_0 < |z| < \rho, \quad |z'| < \rho_1,$$
the inequality $|F_0| > |F_1|$ holds. For all such places we have, on taking logarithmic derivatives of the equation
$$F = F_0\left(1 - \frac{F_1}{F_0}\right),$$
the relation
$$\frac{1}{F}\frac{\partial F}{\partial z} = \frac{1}{F_0}\frac{\partial F_0}{\partial z} - \frac{\partial}{\partial z}\left(\sum_{\lambda=1}^{\infty}\frac{1}{\lambda}\frac{F_1^\lambda}{F_0^\lambda}\right).$$

Now $F_0(z)$ is a regular function of z in a domain round $z = 0$, and it vanishes when $z = 0$; hence the lowest exponent in its expansion must be a positive integer greater than zero, say m. Thus
$$F_0(z) = z^m h(z),$$
where $h(z)$ is a regular function of z in the selected domain and has a constant term; consequently
$$\frac{1}{F_0}\frac{\partial F_0}{\partial z} = \frac{m}{z} + \frac{h'(z)}{h(z)}$$
$$= \frac{m}{z} + G(z),$$
where $G(z)$ is a converging series of positive powers of z in the selected domain. Similarly
$$\frac{F_1^\lambda}{F_0^\lambda} = \sum_{\mu=0}^{\infty} z^{-m\lambda+\mu} G_{\lambda,\mu}(z'),$$

where $G_{\lambda,\mu}(z')$, the coefficients of the powers of z, are converging series of positive integral powers of z'; and because $F_1(z, z')$ vanishes when $z' = 0$ for all values of z, each of these coefficients $G_{\lambda,\mu}(z')$ vanishes when $z' = 0$. Take each power of z, and collect all the terms which involve that power of z in the expansion

$$\sum_{\lambda=1}^{\infty} \frac{1}{\lambda} \frac{F_1^{\lambda}}{F_0^{\lambda}};$$

then we have

$$\sum_{\lambda=1}^{\infty} \frac{1}{\lambda} \frac{F_1^{\lambda}}{F_0^{\lambda}} = \sum_{n=-\infty}^{n=\infty} G_n(z') z^n,$$

while each of the coefficients $G_n(z')$, being a linear combination of the coefficients $G_{\lambda,\mu}(z')$, vanishes when $z' = 0$. Thus

$$\frac{1}{F} \frac{\partial F}{\partial z} = \frac{m}{z} + G(z) - \frac{\partial}{\partial z} \left\{ \sum_{n=-\infty}^{n=\infty} G_n(z') z^n \right\};$$

and the only term on the right-hand side, which involves the power z^{-1}, is the term $\dfrac{m}{z}$.

Now let $\zeta_1, \ldots, \zeta_s$ denote the zeros of $F(z, \zeta')$, regarded as a function of z, when we consider a range of values of z such that $|z| < \rho$, and when we assign to z' a parametric value ζ' such that $|\zeta'| < \rho_1$. Repeated zeros of $F(z, \zeta')$ are given by repetition in the quantities ζ, so that s denotes the tale of zeros of $F(z, \zeta')$ within the range. Then, as $F(z, \zeta')$ is regular for all such values of z, the function

$$\frac{1}{F} \frac{dF(z, \zeta')}{dz} - \sum_{p=1}^{s} \frac{1}{z - \zeta_p}$$

is finite for those values; it can therefore be expanded as a converging series of positive powers of z, say $P(z)$, so that

$$\frac{1}{F} \frac{dF(z, \zeta')}{dz} = \sum_{p=1}^{s} \frac{1}{z - \zeta_p} + P(z).$$

Choose values of z, such that $|z|$ is still less than ρ and is now greater than the greatest of the quantities $|\zeta_1|, \ldots, |\zeta_s|$. The fractions on the right-hand side of the equation can, for such values of z, be expanded in descending powers of z; and the equation, after such expansions, becomes

$$\frac{1}{F} \frac{dF(z, \zeta')}{dz} = P(z) + \frac{s}{z} + \sum_{\tau=1}^{\infty} S_\tau z^{-\tau-1},$$

where

$$S_\tau = \zeta_1^\tau + \ldots + \zeta_s^\tau.$$

As this result is valid for all values of ζ' within the selected z'-range, ζ' being independent of z, we have

$$\frac{m}{z} + G(z) - \frac{\partial}{\partial z} \left\{ \sum_{n=-\infty}^{n=\infty} G_n(\zeta') z^n \right\}$$
$$= \frac{s}{z} + P(z) + \sum_{\tau=1}^{\infty} S_\tau z^{-\tau-1},$$

identically for all values of z; and therefore, among other results, we have
$$s = m, \quad S_\tau = \tau G_{-\tau}(\zeta'),$$
for all values of τ.

The first result shews that, for any given value of z' such that $|z'| < \rho_1$, the function $F(z, z')$ has m zeros in the range $|z| < \rho$, where the number m is the index of the lowest exponent in $F(z, 0)$ when expressed as a regular series of positive powers of z.

The second result then shews that, for all the positive values of τ, the quantity
$$\zeta_1^\tau + \ldots + \zeta_m^\tau$$
is expressible as a regular function of ζ' which vanishes when ζ' is zero. Hence all integral symmetric functions of $\zeta_1, \ldots, \zeta_m$ are regular functions of ζ' which vanish with ζ'; and as ζ' is a parametric value of z', we may (within our range) substitute z' for ζ'. It therefore follows that, if
$$g(z, z') = (z - \zeta_1) \ldots (z - \zeta_m)$$
$$= z^m + g_1 z^{m-1} + \ldots + g_m,$$
the coefficients $g_1, \ldots, g_m$ are regular functions of z' within the selected range, each of them vanishing when $z' = 0$.

Further, from the same equation, we have
$$P(z) = G(z) - \sum_{n=0}^{\infty} (n+1) z^n G_{n+1}(z'),$$
where all the functions are regular. Thus, if
$$\Gamma(z, z') = \int_0^z G(z) \, dz - \sum_{n=0}^{\infty} z^{n+1} G_{n+1}(z'),$$
where $\Gamma(z, z')$ manifestly is a regular function of z and z', and vanishes when $z = 0$ and $z' = 0$, we have
$$P(z) = \frac{\partial}{\partial z} \{\Gamma(z, z')\}.$$
Thus
$$\frac{1}{F} \frac{\partial F}{\partial z} = P(z) + \frac{m}{z} + \sum_{\tau=1}^{\infty} S_\tau z^{-\tau-1}$$
$$= \frac{\partial}{\partial z} \{\Gamma(z, z')\} + \frac{1}{g(z, z')} \frac{\partial}{\partial z} \{g(z, z')\};$$
and therefore
$$F = U g(z, z') e^{\Gamma(z, z')},$$
where U is independent of z.

As U is the same for all values of z, and as F and $g(z, z')$ and $\Gamma(z, z')$ are regular functions of z and z' for the range considered, it follows that U (if variable) is a regular function of z'. When $z' = 0$, let the first term in the expansion of the regular function F_0, which is all of $F(z, z')$ that then survives, be Cz^m; then $g(z, z')$ becomes z^m; and $\Gamma(z, z')$ is then a regular function of z alone. Thus, when $z' = 0$, we have $U = C$; and U, at the utmost, is a regular function of z'; hence

$$U = C(1 + \text{positive powers of } z')$$
$$= Ce^u,$$

where u is a regular function of z' which vanishes when $z' = 0$. Let

$$R(z, z') = u + \Gamma(z, z'),$$

where again $R(z, z')$ is a regular function of z and z' which vanishes when $z = 0$ and $z' = 0$; and we then have

$$F(z, z') = Cg(z, z') e^{R(z, z')},$$

with the defined significance of $g(z, z')$, $R(z, z')$, and C.

The new expression is valid within the assigned range of z, z' in the immediate vicinity of 0, 0. But it must not be assumed—and usually it is not the case in fact—that the new expression is valid over the whole domain where $f(z, z')$ is initially taken as regular.

We thus have the result:—

I. *When a function $f(z, z')$ is regular in some domain of 0, 0, and is such that $f(z, 0) - f(0, 0)$ does not vanish for all values of z in that domain, we have*

$$f(z, z') = f(0, 0) + Cg(z, z') e^{R(z, z')},$$

where

$$g(z, z') = z^m + g_1 z^{m-1} + \ldots + g_m,$$

the quantities $g_1, \ldots, g_m$ being functions of z', each of which is regular in the immediate vicinity of $z' = 0$ and vanishes when $z' = 0$; where Cz^m is the lowest power in the expansion of $f(z, 0) - f(0, 0)$ in positive powers of z; and where $R(z, z')$ is a function of z and z', which is regular in the immediate vicinity of 0, 0 and vanishes when $z = 0$ and $z' = 0$.

62. One important corollary can be at once derived from the preceding result.

Suppose that 0, 0 is a non-zero place for the function $f(z, z')$, so that $f(0, 0)$ is not zero; then we have

$$\frac{f(z, z')}{f(0, 0)} = 1 + \frac{C}{f(0, 0)} g(z, z') e^{R(z, z')}.$$

Now $R(z, z')$ is a regular function of z and z', vanishing when $z = 0$ and $z' = 0$, so that $|e^{R(z, z')}|$ is finite throughout some definite domain round 0, 0. Also $|C/f(0, 0)|$ is finite; and $g(z, z')$, while polynomial in z and regular in z' in the immediate vicinity of $z' = 0$, vanishes at the place 0, 0. It therefore is possible, owing to the regularity of $g(z, z')$ and $R(z, z')$, to choose a non-infinitesimal domain given by

$$|z| < r, \quad |z'| < r',$$

such that, for all the included values of z and z',

$$\left|\frac{C}{f(0,0)}\right| |g(z, z')| |e^{R(z,z')}| \leqslant M < 1,$$

where M is a real positive quantity. For all such values of z and z', we have

$$1 + \frac{C}{f(0,0)} g(z, z') e^{R(z,z')} = e^{\bar{R}(z,z')},$$

where $\bar{R}(z, z')$ is a regular function of z and z', given by the expansion

$$\frac{C}{f(0,0)} g(z, z') e^{R(z,z')} - \tfrac{1}{2} \frac{C^2}{f^2(0,0)} g^2(z, z') e^{2R(z,z')} - \ldots,$$

that is, $\bar{R}(z, z')$ is a regular function in a domain of z and z' and vanishes when $z = 0$ and $z' = 0$. This domain does not include any place that is a zero of $f(z, z')$, because at a zero-place z, z' of $f(z, z')$ we should have

$$\frac{C}{f(0,0)} g(z, z') e^{R(z,z')} = -1,$$

and therefore

$$\left|\frac{C}{f(0,0)}\right| |g(z, z')| |e^{R(z,z')}| = 1,$$

a possibility which is excluded. Hence we must have

$$\frac{f(z, z')}{f(0, 0)} = e^{\bar{R}(z,z')},$$

and therefore

$$f(z, z') = f(0, 0) e^{\bar{R}(z,z')}.$$

Our corollary can therefore be stated as follows:—

When $f(z, z')$ is regular within a finite domain round $0, 0$, and $f(0, 0)$ does not vanish, then there is a domain round $0, 0$—usually more limited than the former domain within which $f(z, z')$ is regular—such that $f(z, z')$ can be expressed in the form

$$f(z, z') = f(0, 0) e^{\bar{R}(z,z')},$$

where $\bar{R}(z, z')$ is a function of z and z', which vanishes when $z = 0$ and $z' = 0$ and is regular within the second domain.

In particular, this expression is valid in the immediate vicinity of $0, 0$, on the supposition adopted.

63. In precisely the same manner and with exactly similar analysis, we can establish the following result which therefore needs only to be stated:—

II. *When a function $f(z, z')$ is regular in some domain of $0, 0$, and is such that $f(0, z') - f(0, 0)$ does not vanish for all values of z' in that domain, we have*

$$f(z, z') = f(0, 0) + K h(z, z') e^{S(z,z')},$$

where

$$h(z, z') = z'^n + h_1 z'^{n-1} + \ldots + h_n,$$

the quantities $h_1, \ldots, h_n$ being functions of z, each of which is regular in the immediate vicinity of $z = 0$ and vanishes when $z = 0$; where $K z'^n$ is the lowest *power in the expansion of $f(0, z') - f(0, 0)$ in positive powers of z'; and where $S(z, z')$ is a function of z and z', which is regular in the immediate vicinity of $0, 0$ and vanishes when $z = 0$ and $z' = 0$.*

The postulated circumstances are not the same in these two theorems. If it should be the case that $f(z, 0) - f(0, 0)$ does not vanish for all values of z within the range, and also the case that $f(0, z') - f(0, 0)$ does not vanish for all values of z' within the range, then both theorems hold. In that event, we have two different expressions for $f(z, z') - f(0, 0)$ which must be equivalent to one another. This equivalence will be illustrated by an example, that will be given after we have discussed the alternative to the initial hypothesis.

64. Secondly, suppose that the function $F(z, 0)$, where
$$F(z, z') = f(z, z') - f(0, 0),$$
vanishes identically for all values of z. Now $F(z, z')$ is a regular function of z and z', within the range considered; as before, it can be expressed, by summation of the uniformly converging series which represents it, in the form
$$F(z, z') = \phi_0(z) + z'\phi_1(z) + z'^2\phi_2(z) + \dots,$$
which itself is a converging series within the range. (As already stated, $\phi_0(z)$ is the $F_0(z)$ of the preceding investigation). If then $F(z, 0)$ vanishes identically for all values of z, then $\phi_0(z)$ vanishes identically. It may happen that other coefficients $\phi_1(z), \phi_2(z), \dots$, vanish identically; let $\phi_t(z)$ be the first that does not thus vanish, t being a finite integer because $F(z, z')$ is presumably not a constant zero. Consequently
$$F(z, z') = z'^t \{\phi_t(z) + z'\phi_{t+1}(z) + \dots\},$$
and the series
$$\phi_t(z) + z'\phi_{t+1}(z) + \dots$$
is a regular function of z and z'; that is, in the suggested circumstance when the function $F(z, 0)$ vanishes identically for all values of z, our function $F(z, z')$ has some power of z' as a factor. Let this factor be z'^t; then t is a positive integer greater than zero, and it is assumed to be the largest positive integer which allows $F(z, z')z'^{-t}$ to be a regular function of z and z' in the vicinity of the place $0, 0$.

The first of the two preceding theorems does not hold as an expression for $f(z, z')$. But if the function $F(0, z')$ does not vanish identically for all values of z', the second of the preceding theorems does hold as an expression for $f(z, z')$. There are, however, limitations upon the forms of the quantities $h_n, h_{n-1}, \dots$; in particular,
$$h_n = 0, \quad h_{n-1} = 0, \quad \dots, \quad h_{n-t+1} = 0.$$
But the momentarily important result is that
$$f(z, z') - f(0, 0) = z'^t G(z, z'),$$
where $G(z, z')$ is regular in the vicinity of $0, 0$, and $G(z, 0)$ does not vanish identically for all values of z.

Next, suppose that the function $F(0, z')$ where (as before)
$$F(z, z') = f(z, z') - f(0, 0),$$
vanishes identically for all values of z'. Then an argument precisely similar to the preceding argument shews that the function $F(z, z')$ has some power of z as a factor. Let this factor be z^s; then s is a positive integer greater than zero, and it is assumed to be the largest positive integer which allows $F(z, z') z^{-s}$ to be a regular function of z and z' in the vicinity of 0, 0.

The second of the two preceding theorems does not now hold as an expression for $f(z, z')$. But if the function $F(z, 0)$ does not vanish identically for all values of z, the first of the preceding theorems does hold as an expression for $f(z, z')$. As before, there are limitations upon the forms of the quantities $g_m, g_{m-1}, \ldots$; in particular,
$$g_m = 0, \quad g_{m-1} = 0, \ldots, \quad g_{m-s+1} = 0.$$
But the momentarily important result is that
$$f(z, z') - f(0, 0) = z^s H(z, z'),$$
where $H(z, z')$ is regular in the vicinity of 0, 0, and $H(0, z')$ does not vanish identically for all values of z'.

Next, again taking
$$F(z, z') = f(z, z') - f(0, 0),$$
suppose that the function $F(z, 0)$ vanishes identically for all values of z and that the function $F(0, z')$ vanishes identically for all values of z'. As in the preceding cases, $F(z, z')$ has a factor which is now of the form $z^s z'^t$, where s and t are positive integers each greater than zero; and it is assumed that each of them, independently of one another, is the largest positive integer which allows $F(z, z') z^{-s} z'^{-t}$ to be a regular function of z and z' in the vicinity of 0, 0.

Neither of the two theorems already proved now holds as an expression for $f(z, z')$. The momentarily important result is that
$$f(z, z') - f(0, 0) = z^s z'^t I(z, z'),$$
where $I(z, z')$ is regular in the vicinity of 0, 0, while $I(z, 0)$ does not vanish identically for all values of z and $I(0, z')$ does not vanish identically for all values of z'.

Thus in each of the cases contemplated, we have
$$f(z, z') - f(0, 0) = z^s z'^t U(z, z'),$$
where s and t are positive integers that are not simultaneous zeros, and $U(z, z')$ is regular in the vicinity of 0, 0, while neither $U(z, 0)$ nor $U(0, z')$ vanishes identically for all values of z or of z' respectively. The alternatives are as follows.

(α) When $U(0, 0)$ is not zero, then, within the sufficiently small domain round 0, 0, we have
$$U(z, z') = U(0, 0) e^{T(z,z')},$$
where $T(z, z')$ is a regular function of z and z', vanishing at 0, 0.

Then we have
$$f(z, z') = f(0, 0) + Cz^s z'^t e^{T(z,z')},$$
where the constant C is the non-zero value of $U(0, 0)$.

(β) When $U(0, 0)$ is zero, the conditions attaching to $U(z, z')$ require that $U(z, 0)$ does not vanish identically for all values of z and that $U(0, z')$ does not vanish identically for all values of z'.

As $U(z, 0)$ does not vanish identically for all values of z and as $U(z, z')$ is a regular function, the first of our two earlier theorems applies to $U(z, z')$; we have an expression of the form
$$U(z, z') = Ag(z, z') e^{R(z,z')},$$
where A is a constant; $g(z, z')$ is a polynomial in z having, as its coefficients, regular functions of z' which vanish with z'; and where $R(z, z')$ is a regular function of z and z' which vanishes when $z = 0$ and $z' = 0$. Then
$$f(z, z') = f(0, 0) + Az^s z'^t g(z, z') e^{R(z,z')}.$$

Also $U(0, z')$ does not vanish identically for all values of z', and $U(z, z')$ is a regular function; hence the second of our two earlier theorems applies to $U(z, z')$. We have an expression of the form
$$U(z, z') = Bh(z, z') e^{S(z,z')},$$
where B is a constant; $h(z, z')$ is a polynomial in z' having, as its coefficients, regular functions of z which vanish with z; and where $S(z, z')$ is a regular function of z and z' which vanishes when $z = 0$ and $z' = 0$. Then
$$f(z, z') = f(0, 0) + Bz^s z'^t h(z, z') e^{S(z,z')}.$$

Summarising these results, we have the theorem:—

III. *When a function $f(z, z')$ is regular in some domain of 0, 0, and is such that either* (i) *$f(z, 0) - f(0, 0)$ vanishes identically for all values of z while $f(0, z') - f(0, 0)$ does not vanish identically for all values of z', or* (ii) *$f(0, z') - f(0, 0)$ vanishes identically for all values of z' while $f(z, 0) - f(0, 0)$ does not vanish identically for all values of z, or* (iii) *$f(z, 0) - f(0, 0)$ vanishes identically for all values of z and $f(0, z') - f(0, 0)$ vanishes identically for all values of z', then expressions for $f(z, z')$ in the immediate vicinity of the place 0, 0 are*
$$f(z, z') = f(0, 0) + Az^s z'^t g(z, z') e^{R(z,z')},$$
$$f(z, z') = f(0, 0) + Bz^s z'^t h(z, z') e^{S(z,z')},$$

where s and t are positive integers such that $s = 0$, $t > 0$ for the first hypothesis; $s > 0$, $t = 0$ for the second hypothesis; and $s > 0$, $t > 0$ for the third hypothesis. The quantities A and B are constants; the functions $R(z, z')$ and $S(z, z')$ are functions of z and z', each of which is regular in the immediate vicinity of $0, 0$ and vanishes when $z = 0$ and $z' = 0$; the function $g(z, z')$ is a polynomial in z of the form

$$z^m + g_1 z^{m-1} + \ldots + g_m,$$

where the coefficients $g_1, \ldots, g_m$ are functions of z' which are regular in the immediate vicinity of $z' = 0$ and vanish with z'; and the function $h(z, z')$ is a polynomial in z' of the form

$$z'^n + h_1 z'^{n-1} + \ldots + h_n,$$

where the coefficients $h_1, \ldots, h_n$ are functions of z which are regular in the immediate vicinity of z and vanish with z. There is a limiting case when both m and n are zero; the expression for $f(z, z')$ in the immediate vicinity of $0, 0$ is

$$f(z, z') = f(0, 0) + C z^s z'^t e^{T(z, z')},$$

where C is a constant, while $T(z, z')$ is a function of z and z' which is regular in the immediate vicinity of $0, 0$ and vanishes when $z = 0$ and $z' = 0$*.

Note. We saw before that, in certain circumstances, both Theorem I and Theorem II are valid, thus providing for the regular function $f(z, z')$ two expressions, which are formally distinct from one another, and must be equivalent to one another.

In Theorem III it follows that, in certain circumstances, the regular function $f(z, z')$ can have two expressions, which are formally distinct from one another and must be equivalent to one another.

In the former case, the two expressions for $f(z, z') - f(0, 0)$ are

$$Cg(z, z') e^{R(z, z')}, \quad Kh(z, z') e^{S(z, z')},$$

where $g(z, z')$ is polynomial in z with coefficients that are regular functions of z' vanishing with z', while $h(z, z')$ is polynomial in z' with coefficients that are regular functions of z vanishing with z. Thus

$$\frac{g(z, z')}{h(z, z')} = \frac{K}{C} e^{S(z, z') - R(z, z')} = L e^{V(z, z')},$$

where L is a constant and $V(z, z')$ is a regular function of z and z' which vanishes when $z = 0$ and $z' = 0$; hence

$$g(z, z') = L e^{V(z, z')} h(z, z'),$$

$$h(z, z') = \frac{1}{L} e^{-V(z, z')} g(z, z').$$

Similar relations hold in the latter case.

---

* This theorem is quite distinct from Weierstrass's second preliminary theorem (p. 141 of his memoir already quoted) for the case $n = 2$; the latter will come hereafter (§ 65).

It follows that, for a regular function $f(z, z')$, when it is not expressed as a power-series valid over a domain round 0, 0, but is expressed for consideration in the immediate vicinity of 0, 0, we usually can obtain two different expressions according as z or z' is taken as the variable for simplifying the representation. Each of the expressions is unique in its form; the two expressions are equivalent to one another.

Ex. Consider an ordinary place of a regular function $f(z, z')$, and let it be 0, 0; and take the general power-series for f, in that domain, in the form

$$f(z, z') - f(0, 0)$$
$$= (a_{10}z + a_{01}z') + (a_{20}z^2 + a_{11}zz' + a_{02}z'^2)$$
$$+ (a_{30}z^3 + a_{21}z^2z' + a_{12}zz'^2 + a_{03}z'^3) + \dots.$$

First, assume that neither a_{10} nor a_{01} vanishes. It is not difficult to establish the following results*:—

$$f(z, z') - f(0, 0) = (a_{10}z + b_{01}z' + b_{02}z'^2 + b_{03}z'^3 + \dots) e^{k_{10}z + k_{01}z' + k_{20}z^2 + k_{11}zz' + k_{02}z'^2 + \dots},$$

where

$$b_{01} = a_{01},$$

$$b_{02} = \frac{1}{a_{10}^2}(a_{02}a_{10}^2 - a_{11}a_{10}a_{01} + a_{20}a_{01}^2),$$

$$b_{03} = \frac{1}{a_{10}^3}(a_{03}a_{10}^3 - a_{12}a_{10}^2 a_{01} + a_{21}a_{10}a_{01}^2 - a_{30}a_{01}^3)$$
$$- \frac{1}{a_{10}^4}(a_{02}a_{10}^2 - a_{11}a_{10}a_{01} + a_{20}a_{01}^2)(2a_{20}a_{01} - a_{11}a_{10}),$$
$$\vdots$$

$$k_{10} = \frac{a_{20}}{a_{10}},$$

$$k_{01} = \frac{1}{a_{10}^2}(a_{11}a_{10} - a_{20}a_{01}),$$

$$k_{20} = \frac{a_{30}}{a_{10}} - \frac{1}{2}\frac{a_{20}^2}{a_{10}^2},$$

$$k_{11} = \frac{1}{a_{10}^2}(a_{21}a_{10} - a_{30}a_{01}) - \frac{a_{20}}{a_{10}^3}(a_{11}a_{10} - a_{20}a_{01}),$$

$$k_{02} = \frac{1}{a_{10}^3}(a_{12}a_{10}^2 - a_{21}a_{10}a_{01} + a_{30}a_{01}^2)$$
$$- \frac{a_{20}}{a_{10}^4}(a_{02}a_{10}^2 - a_{11}a_{10}a_{01} + a_{20}a_{01}^2) - \frac{1}{2}\frac{1}{a_{10}^4}(a_{11}a_{10} - a_{20}a_{01})^2,$$
$$\vdots$$

which is the expression for $f(z, z')$ under Theorem I.

Similarly, as the expression for $f(z, z')$ under Theorem II, we have

$$f(z, z') - f(0, 0) = (a_{01}z' + c_{10}z + c_{20}z^2 + c_{30}z^3 + \dots) e^{l_{10}z + l_{01}z' + l_{20}z^2 + l_{11}zz' + l_{02}z'^2 + \dots},$$

* The expressions suggest that the theory of invariantive forms can be applied to the expansions, in all the cases stated.

where
$$c_{10} = a_{10},$$
$$c_{20} = \frac{1}{a_{01}^2}(a_{02}a_{10}^2 - a_{11}a_{10}a_{01} + a_{20}a_{01}^2),$$
$$c_{30} = \frac{1}{a_{01}^3}(a_{30}a_{01}^3 - a_{21}a_{01}^2 a_{10} + a_{12}a_{01}a_{10}^2 - a_{03}a_{10}^3)$$
$$- \frac{1}{a_{01}^4}(a_{02}a_{10}^2 - a_{11}a_{10}a_{01} + a_{20}a_{01}^2)(2a_{02}a_{10} - a_{11}a_{01})$$
$$\vdots$$
$$l_{10} = \frac{1}{a_{01}^2}(a_{11}a_{01} - a_{02}a_{10}),$$
$$l_{01} = \frac{a_{02}}{a_{01}},$$
$$\vdots$$
$$l_{20} = \frac{1}{a_{01}^3}(a_{21}a_{01}^2 - a_{12}a_{01}a_{10} + a_{03}a_{10}^2)$$
$$- \frac{a_{02}}{a_{01}^4}(a_{02}a_{10}^2 - a_{11}a_{10}a_{01} + a_{20}a_{01}^2) - \frac{1}{2}\frac{1}{a_{01}^4}(a_{11}a_{01} - a_{02}a_{10})^2,$$
$$l_{11} = \frac{1}{a_{01}^2}(a_{12}a_{01} - a_{03}a_{10}) - \frac{a_{02}}{a_{01}^3}(a_{11}a_{01} - a_{02}a_{10}),$$
$$l_{02} = \frac{a_{03}}{a_{01}} - \frac{1}{2}\frac{a_{02}^2}{a_{01}^2},$$
$$\vdots$$

And it is easy to verify that
$$\frac{a_{10}z + a_{01}z' + b_{02}z'^2 + b_{03}z'^3 + \ldots}{a_{10}z + a_{01}z' + c_{20}z^2 + c_{30}z^3 + \ldots} = e^{(l_{10} - k_{10})z + (l_{01} - k_{01})z' + \ldots}.$$

Secondly, when a_{01} vanishes but not a_{10}, the first expression is effective for
$$f(z, z') - f(0, 0),$$
but the second is ineffective. When a_{10} vanishes but not a_{01}, the second expression is effective but the first is ineffective.

Thirdly, when a_{10} and a_{01} both vanish, neither of the expressions is effective. Then
$$f(z, z') - f(0, 0) = a_{20}z^2 + a_{11}zz' + a_{02}z'^2 + a_{30}z^3 + a_{21}z^2z' + a_{12}zz'^2 + a_{03}z'^3 + \ldots;$$
and we find
$$f(z, z') - f(0, 0)$$
$$= \{a_{20}z^2 + z(a_{11}z' + b_{12}z'^2 + \ldots) + z'^2(a_{02} + b_{03}z' + \ldots)\} e^{k_{10}z + k_{01}z' + \ldots},$$
where
$$b_{12} = \frac{1}{a_{20}^2}\{a_{12}a_{20}^2 - a_{21}a_{11}a_{20} + a_{30}(a_{11}^2 - a_{02}a_{20})\},$$
$$b_{03} = \frac{1}{a_{20}^2}\{a_{03}a_{20}^2 - a_{21}a_{02}a_{20} + a_{30}a_{11}a_{02}\},$$
$$\vdots$$
$$k_{10} = \frac{a_{30}}{a_{20}},$$
$$k_{01} = \frac{1}{a_{20}^2}(a_{21}a_{20} - a_{30}a_{11}),$$
$$\vdots$$

We also find
$$f(z, z') - f(0, 0)$$
$$= \{a_{02}z'^2 + z'(a_{11}z + c_{21}z^2 + \ldots) + z^2(a_{20} + c_{30}z + \ldots)\} e^{l_{10}z + l_{01}z' + \ldots},$$
where
$$c_{21} = \frac{1}{a_{02}^2} \{a_{21}a_{02}^2 - a_{12}a_{11}a_{02} + a_{03}(a_{11}^2 - a_{02}a_{20})\},$$
$$c_{30} = \frac{1}{a_{02}^2} \{a_{30}a_{02}^2 - a_{12}a_{02}a_{20} + a_{03}a_{11}a_{20}\},$$
$$\vdots$$
$$l_{10} = \frac{1}{a_{02}^2}(a_{12}a_{02} - a_{03}a_{11}),$$
$$l_{01} = \frac{a_{03}}{a_{02}},$$
$$\vdots$$

The first expression is effective when a_{20} does not vanish; but it is ineffective when a_{20} does vanish. The second expression is effective when a_{02} does not vanish; but it is ineffective when a_{02} does vanish.

When both a_{20} and a_{02} vanish and when a_{11} then does not vanish, another expression must be obtained. In that case, we have
$$f(z, z') - f(0, 0) = a_{11}zz' + a_{30}z^3 + a_{21}z^2z' + a_{12}zz'^2 + a_{03}z'^3 + \ldots,$$
and then we find that
$$f(z, z') - f(0, 0)$$
$$= \{a_{30}z^3 + z^2(b_{21}z' + b_{22}z'^2 + \ldots) + z(b_{11}z' + b_{12}z'^2 + \ldots) + b_{03}z'^3 + b_{04}z'^4 + \ldots\} e^{k_{10}z + k_{01}z' + \ldots},$$
where
$$k_{10} = \frac{a_{40}}{a_{30}},$$
$$k_{01} = \frac{1}{a_{30}^3}(a_{31}a_{30}^2 - a_{21}a_{40}a_{30} - a_{11}a_{30}a_{50} + a_{11}a_{40}^2),$$
$$k_{20} = \frac{1}{a_{30}^2}(a_{30}a_{50} - \tfrac{1}{2}a_{40}^2),$$
$$k_{30} = \frac{1}{a_{30}^3}(a_{30}^2 a_{60} - a_{30}a_{40}a_{50} + \tfrac{1}{3}a_{40}^3),$$
$$k_{11} = k_{10}k_{01} + \frac{1}{a_{30}}\{a_{41} - a_{31}k_{10} - a_{40}k_{01} - a_{21}(k_{20} - \tfrac{1}{2}k_{10}^2) - a_{11}(k_{30} - k_{20}k_{10} + \tfrac{1}{6}k_{10}^3)\},$$
$$\vdots$$
$$b_{11} = a_{11},$$
$$b_{21} = a_{21} - a_{11}k_{10},$$
$$b_{12} = a_{12} - a_{11}k_{01},$$
$$b_{03} = a_{03},$$
$$b_{22} = a_{22} - a_{12}k_{10} - a_{21}k_{01} - a_{11}(k_{11} - k_{10}k_{01}),$$
$$\vdots$$

There is a corresponding expression for $f(z, z') - f(0, 0)$, in which z' is made the dominating variable; it has the form
$$f(z, z') - f(0, 0)$$
$$= \{a_{03}z'^3 + z'^2(c_{21}z + c_{22}z^2 + \ldots) + z'(c_{11}z + c_{12}z^2 + \ldots) + c_{30}z^3 + c_{40}z^4 + \ldots\} e^{l_{10}z + l_{01}z' + \ldots},$$

where

$$l_{10} = \frac{1}{a_{03}{}^3}(a_{13}a_{03}{}^2 - a_{12}a_{04}a_{03} - a_{11}a_{03}a_{05} + a_{11}a_{04}{}^2),$$

$$l_{01} = \frac{a_{04}}{a_{03}},$$

$$l_{02} = \frac{1}{a_{03}{}^2}(a_{03}a_{05} - \tfrac{1}{2}a_{04}{}^2),$$

$$l_{03} = \frac{1}{a_{03}{}^3}(a_{03}{}^2 a_{06} - a_{03}a_{04}a_{05} + \tfrac{1}{3}a_{04}{}^3),$$

$$l_{11} = l_{10}l_{01} + \frac{1}{a_{03}}\{a_{14} - a_{13}l_{01} - a_{04}l_{10} - a_{12}(l_{02} - \tfrac{1}{2}l_{01}{}^2) - a_{11}(l_{03} - l_{02}l_{01} + \tfrac{1}{6}l_{01}{}^3)\},$$

$$\vdots$$

$$c_{11} = a_{11},$$
$$c_{30} = a_{30},$$
$$c_{21} = a_{21} - a_{11}l_{10},$$
$$c_{12} = a_{12} - a_{11}l_{01},$$
$$c_{22} = a_{22} - a_{21}l_{01} - a_{12}l_{01} - a_{11}(l_{11} - l_{10}l_{01}),$$
$$\vdots$$

The first of these is effective when a_{30} does not vanish. The second is effective when a_{03} does not vanish.

The general form of expression for $f(z, z') - f(0, 0)$, when both $f(0, z') - f(0, 0)$ and $f(z, 0) - f(0, 0)$ vanish identically, has been indicated. It then is possible to isolate a factor $z^s z'^t$, where

$$f(z, z') - f(0, 0) = z^s z'^t \bar{f}(z, z'),$$

such that both $\bar{f}(z, 0)$ and $\bar{f}(0, z')$ do not vanish identically; and expressions, similar to those which precede, can be obtained for $\bar{f}(z, z')$.

65. When the function $F(z, 0)$, $=f(z, 0) - f(0, 0)$, vanishes for all values of z, another method of proceeding was given by Weierstrass[*]. It was devised for functions of n variables (when $n > 2$) and some method is needed for them other than the method for functions of two variables, because with n variables it is not generally possible to extract an aggregate factor such as $z^s z'^t$ from the function corresponding to $f(z, z') - f(0, 0)$. Applied to functions of two variables, the Weierstrass method is as follows.

In the double-series expansion of $f(z, z') - f(0, 0)$, valid in a domain round 0, 0, let the terms be gathered together into groups, each group containing all the terms of the same order in z and z' combined; and suppose that the group of lowest order is of order μ, so that we have

$$f(z, z') - f(0, 0) = (z, z')_\mu + (z, z')_{\mu+1} + \dots.$$

Change the variables from z and z' to u and u' by relations of the form

$$z = \alpha u + \beta u', \quad z' = \gamma u + \delta u',$$

where $\alpha, \beta, \gamma, \delta$ are constants such that $\alpha\delta - \beta\gamma$ is not zero, so that u and u' are new independent variables. Then $f(z, z') - f(0, 0)$ becomes a regular

---

[*] See p. 140 of his memoir already quoted.

function of u and u', say $G(u, u')$, the lowest terms in which are of order μ; and
$$G(u, 0) = (\alpha, \gamma)_\mu u^\mu + (\alpha, \gamma)_{\mu+1} u^{\mu+1} + \ldots,$$
so that, choosing $(\alpha, \gamma)_\mu$ to be different from zero, $G(u, 0)$ does not vanish for all values of u.

The first of the preceding theorems can therefore be applied to $G(u, u')$; the result is of the form
$$G(u, u') = (\alpha, \gamma)_\mu \{u^\mu + u^{\mu-1} g_1(u') + \ldots + g_\mu(u')\} e^{I(u, u')},$$
where $(\alpha, \gamma)_\mu$ is the non-vanishing coefficient, $g_1, \ldots, g_\mu$ are regular functions of u' which vanish with u', and $I(u, u')$ is a regular function of u and u' which vanishes when $u = 0$ and $u' = 0$; moreover, as the lowest terms in $G(u, u')$ are of dimensions μ, the regular series for $g_r(u')$ begins with a term in u'^r, for $r = 1, \ldots, \mu$.

When retransformation to the original variables z and z' is effected, we have
$$f(z, z') - f(0, 0)$$
$$= G(u, u')$$
$$= [\{z, z'\}_\mu + \{z, z'\}_{\mu+1} + \ldots] e^{J(z, z')},$$
where $J(z, z')$ is a regular function of z and z' which vanishes when $z = 0$ and $z' = 0$; and by expanding $e^{J(z, z')}$ so as to have the complete series for the new expression, we have
$$\{z, z'\}_\mu = (z, z')_\mu,$$
so that, as is to be expected, the first term in $g(z, z')$, where
$$f(z, z') - f(0, 0) = g(z, z') e^{J(z, z')},$$
is the aggregate $(z, z')_\mu$ in the original double series for $f(z, z') - f(0, 0)$.

Note 1. It may be pointed out that the preceding method is effective, even if $f(z, 0) - f(0, 0)$ does not vanish. Thus for a function it might happen that, in the regular function $f(z, 0) - f(0, 0)$ when it does not vanish for all values of z identically, the term of lowest order is Az^n, while, in $f(z, z') - f(0, 0)$, the terms of lowest order are of dimensions less than n. (As a matter of fact, each of these terms of lowest order will then contain some positive power of z' as a factor). The application of the method will then lead to an expression of the preceding form.

Note 2. In the method, the limitations upon $\alpha, \beta, \gamma, \delta$ are merely exclusive; they are
$$\alpha\delta - \beta\gamma \neq 0, \quad (\alpha, \gamma)_\mu \neq 0.$$
Thus a certain amount of arbitrary element will appear in the result; by varying these constants $\alpha, \beta, \gamma, \delta$, different expressions will be obtained which are equivalent to one another.

Ex. 1. Consider the function*
$$f = zz' + \tfrac{1}{6}(z^3 + z'^3) + \tfrac{1}{24}(z^4 + z'^4) + \dots,$$
the unexpressed terms being of order higher than 4. We take
$$z = u, \quad z' = u + u',$$
so that
$$f = u^2 + uu' + \tfrac{1}{6}(2u^3 + 3u^2 u' + 3uu'^2 + u'^3)$$
$$+ \tfrac{1}{24}(2u^4 + 4u^3 u' + 6u^2 u'^2 + 4uu'^3 + u'^4) + \dots.$$
This must be equal to
$$(u^2 + g_1 u + g_2) e^{a_1 u + b_1 u' + a_2 u^2 + b_2 uu' + c_2 u'^2 + \dots},$$
where
$$g_1 = k_1 u' + k_2 u'^2 + k_3 u'^3 + \dots,$$
$$g_2 = l_2 u'^2 + l_3 u'^3 + l_4 u'^4 + \dots.$$
Expanding, and equating coefficients, we find
$$k_1 = 1, \quad k_2 = \tfrac{1}{3}, \quad k_3 = -\tfrac{1}{36}, \quad \dots;$$
$$l_2 = 0, \quad l_3 = \tfrac{1}{6}, \quad l_4 = \tfrac{1}{72}, \quad \dots;$$
$$a_1 = \tfrac{1}{3}, \quad b_1 = \tfrac{1}{6};$$
$$a_2 = \tfrac{1}{18}, \quad b_2 = 0, \quad c_2 = \tfrac{5}{72};$$
and thus the expression for our function becomes $g(u, u') e^{I(u, u')}$, where
$$g(u, u') = u^2 + u(u' + \tfrac{1}{3} u'^2 - \tfrac{1}{36} u'^3 + \dots) + \tfrac{1}{6} u'^3 + \tfrac{1}{72} u'^4 + \dots,$$
and
$$I(u, u') = \tfrac{1}{3} u + \tfrac{1}{6} u' + \tfrac{1}{72}(4u^2 + 5u'^2) + \dots.$$
When we retransform to the variables z and z' by the relations
$$u = z, \quad u' = z' - z,$$
the terms of the lowest order in $g(u, u')$ become zz', as is to be expected.

But the completely retransformed new expression for f is less effective than the original expression; and the discussion of f in the vicinity of 0, 0 is more effectively made in connection with the expression in terms of z and z'.

Ex. 2. Obtain an expression for the function in the preceding example, when the transformed variables are given by the relations
$$z = u + au', \quad z' = u + \beta u',$$
where the constants a and β are unequal; and prove that, when retransformation takes place, the terms of the first order in $I(u, u')$ become $z + z'$.

This last method of Weierstrass has been outlined, because of its importance when the number of variables is greater than two. When the number of variables is equal to two, the general case for which it was devised falls more simply under the comprehensive results of Theorem III.

We may therefore summarise the results of the whole investigation briefly as follows. Whatever be the detailed form of any function $f(z, z')$, regular in a domain round 0, 0, its general characteristic expression in the immediate vicinity of 0, 0 is
$$f(z, z') - f(0, 0) = z^s z'^t P(z, z') e^{I(z, z')},$$

---

* The expansions under Theorem I and Theorem II arise as special cases of the result given above, p. 104.

where $I(z, z')$ is a function of z and z' which is regular in the immediate vicinity of $0, 0$ and vanishes when $z = 0$ and $z' = 0$. The quantities s and t are positive integers, which may be zero separately or together. When either of these integers is zero, or when both of them are zero, $P(0, 0)$ can be different from zero for special functions; for all other functions, $P(z, z')$ is polynomial in one of its variables, the coefficients of the powers of which are regular functions of the other variable within a limited domain, each such coefficient vanishing when that other variable vanishes.

Level values of a regular function.

66. One immediate deduction of substantial importance can be made from the expression for $f(z, z')$ which has just been obtained, viz.
$$F(z, z') = f(z, z') - f(0, 0) = z^s z'^t A(z, z') e^{B(z, z')},$$
as to the places where $f(z, z')$ acquires the same value as at $0, 0$. When $f(0, 0)$ vanishes, we shall call the place a *zero* for $f(z, z')$. When $f(0, 0)$ does not vanish, we shall call the value $f(0, 0)$ a *level* value for all the places z, z' such that $f(z, z') = f(0, 0)$; all these places are therefore zeros of $F(z, z')$.

As $B(z, z')$ is a regular function of z, z' within a limited domain of $0, 0$, the quantity $e^{B(z, z')}$ cannot vanish at any place in the domain. Consequently the zero-places of $F(z, z')$ within the domain are given by three possible sets.

When the positive integer s does not vanish, zero-places of $F(z, z')$ arise when
$$z = 0, \quad z' = \text{any value within the domain}.$$

When the positive integer t does not vanish, zero-places of $F(z, z')$ arise when
$$z = \text{any value within the domain}, \quad z' = 0.$$

When $A(z, z')$ is not merely the constant $A(0, 0)$, all the places in the domain such that
$$A(z, z') = 0$$
are zero-places for $F(z, z')$.

As regards the first set, we obtain an unlimited number of zero-places of $F(z, z')$ within the domain of $0, 0$; they constitute a continuous two-dimensional aggregate, the continuity being associated with the plane of z' alone.

As regards the second set, we obtain also an unlimited number of zero-places of $F(z, z')$ within the domain of $0, 0$; they too constitute a continuous two-dimensional aggregate, the continuity now being associated with the plane of z alone.

For the third set, there is no additional zero-place for $F(z, z')$, if $A(0, 0)$ is a non-vanishing constant; in that event, either s, or t, or both s and t, must be different from zero. When $A(0, 0)$ does vanish, the function

$A(z, z')$ either is polynomial in z and (usually) transcendental in z', or is polynomial in z' and (usually) transcendental in z; and these alternatives are not mutually exclusive. In the former case, for any assumed value of z' within the domain, there is a limited number (equal to the polynomial degree of A) of values of z, which vanish with z' and usually are transcendental functions of z'; hence, taking a succession of continuous values of z' in the domain, we have, with each value of z', a limited number of associated values of z. All these places taken together constitute a continuous two-dimensional aggregate; the continuity now is associated with both planes, each value of z' having a definite value of z or a limited number of definite values of z associated with it, all within the assigned domain of 0, 0. Similarly, in the latter case, as regards $A(z, z')$; the same result holds when the appropriate interchange of z and z' is made in the statement; and the two-dimensional aggregate is unaltered.

Ex. 1. Among the simplest examples that occur, are those when $A(z, z')$ can be expressed in a form
$$az + P(z'),$$
where a is a constant and $P(z')$ is a regular function of z' given by
$$P(z') = bz' + cz'^2 + \ldots,$$
b not being zero. Then $A(z, z')$, with an appropriate change in $B(z, z')$ which is the function in the exponential, can also be expressed in the form
$$bz' + R(z),$$
where the regular function $R(z)$ is given by
$$R(z) = az + Cz^2 + \ldots,$$
with suitable values of the constants C, ... The zero-values are given by the two-dimensional aggregate
$$-az = P(z'), \quad -bz' = R(z).$$

The result is the generalisation of the known property whereby, in the vicinity of a real non-singular point ξ, η on an analytical curve $f(x, y) = 0$, we have
$$x - \xi = P(y - \eta), \quad y - \eta = R(x - \xi);$$
the linear term in $P(y - \eta)$ combined with $x - \xi$, and the linear term in $R(x - \xi)$ combined with $y - \eta$, give the tangent to the curve at the real ordinary point ξ, η on the curve.

Ex. 2. In both cases that arise out of the alternative forms of A, the actual determination of the set of values of z in terms of z' (or of the set of values of z' in terms of z) can be made as in Puiseux's theory of the algebraical equation $f(w, z) = 0$, the governing terms being selected by the use of Newton's parallelogram. For example, in the case of the zeros of the function
$$f(z, z') - f(0, 0) = a_{11}zz' + a_{30}z^3 + a_{21}z^2z' + a_{12}zz'^2 + a_{03}z'^3 + \ldots$$
within a small domain round 0, 0, we find three values for z in terms of z', viz.

$$\left.\begin{aligned} z &= \left(-\frac{a_{11}}{a_{30}}\right)^{\frac{1}{2}} z'^{\frac{1}{2}} + \frac{1}{2a_{30}^2}(a_{40}a_{11} - a_{21}a_{30})\, z' + \ldots \\ z &= -\left(-\frac{a_{11}}{a_{30}}\right)^{\frac{1}{2}} z'^{\frac{1}{2}} + \frac{1}{2a_{30}^2}(a_{40}a_{11} - a_{21}a_{30})\, z' + \ldots \\ z &= -\frac{a_{03}}{a_{11}} z'^2 + \frac{1}{a_{11}^2}(a_{12}a_{03} - a_{11}a_{04})\, z'^3 + \ldots \end{aligned}\right\};$$

and there are three corresponding values for z' in terms of z, viz.

$$z' = \left(-\frac{a_{11}}{a_{03}}\right)^{\frac{1}{2}} z^{\frac{1}{2}} + \frac{1}{2a_{03}^2}(a_{04}a_{11} - a_{12}a_{03})z + \ldots$$

$$z' = -\left(-\frac{a_{11}}{a_{03}}\right)^{\frac{1}{2}} z^{\frac{1}{2}} + \frac{1}{2a_{03}^2}(a_{04}a_{11} - a_{12}a_{03})z + \ldots$$

$$z' = -\frac{a_{30}}{a_{11}}z^2 + \frac{1}{a_{11}^2}(a_{21}a_{03} - a_{11}a_{40})z^3 + \ldots$$

If a_{30} is zero, the first two series in the earlier pair are not valid; if a_{03} is zero, the first two series in the later pair are not valid. If all the coefficients a_{n0} vanish so that $f(z, 0) - f(0, 0)$ vanishes for all values of z, only the third expression in the earlier pair survives. If the first coefficient a_{n0}, which does not vanish, is a_{r0}, there is a set of $r-1$ expansions in a cycle corresponding to the above two which exist when a_{30} does not vanish. And so on, for the respective cases.

Ex. 3. Quite generally, it may be stated that the detailed determination of the behaviour of $F(z, z')$ in the vicinity of 0, 0, so as to obtain the nature of its zeros as well as the actual positions of its zero-places, has a close resemblance to the method of proceeding in the consideration of an equation $f(w, z) = 0$, which is algebraical both in w and in z, and in the determination of the associated Riemann surface*.

67. All the results relating to the zeros of $F(z, z')$ can apply, in descriptive range, to a determinate finite level value (say α) of a uniform function $f(z, z')$ in a domain where it is regular. Let a, a' be a place where f acquires the value α; so that
$$f(a, a') = \alpha.$$
For places $a + Z$, $a' + Z'$ near a, a' within the domain of a, a', we have
$$f(z, z') = f(a + Z, a' + Z')$$
$$= f(a, a') + \Sigma\Sigma c_{mn} Z^m Z'^n,$$
that is,
$$f(z, z') - \alpha = \Sigma\Sigma c_{mn} Z^m Z'^n.$$
Thus the places within the domain of a, a' where f acquires the level value α are given by the zeros of the double series which itself vanishes when $Z = 0$, $Z' = 0$.

Hence the level places which give a determinate finite value α to a function $f(z, z')$ form a continuous aggregate within the domain of any one such level place.

Manifestly, as we are dealing with properties of a uniform function of f, which is regular within the domain of an ordinary place, the values of f must be finite (for poles do not occur within such a domain) and they must be determinate (for singularities, whether unessential or essential, do not occur within such a domain). The behaviour of a function in the vicinity of a pole and in the vicinity of an unessential singularity will be discussed separately.

---

* For this subject, see Chapter VIII of my *Theory of Functions* for the discussion of the algebraical equation and Chapter XV for the construction of the associated Riemann surface. Reference should also be made to the early chapters of Baker's *Abelian Functions*.

68. Not because of any immediate importance for a single function of two variables but mainly because of the need of estimating the multiplicity of a common zero-place or a common level-place of two functions of two variables, it is worth while assigning integers that shall represent the *orders*, in z and z' respectively, of the zero of $f(z, z') - f(a, a')$ at the place (a, a'). By the preceding proposition, for a place $z = a + u$, $z' = a' + u'$ in the immediate vicinity of a, a', we have

$$f(z, z') - f(a, a') = u^s u'^t G(u, u'),$$

where G is regular in the domain, and the integers s and t can be chosen so that $G(u, 0)$ does not vanish for all values of u and $G(0, u')$ does not vanish for all values of u'. The positive integers s and t can be zero, either separately or together.

As $G(u, 0)$ does not vanish for all values of u, there exists a series

$$Q(u, u') = u^m + u^{m-1} q_1(u') + \ldots + q_m(u'),$$

where $q_1(u'), \ldots, q_m(u')$ are regular functions of u' vanishing with u', such that

$$G(u, u') = KQ(u, u') e^{\overline{Q}(u, u')},$$

where K is a constant and $\overline{Q}(u, u')$ is a regular function of u and u' vanishing with u and u'. Thus for any small value of u', there are m small values of u, making $G(u, u')$ zero.

As $G(0, u')$ does not vanish for all values of u', there exists a series

$$R(u, u') = u'^n + u'^{n-1} r_1(u) + \ldots + r_n(u),$$

where $r_1(u), \ldots, r_n(u)$ are regular functions of u vanishing with u, such that

$$G(u, u') = LR(u, u') e^{\overline{R}(u, u')},$$

where L is a constant and $\overline{R}(u, u')$ is a regular function of u and u' vanishing with u and u'. Thus for any small value of u, there are n small values of u', making $G(u, u')$ zero.

In both of these cases, $G(u, u')$ vanishes when $u = 0$, $u' = 0$; and then neither of the integers m and n is zero. There remains a third case, when $G(0, 0)$ is not zero; then

$$G(u, u') = G(0, 0) e^{I(u, u')},$$

where $I(u, u')$ is a regular function of u and u' vanishing when $u = 0$ and $u' = 0$. Thus no small values of u and u' make $G(u, u')$ vanish; and then both of the integers m and n are zero.

With these explanations, we define the *orders of the zero* of the function

$$f(z, z') - f(a, a')$$

at a, a' as $s + m$ for the variable z and as $t + n$ for the variable z'. But it must be pointed out that the zero of the function at a, a' is not an isolated zero, for it is only a place in a continuous aggregate of zeros; still, a settlement of an order in each variable at a place a, a' is convenient as a preliminary to the settlement of the multiple order (Chap. VII) of such a place when it is a simultaneous and isolated zero of two functions considered together.

Relative divisibility of two regular functions near a common zero.

69. Before proceeding to obtain the expression of any uniform analytic function in the vicinity of a singularity, it is important to consider the behaviour of two uniform functions $f(z, z')$ and $g(z, z')$ simultaneously, both being regular within a common domain which will be taken round 0, 0.

First, suppose that $g(0, 0)$ is not zero; then we have seen that a uniform function $\bar{S}(z, z')$ exists, which vanishes when $z = 0$ and $z' = 0$ and is regular in a domain in the immediate vicinity of 0, 0, and is such that

$$g(z, z') = g(0, 0) e^{\bar{S}(z, z')}$$

for that domain. Also, we know that we can take

$$f(z, z') = f(0, 0) + A\phi(z, z') z^s z'^t e^{R(z, z')},$$

where s and t are non-negative integers, $\phi(z, z')$ is polynomial in z and regular in z', and $R(z, z')$ is a uniform function of z and z' which vanishes when $z = 0$ and $z' = 0$ and is regular in a domain in the immediate vicinity of 0, 0. Consequently

$$\frac{f(z, z')}{g(z, z')} = \frac{1}{g(0, 0)} \{f(0, 0) + A\phi(z, z') z^s z'^t e^{R(z, z')}\} e^{-\bar{S}(z, z')}$$

$$= \frac{f(0, 0)}{g(0, 0)} e^{-\bar{S}(z, z')} + \frac{A}{g(0, 0)} \phi(z, z') z^s z'^t e^{R(z, z') - \bar{S}(z, z')}.$$

The right-hand side, whether $f(0, 0)$ vanishes or not, can be expressed as a regular double series $U(z, z')$; that is,

$$\frac{f(z, z')}{g(z, z')} = U(z, z').$$

When a uniform function $f(z, z')$ is expressed as a double series $P(z, z')$, and another uniform function $g(z, z')$ is expressed also as a double series $Q(z, z')$, and when a third uniform function $U(z, z')$ exists such that

$$\frac{P(z, z')}{Q(z, z')} = U(z, z'),$$

all the functions being regular in a domain round 0, 0, we say, following Weierstrass*, that the series $P(z, z')$ is *divisible* by the series $Q(z, z')$.

---

* *Ges. Werke*, t. ii, p. 142.

It therefore follows that, when $g(0, 0)$ is not zero, the regular function $f(z, z')$ is divisible by the regular function $g(z, z')$, the regularity of both functions extending over a domain round $0, 0$; and the result is true whether $f(0, 0)$ is zero or is not zero.

70. Next, suppose that $g(0, 0)$ is zero; then we know that we can take
$$g(z, z') = B z^\sigma z'^\tau e^{T(z, z')} \chi(z, z'),$$
where B is a constant; σ and τ are non-negative integers; $T(z, z')$ is a function of z and z', regular in the immediate vicinity of $0, 0$ and vanishing when $z = 0$ and $z' = 0$; and $\chi(z, z')$ is a function which is a polynomial in z having functions of z' for its coefficients, these coefficients being regular in the immediate vicinity of $z' = 0$ and vanishing when $z' = 0$. The form of $f(z, z')$ is the same as before. It at once follows that, when $f(0, 0)$ is not zero, we cannot express
$$\frac{f(z, z')}{g(z, z')}$$
in the form of a regular function; in that case, the function $f(z, z')$ is not divisible by $g(z, z')$.

But when $f(0, 0)$ is zero, as also is $g(0, 0)$ under the present hypothesis, then we have
$$\frac{f(z, z')}{g(z, z')} = \frac{A z^s z'^t \phi(z, z') e^{R(z, z')}}{B z^\sigma z'^\tau \chi(z, z') e^{T(z, z')}}$$
$$= \frac{A}{B} \frac{z^s z'^t \phi(z, z')}{z^\sigma z'^\tau \chi(z, z')} e^{R(z, z') - T(z, z')}.$$

Now $R(z, z') - T(z, z')$ is regular in the immediate vicinity of $0, 0$ and vanishes when $z = 0$ and $z' = 0$; hence the exponential factor in the last expression admits the divisibility of $f(z, z')$ by $g(z, z')$. Also this divisibility is admitted, so far as powers of z are concerned, if $s \geqslant \sigma$ and, so far as powers of z' are concerned, if $t \geqslant \tau$. There remains therefore the divisibility of $\phi(z, z')$ by $\chi(z, z')$, where (for the present purpose) we shall assume that both $\phi(z, z')$ and $\chi(z, z')$ are polynomials in z the coefficients in which are regular functions of z' in the immediate vicinity of $z' = 0$ and vanish when $z' = 0$. Manifestly the degree of $\phi(z, z')$ in z cannot be less than that of $\chi(z, z')$, if divisibility is to be possible; accordingly, we suppose that
$$\phi(z, z') = z^m + z^{m-1} g_1 + \ldots + g_m,$$
$$\chi(z, z') = z^n + z^{n-1} h_1 + \ldots + h_n,$$
where $m \geqslant n$, and all the coefficients $g_1, \ldots, g_m, h_1, \ldots, h_n$ are regular functions of z' in the immediate vicinity of $z' = 0$ and vanish when $z' = 0$.

When $\phi(z, z')$ is divisible by $\chi(z, z')$, the quotient is manifestly of the form
$$z^{m-n} + z^{m-n-1} k_1 + \ldots + k_{m-n},$$

F.

where the coefficients $k_1, \ldots, k_{m-n}$ are functions of z'. Also
$$g_1 = h_1 + k_1,$$
$$g_2 = h_2 + h_1 k_1 + k_2,$$
$$\ldots\ldots\ldots\ldots\ldots\ldots\ldots$$
$$g_r = h_r + h_{r-1} k_1 + h_{r-2} k_2 + \ldots,$$
$$\ldots\ldots\ldots\ldots\ldots\ldots\ldots$$
$$g_m = \qquad\qquad\qquad\qquad h_n k_{m-n}.$$

From the first, it follows that the function k_1 is regular and vanishes when $z' = 0$; from the second, that the function k_2 is regular and vanishes when $z' = 0$; and so on, in succession from the first $m - n$ of these relations. Also all the relations are to be satisfied, by appropriate values of $k_1, \ldots, k_{m-n}$, for all values of z' in the immediate vicinity of $z' = 0$. The conditions, necessary and sufficient to satisfy the last requirement, are that, when we form the n independent determinants each of $m - n$ rows and columns from the array

$$\begin{Vmatrix} g_1-h_1, & g_2-h_2, & g_3-h_3, & \ldots, & g_n-h_n, & g_{n+1}, & \ldots, & g_{m-1}, & g_m \\ 1, & h_1, & h_2, & \ldots, & 0, & 0, & \ldots, & 0, & 0 \\ 0, & 1, & h_1, & \ldots, & 0, & 0, & \ldots, & 0, & 0 \\ \ldots & \ldots & \ldots & \ldots & \ldots & \ldots & \ldots & \ldots & \ldots \\ 0, & 0, & 0, & \ldots, & \ldots\ldots, & \ldots, & h_n, & h_{n-1} \\ 0, & 0, & 0, & \ldots, & \ldots\ldots, & \ldots, & 0, & h_n \end{Vmatrix}$$

each of these n determinants must vanish identically for all such values of z'.

Thus there are n conditions. The form of the conditions should, however, be noted. As all the functions g and h are regular functions of z' in the immediate vicinity of $z' = 0$ and vanish when $z' = 0$, each of the n determinants is also a regular function of z' in the immediate vicinity of $z' = 0$ and vanishes when $z' = 0$. Each determinant is to vanish identically for all values of z' in the range round $z' = 0$; and therefore every coefficient, in the power-series which is the expression of the determinant, must vanish. Thus in practice, when the power-series are infinite, the number of relations among the constants would be infinite for each of the conditions; the arithmetic process could not be carried out in general*. But the n analytical conditions among the functions would still remain, in the form of determinants that are to vanish identically.

Thus, in particular, the conditions, that the function
$$z^3 + z^2 g_1 + z g_2 + g_3$$
should be divisible by the function
$$z^2 + z h_1 + h_2,$$
are that the two independent determinants from the array

$$\begin{Vmatrix} g_1-h_1, & g_2-h_2, & g_3 \\ 1, & h_1, & h_2 \end{Vmatrix}$$

---

* In particular cases, it might be feasible, e.g. when there are known scales of relation governing all the coefficients.

shall vanish identically. When the two conditions are satisfied, the quotient is
$$z + \frac{g_3}{h_2}.$$

The general argument shews that the function g_3/h_2 is to be regular and to vanish with z'; a limit upon the orders of the lowest powers of z' in h_2 and g_3 is thereby imposed.

Relative reducibility of functions.

71. Further, it is important to discover whether, even in the case when a function $\phi(z, z')$ is not actually divisible by a function $\chi(z, z')$, both being of the foregoing type, each of them is actually divisible by a function $\psi(z, z')$ also of the same type: that is to say, if $\psi(z, z')$ exists, it is to be a polynomial in z the coefficients of which are regular functions of z' in the immediate vicinity of $z' = 0$ and vanish when $z' = 0$.

A method of determining the fact is as follows. Both $\phi(z, z')$ and $\chi(z, z')$ must vanish for all the places where $\psi(z, z')$ vanishes, if ψ exists. We therefore regard

$$\phi(z, z') = 0, \quad \chi(z, z') = 0,$$

as two simultaneous algebraical equations in z. We eliminate z between these two equations, adopting Sylvester's dialytic process. The resultant is a determinant of $m + n$ rows and columns, every constituent in the determinant (other than the zero constituents) being divisible by z'; and therefore this resultant is of the form

$$z'^\mu \Theta(z'),$$

where μ is a positive integer not less than the smaller of the two integers m and n, and where $\Theta(z')$ is a regular function of z' in the immediate vicinity of $z' = 0$, when it is not an evanescent function.

When $\Theta(z')$ does not become evanescent, the values of z' different from $z' = 0$ which make the resultant vanish are given by the equation

$$\Theta(z') = 0;$$

and these values of z' form a discrete and not a continuous succession. In that event, for each such value of z' and for the specially associated values of z, both ϕ and χ vanish. But their simultaneous zero values are limited to these isolated places; there is no function $\psi(z, z')$ possessing a continuous aggregate of zero-places in the vicinity of 0, 0.

When $\Theta(z')$ is evanescent, the functions $\phi(z, z')$ and $\chi(z, z')$ become zero together, not merely at the place 0, 0, but at all the continuous aggregate of places where some function $\psi(z, z')$, as yet unknown, vanishes; for there is no equation $\Theta(z') = 0$ limiting the values of z' and requiring associated values of z.

In the latter case, $\phi(z, z')$ and $\chi(z, z')$ possess a common factor $\psi(z, z')$, which necessarily will be a polynomial in z of degree less than n; and the polynomial will have functions of z' for its coefficients, all of which are regular in the immediate vicinity of $z' = 0$ and vanish when $z' = 0$. Let

$$\psi(z, z') = z^p + z^{p-1} k_1 + \ldots + k_p;$$

as ψ is a factor of ϕ by hypothesis, and also a factor of χ by hypothesis, our earlier analysis shews that (as already stated) $k_1, \ldots, k_p$ are regular functions of z' in the immediate vicinity of $z' = 0$ and vanish when $z' = 0$.

Accordingly, let

$$\frac{\phi(z, z')}{\psi(z, z')} = z^{m-p} + z^{m-p-1} G_1 + \ldots + G_{m-p},$$

$$\frac{\chi(z, z')}{\psi(z, z')} = z^{n-p} + z^{n-p-1} H_1 + \ldots + H_{n-p},$$

where all the coefficients $G_1, \ldots, G_{m-p}, H_1, \ldots, H_{n-p}$ are regular functions of z' in the immediate vicinity of $z' = 0$ and vanish when $z' = 0$. Consequently the relation

$$(z^m + z^{m-1} g_1 + \ldots + g_m)(z^{n-p} + z^{n-p-1} H_1 + \ldots + H_{n-p})$$
$$= (z^n + z^{n-1} h_1 + \ldots + h_n)(z^{m-p} + z^{m-p-1} G_1 + \ldots + G_{m-p})$$

must be satisfied identically for all values of z and z' within the immediate vicinity of $0, 0$, the common value of the equal expressions being $\phi(z, z') \chi(z, z') \div \psi(z, z')$. Equating the coefficients of the same powers of z in the expressions, we have $m + n - p$ relations, linear in the $(n - p) + (m - p)$ unknown functions $H_1, \ldots, H_{n-p}, G_1, \ldots, G_{m-p}$. When these are eliminated determinantally, we have $m + n - p - (n - p) - (m - p)$, that is, we have p, equations in z' which, being satisfied for all values of z', must become evanescent. The conditions for this evanescence, which are thence derived as existing between the coefficients of ϕ and χ, are the conditions necessary and sufficient for the existence of $\psi(z, z')$.

When these conditions are satisfied, the actual expression of $\psi(z, z')$ can be obtained by constructing the algebraical greatest common measure of $\phi(z, z')$ and $\chi(z, z')$, regarded as polynomials in z.

We thus have analytical tests determining whether two functions $\phi(z, z')$ and $\chi(z, z')$, each polynomial in z and having for the coefficients of powers of z regular functions of z' which vanish when $z' = 0$, are or are not divisible by a common factor of the same type as themselves. To these tests, the same remark applies as in § 70; each condition usually would, in practice with infinite power-series, require an infinite number of arithmetical relations among the constants. Still, the analytical tests remain in the form indicated.

When the tests are satisfied, the two functions are said to be *relatively reducible*; each of them is said to be *reducible* by itself.

Note 1. The processes connected with finding the conditions are those connected with constructing eliminants in algebra. Thus, in order that the functions

$$z^4 + g_1 z^3 + g_2 z^2 + g_3 z + g_4, \quad z^2 + h_1 z^2 + h_2$$

should have a common factor linear in z, all the coefficients of powers of z' in the final expansion of the determinant

$$\begin{vmatrix} g_1 - h_1, & 1, & 1, & 0, & 0 \\ g_2 - h_2, & g_1, & h_1, & 1, & 0 \\ g_3, & g_2, & h_2, & h_1, & 1 \\ g_4, & g_3, & 0, & h_2, & h_1 \\ 0, & g_4, & 0, & 0, & h_2 \end{vmatrix}$$

must vanish identically.

Note 2. In the preceding investigations, we are concerned with the possession by $\phi(z, z')$ and $\chi(z, z')$ of a common factor of the same type as themselves; that is to say, $\phi(z, z')$, $\chi(z, z')$, and the common factor (if it exists) are polynomial in z. We are not concerned with the comparison of expressions

$$\phi(z, z') \quad \text{and} \quad \phi(z, z') e^{R(z, z')},$$

where $R(z, z')$ is regular in the immediate vicinity of 0, 0 and vanishes when $z = 0$ and $z' = 0$; the latter expression, when expressed in a double series, is no longer polynomial in z. The case, when $R(z, z')$ can be such as to make the second expression polynomial in z' alone, has already been discussed (§ 63).

Ex. When two functions

$$(a_0, a_1, a_2 \backslash z, z')^2 + (b_0, b_1, b_2, b_3 \backslash z, z')^3 + \ldots,$$
$$(a_0', a_1', a_2' \backslash z, z')^2 + (b_0', b_1', b_2', b_3' \backslash z, z')^3 + \ldots,$$

possess a common factor of the type

$$z + R(z'),$$

where $R(z')$ is regular in the immediate vicinity of z' and vanishes when $z' = 0$, we can approximate to its expression as follows. (The algebra will illustrate the distinction between the finite number of analytical tests and the infinite number of arithmetical relations between the constants; the latter, of course, cannot be set out explicitly.)

The first function is expressed (§ 64) in the form

$$\{a_0 z^2 + z(a_1 z' + a_2 z'^2 + \ldots) + a_2 z'^2 + \beta_3 z'^3 + \ldots\} e^{\lambda_0 z + \lambda_1 z' + \ldots},$$

where

$$\lambda_0 = \frac{b_0}{a_0}, \quad \lambda_1 = \frac{1}{a_0^2}(a_0 b_1 - a_1 b_0), \quad \ldots,$$

$$a_2 = \frac{1}{a_0}(a_0 b_2 - a_2 b_0) - \frac{a_1}{a_0^2}(a_0 b_1 - a_1 b_0),$$

$$\beta_3 = b_3 - \frac{a_2}{a_0^2}(a_0 b_1 - a_1 b_0),$$

and so on; and the second function is expressed in the similar form

$$\{a_0'z^2 + z(a_1'z' + a_2'z'^2 + \ldots) + a_2'z'^2 + \beta_3'z'^3 + \ldots\} e^{\lambda_0'z + \lambda_1'z' + \ldots},$$

where
$$\lambda_0' = \frac{b_0'}{a_0'}, \quad \lambda_1' = \frac{1}{a_0'^2}(a_0'b_1' - a_1'b_0'), \quad \ldots,$$

$$a_2' = \frac{1}{a_0'}(a_0'b_2' - a_2'b_0') - \frac{a_1'}{a_0'^2}(a_0'b_1' - a_1'b_0'),$$

$$\beta_3' = b_3' - \frac{a_2'}{a_0'^2}(a_0'b_1' - a_1'b_0'),$$

and so on. We then must have the condition or conditions that

$$a_0 z^2 + z(a_1 z' + a_2 z'^2 + \ldots) + a_2 z'^2 + \beta_3 z'^3 + \ldots$$

and
$$a_0' z^2 + z(a_1' z' + a_2' z'^2 + \ldots) + a_2' z'^2 + \beta_3' z'^3 + \ldots$$

should possess a common factor of the type

$$z + R(z'),$$

say
$$z + \gamma_1 z' + \gamma_2 z'^2 + \ldots.$$

Let these two expressions, which are quadratic in z, be denoted by

$$a_0 z^2 + z\xi_1 + \xi_2, \quad a_0' z^2 + z\eta_1 + \eta_2.$$

They both will vanish, if they possess a common factor linear in z and if that factor vanishes. When they vanish, we have

$$a_0 z^2 + z\xi_1 + \xi_2 = 0, \quad a_0' z^2 + z\eta_1 + \eta_2 = 0,$$

simultaneously; and therefore the relations

$$\frac{z^2}{\xi_1\eta_2 - \xi_2\eta_1} = \frac{z}{\xi_2 a_0' - \eta_2 a_0} = \frac{1}{\eta_1 a_0 - \xi_1 a_0'}$$

will be satisfied for the value of z, in terms of z', which makes the common factor vanish. Thus we must have

$$(\xi_1\eta_2 - \xi_2\eta_1)(\eta_1 a_0 - \xi_1 a_0') = (\xi_2 a_0' - \eta_2 a_0)^2,$$

satisfied identically for all values of z'; and the value of z, which would make the common factor vanish, is given by

$$z = \frac{\xi_2 a_0' - \eta_2 a_0}{\eta_1 a_0 - \xi_1 a_0'}.$$

Now
$$\xi_1\eta_2 - \xi_2\eta_1 = z'^3\{(a_1 a_2' - a_1' a_2) + (a_1\beta_3' - a_1'\beta_3 + a_2 a_2' - a_2' a_2) z' + \ldots\},$$

$$\xi_2 a_0' - \eta_2 a_0 = z'^2\{(a_0' a_2 - a_2' a_0) + (a_0'\beta_3 - a_0\beta_3') z' + \ldots\},$$

$$\eta_1 a_0 - \xi_1 a_0' = z'\{a_0 a_1' - a_1 a_0' + (a_0 a_2' - a_0' a_2) z' + \ldots\};$$

and therefore, disregarding the factor z'^4, the expression

$$\{a_0' a_2 - a_2' a_0 + (a_0'\beta_3 - a_0\beta_3') z' + \ldots\}^2$$
$$- \{(a_1 a_2' - a_1' a_2) + (a_1\beta_3' - a_1'\beta_3 + a_2 a_2' - a_2' a_2) z' + \ldots\}\{(a_0 a_1' - a_1 a_0') + (a_0 a_2' - a_0' a_2) z' + \ldots\}$$

must vanish identically, for all values of z'. Let the expression be denoted by

$$C_0 + C_1 z' + \ldots;$$

then we must have
$$C_0 = 0, \quad C_1 = 0, \quad \ldots,$$

as the arithmetical relations between the constants.

Also the value of z, which makes the common factor vanish, is

$$z = \frac{\xi_2 a_0' - \eta_2 a_0}{\eta_1 a_0 - \xi_1 a_0'}$$
$$= z' \frac{a_0' a_2 - a_2' a_0 + (a_0' \beta_3 - a_0 \beta_3') z' + \ldots}{a_0 a_1' - a_1 a_0' + (a_0 a_2' - a_0' a_2) z' + \ldots}.$$

Consequently, when all the relations between the constants are satisfied, the common factor is

$$z + \gamma_1 z' + \gamma_2 z'^2 + \ldots,$$

where

$$\gamma_1 = \frac{a_0' a_2 - a_0 a_2'}{a_0' a_1 - a_0 a_1'},$$
$$\gamma_2 = \frac{(a_0' a_2 - a_2' a_0)(a_0 a_2' - a_0' a_2) - (a_0 a_1' - a_1 a_0')(a_0' \beta_3 - a_0 \beta_3')}{(a_0' a_1 - a_0 a_1')^2},$$

and so on.

It is clear that, in the absence of general laws giving relations between the coefficients in each of the two functions, we cannot set out the aggregate of relations $C = 0$ and the aggregate of constants γ.

Expressions of functions near a pole or an accidental singularity.

72. The non-ordinary places of a uniform function have been sorted into three classes, the poles (or accidental singularities of the first kind), the unessential singularities (or accidental singularities of the second kind), and the essential singularities.

The simplest of these, in their analytical character and in their effect upon the function, are the *poles*. Let p, p' be a pole of a uniform function $f(z, z')$; then, after the definition, some series of positive powers of $z - p$, $z' - p'$ exists, say $F(z - p, z' - p')$, which is regular in the immediate vicinity of p, p' and vanishes when $z = p$ and $z' = p'$, and is such that the product

$$f(z, z') F(z - p, z' - p')$$

is regular in the vicinity of p, p' and does not vanish when $z = p, z' = p'$. Thus the function $f(z, z')$ acquires a unique infinite value at a pole; that is, the infinite value is acquired no matter by what laws of variation the variables z and z' tend towards, and ultimately reach, the place p, p'. Further, the pole-annulling factor $F(z - p, z' - p')$ is not unique; a factor

$$F(z - p, z' - p') e^{R(z - p, z' - p')},$$

where $R(z - p, z' - p')$ is any regular function of $z - p$ and $z' - p'$, would have the same effect. All such factors we shall (for the present purpose) regard as equivalent to one another; they can be represented by $F(z - p, z' - p')$. Moreover, there cannot be more than one such representative factor for $f(z, z')$ at a pole; if there were two, say $F(z - p, z' - p')$ and $G(z - p, z' - p')$, we should have

$f(z, z') F(z - p, z' - p') =$ regular function, not vanishing when $z = p$ and $z' = p'$,
$f(z, z') G(z - p, z' - p') = \ldots\ldots\ldots\ldots\ldots\ldots\ldots\ldots\ldots\ldots\ldots\ldots\ldots\ldots\ldots\ldots\ldots\ldots$,

and therefore p, p' would be an ordinary non-zero place for the quotient
$$\frac{F(z-p, z'-p')}{G(z-p, z'-p')},$$
which is impossible unless F is divisible by G, and it would be an ordinary non-zero place for the reciprocal of this function, which is impossible unless G is divisible by F.

Hence, denoting the representative factor by F, we have
$$f(z, z')\, F(z-p, z'-p') = k_{00} + k_{10}(z-p) + k_{01}(z'-p') + \ldots,$$
the series on the right-hand side being a regular function in a domain of p, p'; and therefore
$$\frac{1}{f(z, z')} = \frac{F(z-p, z'-p')}{k_{00} + k_{10}(z-p) + k_{01}(z'-p') + \ldots}$$
= a regular function (§ 69) of z and z' in a domain of p, p', vanishing when $z = p$, $z' = p'$.

It therefore follows that a pole of $f(z, z')$ is a zero of $\dfrac{1}{f(z, z')}$, so that the place p, p' is an ordinary place for the function $\dfrac{1}{f(z, z')}$. Hence, in the vicinity of a pole of $f(z, z')$, it is convenient to consider the reciprocal function, say
$$\phi(z, z') = \frac{1}{f(z, z')};$$
and then the behaviour of $f(z, z')$ in the vicinity of the pole p, p' can be described by the behaviour of $\phi(z, z')$ which is regular in the vicinity of its zero there. Moreover, any zero of $f(z, z')$ in a domain of p, p' is a pole of $\phi(z, z')$; hence the domain of p, p', within which $\phi(z, z')$ is regular, does not extend so far as to include any zero of $f(z, z')$.

As $\phi(z, z')$ is regular in this domain of p, p', and as it vanishes at p, p', it has an unlimited number of zero-values in the immediate vicinity of p, p', and these occur at places forming a continuous two-dimensional aggregate that includes p, p'. Hence *in the immediate vicinity of any pole of a uniform analytic function, there is an unlimited number of poles forming a continuous two-dimensional aggregate that includes the given pole.*

Further, we have definite integers as the orders of the zero of $\phi(z, z')$ in the two variables at p, p', the integer being derived from the equivalent expressions of $\phi(z, z')$ in the immediate vicinity of p, p'; these integers will be taken as *the orders of the pole* of $f(z, z')$ in the two variables at p, p'.

Cor. Manifestly, a pole of $f(z, z')$ of any order is a pole of $f(z, z') - \alpha$ of the same order, where $|\alpha|$ is finite.

73. An *unessential singularity* (an accidental singularity of the second kind, to use Weierstrass's fuller phrase) of a uniform function $f(z, z')$ at a place s, s' is defined by the property that there exists a power-series $F(z-s, z'-s')$, which is a regular function of z and z' in the immediate vicinity of s, s' and vanishes at s, s', and is such that the product

$$f(z, z') F(z-s, z'-s')$$

is a regular function in the immediate vicinity of s, s', and vanishes at s, s'. Let this latter regular function be denoted by $H(z-s, z'-s')$. No generality is lost by assuming that the functions F and H have no common factor vanishing when $z = s$, $z' = s'$. We then have a fractional expression for f, viz.

$$f(z, z') = \frac{H(z-s, z'-s')}{F(z-s, z'-s')}.$$

As in the case of a pole of $f(z, z')$ at p, p', the function $F(z-p, z'-p')$ was representative and unique, so here each of the functions $H(z-s, z'-s')$ and $F(z-s, z'-s')$ is representative and unique, when H and F have no common factor vanishing when $z = s$, $z' = s'$. The functions H and F can of course have any number of exponential factors, each exponent being a regular function of $z-s$, $z'-s'$; but no factor of that type affects the characteristic variations of f in the immediate vicinity of that place. Thus, in our expression for $f(z, z')$, we can regard the representative functions H and F as unique.

To consider the behaviour of f at, and near, the accidental singularity, write

$$z - s = \sigma, \quad z' - s' = \sigma';$$

then we have expressions of the form

$$H(z-s, z'-s') = E\sigma^m \sigma'^{m'} \{\sigma^l + \sigma^{l-1} h_1(\sigma') + \ldots + h_l(\sigma')\} e^{\overline{H}(\sigma, \sigma')},$$

$$F(z-s, z'-s') = D\sigma^n \sigma'^{n'} \{\sigma^k + \sigma^{k-1} f_1(\sigma') + \ldots + f_k(\sigma')\} e^{\overline{F}(\sigma, \sigma')},$$

where E and D are constants: m, m', n, n' are positive integers, each zero in the simplest cases: l and k are positive integers, each greater than zero in the simplest cases; $h_1, \ldots, h_l, f_1, \ldots, f_k$ are regular functions of σ' in the immediate vicinity of $\sigma' = 0$ and vanish with σ'; and $\overline{H}, \overline{F}$ are regular functions of σ and σ' in the immediate vicinity of $\sigma = 0$, $\sigma' = 0$ and vanish with σ and σ', so that neither H nor F can acquire a zero value or an infinite value from the factors $e^{\overline{H}}$ and $e^{\overline{F}}$. Moreover, H and F are devoid of any common factor: so that either m or n (or both) must be zero, and m' or n' (or both) must be zero. Also

$$\sigma^l + \sigma^{l-1} h_1(\sigma') + \ldots + h_l(\sigma'), \quad \sigma^k + \sigma^{k-1} f_1(\sigma') + \ldots + f_k(\sigma')$$

have no common zero in the immediate vicinity (defined as a region round σ' of radius less than the modulus of the smallest root of the resultant of these two polynomials) of $\sigma = 0$, $\sigma' = 0$ save actually at $0, 0$; for their eliminant is a function $\sigma'^\mu \Theta(\sigma')$ which does not vanish for small values of σ' other than $\sigma' = 0$.

Manifestly, the value of $f(z, z')$ at s, s' is *not definite*; it can be made to acquire any value by assigning appropriate laws for the approach of z to s and of z' to s'. In the immediate vicinity of $s, s', f(z, z')$ possesses

(i) an unlimited number of zeros, given by zero-values, other than at $0, 0$, of $\sigma^l + \sigma^{l-1} h_1(\sigma') + \ldots + h_l(\sigma')$;

(ii) an unlimited number of poles, given by zero-values, other than at $0, 0$, of $\sigma^k + \sigma^{k-1} f_1(\sigma') + \ldots + f_k(\sigma')$;

(iii) an unlimited number of places at which it assumes a level value of finite modulus;

but $\sigma = 0$ and $\sigma' = 0$ is the only place in the immediate vicinity of $0, 0$, where the value of $f(z, z')$ is not unique and definite. Hence we have the result:—

The unessential singularities of a uniform function $f(z, z')$ are isolated places in the domain of existence of $f(z, z')$; the value of f at an unessential singularity is not definite; and, in the immediate vicinity of any unessential singularity, there is an unlimited number of places where f can assume any assigned definite value, zero, finite, or infinite.

Further, let the unessential singularities (each of them being an isolated place) of a uniform analytic function be represented by a_m, a'_m, where $m = 1, 2, \ldots$. They may be finite in number or infinite in number. When they are infinite in number, the places a_m, a'_m must have one or more limit-places; let such a limit-place be b, b'. As regards the function in a small domain round b, b', it cannot be represented by any of the different foregoing expressions, suitable to the respective vicinities of an ordinary place, a pole, and an isolated unessential singularity. The limit-place must therefore be an essential singularity of the function.

Expression near an essential singularity.

74. The definition of an *essential singularity* of a uniform function, that has been adopted after Weierstrass, is mainly of an uninforming character—to the effect that, in the immediate vicinity of such a place, no power-series $U(z, z')$ representing a regular function and vanishing at the place can be obtained such that the product

$$f(z, z') U(z, z')$$

is a regular function of z and z'. But, as is known to be the fact with uniform functions of a single variable, essential singularities cannot effectively be sorted together in one class: there can be points, or lines, or spaces, of essential singularity for a uniform function of a single variable. The conception of added complications, when we deal with uniform analytic functions of more than one variable, needs no argument for postulation, though it gives no substantial assistance towards analytical formulation.

It may however be added that one large question dealing with the essential singularities of a uniform analytical function has occupied a number of memoirs published in recent years.

We have seen that the zeros of an analytical function of two variables constitute a two-dimensional aggregate, and likewise that its poles constitute a two-dimensional aggregate. We have also seen that its unessential singularities are isolated places.

The question just mentioned relates to the aggregate constituted by the essential singularities of a uniform analytical function; for its discussion, as well as for other matters, we shall refer to the memoirs indicated*.

---

* The chief memoirs are those by Hartogs, viz. *Math. Ann.*, t. lxii (1906), pp. 1—88 ; *Münch. Sitzungsb.*, t. xxxvi (1906), pp. 223—242 ; *Jahresb. d. Deutscher Math. Vereinigung*, t. xvi (1907), pp. 223—240 ; *Acta Math.*, t. xxxii (1909), pp. 57—79 ; *Math. Ann.*, t. lxx (1911), pp. 207—222.
See also a memoir by E. E. Levi, *Annali di Mat.*, Ser. iii, t. xvii (1910), pp. 61—87.

CHAPTER V

Two Theorems on the Expression of a Function without Essential Singularities in the Finite Part of the Field

75. We now come to the consideration of a couple of theorems relating to the expression of a uniform analytic function of two variables. In the first of them, we have to deal with a function that has no essential singularities within the whole range of the field of variation of z and z'; the function then has the form of a rational function of the variables. In the second of them, we have to deal with a function that has no essential singularities within the range of the field of variation of z and z' such that $|z| \leqslant R, |z'| \leqslant R'$, where R and R' can be taken as large as we please; the function then has the form of the quotient of two functions, each of which is a regular function of z and z' for the values of z considered*.

76. First of all, consider a polynomial in z and z', say
$$p(z, z') = \zeta_0 z^n + \zeta_1 z^{n-1} + \ldots + \zeta_n,$$
where $\zeta_0, \zeta_1, \ldots, \zeta_n$ are themselves polynomials in z'. Then we at once have the results:—

(i) every finite place is ordinary for $p(z, z')$;

(ii) with every finite value z', that is not a zero of ζ_0, can be associated n finite values of z, such that each of the n places thus constituted is a zero for $p(z, z')$, repetition of values of z causing multiplicity of zero-places for $p(z, z')$;

(iii) with every finite value z', that is a zero of ζ_0 and is such that $\zeta_r (r > 0)$ is the first coefficient of powers of z in $p(z, z')$ which does not vanish, can be associated $n - r$ finite values of z, such that each of the $n - r$ places thus constituted is a zero for $p(z, z')$;

(iv) the poles of $p(z, z')$ are given by infinite values of $|z|$ and finite values of z' other than the roots of ζ_0, and by infinite values of $|z'|$ and finite values of z other than the roots of the coefficient

---

* Both theorems were enunciated by Weierstrass for n variables, but without proof; references will be given later.

of the highest power of z' in $p(z, z')$ arranged in powers of z', and by infinite values of $|z|$ and of $|z'|$;

(v) the unessential singularities of $p(z, z')$, if any, are given by infinite values of $|z|$ and by the roots of ζ_0, but each such place is an unessential singularity only if other conditions are satisfied; and similarly for infinite values of $|z'|$ and by the finite values of z excepted in (iv), but each such place is an unessential singularity only if other conditions are satisfied: so that, in general, $p(z, z')$ has no unessential singularities; and

(vi) there are no essential singularities of $p(z, z')$.

77. In the next place, consider an irreducible rational function of z and z', say
$$R(z, z') = \frac{p(z, z')}{q(z, z')},$$
where $p(z, z')$ and $q(z, z')$ are polynomials in z and z',
$$p(z, z') = \zeta_0 z^n + \zeta_1 z^{n-1} + \ldots + \zeta_n,$$
$$q(z, z') = \eta_0 z^m + \eta_1 z^{m-1} + \ldots + \eta_m,$$
while $\zeta_0, \ldots, \zeta_n, \eta_0, \ldots, \eta_m$ are polynomials in z' alone. Then it is easy to infer the following results:—

(i) every finite place, that is not a zero of $q(z, z')$, is ordinary for $R(z, z')$;

(ii) every zero of $p(z, z')$, that is not a zero of $q(z, z')$, is a zero of $R(z, z')$;

(iii) every zero of $q(z, z')$, that is not a zero of $p(z, z')$, is a pole of $R(z, z')$;

(iv) every place, that is a simultaneous zero of $p(z, z')$ and of $q(z, z')$ which have no common factor because our rational function is irreducible, is an unessential singularity of $R(z, z')$;

(v) the behaviour of $R(z, z')$ for infinite values of $|z|$ or of $|z'|$ or of both $|z|$ and $|z'|$, depends upon the degrees of $p(z, z')$ and $q(z, z')$ in z and in z', while every such place is either a zero, or ordinary, or a pole, or an unessential singularity; and

(vi) the rational function $R(z, z')$ has no essential singularities.

Functions entirely devoid of essential singularities.

78. Now we know that not a few of the important properties of uniform analytic functions of a single variable are deduced from those expressions of the function which arise when special regard is paid to its singularities; and occasionally some classification of functions can be secured according to the number and nature of these points*. In particular, we know that a uniform function, devoid of essential singularities throughout the whole field of variation of the variable z, is a rational function of z. Of this result, there is the generalisation, given by the theorem†:—

A uniform analytic function of two complex variables z and z', having no essential singularity in the whole field of their variation, is a rational function of z and z'.

To establish this theorem, we proceed as follows.

Let $f(z, z')$ be a uniform function of z and z', entirely devoid of essential singularities; and let any ordinary place (say 0, 0) be chosen which is a non-zero place of the function. In the vicinity of 0, 0, let the expansion of $f(z, z')$ be

$$f(z, z') = \sum_{m=0}^{\infty} \sum_{n=0}^{\infty} c_{m,n} z^m z'^n;$$

and suppose that this series converges absolutely within a domain $|z| < r$, $|z'| < r'$. Manifestly, after the supposition as to $f(0, 0)$, the quantity c_{00} is not zero.

Within the domain, we have

$$f(z, z') = \sum_{m=0}^{\infty} \left(\sum_{n=0}^{\infty} c_{m,n} z'^n \right) z^m,$$

because the double series converges absolutely; so, writing

$$g_m(z') = \sum_{n=0}^{\infty} c_{m,n} z'^n,$$

we have

$$f(z, z') = \sum_{m=0}^{\infty} z^m g_m(z').$$

Consequently, for all values 0, 1, ... of m, and for all values of z' within the domain, we have

$$\frac{1}{m!} \left\{ \frac{\partial^m f(z, z')}{\partial z^m} \right\}_{z=0} = g_m(z').$$

Now $f(z, z')$ is everywhere a uniform analytic function without essential singularities; consequently every derivative of $f(z, z')$, at every place in the

---

* Of course, there are other classifications, such as those connected with the kinds of aggregate of the zeros of a uniform analytic function of a single variable, leading to the *class* (*genre*) question that has been the subject of many investigations in recent years, initiated by Laguerre, Poincaré, Hadamard, Borel, and others.

† It is the first of the two theorems which, as already stated, were enunciated by Weierstrass without proof. His enunciation, given for n variables instead of two only, is to be found *Ges. Werke*, t. ii, p. 129.

A proof is given by Hurwitz, *Crelle*, t. xcv (1883), pp. 201—206, for n variables; and this proof is followed by Dautheville, *Étude sur les séries entières par rapport à plusieurs variables imaginaires indépendantes* (Thèse, Paris, 1885). Hurwitz's proof, modified for the case of two variables, and amplified, is substantially adopted in my text.

field, also is a uniform analytic function without essential singularities. At the places $0, z'$ within the domain, the converging series denoted by $g_m(z')$ represents a derivative of $f(z, z')$; it is therefore an element of a function of a single variable z', which is uniform, analytic, and devoid of essential singularities. But we know* that such a function of a single variable is a rational function of the variable; and therefore $g_m(z')$ is an element of a rational function of z'. Denoting this rational function by $A_m(z')$, or by A_m, for all values of m, we have

$$g_m(z') = A_m(z'),$$

for all values of z' within the domain; and so, within that domain, we have

$$f(z, z') = A_0 + A_1 z + A_2 z^2 + \ldots,$$

where now $A_0, A_1, A_2, \ldots$ are rational functions of z' which have no pole anywhere within our domain.

Moreover, when $z = 0$, $z' = 0$, the quantity c_{00} is not zero, so that $A_0(0)$ is different from zero. Hence we can choose a more restricted domain given by $|z| \leqslant \delta$ and $|z'| \leqslant \delta'$, where δ and δ' are not infinitesimal, such that the uniform analytic function $f(z, z')$ is everywhere regular and different from zero.

Assign an arbitrary value a' to z' in this restricted domain, that is, such that $|a'| \leqslant \delta'$. Then $f(z, a')$ is a function of a single variable only; it is uniform; and it possesses no essential singularity; it is therefore a rational function of z, so that we may write

$$f(z, a') = \frac{B_0 + B_1 z + \ldots + B_r z^r}{C_0 + C_1 z + \ldots + C_r z^r}.$$

As a rational function of z has a limited number of zeros and of poles, the highest index of z in the numerator and the denominator combined is finite: that is, r is a finite integer. No generality is lost by assuming that B_r and C_r are not zero together. If B_0 were zero, then $z = 0$ and $z' = a'$ would be a zero of $f(z, z')$, contrary to the supposition that f does not vanish within the selected domain; if C_0 were zero, then $z = 0$ and $z' = a'$ would be a pole of $f(z, z')$, contrary to the supposition that f is regular within the selected domain; hence neither B_0 nor C_0 is zero.

Let $K_0, K_1, K_2, \ldots$ respectively denote the values of the rational functions $A_0, A_1, A_2, \ldots$ when $z' = a'$. Then a converging series for $f(z, a')$ is given by

$$f(z, a') = K_0 + K_1 z + K_2 z^2 + \ldots,$$

so that, from the two expressions of $f(z, a')$, we have

$$(K_0 + K_1 z + K_2 z^2 + \ldots)(C_0 + C_1 z + \ldots + C_r z^r) = B_0 + B_1 z + \ldots + B_r z^r,$$

holding for all values of z such that $|z| \leqslant \delta$. The two coefficients of each power of z on the two sides must be equal to one another; and therefore, as

---

* See my *Theory of Functions*, § 48.

z^{r+n} (for $n \geqslant 1$) does not occur on the right-hand side, we have the coefficient of z^{r+n} on the left-hand side equal to zero. Thus all the determinants

$$\begin{Vmatrix} K_1, & K_2, & K_3, & \ldots \\ K_2, & K_3, & K_4, & \ldots \\ \cdots\cdots\cdots\cdots\cdots\cdots\cdots\cdots \\ K_{r+1}, & K_{r+2}, & K_{r+3}, & \ldots \end{Vmatrix}$$

must vanish.

With each value of a', some finite integer r must be associated because $f(z, a')$ is rational in z. But with at least one value (and, it may be, with more than one value) of r, an infinite number of values of a' must be associated; for otherwise, if with each value of r only a finite number of values of a' could be associated and as every admissible integer r is finite, there would in all be only a finite number of values of a', contrary to the fact that a' is any place in the domain $|z'| \leqslant \delta'$.

Consequently, taking r to be the greatest integer for any value of a' in the domain determined by δ', all the preceding determinants vanish for the infinite number of values of a' in the domain. Hence there must exist functions of z' (to be denoted by $F_0, F_1, \ldots, F_r$), such that the equations

$$F_r A_1 + F_{r-1} A_2 + \ldots + F_0 A_{r+1} = 0,$$
$$F_r A_2 + F_{r-1} A_3 + \ldots + F_0 A_{r+2} = 0,$$
$$\cdots\cdots\cdots\cdots\cdots\cdots\cdots\cdots\cdots\cdots$$

are satisfied for an infinite number of values of z'; and not all the functions F can vanish. Moreover, the functions A are rational and, at most, only some of them (limited in number) are evanescent; hence, as the functions $F_0, F_1, \ldots, F_r$ can be taken as equal to determinants the constituents of which are rational functions of z', they are themselves rational functions of z'.

Consider the function

$$(F_0 + zF_1 + \ldots + z^r F_r) f(z, z') - (G_0 + zG_1 + \ldots + z^r G_r),$$

where

$$G_0 = A_0 F_0, \quad G_1 = A_1 F_0 + A_0 F_1, \ldots, \quad G_r = A_0 F_r + A_1 F_{r-1} + \ldots + A_r F_0;$$

and denote it by $\Phi(z, z')$, which may or may not vanish identically. The quantities $G_0, \ldots, G_r$, being lineo-linear in the rational functions A and F, are themselves rational functions of z'; and not all the functions G can vanish. Then the function $\Phi(z, z')$ is a regular function of z and z' within the domain $|z| \leqslant \delta$ and $|z'| \leqslant \delta'$, because all its components are regular within that domain. The foregoing analysis shews that, for all values of z in the range $|z| \leqslant \delta$, there is an infinite number of values of z' in the range $|z'| \leqslant \delta'$ for which $\Phi(z, z')$ vanishes. If $\Phi(z, z')$ does not vanish identically, we take any special value of z within the range $|z| \leqslant \delta$, say $z = c$; then $\Phi(c, z')$ is a regular function of z' within the range $|z'| \leqslant \delta'$, and (after what precedes) there is an infinite number of values of z' within that range where $\Phi(c, z')$ vanishes. It is a known property* of regular functions of one variable that the number of its zeros, within any finite region where the function is regular, is necessarily finite; and the preceding result, based immediately upon the hypothesis that $\Phi(z, z')$ does not vanish identically, does not accord with this requirement. Accordingly, the hypothesis must be abandoned; the function $\Phi(z, z')$ vanishes identically; and therefore, for all values of z and z' within the selected domain, we have

$$(F_0 + zF_1 + \ldots + z^r F_r) f(z, z') = G_0 + zG_1 + \ldots + z^r G_r,$$

where $F_0, F_1, \ldots, F_r, G_0, G_1, \ldots, G_r$ are rational functions of z'.

The function F_0 and the function G_0 do not vanish under our initial hypothesis that the ordinary place $0, 0$ is not a zero of $f(z, z')$; some (but not all) of the other functions $F_1, \ldots, F_r, G_1, \ldots, G_r$ may vanish.

We thus have

$$f(z, z') = \frac{G_0 + zG_1 + \ldots + z^r G_r}{F_0 + zF_1 + \ldots + z^r F_r};$$

that is, $f(z, z')$ is a rational function of z and z'. The proposition is thus established.

79. One provisional remark will be made at this stage. Let $f(z, z')$ be a uniform function which, within some limited region of its existence, has no essential singularities and, within that region, does possess zeros, and poles, and unessential singularities.

Suppose that a uniform function exists, which has those zeros, those poles, and those unessential singularities, all in precisely the same fashion as $f(z, z')$, and which possesses no others within the region; and suppose that this function has no essential singularity anywhere in the whole field of variation of z and z'. The preceding proposition shews that it must be a rational function of z and z'. (Examples can easily be constructed, in the case of definite simple assignments of such places). We shall, for the moment, assume the possible existence of such a rational function; and then, denoting it by $r(z, z')$, we write

$$g(z, z') = \frac{f(z, z')}{r(z, z')}.$$

Within the region, the function $g(z, z')$ has no zeros and it has no singularities of any kind; hence, within the domain of every place in that region, the two functions g_1 and g_2, where

$$g_1 = \frac{1}{g} \frac{\partial g}{\partial z}, \quad g_2 = \frac{1}{g} \frac{\partial g}{\partial z'},$$

can be expressed as absolutely converging power-series, which are elements

* See my *Theory of Functions*, § 37.

of two regular functions. Moreover, as regards these two power-series for g_1 and g_2, we obviously must have
$$\frac{\partial g_1}{\partial z'} = \frac{\partial g_2}{\partial z}$$
identically; so we denote the common value of these two quantities by
$$\frac{\partial^2 P(z, z')}{\partial z\, \partial z'},$$
where $P(z, z')$ is itself a double series converging absolutely in the domain, and is an element of a single regular function, which may be denoted by $Q(z, z')$. Then
$$\frac{1}{g}\frac{\partial g}{\partial z} = \frac{\partial P(z, z')}{\partial z}, \quad \frac{1}{g}\frac{\partial g}{\partial z'} = \frac{\partial P(z, z')}{\partial z'},$$
and therefore
$$g = e^{P(z, z')},$$
within the domain. Now $g(z, z')$ is regular throughout the region; and, for each domain within the region, $P(z, z')$ is the element of the regular function $Q(z, z')$. Consequently, on the assumption that the rational function $r(z, z')$ exists, we have
$$r(z, z')\, e^{Q(z, z')}$$
as a representation of $f(z, z')$ within the region, $Q(z, z')$ denoting a function that is regular within the region.

The definite existence of the function, denoted by $r(z, z')$, has not been established in general. The assumption that has been made raises the question as to whether rational functions exist, defined by the possession solely of assigned zeros, assigned poles, and assigned unessential singularities. Also, that question raises the further question as to what are the limitations (if any) upon the arbitrary assignment of zeros, poles, and unessential singularities, in order that it may lead to the existence of a rational function.

These questions initiate a subject of separate enquiry which will not be pursued here.

Functions having essential singularities only in the infinite part of the field.

80. The other of the theorems already mentioned relates to the expression of a uniform analytic function, of which all the essential singularities arise for infinite values of one or other or both of the variables. It was adumbrated by Weierstrass[*]; the following proof is based upon a memoir by Cousin[†]. We have to establish the theorem:—

A uniform analytic function of two variables, all the essential singularities of which arise for infinite values of either of the variables or of

---
[*] *Ges. Werke*, t. ii, p. 163.
[†] *Acta Math.*, t. xix (1895), pp. 1—62; it applies to *n* variables.
It may be added that a proof is given by Poincaré, *Acta Math.*, t. ii (1883), pp. 97—113;

both of the variables, can be expressed as the quotient of two functions which are everywhere regular for finite values of the variables.

For this purpose, Cousin uses the Cauchy method of contour integrals.

81. Consider an integral, the variable of integration Z' being taken in the plane of z', as given by

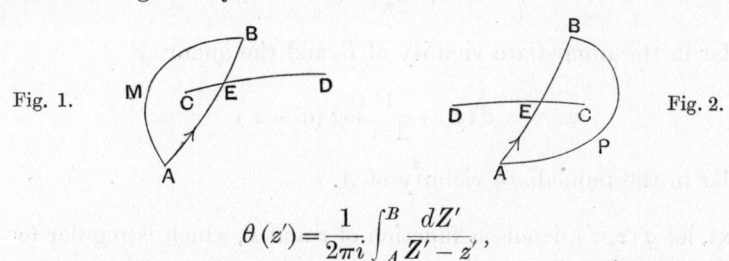

Fig. 1. Fig. 2.

$$\theta(z') = \frac{1}{2\pi i} \int_A^B \frac{dZ'}{Z' - z'},$$

where the integration extends along an arc AB from A as the lower limit to B as the upper limit. When we take a closed contour of which AB is a portion, AB is the positive direction of description in figure 1 and is the negative direction of description in figure 2.

Now in figure 1, we have

$$\theta(z') = 1 + \frac{1}{2\pi i} \int_{AMB} \frac{dZ'}{Z' - z'}$$

for all points z' within the contour $AEBMA$, and

$$\theta(z') = \frac{1}{2\pi i} \int_{AMB} \frac{dZ'}{Z' - z'}$$

for all points z' without the same contour. For all points within the contour, and for all points without the contour, $\theta(z')$ is a regular function of z'. Consequently the line AEB is a *section** for the function; the continuation $\theta(D)$, taken from the inside point C to the outside point D across the section AB when the latter is described positively for the area, is $-1 + \theta(C)$.

In the same way for figure 2, the continuation $\theta(D)$, taken from the inside point C to the outside point D across the section AB when the latter is described negatively for the area, is $1 + \theta(C)$.

---

it is based upon the properties of potential functions. The following memoirs may also be consulted:—

Poincaré, *Acta Math.*, t. xxii (1899), pp. 89—178; *ib.*, t. xxvi (1902), pp. 43—98.

Baker, *Camb. Phil. Trans.*, vol. xviii (1899), p. 431; *Proc. Lond. Math. Soc.*, 2nd Ser., vol. i (1903), pp. 14—36.

Hartogs, *Jahresb. d. deutschen Mathematikervereinigung*, t. xvi (1907), pp. 223—240; and the memoir by Dautheville already (p. 126) quoted.

* See my *Theory of Functions*, § 103; the notion is due to Hermite, who called such a line a *coupure*.

The general value, of course, is

$$\theta(z') = \frac{1}{2\pi i} \log \frac{b'-z'}{a'-z'},$$

where a' and b' are the variables of A and B. Clearly the quantity

$$\theta(z') - \frac{1}{2\pi i} \log(b'-z')$$

is regular in the immediate vicinity of B, and the quantity

$$\theta(z') + \frac{1}{2\pi i} \log(a'-z')$$

is regular in the immediate vicinity of A.

Next, let $g(z, z')$ denote a function of z and z', which is regular for ranges of z and z' that have finite values; and consider an integral

$$\chi(z, z') = \frac{1}{2\pi i} \int_A^B \frac{g(z, Z')}{Z'-z'} dZ',$$

taken precisely as for the preceding integral $\theta(z')$. Then $\chi(z, z')$ is a regular function of z and z', except when z' lies upon the line AEB; and AEB is a section for the function $\chi(z, z')$. Now let

$$G(z, z', Z') = \frac{g(z, Z') - g(z, z')}{Z'-z'};$$

as $g(z, z')$ is a regular function of z and z', it is easy to see* that $G(z, z', Z')$ is a regular function of z, z', Z'. Hence

$$\chi(z, z') = \frac{1}{2\pi i} \int_A^B G(z, z', Z') dZ' + \frac{g(z, z')}{2\pi i} \int_A^B \frac{dZ'}{Z'-z'}$$
$$= H(z, z') + \theta(z') g(z, z'),$$

where $H(z, z')$ is a regular function of z and z' for all the values of z and z' included, and $\theta(z')$ is the preceding integral already considered. Consequently $\chi(z, z')$ is a regular function of z and z' for all points z' that do not lie upon the section AEB; and the change in the analytical continuation of $\chi(z, z')$

---

* If we take
$$g(z, Z') = g_0(z) + Z' g_1(z) + Z'^2 g_2(z) + \ldots,$$
then
$$G(z, z', Z') = g_1(z) + (Z'+z') g_2(z) + \ldots,$$
so that
$$|G(z, z', Z')| \leqslant |g_1(z)| + 2r'|g_2(z)| + 3r'^2|g_3(z)| + \ldots,$$
for values of z' and Z' such that
$$|z'| < r', \quad |Z'| < r' < R'.$$
With the properties of a regular function such as $g(z, z')$, which have been established earlier, the series on the right-hand side converges absolutely; hence $G(z, z', Z')$ is regular.

across the section AEB is $-g(z, z')$ or $+g(z, z')$ according as AEB, when crossed, is being described negatively or positively. Moreover, the function

$$\chi(z, z') - \frac{1}{2\pi i} g(z, z') \log(b' - z')$$

is regular in the immediate vicinity of b', and the function

$$\chi(z, z') + \frac{1}{2\pi i} g(z, z') \log(a' - z')$$

is regular in the immediate vicinity of a'.

Next, take in order a finite number of lines $A_1 B, A_2 B, \ldots$ in the plane of z', such that they have a common extremity B, do not meet except at B, and all lie within the z, z' domain considered. Associated with each of the lines $A_r B$, we take a regular function $g_r(z, z')$, occurring precisely as $g(z, z')$ occurred in the preceding discussion of the function $\chi(z, z')$ over its section; and write

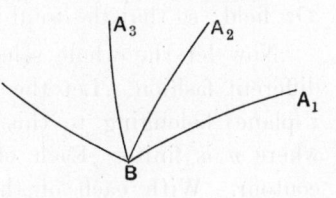

$$\chi_r(z, z') = \frac{1}{2\pi i} \int_{A_r}^{B} \frac{g_r(z, Z')}{Z' - z'} dZ',$$

the integral being taken from A_r to B. The character of $\chi(z, z')$ is known from the earlier investigation.

Let a new function $\Phi(z, z')$ be defined by the equation

$$\Phi(z, z') = \sum_{r=1} \chi_r(z, z').$$

For all places not lying upon any one of the lines, the function $\Phi(z, z')$ is regular. In the immediate vicinity of the place B common to all the lines, the function

$$\Phi(z, z') - \frac{1}{2\pi i} \{\log(b' - z')\} \sum_{r=1} g_r(z, z')$$

is regular; hence, if $\Phi(z, z')$ is regular in the immediate vicinity of B, it is necessary and sufficient that

$$\sum_{r=1} g_r(z, z')$$

should vanish at B. Moreover, if

$$\sum_{r=1} g_r(z, z') = 2k\pi i$$

at B, where k is a constant, then

$$\Phi(z, z') - k \log(b' - z')$$

is regular at B.

82. We are to deal with a uniform analytic function $f(z, z')$, which has no essential singularity in the finite part of the z, z' field. In this field, take any finite domain. Within the selected domain, $f(z, z')$ deviates from regularity at or in the immediate vicinity of poles, and at or in the immediate vicinity of unessential singularities. At a pole and in its vicinity, there is one definite type of representation of $f(z, z')$ which is valid for some region round the pole. At an unessential singularity and in its vicinity, there is another definite type of representation of $f(z, z')$ which likewise is valid for some region round the unessential singularity. At an ordinary place and within some limited region of the place, $f(z, z')$ is regular; within that region, there is another definite type of representation of $f(z, z')$ which likewise is valid for the limited region.

When any two of these respective regions have any area in common, the respective representations of our uniform function $f(z, z')$ are equivalent to one another over that area. Moreover, we have selected a finite domain in the z, z' field; so that the total number of these regions in this domain is finite.

Now let the whole selected domain in the z, z' field be divided up in different fashion. Let the whole region in one of the two planes (say the z'-plane) belonging to this domain in the field be divided into n regions, where n is finite. Each of these regions is to be bounded by a simple contour. With each of these n regions in the z'-plane, we combine the whole of the z-plane that belongs to the selected domain; so that we now have n domains within the single selected finite domain in the z, z' field. At every place in each of these n domains, our function $f(z, z')$ is defined. Let $f_1(z, z')$ denote the whole representation of $f(z, z')$ in one domain, $f_2(z, z')$ the whole representation in another domain; and so on for the n domains, up to $f_n(z, z')$. With each region in the z'-plane, we associate the function $f_m(z, z')$ giving the representation of $f(z, z')$ for the domain which includes that particular z'-region.

It may happen that two such regions have a common area, so that the respective functions belonging to the regions coexist over that area; we shall assume that, if deviations from regularity occur within the area, such deviations are the same for the two functions, say $f_k(z, z')$ and $f_l(z, z')$, so that

$$f_k(z, z') - f_l(z, z')$$

is a regular function over the area.

When two functions are such that their difference over an area is a regular function, they are said* to be *equivalent* over the area; if their difference is a regular function in the immediate vicinity of a point, they are said to be equivalent at the point.

Denote the regions in the z'-plane by $R_1, R_2, \ldots, R_n$ with which $f_1(z, z')$, $f_2(z, z'), \ldots, f_n(z, z')$ are respectively associated. Further, denote by l_{12} the boundary between R_1 and R_2, such that when z' passes from R_1 to R_2 by crossing l_{12}, this line is described positively for the boundary of R_2; and similarly for the boundary between any two contiguous regions. Lastly, there will be points where three or more boundary lines are concurrent.

* Cousin, *l. c.*, p. 10.

When a point P' lies within the region R_k, then $f_k(z, z')$ is the function associated with P'. When a point Q' lies on the boundary between two contiguous regions R_k and R_l, then either of the functions $f_k(z, z')$ and $f_l(z, z')$ is the function associated with Q'. When a point S' is a point of concurrence of more than two boundary lines of regions $R_j, R_k, R_l, \ldots$, then any one of the functions $f_j(z, z'), f_k(z, z'), f_l(z, z'), \ldots$, is the function associated with S'.

83. Consider the integral

$$I_{km} = \frac{1}{2\pi i} \int \frac{f_m(z, Z') - f_k(z, Z')}{Z' - z'} dZ'$$

taken along the line l_{km} between two contiguous regions, the order of the suffixes in I_{km} being the same as their order in l_{km}. Manifestly

$$I_{km} = I_{mk}.$$

As the function $f_m(z, Z') - f_k(z, Z')$ is regular everywhere along the path of integration, the integral is of the same character as the integral previously denoted by $\chi_r(z, z')$; the line l_{km} is a section for the function I_{km}.

Now take all these integrals I_{km} which arise for contiguous regions, and write

$$\Phi(z, z') = \Sigma I_{km},$$

where the summation is for all pairs of suffixes that correspond to contiguous regions. The function $\Phi(z, z')$ has each line l_{km} as a section; at every place that does not lie upon a section, $\Phi(z, z')$ is regular.

Next, we take a set of functions $\phi_1(z, z'), \phi_2(z, z'), \ldots, \phi_n(z, z')$, associated with the respective regions $R_1, R_2, \ldots, R_n$; and we define $\phi_p(z, z')$ as the value of $\Phi(z, z')$ within the region R_p. A point P' in the z'-plane may lie within a region; it may lie upon the boundary of two contiguous regions; and it may be a point of concurrence of several such boundaries.

When the point P' lies within the region R_p, the function $\phi_p(z, z')$ as defined is regular, because the sections of $\Phi(z, z')$ are only the boundaries of regions.

When the point P' lies on a boundary of the region R_p, say on the line l_{pq} so that R_q is the contiguous region, and when P' does not lie at either extremity of l_{pq}, the analytical continuation of $\phi_p(z, z')$ through the point P' remains regular. For, writing

$$g_{pq}(z, z') = f_q(z, z') - f_p(z, z'),$$

so that $g_{pq}(z, z')$ is regular for all the values of z and z' considered, the earlier investigation shews that, in crossing the section l_{pq}, the change in the analytical continuation of I_{pq} is $-g_{pq}(z, z')$ when l_{pq}, as it is crossed, is being described positively. For this position of P', every element in the sum of the functions I_{km} is regular except I_{pq}; and therefore the change in the analytical continuation of $\Phi(z, z')$ is $-g_{pq}(z, z')$. But the new function $\phi_q(z, z')$ is the value of $\Phi(z, z')$ in the region R_q; hence

$$\phi_q(z, z') = \phi_p(z, z') - g_{pq}(z, z'),$$

and therefore
$$\phi_q(z, z') + f_q(z, z') = \phi_p(z, z') + f_p(z, z'),$$
where R_p and R_q are contiguous regions.

When the point P' is a point of concurrence of several boundaries, the regions may be taken as in the figure. Our function $\Phi(z, z')$ can be rearranged in its summation. We group together all the integrals I_{km} which have no section passing through P'; and we call this group $\Phi_1(z, z')$. We group together all the remaining integrals, the section of each of which passes through P'; and we call this group $\Phi_2(z, z')$. Thus
$$\Phi(z, z') = \Phi_1(z, z') + \Phi_2(z, z').$$

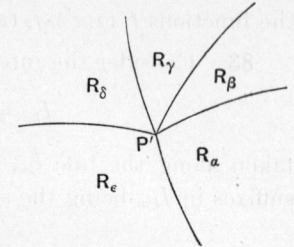

The sum $\Phi_1(z, z')$ is regular at P', because every element I in the sum is regular.

As regards the sum $\Phi_2(z, z')$, our earlier investigation shews that the function
$$\Phi_2(z, z') - \frac{1}{2\pi i} \{\log(P' - z')\} \Sigma g(z, z')$$
is regular at P'. But the functions $g(z, z')$, for the various elements I in $\Phi_2(z, z')$ taken as in the figure, are
$$f_\beta(z, z') - f_\alpha(z, z'),$$
$$f_\gamma(z, z') - f_\beta(z, z'),$$
$$f_\delta(z, z') - f_\gamma(z, z'),$$
$$f_\epsilon(z, z') - f_\delta(z, z'),$$
$$f_\alpha(z, z') - f_\epsilon(z, z'),$$
that is, the quantity $\Sigma g(z, z')$ is identically zero. Hence the sum $\Phi_2(z, z')$ is regular at P'.

Consequently, the function $\Phi(z, z')$ is regular at P', in this third case; and therefore all the functions $\phi(z, z')$, equivalent to one another at P', are regular at that point.

We thus have a set of functions $\phi(z, z')$. Each of them is regular within its own region. Each of them is regular at any point of concurrence of the boundaries of several regions. The change in the analytical continuation, from the function $\phi_p(z, z')$ belonging to a region R_p, to the function $\phi_q(z, z')$ belonging to a contiguous region R_q, is known; we have
$$\phi_q(z, z') - \phi_p(z, z') = f_p(z, z') - f_q(z, z').$$

The last relation gives
$$\phi_p(z, z') + f_p(z, z') = \phi_q(z, z') + f_q(z, z')$$

as a relation holding between two contiguous regions R_p and R_q. Let R_r be a region contiguous to R_q and distinct from R_p; then

$$\phi_q(z, z') + f_q(z, z') = \phi_r(z, z') + f_r(z, z').$$

And so on, for each region in succession, until the whole domain considered is covered.

Accordingly, we define a new function $F(z, z')$, by the relation

$$F(z, z') = \phi_r(z, z') + f_r(z, z')$$

for every region R_r. But all these different expressions for $F(z, z')$ are the same, because the relation

$$\phi_l(z, z') + f_l(z, z') = \phi_m(z, z') + f_m(z, z')$$

holds for any two contiguous regions within the domain. This final function $F(z, z')$, at every place within the domain, is equivalent to the assigned function $f_m(z, z')$ belonging to the region which, within that domain, includes the place; and the expression for this function $F(z, z')$ is

$$F(z, z') = f_m(z, z') + \phi_m(z, z'),$$

where $\phi_m(z, z')$ is regular in the domain of the place. The expression for $F(z, z')$ is valid over the domain considered; and the argument establishes the existence of the function $F(z, z')$, possessing the property that it is equivalent to each of the functions $f_1, \ldots, f_n$ in their respective domains.

84. The result can be extended. We can substitute a single function $F(z, z')$ for the aggregate of functions $f_m(z, z')$ within the aggregate of regions $R_1, \ldots, R_n$. When this aggregate of regions is denoted by S, we infer that a function $F(z, z')$ exists which, within this aggregate region S, possesses all the characteristics of the functions $f_m(z, z')$; it is subject to an additive function $\phi(z, z')$ which is regular throughout the region S.

Now take a number of these corporate regions S. It is not difficult to see that all the conditions for the individual functions $f_m(z, z')$ can be transferred, in each such region S, to the function $F(z, z')$ for these regions. The functions $F(z, z')$ for the different regions S are then taken as the elements for the composition of a new function which may be denoted by $\mathfrak{F}(z, z')$; and this new function $\mathfrak{F}(z, z')$ is equivalent, over the whole aggregate of these corporate regions, to the functions $f_m(z, z')$ which exist in any part of it. Thus we infer the existence of a function $\mathfrak{F}(z, z')$ which is such that, in the vicinity of any place in the finite part of the field of variation where a uniform analytic function $f_m(z, z')$ is not regular, the quantity

$$\mathfrak{F}(z, z') - f_m(z, z')$$

is a regular function of the variables. But it must be remembered that only a finite part of the field is considered and that the whole number of functions $f_m(z, z')$ is finite.

85. In the establishment of the preceding result, which is of the nature of a summation theorem, all the functions $f_r(z, z')$ were assumed to be uniform and analytic. There is a corresponding result, which is of greater importance for our investigation; it is of the nature of a product theorem, and the associated functions are logarithms of regular functions.

The z'-plane is divided into regions $R_1, \ldots, R_n$ as before; with each region R_k we associate a regular function $u_k(z, z')$, and we take

$$f_k(z, z') = \log u_k(z, z'),$$

so that the value of $f_k(z, z')$ is subject to additive integer multiples of $2\pi i$, and otherwise is a regular function of z and z' except at places which are zero-places of $u_k(z, z')$.

As regards the functions $u_1(z, z'), \ldots, u_n(z, z')$, we assume that, over any area common to two contiguous regions R_k and R_m or, if no area is common, along the part of their boundary which is common to them, the function

$$\frac{u_k(z, z')}{u_m(z, z')}$$

is regular and different from zero. Consequently the function

$$f_k(z, z') - f_m(z, z')$$

is regular for the same range of the variables, subject to a possible additive integer multiple of $2\pi i$.

We now proceed as before. We again form the integrals

$$I_{km} = \frac{1}{2\pi i} \int \frac{f_m(z, Z') - f_k(z, Z')}{Z' - z'} dZ',$$

taken along the line l_{km} which is the boundary common to two contiguous regions; the order of the suffixes in I_{km} is the same as their order in l_{km}, and clearly

$$I_{km} = I_{mk}.$$

The function $f_m(z, Z') - f_k(z, Z')$ is regular along the line l_{km}, and there is nothing to cause a change in the additive multiple of $2\pi i$ when once this multiple has been assigned; thus the integral is of the same character as the integral previously denoted by $\chi(z, z')$, and the line l_{km} is a section for the integral I_{km}.

Again, as before, we take

$$\Phi(z, z') = \Sigma I_{km},$$

where the summation is for all pairs of suffixes that correspond to contiguous regions. The function $\Phi(z, z')$ has each line l_{km} as a section.

At any point P' lying within a region, the function $\Phi(z, z')$ is regular.

At any point P', which lies on a boundary of the region R_p (say on the line l_{pq} so that R_q is the contiguous region) and does not lie at either extremity of l_{pq}, the analytical continuation of $\Phi(z, z')$ from R_p to R_q through z' is regular, the function in R_q being

$$\Phi(z, z') - \{f_q(z, z') - f_p(z, z')\},$$

where the additive multiple of $2\pi i$ is the same as in the integral I_{pq}.

When the point P' is at b', a point of concurrence of several boundaries which may be taken as before, it is again necessary to rearrange the summation of $\Phi(z, z')$. We group together all the integrals having no section passing through b', and call the sum of this group $\Phi_1(z, z')$. We then group together all the remaining integrals, the section of each of which passes through b'; and we call the sum of this group $\Phi_2(z, z')$. Thus

$$\Phi(z, z') = \Phi_1(z, z') + \Phi_2(z, z').$$

Each element I in the first sum $\Phi_1(z, z')$ is regular at b'; and therefore $\Phi_1(z, z')$ itself is regular at b'.

As regards $\Phi_2(z, z')$, our earlier investigation shews that the function

$$\Phi_2(z, z') - \frac{1}{2\pi i} \{\log(b' - z')\} \Sigma g(z, z')$$

is regular at b', the summation being over all the lines l which meet at b'. Now these functions $g(z, z')$, for the various elements I in $\Phi_2(z, z')$ taken as in the former figure (§ 83), are

$$f_\beta(z, z') - f_\alpha(z, z'),$$
$$f_\gamma(z, z') - f_\beta(z, z'),$$
$$f_\delta(z, z') - f_\gamma(z, z'),$$
$$f_\epsilon(z, z') - f_\delta(z, z'),$$
$$f_\alpha(z, z') - f_\epsilon(z, z'),$$

respectively, subject—for each of the functions $g(z, z')$—to an additive integer multiple of $2\pi i$. Accordingly, the quantity $\Sigma g(z, z')$ is some integer multiple of $2\pi i$; let it be denoted by $k \cdot 2\pi i$. It follows that the function

$$\Phi_2(z, z') - k \log(b' - z')$$

is regular at the place b'.

We have seen that $\Phi_1(z, z')$ is regular at b'; hence

$$\Phi(z, z') - k \log(b' - z')$$

is regular at the place b'.

At any point of concurrence of boundaries b'', other than b', the function $\log(b' - z')$ is regular, subject to an added multiple of $2\pi i$. Consequently, the function
$$\Phi(z, z') - \Sigma\{k \log(b' - z')\},$$
where the summation is taken over all the points of concurrence of the boundaries of regions, is regular for all places z' in the range considered; its expression being always subject to an additive integer multiple of $2\pi i$. Let this function be denoted by $\psi(z, z')$; then
$$\psi(z, z') = \Phi(z, z') - \Sigma\{k \log(b' - z')\}.$$
Subject to the added multiple of $2\pi i$, the function $\psi(z, z')$ is regular for the z'-region considered: and its sections are the lines l_{pq}.

Having constructed this function $\psi(z, z')$, we now take functions $\psi_1(z, z')$, $\psi_2(z, z'), \ldots, \psi_n(z, z')$, associating them with the regions $R_1, R_2, \ldots, R_n$ respectively, and defining them by the condition that the relation
$$\psi_m(z, z') = \psi(z, z')$$
is satisfied within and on the boundary of R_m, for all the values of m. When we pass across the boundary of R_m into a contiguous region R_p, we change to another function $\psi_p(z, z')$. But, as we have seen, the analytical change in $\psi(z, z')$ in passing over a line l_{mp} is
$$-\{f_p(z, z') - f_m(z, z')\},$$
and so the analytical continuation of $\psi_m(z, z')$ is
$$\psi_m(z, z') - \{f_p(z, z') - f_m(z, z')\}.$$
As this is the function $\psi_p(z, z')$, we have
$$\psi_p(z, z') = \psi_m(z, z') - \{f_p(z, z') - f_m(z, z')\},$$
there always being an additive multiple of $2\pi i$ on the right-hand side. Hence, subject to this additive multiple, we have
$$\psi_m(z, z') + f_m(z, z') = \psi_p(z, z') + f_p(z, z'),$$
for contiguous regions R_m and R_p.

Now pass from R_p to another contiguous region R_q, distinct from R_m; then, again subject to an additive multiple of $2\pi i$, we have
$$\psi_p(z, z') + f_p(z, z') = \psi_q(z, z') + f_q(z, z').$$
And so on, for the full succession of contiguous regions, until the whole z'-range is covered. It follows then that, for any two regions R_m and R_μ, we have the relation
$$\psi_m(z, z') + f_m(z, z') = \psi_\mu(z, z') + f_\mu(z, z'),$$
always subject to an additive integer multiple of $2\pi i$; and each of the functions ψ is regular within its own region.

Accordingly, we define a new function $G(z, z')$ by the equation

$$G(z, z') = \psi_m(z, z') + f_m(z, z'),$$

for every region R_m. But all these different expressions for $G(z, z')$ are the same as one another (save for an additive multiple of $2\pi i$ which may change from region to region), because the relation

$$\psi_m(z, z') + f_m(z, z') = \psi_\mu(z, z') + f_\mu(z, z')$$

is satisfied for all values of m and μ.

Finally, take a new function $U(z, z')$ defined by the equation

$$U(z, z') = e^{G(z, z')}.$$

The added integer multiple of $2\pi i$ in $G(z, z')$ does not affect the character of $U(z, z')$; and so we have

$$U(z, z') = e^{G(z, z')}$$
$$= e^{\psi_m(z, z') + f_m(z, z')}$$
$$= u_m(z, z') e^{\psi_m(z, z')}$$

within the region R_m. We thus have established the result:—

A function $U(z, z')$ exists, regular throughout the whole finite region considered, such that the quotient

$$\frac{U(z, z')}{u_m(z, z')}$$

is a regular function of z and z' within the region R_m and is different from zero, $u_m(z, z')$ being itself a regular function within that region; and this holds for all the n values of m.

Again it must be remembered that n, the number of functions $u_m(z, z')$, is finite.

The general theorem.

86. After these two propositions, which are general in character and the second of which is immediately useful for our purpose, we can proceed to the establishment of the general theorem, stated by Weierstrass, as to the expression of a function of two variables, of which the essential singularities occur only for infinite values of either or of both the variables.

It has been proved that, in the immediate vicinity of a zero-place of a uniform analytic function $f(z, z')$, we have

$$f(z, z') = P e^R,$$

where P is a polynomial in z having, as coefficients of powers of z, regular functions of z', or conversely as between z and z', and where R is a regular function of z and z' which vanishes when $z = 0$ and $z' = 0$.

We have defined a pole of a uniform analytic function $F(z, z')$ as a place, where a function $f(z, z')$ of the preceding form exists such that

$$F(z, z') f(z, z')$$

is a regular function of z and z', which does not vanish at the supposed pole or in its immediate vicinity.

We have defined an unessential singularity of a uniform analytic function $F(z, z')$ as a place, where two functions $f(z, z')$ and $g(z, z')$ of the preceding type, and irreducible relatively to one another, are such that

$$F(z, z') \frac{g(z, z')}{f(z, z')}$$

is a regular function of z and z' which does not vanish at the supposed singularity.

Suppose, then, that a function $P(z, z')$ is defined as being uniform and analytic over the whole field of variation: that it has poles and unessential singularities of defined type within that field: that it has no essential singularities except within the infinite parts of the field of variation of the two complex variables: and that, except for the poles, and for the unessential singularities, the function otherwise is regular for finite values of the variables z and z'.

For the expression of the function, we need take account only of functions $f(z, z')$ which give rise to poles, and of functions $f(z, z')$ and $g(z, z')$ which give rise to unessential singularities. We range these functions in two classes. In one class, we include all the denominator functions $f(z, z')$; in the other class, we include all the numerator functions $g(z, z')$.

Let $f(z, z')$ be typical of all the denominators, which occur in the expression of the function at a pole and its immediate vicinity; and let $\bar{f}(z, z')$ be typical of all the denominators, which occur in the expression of the function at an unessential singularity. We proceed to construct a function $G(z, z')$ such that, in the immediate vicinity of any of these places, the quotient

$$\frac{G(z, z')}{f(z, z')} \quad \text{or} \quad \frac{G(z, z')}{\bar{f}(z, z')}$$

is regular and different from zero; the function $G(z, z')$ exists, and is regular, in the whole finite part of the field of variation.

Again, let $g(z, z')$ be typical of all the numerators which occur in the expression of the function at an unessential singularity. Analysis, precisely similar to that used for the establishment of the function $G(z, z')$, enables us to establish the existence of a function $\bar{G}(z, z')$ such that, in the immediate vicinity of any such place, the quotient

$$\frac{\bar{G}(z, z')}{g(z, z')}$$

is regular and different from zero; the function $\bar{G}(z, z')$ exists, and is regular, in the whole finite part of the field of variation.

Accordingly, we consider the possibility of the existence of the functions $G(z, z')$, $\bar{G}(z, z')$.

87. Imagine a succession of regions in the field of variation, each region enclosing the one before it in the succession. We shall take, as the boundaries of the regions, concentric circles in the respective planes; and these may be denoted by (C_1, C_1'), (C_2, C_2'), ..., which may be unlimited in number, as we proceed to cover the whole field of variation. We also take the common centres of the circles at the respective origins.

For the first region, there is only a limited number of functions $f_m(z, z')$, each of which is regular at, and in the immediate vicinity of, its place of definition. Hence, by § 85, there is a function, say U_1, which is regular throughout the region and is such that the quotient

$$\frac{U_1}{f_m(z, z')}$$

is a regular function of z and z' within the region and is different from zero; and this holds for each of the functions $f_m(z, z')$ defined within the region.

For the second region, there are all the functions $f_m(z, z')$, which are defined for places in the first region; and there are the additional functions, which lie in the belt between the two regions (including the boundary of the first region). Then, again by § 85, there is a function U_2 which is regular throughout the second region and is such that, (i) the quotient $\dfrac{U_2}{U_1}$ is a regular function throughout the region and is different from zero, and (ii) the quotient

$$\frac{U_2}{f_n(z, z')},$$

where $f_n(z, z')$ is any one of the newly included additional functions, is a regular function of z and z' within the region and is different from zero; and this holds for each of these functions $f_n(z, z')$.

And so on, from each region to the region next in succession; we obtain a gradual succession of functions $U_1, U_2, \ldots, U_r, \ldots$, each regular in its region, and having the properties, (i) that $\dfrac{U_{r+1}}{U_r}$ is a regular function throughout the region (C_r, C_r') and is different from zero, and (ii) that, for each of the functions $f_s(z, z')$ defined for the region (C_{r+1}, C'_{r+1}) but not for the region (C_r, C_r'), the quotient

$$\frac{U_{r+1}}{f_s(z, z')}$$

is regular for the region (C_{r+1}, C'_{r+1}) and is different from zero.

88. Take a converging series of positive quantities $\alpha_1, \alpha_2, \ldots, \alpha_r, \ldots,$ associating them in order with the successive regions, so that α_r is associated with the region (C_r, C_r'). Also, let

$$\frac{U_{r+1}}{U_r} = \rho_r;$$

then the regular functions $U_1, U_2, \ldots$ can be chosen so as to give

$$|\rho_r| < e^{\alpha_r},$$

for each value of r.

Suppose that $U_1, \ldots, U_s$ have been chosen so as to satisfy this relation for $r = 1, \ldots, s-1$. The function U_{s+1}/U_s is regular throughout the region (C_s, C_s') and is different from zero there; and therefore

$$\log U_{s+1} - \log U_s$$

is (save as to an additive integer multiple of $2\pi i$) a regular function of z and z' throughout the region. This regular function, save as to the additive multiple of $2\pi i$, can be expressed as a double power-series in z and z' converging absolutely within the region. Let this series be denoted by

$$\sum_{m=0}^{\infty} \sum_{n=0}^{\infty} c_{m,n} z^m z'^n;$$

let M be the (finite) greatest value of its modulus within the region; and let R and R' be the radii of the circles C_s, C_s'. Choose values, μ_s of m, and ν_s of n, sufficiently large to secure that

$$\frac{M}{\left\{1 - \frac{|z|}{R}\right\}\left\{1 - \frac{|z'|}{R'}\right\}} \left\{\frac{|z|}{R}\right\}^{\mu_s} < \tfrac{1}{3}\alpha_s,$$

$$\frac{M}{\left\{1 - \frac{|z|}{R}\right\}\left\{1 - \frac{|z'|}{R'}\right\}} \left\{\frac{|z'|}{R'}\right\}^{\nu_s} < \tfrac{1}{3}\alpha_s,$$

$$\frac{M}{\left\{1 - \frac{|z|}{R}\right\}\left\{1 - \frac{|z'|}{R'}\right\}} \left\{\frac{|z|}{R}\right\}^{\mu_s+1} \left\{\frac{|z'|}{R'}\right\}^{\nu_s+1} < \tfrac{1}{3}\alpha_s,$$

the third of the inequalities being satisfied when the first two are satisfied. Then, writing

$$P_s = \sum_{m=0}^{\mu_s} \sum_{n=0}^{\nu_s} c_{m,n} z^m z'^n,$$

so that P_s is a polynomial in z and z'; and also

$$Q_s = \left(\sum_{m=\mu_s}^{\infty} \sum_{n=0}^{\infty} + \sum_{m=0}^{\infty} \sum_{n=\nu_s}^{\infty} - \sum_{m=\mu_s+1}^{\infty} \sum_{n=\nu_s+1}^{\infty}\right) c_{m,n} z^m z'^n,$$

so that

$$|Q_s| < \tfrac{1}{3}\alpha_s + \tfrac{1}{3}\alpha_s + \tfrac{1}{3}\alpha_s < \alpha_s;$$

we have

$$\log U_{s+1} - \log U_s = P_s + Q_s,$$

save as to an additive integer multiple of $2\pi i$. Consequently
$$\frac{U_{s+1} e^{-P_s}}{U_s} = e^{Q_s},$$
where now the multiple of $2\pi i$ no longer affects the functions concerned. Let
$$U'_{s+1} = U_{s+1} e^{-P_s},$$
so that
$$\frac{U'_{s+1}}{U_s} = e^{Q_s}.$$

The function U'_{s+1}, within the region (C_s, C_s'), possesses all the properties of U_{s+1}, because e^{-P_s} within that region is a regular function of z and z' which vanishes nowhere in the finite part of the field; thus U'_{s+1}/U_s is everywhere regular in that region and nowhere vanishes there, and the quotient
$$\frac{U'_{s+1}}{f_k(z, z')},$$
for each of the functions $f_k(z, z')$ defined for the region between (C_{s+1}, C'_{s+1}) and (C_s, C_s'), is everywhere regular for the region (C_{s+1}, C'_{s+1}) and vanishes nowhere in the region. Accordingly, we substitute U'_{s+1} for U_{s+1}; we write
$$e^{Q_s} = \rho_s,$$
so that
$$|\rho_s| < e^{a_s};$$
and we now have
$$\frac{U'_{s+1}}{U_s} = \rho_s,$$
with the condition $|\rho_s| < e^{a_s}$ satisfied.

89. For any region (C_q, C_q'), we define a function $G_q(z, z')$ by the form
$$G_q(z, z') = U_q' \prod_{t=1}^{\infty} \rho_{q+t}.$$

The function U_q' is regular everywhere within the region. The product
$$\prod_{t+1}^{\infty} \rho_{q+t}$$
is regular there; for its modulus
$$= \prod_{t+1}^{\infty} |\rho_{q+t}|$$
$$< e^{\Sigma a_{q+t}},$$
which is a finite quantity because of the convergence of the series of positive quantities $a_1, a_2, \ldots$; and, within the region, no one of the quantities ρ_{q+1}, $\rho_{q+2}, \ldots$ vanishes, while each of them is regular there. Thus within the region, the function
$$\frac{G_q(z, z')}{f_q(z, z')}$$
is everywhere regular, and nowhere zero, within the region (C_q, C_q'), for each of the functions $f_l(z, z')$ defined within the region.

F.

Next, take a function $G_{q+p}(z, z')$, defined for the region (C_{q+p}, C'_{q+p}). We have
$$G_{q+p}(z, z') = U'_{q+p} \prod_{t=1}^{\infty} \rho_{q+p+t}.$$
Also
$$G_q(z, z') = U'_q \prod_{t'=1}^{\infty} \rho_{q+t'}$$
$$= U'_q \prod_{t'=1}^{p} \rho_{q+t'} \prod_{t=1}^{\infty} \rho_{p+q+t}$$
$$= U'_q \cdot \frac{U'_{q+1}}{U'_q} \cdot \ldots \cdot \frac{U'_{q+p}}{U'_{q+p-1}} \prod_{t=1}^{\infty} \rho_{p+q+t}$$
$$= G_{q+p}(z, z').$$

Thus all the functions G_q are one and the same; let this function, the same for all the regions, be denoted by $G(z, z')$. Then the function $G(z, z')$ exists; it is regular everywhere over the field of variation considered, that is, for all finite values of the variables z and z'; and it is such that at, and in the immediate vicinity of, any place where a typical function $f(z, z')$ is defined, the quotient
$$\frac{G(z, z')}{f(z, z')}$$
is regular and different from zero.

We thus have established the existence of the function denoted by $G(z, z')$.

In precisely the same way, we can establish the existence of the function denoted by $\bar{G}(z, z')$.

90. Now take the quotient
$$\Theta(z, z') = \frac{\bar{G}(z, z')}{G(z, z')}.$$

This function $\Theta(z, z')$ has unessential singularities at all the places where $\bar{G}$ and G vanish simultaneously, that is, at all the places where associated functions $g(z, z')$ and $\bar{f}(z, z')$ vanish simultaneously; in other words, $\Theta(z, z')$ possesses, in exact and precise form for each of them, all the unessential singularities possessed by the function $P(z, z')$ of § 86. Again $\Theta(z, z')$ has poles at all the places where $G(z, z')$ is zero while $\bar{G}(z, z')$ is different from zero, that is, at all the places, where the functions $f(z, z')$ vanish while the functions $g(z, z')$ do not vanish: in other words, $\Theta(z, z')$ possesses, in exact and precise form, all the poles possessed by the function $P(z, z')$. Neither $\Theta(z, z')$ nor, by hypothesis, $P(z, z')$ has any essential singularity for finite values of z and z'; and at all places, other than isolated unessential singularities and other than the continuous aggregates of poles, both $\Theta(z, z')$ and $P(z, z')$ are regular functions. Hence
$$\frac{P(z, z')}{\Theta(z, z')}$$

is a function that is regular everywhere in the domain constituted by all finite values of z and z'; denoting this regular function by $R(z, z')$, we have

$$P(z, z') = \Theta(z, z') R(z, z')$$
$$= \frac{\bar{G}(z, z') R(z, z')}{G(z, z')}.$$

Now $\bar{G}(z, z')$ is a function that is regular for all finite values of z and z'; consequently the product $\bar{G}(z, z') R(z, z')$ is a function that is regular for all finite values of z and z'. Denoting this product by $H(z, z')$, we have

$$P(z, z') = \frac{H(z, z')}{G(z, z')}$$

as the final expression of our function; and, in this expression, the functions $H(z, z')$ and $G(z, z')$ are regular for all finite values of z and z'. We thus have the theorem:—

When a uniform analytic function of two variables possesses only unessential singularities for finite values of the variables, it can be expressed as the quotient of two functions, each of which is regular for all finite values of the variables; and the quotient is irreducible.

The last statement in the theorem follows from the construction of the functions $\bar{G}(z, z')$ and $G(z, z')$. A quotient $g(z, z') \div \bar{f}(z, z')$ is irreducible at an unessential singularity; there is no question of the reducibility of a function $\{f(z, z')\}^{-1}$ in the vicinity of any pole; and $R(z, z')$ is regular for all finite values of z and z'.

Note. In the particular case where the uniform analytic function has no essential singularity within the whole field of variation of z and z', both the functions $H(z, z')$ and $G(z, z')$ are devoid of essential singularities within that whole field; that is, they must be polynomials in z and z'. We thus again have the earlier theorem already (§ 78) established.

For further developments from the results now proved, reference should be made to Cousin's memoir.

Appell's Examples.

91. Such is the general existence-theorem, obtained in the product-form. There is a corresponding theorem, in a sum-form. Simpler expressions may be obtainable in particular cases, when the functions $f_m(z, z')$ or $u_k(z, z')$ are known.

As an example of the sum-theorem, for a particular class of functions, Appell[*] proceeds as follows, in a generalisation of Weierstrass's proof of Mittag-Leffler's theorem on functions of a single variable[†]. The set of

---

[*] *Acta Math.*, t. ii (1883), pp. 71—80.
[†] For references, see my *Theory of Functions*, ch. vii.

uniform analytic functions $f_1(z, z')$, $f_2(z, z')$, ... is supposed to have the property that for all integers n, greater than some definite integer N, we can assign a magnitude r_n such that $f_n(z, z')$ is holomorphic for all values of z and z' given by $|z| < r_n$, $|z'| < r_n$, and such also that r_n increases indefinitely with n.

Let $\epsilon_1, \epsilon_2, ..., \epsilon_n, ...$ be a converging series of positive quantities, and let ϵ denote a positive quantity less than unity. Take first the sum of the functions $f_1(z, z'), f_2(z, z'), ..., f_N(z, z')$; and write

$$F_1(z, z') = \sum_{m=1}^{N} f_m(z, z').$$

Next, consider the functions $f_n(z, z')$ such that $n > N$; as each of them is regular for values of z and z' such that

$$|z| \leqslant \epsilon r_n, \quad |z'| \leqslant \epsilon r_n,$$

we can express $f_n(z, z')$ in a form

$$f_n(z, z') = \sum_{p=0}^{\infty} \sum_{q=0}^{\infty} c_{p,q}^{(n)} z^p z'^q,$$

where the double series converges absolutely. As in § 88, we can assign a positive integer μ_n, taking μ_n to be the greater of the two integers μ_s and ν_s there assigned, such that

$$\left| \left\{ \sum_{p=\mu_n}^{\infty} \sum_{q=0}^{\infty} + \sum_{p=0}^{\infty} \sum_{q=\mu_n}^{\infty} - \sum_{p=1+\mu_n}^{\infty} \sum_{q=1+\mu_n}^{\infty} \right\} c_{p,q}^{(n)} z^p z'^q \right| \leqslant \epsilon_n,$$

for all the values of z and z' considered. Hence, denoting by $\phi_n(z, z')$ the polynomial

$$\phi_n(z, z') = \sum_{p=0}^{\mu_n-1} \sum_{q=0}^{\mu_n-1} c_{p,q}^{(n)} z^p z'^q,$$

and constructing a function

$$F_2(z, z') = \sum_{n=N+1}^{\infty} \{f_n(z, z') - \phi_n(z, z')\},$$

we have, on the right-hand side, a series which converges absolutely for the values of z and z' considered.

Now consider the sum

$$F(z, z') = F_1(z, z') + F_2(z, z').$$

The function

$$F(z, z') - f_m(z, z')$$

is regular at all the singularities of $f_m(z, z')$; and so the function $F(z, z')$ is regular at all places in the field of variation which are not singularities of any of the functions $f_1(z, z'), f_2(z, z'), ...$; and $F(z, z')$, at places which are singularities of a function $f(z, z')$, is non-regular in the same way as $f(z, z')$.

92. As a special instance of this sum-theorem, Appell adduces the case when
$$f_{mn}(z, z') = \frac{1}{\{(z+m)^2 + (z'+n)^2 + a^2\}^s},$$
where s is a positive integer, a is a constant, and the different functions $f_{mn}(z, z')$ arise by assigning to m and to n, independently of one another, all integer values from $-\infty$ to $+\infty$.

We have
$$|(z+m)^2 + (z'+n)^2 + a^2| > |(z+m)^2 + (z'+n)^2| - |a|^2.$$
Also
$$(z+m)^2 + (z'+n)^2 = (z + iz' + m + in)(z - iz' + m - in).$$
But
$$|z + iz' + m + in| > |m + in| - |z + iz'|$$
$$> (m^2 + n^2)^{\frac{1}{2}} - |z| - |z'|,$$
and
$$|z - iz' + m - in| > (m^2 + n^2)^{\frac{1}{2}} - |z| - |z'|.$$
Hence, if
$$|z| \leqslant \tfrac{1}{2} \{(m^2 + n^2)^{\frac{1}{2}} - |a| - c\},$$
$$|z'| \leqslant \tfrac{1}{2} \{(m^2 + n^2)^{\frac{1}{2}} - |a| - c\},$$
we have
$$|(z+m)^2 + (z'+n)^2| > \{|a| + c\}^2;$$
and therefore
$$|(z+m)^2 + (z'+n)^2 + a^2| > \{|a| + c\}^2 - |a|^2$$
$$> 2c|a| + c^2.$$

Consequently, for all values of z and z' within a range that increases indefinitely with m and n, as given by the foregoing limits, $|f_{mn}(z, z')|$ remains smaller than an assigned quantity; and so for those values, $f_{mn}(z, z')$ is a regular function. Thus the set of conditions for the function $f_{mn}(z, z')$ is satisfied.

When the integer s is greater than unity, the series
$$\sum_{-\infty}^{m=\infty} \sum_{-\infty}^{n=\infty} \frac{1}{\{(z+m)^2 + (z'+n)^2 + a^2\}^s}$$
converges absolutely. We therefore take
$$F(z, z') = \sum_{-\infty}^{m=\infty} \sum_{-\infty}^{n=\infty} \frac{1}{\{(z+m)^2 + (z'+n)^2 + a^2\}^s}.$$
The function $F(z, z')$ has poles at all the places
$$z = -m + ia \cos\theta, \quad z' = -n + ia \sin\theta,$$
for the continuous succession of values of θ and for all values of m and of n. Elsewhere, at all places in the field of variation, the function $F(z, z')$ is regular. In this case, there is no need to take polynomials corresponding to the functions $\phi_n(z, z')$ in the general investigation.

When the integer s is equal to unity, the expression of the function is not so simple, because the series, of which the general term is

$$\frac{1}{(z+m)^2+(z'+n)^2+a^2},$$

does not converge absolutely. We then take all the values of m and n, which are finite in number and are such that

$$(m^2+n^2)^{\frac{1}{2}} \leqslant |a|+c;$$

selecting all the functions $f_{mn}(z, z')$ given by these values of m and n, we denote their sum by $F_1(z, z')$.

Next, take the values of m and n which are such that

$$(m^2+n^2)^{\frac{1}{2}} > |a|+c,$$

and expand $f_{mn}(z, z')$, for any such pair of values, in powers of z and z', valid in a range

$$|z| \leqslant \tfrac{1}{2}\{(m^2+n^2)^{\frac{1}{2}} - |a| - c\}, \quad |z'| \leqslant \tfrac{1}{2}\{(m^2+n^2)^{\frac{1}{2}} - |a| - c\}.$$

Thus

$$f_{mn}(z, z') = \frac{1}{m^2+n^2+a^2} - \frac{2mz+2nz'}{(m^2+n^2+a^2)^2} + \dots.$$

For our purpose, it is sufficient to take the desired polynomial $\phi_{mn}(z, z')$ as equal merely to the constant term in the expansion; for the series

$$F_2(z, z') = \Sigma\Sigma \left\{ \frac{1}{(z+m)^2+(z'+n)+a^2} - \frac{1}{m^2+n^2+a^2} \right\},$$

for all such values of z and z', and for the doubly infinite set of values of m and n, converges absolutely. Our required function is

$$F(z, z') = F_1(z, z') + F_2(z, z').$$

It has poles at all the places

$$z = -m + ia\cos\theta, \quad z' = -n + ia\sin\theta,$$

for the continuous succession of values of θ, and for all integer values of m and n. At all other places in the finite part of the field of variation, the function $F(z, z')$ is regular.

93. As an example of the product-theorem, let $u_1(z, z')$, $u_2(z, z')$, ... denote a set of regular functions of z and z', and let them have the property that for all integers n, greater than some definite integer N, we can assign a magnitude r_n so that $u_n(z, z')$ is distinct from zero for values of z and z' such that $|z| < r_n$, $|z'| < r_n$ and such also that r_n increases indefinitely with n. Then denoting by $k_1, k_2, \dots$ a succession of positive integers, we can form a regular function $G(z, z')$, vanishing for all the values of z and z' which make $g_m(z, z')$ vanish, and vanishing in such a way as to make the quotient

$$\frac{G(z, z')}{\{g_m(z, z')\}^{k_m}}$$

finite and different from zero for those values.

This function $G(z, z')$ is of the form

$$G_1(z, z') G_2(z, z'),$$

where

$$G_1(z, z') = \prod_{m=1}^{N} \{g_m(z, z')\}^{k_m},$$

$$G_2(z, z') = \prod_{N+1}^{\infty} \{g_n(z, z')\}^{k_n} e^{\psi_n(z, z')},$$

while $\psi_n(z, z')$ is an appropriate polynomial in z and z'.

Ex. 1. Shew that, when

$$g_{mn}(z, z') = (z+m)^2 + (z'+n)^2 + a^2,$$

where m and n vary independently of one another through all integer values from $-\infty$ to $+\infty$, a function $G(z, z')$, regular everywhere in the finite part of the field and vanishing like $g_{mn}(z, z')$, can be constructed as follows. Take all the values of m and n, finite in number, such that

$$(m^2 + n^2)^{\frac{1}{2}} \leqslant |a| + c,$$

where a is any assumed finite quantity; and write

$$G_1(z, z') = \Pi\Pi \{(z+m)^2 + (z'+n)^2 + a^2\},$$

where the product extends over all these values of m and n.

Take all the values of m and n, doubly infinite in number, such that

$$(m^2 + n^2)^{\frac{1}{2}} > |a| + c,$$

and write

$$G_2(z, z') = \Pi\Pi \left\{ \frac{(z+m)^2 + (z'+n)^2 + a^2}{m^2 + n^2 + a^2} e^{-\psi_{mn}(z, z')} \right\},$$

where the product extends over all these values of m and n, and where

$$\psi_{mn}(z, z') = \frac{2mz + 2nz' + z^2 + z'^2}{m^2 + n^2 + a^2} - \frac{1}{2} \left(\frac{2mz + 2nz' + z^2 + z'^2}{m^2 + n^2 + a^2} \right)^2.$$

The required function is given by

$$G(z, z') = G_1(z, z') G_2(z, z').$$

Ex. 2. Verify that, when a is zero, the function $G(z, z')$ can be expressed by means of two Weierstrass's σ-functions.

CHAPTER VI

Integrals; in particular, Double Integrals

As regards the matter of this chapter and, above all, as regards integrals of algebraic functions of two variables, the student should pay special attention to various sections in the treatise (which usually is quoted here in Picard's name) Picard et Simart, *Théorie des fonctions algébriques de deux variables indépendantes*, t. i (1897), t. ii (1906). Other references will be found in the course of this chapter.

It may be noted initially, as regards algebraic functions of two variables, that I have chosen, for reasons already stated, to take two fundamental equations defining two independent algebraic functions of the variables, instead of only a single equation defining only a single algebraic function. If three (or more) equations were taken defining the same number of algebraic functions, these would not be independent; so it is sufficient to take not more than two fundamental equations.

94. In the theory of functions of a single variable, many important results are derived through the use of Cauchy's theorems concerning contour integrals. It is natural to attempt some extension of theorems so as similarly to derive results in the theory of functions of more than one variable. Here we shall restrict the discussion to the case of a couple of complex variables.

The integral of a function of two independent complex variables may be single or may be double. The definition of a single integral is the same as in the customary theory of functions of one complex variable; but there is the added complication through the occurrence of two complex variables. Either there is variation, within the range of the integral, of only one of the two variables; or within that range, there is a definitely connected and simultaneous variation of both variables.

Of double integrals, there are two classes. In one class, the integration with regard to each variable is entirely independent of the integration with regard to the other, so that the integrations can be performed in either order. In each integration, only one variable is subject to variation. Thus the double integral is effectively only a double operation of single integration. We have already had some examples, at an earlier stage, of this class of double integrals.

Ex. A function $f(\psi, \theta)$ is periodic in ψ, with period 2π, and is also periodic in θ, with period 2π; and it is regular for all values of the variables within the ranges of two complete respective periods. Let $u(r, r', \phi, \phi')$ denote the integral

$$\frac{1}{4\pi^2} \int_0^{2\pi} \int_0^{2\pi} f(\psi, \theta) \frac{(1-r^2)(1-r'^2)}{\{1 - 2r\cos(\psi-\phi)+r^2\}\{1 - 2r'\cos(\theta-\phi')+r'^2\}} d\psi d\theta.$$

Prove that, when $r < 1$ and $r' < 1$, the function $u(r, r', \phi, \phi')$ is regular; and that, in the limit when $r = 1$ and $r' = 1$, the function $u(r, r', \phi, \phi')$ is equal to $f(\phi, \phi')$.

Shew also that, if

$$z = re^{\phi i}, \quad z' = r'e^{\phi' i},$$

$u(r, r', \phi, \phi')$ is expressible as the real part of a regular function of the complex variables z and z'.

Note. This result will be noted as the extension of the simplest result, relating to potential functions of two real variables, in Schwarz's establishment of the existence of a function of one complex variable satisfying conditions of specified assigned types*.

95. In the other class of double integrals, the variations are not independent of one another; if either can be performed alone, usually the range of variation for the variable is affected by the other variable; and, in the general case, such integration cannot be performed for one variable alone. It then becomes imperative to define precisely what is the meaning assigned to the double integral. For this purpose, we adopt the procedure initiated by Poincaré †, using space of four dimensions in real variables.

As usual, we take

$$z = x + iy, \quad z' = x' + iy',$$

where x, y, x', y' are real and are the coordinates of a point in this space. Without further limitation, the variables x, y, x', y' are independent of one another.

For our immediate purpose, we now make two successive suppositions consistent with one another, so as to secure a working definition of a double integral.

First, let X, Y, Z be real variables of a point in ordinary space; and suppose that x, y, x', y' are limited in variation so as to be expressible in forms

$$x = F_1(X, Y, Z), \quad y = F_2(X, Y, Z), \quad x' = F_3(X, Y, Z), \quad y' = F_4(X, Y, Z),$$

where (for purposes of description) we assume that F_1, F_2, F_3, F_4 are rational functions of X, Y, Z not becoming infinite for real values of these variables. Eliminating X, Y, Z, we shall have an (algebraical) relation

$$\Phi(x, y, x', y') = 0,$$

---

* See my *Theory of Functions*, chap. xvii.

† *Acta Math.*, t. ix (1887), pp. 321—380. It is followed, in part, by Picard who has made great extensions, as also by other methods, of the properties of double integrals specially connected with algebraic functions; see his *Traité d'Analyse*, t. ii, ch. ix, and his *Théorie des fonctions algébriques de deux variables indépendantes*, already quoted.

which represents a three-dimensional continuum in the four-dimensional space.

Next, let X, Y, Z describe a surface S, or a portion of a surface S, in ordinary space. Again for purposes of illustration, we shall assume S, or the selected portion of S, to be devoid of singularities. We can take X, Y, Z as functions of two real parameters p and q, valid over the surface S or the portion of it; and we then have equations

$$x = g_1(p, q), \quad y = g_2(p, q), \quad x' = g_3(p, q), \quad y' = g_4(p, q).$$

These relations imply two equations, say

$$U(x, y, x', y') = 0, \quad V(x, x', y, y') = 0,$$

which represent a two-dimensional continuum (the surface S, as in § 5) in our four-dimensional space. We take a simple closed area in the plane of the variables p and q, represented by an equation

$$F(p, q) = 0;$$

and for the double integral, we allow all values of p and q within this area, representing them by the relation

$$F(p, q) \leqslant 0.$$

Then the limit of the range of integration on the surface S is given by $F(p, q) = 0$; and this limit will lead to three equations of the form

$$P_s(x, y, x', y') = 0, \quad (s = 1, 2, 3),$$

representing a curve in the four-dimensional space.

Now let $f(z, z')$ be the function, to be "doubly integrated" in the sense that a meaning has to be assigned to the double integral

$$I = \iint f(z, z') \, dz \, dz'.$$

As $f(z, z')$ is a complex function, we resolve it into its real and imaginary parts; let

$$f(z, z') = P + iQ,$$

where P and Q are real functions of x, y, x', y'. Then

$$I = \iint (P + iQ)(dx + idy)(dx' + idy')$$

$$= \iint \{(P + iQ) \, dx \, dx' + (iP - Q) \, dx \, dy' + (iP - Q) \, dy \, dx' - (P + iQ) \, dy \, dy'\}.$$

Manifestly I, whatever its value, can be a complex variable; so writing

$$I = I_1 + iI_2,$$

where I_1 and I_2 are real, we have

$$I_1 = \iint \{P(dx\,dx' - dy\,dy')\} - \iint \{Q(dx\,dy' + dy\,dx')\},$$

$$I_2 = \iint \{Q(dx\,dx' - dy\,dy')\} + \iint \{P(dx\,dy' + dy\,dx')\}.$$

And now, I_1 and I_2 are ordinary double integrals involving only real variables, for the real quantities x, y, x', y' are functions of only the real variables p and q; and these double integrals are taken over the limited area $F(p, q) \leqslant 0$ in the plane of the variables p and q.

Both integrals are of the form

$$\iint (A\,dx\,dx' + B\,dx\,dy' + C\,dy\,dx' + D\,dy\,dy'),$$

where all the quantities concerned are real—there being, of course, limitations upon the forms of A, B, C, D and also of their differential relations to one another. When we give explicit expression to the functionality of x, y, x', y' in terms of p and q, the integral becomes

$$\iint \left\{ AJ\left(\frac{x, x'}{p, q}\right) + BJ\left(\frac{x, y'}{p, q}\right) + CJ\left(\frac{y, x'}{p, q}\right) + DJ\left(\frac{y, y'}{p, q}\right) \right\} dp\,dq\,;$$

but for our purposes it will suffice to take the first form.

Our object is the generalisation, if generalisation be possible, of the fundamental theorem of Cauchy which asserts that, under appropriate conditions as to $f(z)$, the integral $\int f(z)\,dz$ taken round a closed contour is zero: it is a consequence that the integral $\int f(z)\,dz$, between two points in the plane, has a value independent (subject to restrictions) of the z-path between the points. Suppose that, instead of the former values of x, y, x', y', we take

$$x = h_1(p, q), \quad y = h_2(p, q), \quad x' = h_3(p, q), \quad y' = h_4(p, q),$$

so that we could have a new surface T different from S; and suppose that, corresponding to the former equation $F(p, q) = 0$ limiting the range of integration, the range of integration in T is still limited by $F(p, q) = 0$, and that the limiting curve connected with T in our four-dimensional space is given by the same equations

$$P_s(x, y, x', y') = 0, \quad (s = 1, 2, 3),$$

as the limiting curve connected with S. We thus should have two different surfaces passing through the same contour. Then the generalisation would be that the integral $\iint f(z, z')\,dz\,dz'$ should remain invariable if only the surface over which the integration extends is made to pass through an assigned fixed contour; or, if we take a completely closed surface through the fixed contour, the integral $\iint f(z, z') \, dz \, dz'$ taken over the whole of this surface vanishes.

96. Accordingly, we consider an integral

$$\Sigma\Sigma \iint A_{mn} \, dx_m \, dx_n,$$

where the summation is taken over all pairs of values $m, n = 1, 2, 3, 4$, and where x_1, x_2, x_3, x_4 take the place of x, y, x', y'. We define the integral for the four-dimensional space as above; consequently, because

$$\iint A_{mn} \, dx_m \, dx_n = \iint A_{mn} J\left(\frac{x_m, x_n}{x_n, x_m}\right) dx_n \, dx_m$$

with the foregoing interpretation, we have

$$\iint A_{mn} \, dx_m \, dx_n = -\iint A_{mn} \, dx_n \, dx_m,$$

and

$$\iint A_{nm} \, dx_n \, dx_m = -\iint A_{nm} \, dx_m \, dx_n;$$

that is, taking account of the whole integral and of the combinations of m and n instead of the permutations, we shall assume that

$$A_{mn} = -A_{nm},$$

so that we need only consider the combination $\iint A_{mn} \, dx_m \, dx_n$. Moreover, this process of regarding the integral obviously involves the additional assumptions

$$A_{mm} = 0,$$

for all the values of m.

Next, we take* x_1, x_2, x_3, x_4 as expressed in terms of the three variables X, Y, Z, so that our double integral becomes

$$\Sigma\Sigma \left[A_{mn} \left\{ J\left(\frac{x_m, x_n}{Y, Z}\right) dY \, dZ + J\left(\frac{x_m, x_n}{Z, X}\right) dZ \, dX + J\left(\frac{x_m, x_n}{X, Y}\right) dX \, dY \right\} \right],$$

that is,

$$\iint (\xi \, dY \, dZ + \eta \, dZ \, dX + \zeta \, dX \, dY),$$

where

$$\xi = \Sigma\Sigma A_{mn} J\left(\frac{x_m, x_n}{Y, Z}\right),$$

$$\eta = \Sigma\Sigma A_{mn} J\left(\frac{x_m, x_n}{Z, X}\right),$$

$$\zeta = \Sigma\Sigma A_{mn} J\left(\frac{x_m, x_n}{X, Y}\right).$$

---

* Here Picard's proof (*Traité d'Analyse*, t. ii, p. 270) is followed exactly.

The integral is to extend over the surface in the X, Y, Z ordinary space.

We therefore require the condition necessary and sufficient that such an integral
$$\iint (\xi\, dY\, dZ + \eta\, dZ\, dX + \zeta\, dX\, dY),$$
over any surface which passes through an assigned contour in the p, q plane, shall depend solely upon the contour. This condition is well known; we must have*
$$\frac{\partial \xi}{\partial X} + \frac{\partial \eta}{\partial Y} + \frac{\partial \zeta}{\partial Z} = 0.$$

Accordingly, the condition is
$$\frac{\partial}{\partial X}\left\{\Sigma\Sigma A_{mn} J\left(\frac{x_m,\ x_n}{Y,\ Z}\right)\right\} + \frac{\partial}{\partial Y}\left\{\Sigma\Sigma A_{mn} J\left(\frac{x_m,\ x_n}{Z,\ X}\right)\right\}$$
$$+ \frac{\partial}{\partial Z}\left\{\Sigma\Sigma A_{mn} J\left(\frac{x_m,\ x_n}{X,\ Y}\right)\right\} = 0.$$

In this expression, the coefficient of A_{mn} is
$$\frac{\partial}{\partial X}\left\{J\left(\frac{x_m,\ x_n}{Y,\ Z}\right)\right\} + \frac{\partial}{\partial Y}\left\{J\left(\frac{x_m,\ x_n}{Z,\ X}\right)\right\} + \frac{\partial}{\partial Z}\left\{J\left(\frac{x_m,\ x_n}{X,\ Y}\right)\right\},$$
which vanishes identically.

As regards the derivatives of A_{mn}, we have
$$\frac{\partial A_{mn}}{\partial X} = \sum_{l=1}^{4} \frac{\partial A_{mn}}{\partial x_l} \frac{\partial x_l}{\partial X},$$
and so for the others. Hence, in the foregoing expression, the coefficient of $\frac{\partial A_{mn}}{\partial x_m}$, and the coefficient of $\frac{\partial A_{mn}}{\partial x_n}$, both vanish identically; and the non-vanishing coefficients are the sum of terms of the form
$$\left(\frac{\partial A_{mn}}{\partial x_l} + \frac{\partial A_{nl}}{\partial x_m} + \frac{\partial A_{lm}}{\partial x_n}\right) J\left(\frac{x_l,\ x_m,\ x_n}{X,\ Y,\ Z}\right).$$

Consequently, the condition becomes
$$\sum_{l=1}^{4}\sum_{m=1}^{4}\sum_{n=1}^{4}\left\{\left(\frac{\partial A_{mn}}{\partial x_l} + \frac{\partial A_{nl}}{\partial x_m} + \frac{\partial A_{lm}}{\partial x_n}\right) J\left(\frac{x_l,\ x_m,\ x_n}{X,\ Y,\ Z}\right)\right\} = 0,$$

---

* When the condition is satisfied, we can take
$$\xi = \frac{\partial \gamma}{\partial Y} - \frac{\partial \beta}{\partial Z}, \quad \eta = \frac{\partial \alpha}{\partial Z} - \frac{\partial \gamma}{\partial X}, \quad \zeta = \frac{\partial \beta}{\partial X} - \frac{\partial \alpha}{\partial Y};$$
and then the integral can be expressed in the form
$$\int (\alpha\, dx + \beta\, dy + \gamma\, dz),$$
taken round the contour in the p, q plane. The result was first enunciated as a problem by Stokes, in the old examination for the Smith's Prizes at Cambridge in the year 1854; see Stokes, *Math. and Phys. Papers*, vol. v, p. 320, with a note by Prof. Sir J. Larmor.

a condition which must be satisfied identically, whatever be the surface over which the integration extends, subject to its passing through the contour.

The quantities x_l, x_m, x_n, x_p are functions of X, Y, Z such that, away from the contour, any three of them are independent of one another; and therefore the quantities

$$J\left(\frac{x_l, x_m, x_n}{X, Y, Z}\right),$$

except along the contour and individually at special places in space, are different from zero. It follows that we must have

$$\frac{\partial A_{mn}}{\partial x_l} + \frac{\partial A_{nl}}{\partial x_m} + \frac{\partial A_{lm}}{\partial x_n} = 0,$$

for all the combinations $l, m, n = 1, 2, 3, 4$. Moreover, it is easy to see that this set of four conditions is sufficient, as well as necessary, to secure that the value of the integral

$$\Sigma\Sigma \iint A_{mn} dx_m dx_n$$

depends only upon the contour.

97. Now let us apply all the conditions to the integrals I_1 and I_2. We have

$$I_1 = \iint (P dx dx' - Q dx dy' - Q dy dx' - P dy dy'),$$

and we take

$$x, y, x', y' = x_1, x_2, x_3, x_4,$$

respectively. We have

$$A_{12} = 0, \quad A_{13} = P, \quad A_{14} = -Q, \quad A_{23} = -Q, \quad A_{24} = -P, \quad A_{34} = 0$$

Consider the conditions

$$\frac{\partial A_{mn}}{\partial x_l} + \frac{\partial A_{nl}}{\partial x_m} + \frac{\partial A_{lm}}{\partial x_n} = 0,$$

for the combinations $l, m, n = 1, 2, 3, 4$. They require the relation

$$-\frac{\partial Q}{\partial x} - \frac{\partial P}{\partial y} = 0,$$

for $l, m, n = 1, 2, 3$; the relation

$$-\frac{\partial Q}{\partial y'} + \frac{\partial P}{\partial x'} = 0,$$

for $l, m, n = 2, 3, 4$; the relation

$$\frac{\partial Q}{\partial x'} + \frac{\partial P}{\partial y'} = 0,$$

for $l, m, n = 3, 4, 1$; and the relation
$$-\frac{\partial P}{\partial x} + \frac{\partial Q}{\partial y} = 0,$$
for $l, m, n = 4, 1, 2$.

Similarly, we have
$$I_2 = \iint \{Q\,dx\,dx' + P\,dx\,dy' + P\,dy\,dx' - Q\,dy\,dy'\},$$
so that we can take
$$A_{12} = 0, \quad A_{13} = Q, \quad A_{14} = P, \quad A_{23} = P, \quad A_{24} = -Q, \quad A_{34} = 0.$$
The general conditions require the relation
$$\frac{\partial P}{\partial x} - \frac{\partial Q}{\partial y} = 0,$$
for the combination $l, m, n = 1, 2, 3$; the relation
$$\frac{\partial P}{\partial y'} + \frac{\partial Q}{\partial x'} = 0,$$
for the combination $l, m, n = 2, 3, 4$; the relation
$$-\frac{\partial P}{\partial x'} + \frac{\partial Q}{\partial y'} = 0,$$
for the combination $l, m, n = 3, 4, 1$; and the relation
$$-\frac{\partial P}{\partial y} - \frac{\partial Q}{\partial x} = 0,$$
for the combination $l, m, n = 4, 1, 2$.

Thus all the conditions are satisfied if only
$$\frac{\partial P}{\partial x} = \frac{\partial Q}{\partial y}, \quad \frac{\partial P}{\partial y} = -\frac{\partial Q}{\partial x}, \quad \frac{\partial P}{\partial x'} = \frac{\partial Q}{\partial y'}, \quad \frac{\partial P}{\partial y'} = -\frac{\partial Q}{\partial x'}.$$
But, by definition, we have
$$P + iQ = f(z, z') = f(x + iy, x' + iy'),$$
where P, Q, x, y, x', y' are real; and so these four relations are satisfied.

It follows, then, that I_1 and I_2 depend solely upon the contour; and therefore $I, = I_1 + iI_2$, also depends solely upon the contour. And we have, throughout, assumed that the quantities P and Q,—that is, also the function $f(z, z')$—are free from singularities. Hence we have Poincaré's extension of Cauchy's theorem:—

If, within the closed surface S, which is taken in the space of three dimensions X, Y, Z, and points on which are given by equations of the form
$$X = f_1(p, q), \quad Y = f_2(p, q), \quad Z = f_3(p, q),$$
so that, along the surface,
$$x = F_1(X, Y, Z) = g_1(p, q), \quad y = F_2(X, Y, Z) = g_2(p, q),$$
$$x' = F_3(X, Y, Z) = g_3(p, q), \quad y' = F_4(X, Y, Z) = g_4(p, q),$$

there is no place X, Y, Z, where the function $f(z, z')$ ceases to be regular, the value of the integral $\iint f(z, z') \, dz \, dz'$ taken over the whole of the closed surface is zero.

Again, for such a function and over such a space, the value of the integral $\iint f(z, z') \, dz \, dz'$ taken over any portion of any such surface S bounded by a contour, the surface and the contour lying within the domain, depends only upon the contour.

Further, it follows that the value of the integral $\iint f(z, z') \, dz \, dz'$, taken over any such closed surface, remains unaltered during deformations of the surface provided they occur in the domain of X, Y, Z, and cross no place giving rise to no singularity of $f(z, z')$.

98. Now consider the singularities, or other deviations from regularity, of a function $f(z, z')$. We take the preceding surface S existing, as in § 95, in an ordinary space of three dimensions, the representation of the variables being
$$x = F_1(X, Y, Z), \quad y = F_2(X, Y, Z), \quad x' = F_3(X, Y, Z), \quad y' = F_4(X, Y, Z).$$
The singularities of $f(z, z')$ may be given by a set of single equations, typified for each of them by
$$\theta(z, z') = 0,$$
or by sets of two independent equations, typified for each set by
$$\theta(z, z') = 0, \quad \phi(z, z') = 0.$$
The former will lead to two equations, say
$$\vartheta_1(x, y, x', y') = 0, \quad \vartheta_2(x, y, x', y') = 0;$$
so, in our X, Y, Z space, they will be given by equations
$$\Theta_1(X, Y, Z) = 0, \quad \Theta_2(X, Y, Z) = 0.$$
These two equations represent a curve C in that space; at every point on the curve there is a singularity of $f(z, z')$.

The latter will lead to four equations, which may be regarded as defining an isolated place or an aggregate of isolated places determined by the values of x, y, x', y'. Such places may or may not exist in our X, Y, Z space.

Take a closed surface S in the space, containing no place or places X, Y, Z, giving rise to an isolated singularity of $f(z, z')$, to any curve C, or to any part of such a curve. The integral $\iint f(z, z') \, dz \, dz'$ taken over S is zero.

Take two closed surfaces S and S' in the space X, Y, Z, such that S can be continuously deformed into S', without passing over any place giving rise to an isolated singularity of $f(z, z')$, or over any curve C, or any part of such a curve C. The value of the integral taken over the surface S is equal to its value taken over the surface S'.

Take two closed surfaces S and S' in the space X, Y, Z, such that they enclose places giving rise to exactly the same isolated singularities of $f(z, z')$, to exactly the same curves C and to exactly the same portions of curves C. The value of the integral taken over the surface S is equal to its value taken over the surface S'.

Thus the value of the double integral $\iint f(z, z')\, dz\, dz'$, taken over the closed surface S, is zero when the surface encloses no place X, Y, Z, where $f(z, z')$ ceases to be regular. When the surface does enclose places X, Y, Z, where $f(z, z')$ ceases to be regular, the value of the integral depends upon these enclosed places; we cannot assert that its value is zero.

99. The theorem can be enunciated in similar terms when a two-plane representation of z and z' is adopted. Thus, very specially, within a circular ring in the z-plane and within a circular ring in the z'-plane, let a function $f(z, z')$ be everywhere regular; then the value of $\iint f(z, z')\, dz\, dz'$ is the same, whether the integral be taken positively round the outer circles in the two planes, or be taken positively round the inner circles in the two planes. But such a case is exceedingly special; and, as was indicated earlier in the lectures (§ 19), the frontier of a domain of variation for z and z' is of a more complicated character than in the result just enunciated.

100. We proceed to consider some of the simplest cases when the subject of integration in a double integral $\iint f(z, z')\, dz\, dz'$ possesses either isolated singularities or any continuous aggregate of singularities within an assigned domain. In passing to these examples, it may be remarked that the whole subject of double integrals of uniform analytic functions, possessing singularities of the known types, offers a field of research, in which many of the results already obtained are of a tentatively exploratory character.

In the examples that will be considered, we shall use the two-plane representation of z and z', and we shall deal only with a finite part of the whole field of variation of z and z'; that is, for all the variations, $|z|$ and $|z'|$ will be kept finite. To these examples*, all of which involve only rational functions of z and z', we now proceed in order.

EXAMPLE I. Let $F(z, z')$ denote a function that is regular everywhere within an assigned finite domain; let a, a' denote any place within that domain. Then we consider the integral

$$\iint \frac{F(z, z')}{(z-a)(z'-a')}\, dz\, dz',$$

---

* In this connection, reference should be made to Picard, *Fonctions algébriques de deux variables*, t. i, ch. iii.

taken over the closed frontier given by the equations $|z - a| = R$, $|z' - a'| = R'$, so that it encloses the place a, a'.

The singularities of the subject of integration are given by

(i) $z = a$, $z' =$ any enclosed value of z';

(ii) $z =$ any enclosed value of z, $z' = a'$.

By our general theorem, we can deform the closed frontier without changing the value of the double integral, provided the deformation causes no transition through any of these places. Accordingly, let the closed frontier be deformed until it encloses only the small domain, composed of the interior of the circles

$$z - a = re^{\theta i}, \quad z' - a' = r'e^{\theta' i},$$

where r and r' are small real positive constant quantities. Then

$$\iint \frac{F(z, z')}{(z-a)(z'-a')} \, dz \, dz' = -\iint F(a + re^{\theta i}, a' + r'e^{\theta' i}) \, d\theta \, d\theta',$$

the integration extending over a θ-range from 0 to 2π and over a θ'-range from 0 to 2π. Now $F(z, z')$ is regular throughout the domain; hence

$$F(a + re^{\theta i}, a' + r'e^{\theta' i}) = \sum_{m=0}^{\infty} \sum_{n=0}^{\infty} \frac{1}{m! \, n!} \frac{\partial^{m+n} F(a, a')}{\partial a^m \partial a'^n} r^m r'^n e^{(m\theta + n\theta')i}.$$

But for positive integer values of m and n, such that either m or n is greater than zero, we have

$$\iint e^{(m\theta + n\theta')i} \, d\theta \, d\theta' = 0;$$

and

$$\iint d\theta \, d\theta' = 4\pi^2.$$

Hence

$$\iint F(a + re^{\theta i}, a' + r'e^{\theta' i}) \, d\theta \, d\theta' = 4\pi^2 F(a, a');$$

and therefore, with our hypothesis as to the regular character of $F(z, z')$ within the domain, we have

$$-\frac{1}{4\pi^2} \iint \frac{F(z, z')}{(z-a)(z'-a')} \, dz \, dz' = F(a, a'),$$

taken over the closed frontier of integration $|z - a| = R$, $|z' - a'| = R'$.

Corollary. With the preceding assumptions concerning the regular function $F(z, z')$, we have

$$-\frac{1}{4\pi^2} \iint \frac{F(z, z')}{z - a} \, dz \, dz' = 0,$$

$$-\frac{1}{4\pi^2} \iint \frac{F(z, z')}{z' - a'} \, dz \, dz' = 0,$$

taken over the closed frontier of integration $|z - a| = R$, $|z' - a'| = R'$.

Note. When the integrals are taken over a closed frontier of integration which does not enclose the place a, a', all the three integrals have a zero value.

EXAMPLE II. As before, let $F(z, z')$ be regular everywhere within an assigned finite domain; and let a, a' be any place within that domain. We consider the integral

$$\iint \frac{F(z, z')}{(z-a)^{m+1}(z'-a')^{n+1}}\, dz\, dz',$$

taken over the same closed frontier in that domain, the frontier enclosing the place a, a', and the quantities m and n denoting positive integers, zero included.

We proceed exactly as in the preceding example. Because

$$\iint e^{(-m+\mu)\theta i + (-n+\nu)\theta' i}\, d\theta\, d\theta' = 0,$$

for the range 0 to 2π for θ and for θ', except only when $m = \mu$ and $n = \nu$, we find

$$-\frac{1}{4\pi^2}\iint \frac{F(z, z')}{(z-a)^{m+1}(z'-a')^{n+1}}\, dz\, dz' = \frac{1}{m!\, n!}\left\{\frac{\partial^{m+n} F(z, z')}{\partial z^m \partial z'^n}\right\}_{z=a,\, z'=a'},$$

for all integer values of m and n that are not negative.

EXAMPLE III. Let $\alpha, \beta, \gamma, \delta$ denote four constants such that $\alpha\delta - \beta\gamma$ is not zero; and consider the double integral

$$\iint \frac{dz\, dz'}{(\alpha z + \beta z')(\gamma z + \delta z')},$$

taken over a frontier that encloses the place 0, 0.

For a given value of z', the quantity $\alpha z + \beta z'$ vanishes if $z = z_1$, and the quantity $\gamma z + \delta z'$ vanishes if $z = z_2$, where

$$z_1 = -\frac{\beta}{\alpha} z', \quad z_2 = -\frac{\delta}{\gamma} z'.$$

The values of z_1 and z_2 are unequal except only when $z' = 0$.

First, let integration with regard to z be effected before integration with regard to z'. Take in the z-plane a small simple curve enclosing z_1 and excluding z_2, say a circle centre z_1 and of radius $< |z_1 - z_2|$; and effect the integration round this circle in the z-plane while z' is supposed invariable. Then, as

$$\frac{1}{(\alpha z + \beta z')(\gamma z + \delta z')} = \frac{1}{\alpha\gamma (z - z_1)(z - z_2)}$$

$$= \frac{1}{(\alpha\delta - \beta\gamma) z'}\left(\frac{1}{z - z_1} - \frac{1}{z - z_2}\right),$$

we have (when the indicated integration is effected)

$$\int \frac{dz}{(\alpha z + \beta z')(\gamma z + \delta z')} = \frac{2\pi i}{(\alpha\delta - \beta\gamma) z'},$$

because

$$\int \frac{dz}{z - z_1} = 2\pi i, \quad \int \frac{dz}{z - z_2} = 0,$$

taken round the z-circle. Now let the integration with respect to z' be effected round a small circle, the circumference of which passes through z' and the centre of which is at $z' = 0$; then, as

$$\int \frac{dz'}{z'} = 2\pi i$$

for this integration, we have

$$-\frac{1}{4\pi^2} \iint \frac{dz\, dz'}{(\alpha z + \beta z')(\gamma z + \delta z')} = \frac{1}{\alpha\delta - \beta\gamma}.$$

Writing

$$\zeta = \alpha z + \beta z', \quad \zeta' = \gamma z + \delta z',$$

$$J\left(\frac{\zeta, \zeta'}{z, z'}\right) = J(\zeta, \zeta') = \alpha\delta - \beta\gamma,$$

we have

$$-\frac{1}{4\pi^2} \iint \frac{dz\, dz'}{\zeta \zeta'} = \frac{1}{J(\zeta, \zeta')},$$

when integration is effected, first with regard to z round a small simple z-curve enclosing a root of ζ for a given value of z' but not a root of ζ', and then with regard to z' round a simple z'-curve through that value of z' enclosing the origin $z' = 0$.

Similarly, we have

$$-\frac{1}{4\pi^2} \iint \frac{dz\, dz'}{\zeta \zeta'} = \frac{1}{J(\zeta', \zeta)},$$

when integration is effected, first with regard to z round a small simple z-curve enclosing a root of ζ' for a given value of z' but not a root of ζ, and then with regard to z' round a simple z'-curve, passing through that value of z' and enclosing the origin $z' = 0$.

Similarly, we have

$$-\frac{1}{4\pi^2} \iint \frac{dz\, dz'}{\zeta \zeta'} = 0,$$

when integration is effected first with regard to z round a z-curve enclosing both a root of ζ and a root of ζ' for a given value of z', and then with regard to z' round a z'-curve passing through that value of z' and enclosing the origin $z' = 0$. For we then have

$$\int \frac{dz}{z - z_1} = 2\pi i, \quad \int \frac{dz}{z - z_2} = 2\pi i,$$

so that

$$\int \frac{dz}{(\alpha z + \beta z')(\gamma z + \delta z')} = \frac{1}{(\alpha\delta - \beta\gamma) z'} \int \left(\frac{dz}{z - z_1} - \frac{dz}{z - z_2} \right)$$
$$= 0.$$

Next, let integration with regard to z' be effected before integration with regard to z. Indicating this order in the same way as before, we consider

$$\iint \frac{dz'\,dz}{(\alpha z + \beta z')(\gamma z + \delta z')}$$

and then, from the definition of the significance of a double integral, we have

$$I = \iint \frac{dz\,dz'}{(\alpha z + \beta z')(\gamma z + \delta z')} = -\iint \frac{dz'\,dz}{(\alpha z + \beta z')(\gamma z + \delta z')}$$
$$= -\iint \frac{dz'\,dz}{\zeta \zeta'}.$$

Take in the z'-plane a small simple z'-curve enclosing a root z_1' of ζ but not a root z_2' of ζ', for a given value of z, where

$$z_1' = -\frac{\alpha}{\beta}z, \quad z_2' = -\frac{\gamma}{\delta}z;$$

effect the integration with regard to z' round this curve; and then effect the integration with regard to z round a simple curve through the given value of z enclosing the z-origin; then

$$-\frac{1}{4\pi^2} \iint \frac{dz'\,dz}{\zeta \zeta'} = -\frac{1}{J(\zeta, \zeta')},$$

and so

$$-\frac{1}{4\pi^2} \iint \frac{dz\,dz'}{(\alpha z + \beta z')(\gamma z + \delta z')} = \frac{1}{J(\zeta, \zeta')},$$

in this case also.

Similarly, when integration with regard to z' is effected first, round a small simple z'-curve enclosing a root of ζ' but not a root of ζ for a given value of z, and then integration is effected with regard to z round a simple curve through the value of z enclosing the z-origin, we find

$$-\frac{1}{4\pi^2} \iint \frac{dz\,dz'}{(\alpha z + \beta z')(\gamma z + \delta z')} = \frac{1}{J(\zeta', \zeta)}.$$

Lastly, when integration with regard to z' is effected first, round a small simple z'-curve enclosing both a root of ζ and a root of ζ' for a given value of z, and afterwards integration is effected with regard to z round a simple curve, passing through the value of z and enclosing the z-origin, we find

$$-\frac{1}{4\pi^2} \iint \frac{dz\,dz'}{(\alpha z + \beta z')(\gamma z + \delta z')} = 0.$$

Summing up, we can say *that the value of the double integral*

$$-\frac{1}{4\pi^2} \iint \frac{dz\,dz'}{(\alpha z + \beta z')(\gamma z + \delta z')}$$

is independent of the order of integration; that it is $\dfrac{1}{J(\zeta, \zeta')}$, *where*

$$J(\zeta, \zeta') = \alpha\delta - \beta\gamma,$$

when integration is effected round a curve enclosing a root of ζ, where $\zeta = \alpha z + \beta z'$, but not a root of ζ', where $\zeta' = \gamma z + \delta z'$; that it is $\dfrac{1}{J(\zeta', \zeta)}, = -\dfrac{1}{J(\zeta, \zeta')}$, when integration is effected round a curve enclosing a root of ζ' but not a root of ζ; and that it is zero when integration is effected round a curve enclosing both a root of ζ and a root of ζ'.

And, of course, the value is zero when the integration is effected round a region that does not enclose any zero of ζ or of ζ'.

EXAMPLE IV. The preceding result cannot be applied when the initial assumption, viz. that $\alpha\delta - \beta\gamma$ is different from zero, is not satisfied. In that case, we have to deal with

$$\iint \frac{dz\,dz'}{(\alpha z + \beta z')^2}.$$

When the integral is taken round the place 0, 0, in either of the ways indicated in the construction of the last result, the value of the double integral is zero.

EXAMPLE V. From III and IV, we infer the following results relating to the double integral

$$-\frac{1}{4\pi^2} \iint \frac{dz\,dz'}{\lambda z^2 + 2\mu zz' + \rho z'^2}.$$

There are two cases, according as μ^2 is not, or is, equal to $\lambda\rho$.

(i) Suppose that $\mu^2 - \lambda\rho$ is not zero. When integration is effected in either plane, round a small simple curve enclosing the root of $\lambda z + \{\mu + (\mu^2 - \lambda\rho)^{\frac{1}{2}}\} z' = 0$ but not the root of $\lambda z + \{\mu - (\mu^2 - \lambda\rho)^{\frac{1}{2}}\} z' = 0$, and then round a small simple curve enclosing the origin in the other plane, *the value of the double integral is*

$$-\tfrac{1}{2}(\mu^2 - \lambda\rho)^{-\frac{1}{2}}.$$

When integration is effected in either plane, round a small simple curve enclosing the root of $\lambda z + \{\mu - (\mu^2 - \lambda\rho)^{\frac{1}{2}}\} z' = 0$ but not the root of $\lambda z + \{\mu + (\mu^2 - \lambda\rho)^{\frac{1}{2}}\} z' = 0$, and then round a small simple curve enclosing the origin in the other plane, *the value of the double integral is*

$$\tfrac{1}{2}(\mu^2 - \lambda\rho)^{-\frac{1}{2}}.$$

And when integration is effected in either plane, round a small simple curve enclosing both roots of $\lambda z^2 + 2\mu zz' + \rho z'^2 = 0$, and then round a small simple curve enclosing the origin in the other plane, *the value of the double integral is zero*.

(ii) Suppose that $\mu^2 - \lambda\rho = 0$. When the integral is taken round the place 0, 0 in any of the ways indicated for the preceding case, *the value of the double integral is zero*.

EXAMPLE VI. Let
$$P = z'^m(\gamma_0 + \gamma_1 z' + \ldots), \quad Q = z'^n(\delta_0 + \delta_1 z' + \ldots),$$
where γ_0 and δ_0 are different from zero and (for the immediate purpose) m and n are positive real quantities, not necessarily integers. We require the value of
$$-\frac{1}{4\pi^2}\iint \frac{J(u,v)}{uv}\, dz\, dz',$$
where $u = \alpha z + P$, $v = \beta z + Q$, when the integration is effected, first, with regard to z round a small simple closed z-curve enclosing a root of u (but not a root of v) for a value of z', and, then, with regard to z' round a small simple closed curve, passing through that value of z' and enclosing the z'-origin. We also assume that $\alpha Q - \beta P$ does not vanish identically. Now
$$J = \alpha z'^{n-1}\{n\delta_0 + (n+1)\delta_1 z' + \ldots\} - \beta z'^{m-1}\{m\gamma_0 + (m+1)\gamma_1 z' + \ldots\}.$$
Thus, if $m < n$, the lowest power in J is $-m\beta\gamma_0 z'^{m-1}$; if $m > n$, the lowest power is $n\alpha\delta_0 z'^{n-1}$; if $m = n, = l$ say, the value of J is
$$lz'^{n-1}(\alpha\delta_0 - \beta\gamma_0) + (l+1)z'^m(\alpha\delta_1 - \beta\gamma_1) + \ldots.$$
For any small value of z', such that $|z'|$ is less than the modulus of the smallest root of P or Q other than $z' = 0$, let
$$\alpha z_1 + P = 0, \quad \beta z_2 + Q = 0.$$
Then the double integral
$$= -\frac{1}{4\pi^2}\iint \frac{dz\, dz'}{\alpha\beta(z-z_1)(z-z_2)} J$$
$$= -\frac{2\pi i}{4\pi^2}\iint \frac{J}{\alpha Q - \beta P}\, dz'.$$

When $m < n$, the value of the right-hand side is n.

When $m > n$, the value of the right-hand side is m.

When $m = n, = l$, the value of the right-hand side is $l + k$, where $\alpha\delta_k - \beta\gamma_k$ is the first of the coefficients $\alpha\delta_0 - \beta\gamma_0$, $\alpha\delta_1 - \beta\gamma_1$, ... which does not vanish.

In each of the three alternatives, *the value of the integral is the degree of the lowest power of z' in the eliminant of $\alpha z + P$ and $\beta z + Q$, when z is eliminated.* Moreover, *when m and n are integers, the value of the integral is then the multiplicity of $0, 0$,* as the sole isolated simultaneous zero of the uniform functions
$$\alpha z + P, \quad \beta z + Q,$$
enclosed by the frontier of integration.

EXAMPLE VII. Next, let
$$u = z^m + z^{m-1}f_1(z') + \ldots + f_m(z'),$$
$$v = z^n + z^{n-1}g_1(z') + \ldots + g_n(z'),$$

where the functions u and v are independent and have no common factor of their own form, and all the coefficients $f_1, \ldots, f_m, g_1, \ldots, g_n$ are functions of z' which are regular in the vicinity of $z' = 0$ and vanish with z'. We require the value of the double integral

$$-\frac{1}{4\pi^2} \iint \frac{J(u, v)}{uv} \, dz \, dz',$$

taken (as have been the preceding integrals) round a frontier, which encloses the place 0, 0, and encloses no other simultaneous zero of u and v. Let

$$u = (z - z_1)(z - z_2) \ldots (z - z_m), \quad v = (z - \zeta_1)(z - \zeta_2) \ldots (z - \zeta_n),$$

where each of the quantities $z_1, \ldots, z_m, \zeta_1, \ldots, \zeta_n$ is a regular function of positive powers of z'^μ; where μ is a positive rational fraction; and where each of these quantities vanishes with z'. The eliminant of u and v is

$$\prod_{r=1}^{m} \prod_{s=1}^{n} (z_r - \zeta_s);$$

if, when $z_r - \zeta_s$ is arranged in ascending (fractional or integral) powers of z', the lowest power of z' has an index $\mu_{r,s}$, and if

$$\sum_{r=1}^{m} \sum_{s=1}^{n} \mu_{r,s} = M,$$

the eliminant of u and v is

$$z'^M \phi(z'),$$

where $\phi(0)$ is not zero. The magnitude M is an integer, manifestly finite: it is the measure of the multiplicity of 0, 0, as an isolated zero common to u and v.

For the range of integration, first take a value z' of modulus smaller than the root of $\phi(z')$ which has the smallest modulus. In the z-plane mark all the quantities $z_1, \ldots, z_m, \zeta_1, \ldots, \zeta_n$, which are functions of this value of z'; and draw a simple closed z-curve, enclosing all the places $z_1, \ldots, z_m$ and none of the places $\zeta_1, \ldots, \zeta_n$. We take the integral round this z-curve; when this first integration has been effected, we integrate with regard to z' along a small simple closed z'-curve, through the place for the assigned value of z' and enclosing the z'-origin.

We have

$$\frac{J}{uv} = \sum_{r=1}^{m} \sum_{s=1}^{n} \frac{-\zeta_s' + z_r'}{(z - z_r)(z - \zeta_s)},$$

where $z_r' = \frac{dz_r}{dz'}$ and $\zeta_s' = \frac{d\zeta_s}{dz'}$; hence

$$-\frac{1}{4\pi^2} \iint \frac{J(u, v)}{uv} \, dz \, dz' = -\frac{2\pi i}{4\pi^2} \sum_{r=1}^{m} \sum_{s=1}^{n} \int \frac{z_r' - \zeta_s'}{z_r - \zeta_s} \, dz'.$$

But the lowest power of z' in $z_r - \zeta_s$ is $z'^{\mu_{rs}}$. Hence

$$-\frac{1}{4\pi^2} \iint \frac{J(u, v)}{uv} \, dz \, dz' = \sum_{r=1}^{m} \sum_{s=1}^{n} \mu_{r,s} = M;$$

that is, *the value of the double integral, taken over the range indicated, is the measure of the multiplicity of* 0, 0, *as an isolated simultaneous zero of the functions u and v, which are supposed to be independent and to be devoid of any common factor of their own form.*

Corollary. Two or more of the quantities $z_1, \ldots, z_m$ may be equal, or they may be equal in groups; and, similarly, two or more of the quantities $\zeta_1, \ldots, \zeta_n$ may be equal, or they may be equal in groups; while, after the hypothesis as to the functions u and v, no one of the quantities ζ is equal to any of the quantities $z_1, \ldots, z_m$. *The value of the double integral over the indicated range still is* M.

Note 1. If the range of integration, enclosing 0, 0 and no other simultaneous zero of u and v, is chosen so that the z-curve (for a value of z') encloses all the places $\zeta_1, \ldots, \zeta_n$ and no one of the places $z_1, \ldots, z_m$, and the z'-curve is drawn as before, the value of the double integral becomes $-M$.

Note 2. We have
$$-\frac{1}{4\pi^2} \iint \frac{J(u,v)}{uv} dz\, dz' = \frac{1}{4\pi^2} \iint \frac{J(u,v)}{uv} dz'\, dz.$$
When integration is effected first with regard to z', round a curve enclosing all the roots of $u=0$ and no root of $v=0$ for an assigned value of z, and then round a z-curve through this value and enclosing the z-origin, we still have
$$-\frac{1}{4\pi^2} \iint \frac{J(u,v)}{uv} dz\, dz' = M.$$
In other words, *the value of the double integral is independent of the order of integration.*

EXAMPLE VIII. *Let α and β be non-variable quantities, of finite moduli; let c, c' be a level place for two regular functions, f and g, such that*
$$f(c, c') - \alpha = 0, \quad g(c, c') - \beta = 0;$$
and let $f(z, z') - \alpha$, $g(z, z') - \beta$, be independent, and have no common factor which vanishes at c, c'. Then the place c, c' is isolated; its multiplicity is the value of the double integral
$$-\frac{1}{4\pi^2} \iint \frac{J(f, g)}{\{f(z, z') - \alpha\}\{g(z, z') - \beta\}} dz\, dz',$$
taken first round a small simple closed curve in the z-plane which, for an assigned small value of z', encloses all the roots of $f(z, z') = \alpha$ and none of the roots of $g(z, z') = \beta$, and then round a small simple closed curve, through that value of z' and enclosing the z'-origin.

The result follows from the last example by writing
$$u = f(z, z') - \alpha, \quad v = g(z, z') - \beta;$$
the multiplicity of c, c' as a level place for f and g is its multiplicity as a zero for u and v*.

---

* In connection with double integrals of the preceding types and taken over such ranges of integration, the reader should consult Picard's treatise, t. i, ch. iii, quoted p. 161.

Algebraic functions in general.

101. Hitherto, all the subjects of integration in the double integrals that have been considered, have been uniform functions. Bearing in mind the extraordinary importance of Riemann's investigations connected with the simple integrals of algebraic functions, we should naturally seek the generalisation of that work for algebraic functions of two variables.

Into that theory I do not propose to enter in detail. In one sense, it is enough for me to refer to the long series of valuable researches by Picard[*]. All that will be done here is to submit one or two simple propositions, when there is a single dependent variable, partly from the standpoint of the general theory of functions and without regard to the theory of the singularities of surfaces, partly also to state the corresponding propositions when we have to deal with the case when the fundamental algebraic equations provide two dependent variables and not one alone, the number of independent variables always being two.

Suppose then that we have, in the first place, a single irreducible algebraic equation
$$f(w, z, z') = 0,$$
expressing w as an algebraic function of z and z'; and assume that the equation is of order m in w, so that w is m-valued. Any rational function in the field of variation is of the form $R(w, z, z')$, where R is the quotient of two polynomials in all the variables w, z, z'. To this rational function $R(w, z, z')$ a canonical and recognisable form can be given; the proposition, stating its form, can be established in the same kind of way as for the corresponding proposition when there is only a single independent variable.

Let the m roots of the fundamental equation $f(w, z, z') = 0$ be denoted by $w_1, w_2, \ldots, w_m$. Then, for any positive integer n, the quantity
$$w_1^n R(w_1, z, z') + w_2^n R(w_2, z, z') + \ldots + w_m^n R(w_m, z, z')$$
is a symmetric function of the roots $w_1, \ldots, w_m$ of the fundamental equation, having rational functions of z and z' for the various symmetric combinations of the roots; it is therefore a rational function of z and z'. Denoting this rational function by $P_n(z, z')$, we have
$$\sum_{r=1}^{m} w_r^n R(w_r, z, z') = P_n(z, z').$$

This result holds for all integers n; hence, taking it for $n = 0, 1, \ldots, m-1$, we have m equations, each linear in the m quantities $R(w_1, z, z'), \ldots, R(w_m, z, z')$.

---

[*] They are expounded fully in his treatise already quoted (pp. 161, 169); and in that treatise full references will be found to the work of Nœther, Enriques, Castelnuovo, Severi, Humbert, Berry, and others, in especial connection with the analytical developments associated with surfaces in ordinary real space.

Solving these m linear equations for the m functions $R(w_r, z, z')$, we have

$$\begin{vmatrix} 1, & 1, & \ldots, & 1 \\ w_1, & w_2, & \ldots, & w_m \\ \cdots & & & \\ w_1^{m-1}, & w_2^{m-1}, & \ldots, & w_m^{m-1} \end{vmatrix} R(w_1, z, z') = \begin{vmatrix} P_0(z, z'), & 1, & \ldots, & 1 \\ P_1(z, z'), & w_2, & \ldots, & w_m \\ \cdots & & & \\ P_{m-1}(z, z'), & w_2^{m-1}, & \ldots, & w_m^{m-1} \end{vmatrix}.$$

The determinant on the left-hand side is the product of the differences of all the roots of the fundamental equation $f(w, z, z') = 0$ regarded as an equation in w, and is usually denoted by

$$\zeta(w_1, w_2, \ldots, w_m),$$

so that, from this definition of ζ, we have

$$\pm \zeta(w_1, w_2, \ldots, w_m) = (w_1 - w_2)(w_1 - w_3) \ldots (w_1 - w_m) \zeta(w_2, \ldots, w_m).$$

On the right-hand side, each of the quantities $P_r(z, z')$ has, as its coefficient, a determinant of the roots $w_2, \ldots, w_m$; and in each case, this determinant can be expressed as a product of $\zeta(w_2, \ldots, w_m)$ and a symmetric function of $w_2, \ldots, w_m$. Thus the coefficient of $P_0(z, z')$ is $w_2 w_3 \ldots w_m \zeta(w_2, \ldots w_m)$; the coefficient of $P_1(z, z')$ is $-w_2 w_3 \ldots w_m \left(\sum_{r=2}^{m} \frac{1}{w_r}\right) \zeta(w_2, \ldots, w_m)$; and so on. Hence dividing out by $\zeta(w_2, \ldots, w_m)$, we have

$$(w_1 - w_2)(w_1 - w_3) \ldots (w_1 - w_m) R(w_1, z, z')$$
$$= P_0 s_0 + P_1 s_1 + \ldots + P_{m-1} s_{m-1},$$

where $s_0, s_1, \ldots, s_{m-1}$ are the symmetric functions of $w_2, \ldots, w_m$.

Now by the algebraic equation $f(w, z, z') = 0$, each symmetric function of $w_2, \ldots, w_m$ can be expressed as a polynomial in w_1, having rational functions of z for its coefficients. Also

$$A(w_1 - w_2)(w_1 - w_3) \ldots (w_1 - w_m) = \left(\frac{\partial f}{\partial w}\right)_{w=w_1},$$

where A is the coefficient of w_1^m in $f(w, z, z')$. Hence

$$\left(\frac{\partial f}{\partial w}\right)_1 R(w_1, z, z') = \Theta(w_1, z, z'),$$

where Θ is a polynomial in w_1, which can always be made of degree $\leqslant m - 1$ by use of the equation $f(w, z, z') = 0$; and the coefficients in this polynomial are rational functions of z and z'.

A corresponding expression holds for each of the functions $R(w_2, z, z')$, $\ldots, R(w_m, z, z')$, all the polynomials $\Theta(w, z, z')$ having the same coefficients in the form of rational functions of z and z'. Consequently, when we denote any root of our algebraic equation

$$f(w, z, z') = 0$$

simply by w, any rational function $R(w, z, z')$ of all the variables can be expressed in the form

$$R(w, z, z') = \frac{\Theta(w, z, z')}{\frac{\partial f}{\partial w}},$$

where $\Theta(w, z, z')$ is a polynomial in w of degree $\leqslant m - 1$, the degree of $f(w, z, z') = 0$ in w being m, and where the polynomial has rational functions of z and z' for the coefficients of the powers of w.

This is the generalisation of the well-known theorem of Riemann on the expression of functions that are uniform functions of position on a Riemann surface*.

Ex. 1. Let the fundamental equation be
$$w^2 + z^2 + z'^2 = 1;$$
and let
$$R = \frac{Az + A'z' + Cw}{az + a'z' + cw}.$$
There are two values of R, viz. the expressed value, and R', where
$$R' = \frac{Az + A'z' - Cw}{az + a'z' - cw}.$$
Hence, following the general argument, we have
$$R + R' = 2\frac{(Az + A'z')(az + a'z') - cCw^2}{(az + a'z')^2 - c^2w^2} = 2P,$$
where P is a rational function of z and z'; and
$$wR - wR' = -2w^2 \frac{c(Az + A'z') - C(az + a'z')}{(az + a'z')^2 - c^2w^2} = 2Q,$$
where Q is a rational function of z and z'. Hence
$$R = \frac{wP + Q}{w},$$
which establishes the proposition.

Ex. 2. When the fundamental equation is
$$w^3 + z^3 + z'^3 = 1,$$
obtain canonical expressions for

(i) $\dfrac{Az + Bz' + Cw}{az + bz' + cw}$,

(ii) $\dfrac{az^2 + bzw + cw^2}{a'z'^2 + b'z'w + c'w^2}$.

Note. There are of course particular methods better adapted to particular cases than is the general method which applies to all cases.

Thus the function
$$R(w, z) = \frac{Az + A'z' + Cw}{az + bz' + cw},$$
when $w^3 + z^3 + z'^3 = 1$ is the governing algebraic equation, gives
$$R(w, z) = \frac{(Az + A'z' + Cw)\{(az + bz')^2 - (az + bz')cw + c^2w^2\}}{(az + bz')^3 + c^3w^3};$$
and so
$$w^2 R(w, z) = \frac{L + Mw + Nw^2}{(az + bz')^3 + c^3(1 - z^3 - z'^3)},$$
where L, M, N are polynomials in z and z' of degrees five, four, three respectively.

102. When we have to deal with the case, in which there are a couple of algebraic functions w and w' given by two algebraic equations
$$f(w, w', z, z') = 0, \quad g(w, w', z, z') = 0,$$

* See my *Theory of Functions*, § 399.

it is desirable to have a canonical form of the most general rational function; we shall prove that this canonical form is

$$\frac{\Theta(w, w', z, z')}{J\left(\dfrac{f, g}{w, w'}\right)},$$

where Θ is a polynomial in w and w', having rational functions of z and z' for its coefficients.

Let f be of degree m in w and w' combined, and g of degree n in w and w' combined: that is to say, if w and w' were Cartesian plane real coordinates, and if $f = 0$ and $g = 0$ were loci in that w, w' plane, $f = 0$ and $g = 0$ would be plane curves of degrees m and n respectively. Construct the w-eliminant of f and g by eliminating w' between $f = 0$ and $g = 0$, and denote it by W; then from the ordinary processes of algebra, we know that

$$W = Af + Bg,$$

where A is a polynomial in w of degree $mn - m$, and in w' of degree $n - 1$; B is a polynomial in w of degree $mn - n$, and in w' of degree $m - 1$; and W, not containing w', is of degree mn in w. Similarly, the w'-eliminant of f and g, obtained by eliminating w between $f = 0$ and $g = 0$, can be put into the form

$$W' = Cf + Dg,$$

where W' is of degree mn in w' alone, and does not involve w.

There are mn roots of $W = 0$, expressing each w as one of mn functions of z and z'; and there are likewise mn roots of $W' = 0$. The mn combinations of one root of $W = 0$ with one root of $W' = 0$, which make

$$f = 0, \quad g = 0$$

simultaneously, are called the congruous pairs: the combinations are determined by the ordinary processes of algebra. The remaining $mn(mn - 1)$ combinations of roots of $W = 0$ and $W' = 0$ are called the non-congruous pairs; they all satisfy $\Delta = 0$, where

$$\Delta = AD - BC.$$

Now take a congruous pair of roots, say w_1 and w_1'; they satisfy $f = 0$, $g = 0$, $W = 0$. We have

$$W = Af + Bg$$

identically; hence differentiating with respect to w and w', and inserting the pair of congruous roots after differentiation, we have

$$\frac{\partial W}{\partial w_1} = A\frac{\partial f}{\partial w_1} + B\frac{\partial g}{\partial w_1}, \quad 0 = A\frac{\partial f}{\partial w_1'} + B\frac{\partial g}{\partial w_1'}.$$

Similarly we have

$$0 = C\frac{\partial f}{\partial w_1} + D\frac{\partial g}{\partial w_1}, \quad \frac{\partial W'}{\partial w_1'} = C\frac{\partial f}{\partial w_1'} + D\frac{\partial g}{\partial w_1'}.$$

Hence, for the congruous pair of roots, we have

$$\begin{vmatrix} \dfrac{\partial W}{\partial w_1}, & 0 \\ 0, & \dfrac{\partial W'}{\partial w_1'} \end{vmatrix} = \begin{vmatrix} A\dfrac{\partial f}{\partial w_1} + B\dfrac{\partial g}{\partial w_1}, & A\dfrac{\partial f}{\partial w_1'} + B\dfrac{\partial g}{\partial w_1'} \\ C\dfrac{\partial f}{\partial w_1} + D\dfrac{\partial g}{\partial w_1}, & C\dfrac{\partial f}{\partial w_1'} + D\dfrac{\partial g}{\partial w_1'} \end{vmatrix},$$

that is,

$$\dfrac{\partial W}{\partial w_1}\dfrac{\partial W'}{\partial w_1'} = \Delta_1 J\left(\dfrac{f, g}{w_1, w_1'}\right) = \Delta_1 J_1,$$

say, where Δ_1 is the value of Δ for the congruous pair of roots w_1 and w_1', and likewise for J_1.

Similarly for each congruous pair.

Let our rational function of w, w', z, z', which is to be expressed in a canonical form as stated, be denoted initially by $R(w, w', z, z')$; and let its value, for a congruous pair of roots w_μ and w_μ', be denoted by R_μ. Then, taking all the congruous pairs of roots, we have

$$\sum_{\mu=1}^{mn} w_\mu{}^r R_\mu = \text{a rational function of } z \text{ and } z'$$
$$= P_\nu(z, z'),$$

say; the value of $P_\nu(z, z')$ is obtainable by the usual processes of algebra; and the result holds for all integer values of r. Hence, taking $r = 0, 1, \ldots, mn-1$ in succession, we have

$$R_1 + R_2 \quad + \ldots\ldots + R_{mn} \qquad = P_0,$$
$$w_1 R_1 + w_2 R_2 \quad + \ldots\ldots + w_{mn} R_{mn} \qquad = P_1,$$
$$\ldots\ldots\ldots\ldots\ldots\ldots\ldots\ldots\ldots\ldots\ldots\ldots\ldots\ldots$$
$$w_1{}^{mn-1} R_1 + w_2{}^{mn-1} R_2 + \ldots\ldots + w_{mn}{}^{mn-1} R_{mn} = P_{mn-1}.$$

These equations can be solved for the $mn - 1$ quantities $R_1, R_2, \ldots$ which occur linearly. Proceeding as before in § 101, we find

$$R_1 = \dfrac{\Phi(w_1, z, z')}{\dfrac{\partial W}{\partial w_1}},$$

where Φ is a polynomial in w_1, having rational functions of z and z' for its coefficients. Multiplying the denominator and the numerator by $\dfrac{\partial W'}{\partial w_1'}$, we have

$$R_1 = \dfrac{\Phi(w_1, z, z')\dfrac{\partial W'}{\partial w_1'}}{\dfrac{\partial W}{\partial w_1}\dfrac{\partial W'}{\partial w_1'}}$$

$$= \dfrac{S(w_1, w_1', z, z')}{\dfrac{\partial W}{\partial w_1}\dfrac{\partial W'}{\partial w_1'}},$$

where S is a polynomial in w_1 and w_1', having rational functions of z and z' for its coefficients. But
$$\frac{\partial W}{\partial w_1}\frac{\partial W'}{\partial w_1'} = J_1 \Delta_1;$$
and therefore
$$R_1 = \frac{S(w_1, w_1', z, z')}{J_1} \cdot \frac{1}{\Delta_1}.$$
Now
$$\Delta_1 \Delta_2 \ldots \Delta_{mn}$$
is a symmetric function of w_1 and w_1', w_2 and w_2', ..., the pairs of congruous roots; and it is therefore expressible as a rational function of z and z', say
$$\Delta_1 \Delta_2 \ldots \Delta_{mn} = T(z, z').$$
Similarly
$$\Delta_2 \ldots \Delta_{mn}$$
is a symmetric function of all the congruous pairs of roots other than the pair w_1 and w_1'; hence it is expressible as a polynomial function of w_1, w_1', having rational functions of z and z' for its coefficients, say
$$\Delta_2 \ldots \Delta_{mn} = Q(w_1, w_1', z, z').$$
Consequently
$$\frac{1}{\Delta_1} = \frac{Q(w_1, w_1', z, z')}{T(z, z')}.$$
Hence
$$R_1 = \frac{S(w_1, w_1', z, z') Q(w_1, w_1', z, z')}{T(z, z') J_1}$$
$$= \frac{\Theta(w_1, w_1', z, z')}{J_1},$$
on multiplying the polynomials S and Q, and absorbing the rational function $T(z, z')$ into the coefficients of the product.

The same conclusion holds for every congruous pair of roots. We therefore infer that every function, rational in the algebraic field of w, w', z, z', where w and w' are given by algebraic equations
$$f(w, w', z, z') = 0, \quad g(w, w', z, z') = 0,$$
can be expressed in the form
$$\frac{\Theta(w, w', z, z')}{J\left(\dfrac{f, g}{w, w'}\right)},$$
where Θ is polynomial in w and w', having rational functions of z and z' for its coefficients.

Modifications in the degree of Θ in w and of its degree in w' may sometimes be effected by the use of the equations $f = 0$ and $g = 0$. These modifications, when they are possible, do not affect the denominator J, and only give equivalent expressions for the polynomial Θ; it is for this reason that the form is called canonical, even though the expression for Θ may happen to be not unique.

Note. In establishing the preceding form for the rational function, two theorems concerning symmetric functions have been quoted. In actual practice, we can proceed as follows.

Take
$$t = \lambda w + \lambda' w';$$
eliminate w from f and g, so that they become
$$F(t, w', z, z') = 0, \quad G(t, w', z, z') = 0,$$
of the same degrees in t and w' combined as are f and g respectively. Eliminate w' between $F = 0$ and $G = 0$, so as to give an equation
$$T = 0,$$
of degree mn in t, having rational functions (frequently polynomial functions) of z and z' for its coefficients.

In the product $\Delta_1 \Delta_2 \ldots \Delta_{mn}$, we have symmetric functions of the congruous pairs of roots; let such an one be
$$\Sigma w_1^{m_1} w_1'^{n_1} w_2^{m_2} w_2'^{n_2} \ldots,$$
where the summation is over all the like terms obtained by permuting the congruous pairs in all possible ways. We then form the symmetric function of the roots of the equation $T = 0$ represented by
$$\Sigma t_1^{m_1 + n_1} t_2^{m_2 + n_2} \ldots.$$
In its expression we select the coefficient of
$$\lambda^{m_1 + m_2 + \ldots} \lambda'^{n_1 + n_2 + \ldots},$$
and remove the multinomial numerical factor
$$\frac{(m_1 + n_1)!}{m_1! \, n_1!} \cdot \frac{(m_2 + n_2)!}{m_2! \, n_2!} \ldots;$$
the result is the symmetric function required.

Again, in the product $\Delta_2 \ldots \Delta_{mn}$, we have symmetric functions of all the congruous pairs of roots except only the pair w_1 and w_1'. Let
$$T = (t - t_1) \, T',$$
so that $t_2, \ldots, t_{mn}$ are the roots of $T' = 0$. The coefficients in T' are linear in the coefficients of T and are polynomials in t_1; thus, if
$$T = \theta_0 t^{mn} + \theta_1 t^{mn-1} + \theta_2 t^{mn-2} + \ldots,$$
$$T' = \theta_0 t^{mn-1} + \phi_1 t^{mn-2} + \phi_2 t^{mn-3} + \ldots,$$
we have
$$\phi_1 - t_1 \theta_0 = \theta_1, \quad \phi_2 - t_1 \phi_1 = \theta_2, \quad \phi_3 - t_1 \phi_2 = \theta_3, \quad \ldots,$$
and therefore
$$\phi_1 = \theta_1 + t_1 \theta_0,$$
$$\phi_2 = \theta_2 + t_1 \theta_1 \theta_0 + t_1^2 \theta_0^2,$$
$$\phi_3 = \theta_3 + t_1 \theta_2 \theta_0 + t_1^2 \theta_1 \theta_0^2 + t_1^3 \theta_0^3,$$
and so on.

As was the case with $\Delta_1 \Delta_2 \ldots \Delta_{mn}$, which is a sum of coefficients in a polynomial function of the coefficients of T divided by a power of θ_0, so also the symmetric product $\Delta_2 \ldots \Delta_{mn}$ is a sum of coefficients of powers of λ and λ' in a polynomial function of the coefficients of T' divided by a power of θ_0; that is, $\Delta_2 \ldots \Delta_{mn}$ is a polynomial function of the coefficients of T', itself also polynomial in t_1 (that is, in w_1 and w_1') divided by a power of θ_0.

These are the two theorems used.

Ex. For particular equations, a given rational function is most easily discussed in an initial form, not in a canonical form; it is for the general theory that a canonical form is required, as it includes all rational functions. We may however take an example, to shew the outline of the reduction to a canonical form; but the process is only an exercise in algebra.

Let the two fundamental equations be
$$f = w^3 - w'^3 - A = 0, \quad g = w^2 + w'^2 - B = 0,$$
where A and B are given functions of z and z' only. Their Jacobian J, on the omission of a factor 6, is
$$J = ww'(w + w').$$

We take the simple rational function
$$R = \frac{1}{w + Z},$$
where Z is any rational function of z and z'; and we proceed to express it in a canonical form
$$\frac{P(w, w', z, z')}{J},$$
where P is a polynomial in w and w', having rational functions of z and z' for its coefficients.

The W-eliminant of f and g is
$$W = 2w^6 - 2Aw^3 + A^2 - 3Bw^4 + 3B^2w^2 - B^3 = 0.$$
Let
$$w + Z = t;$$
then the six values of t are given by the equation
$$2(t-Z)^6 - 3B(t-Z)^4 - 2A(t-Z)^3 + 3B^2(t-Z)^2 + A^2 - B^3 = 0.$$
Let
$$\Theta = 2Z^6 - 3BZ^4 + 2AZ^3 + 3B^2Z^2 + A^2 - B^3,$$
being the term independent of t in the last equation; then
$$-\frac{\Theta}{t} = 2\frac{w^6 - Z^6}{w + Z} - 3B\frac{w^4 - Z^4}{w + Z} - 2A\frac{w^3 + Z^3}{w + Z} + 3B\frac{w^2 - Z^2}{w + Z}$$
$$= 2w^5 - 2Zw^4 + (2Z^2 - 3B)w^3 + (3BZ - 2A - 2Z^3)w^2$$
$$+ (3B - 3BZ + 2AZ + 2Z^4)w + 3BZ^3 - 3BZ - 2AZ^2 - 2Z^5$$
$$= \Phi, \text{ say.}$$
Consequently
$$-\frac{\Theta}{w_1 + Z}w_1(w_1 + w_1') = (w_1^2 + w_1 w_1')\Phi_1.$$

All terms in the right-hand side, which are of degree six and higher, can be removed by using the equation $W_1 = 0$. These terms are
$$2w_1^7 + (2w_1' - 2Z)w_1^6.$$
The term $2w_1^7$ is to be replaced by
$$3Bw_1^5 + 2Aw_1^4 - 3B^2w_1^3 - (A^2 - B^3)w_1,$$
and the terms $(2w_1' - 2Z)w_1^6$ by
$$(w_1' - Z)\{3Bw_1^4 + 2Aw_1^3 - 3B^2w_1^2 - A^2 + B^3\}.$$
When these changes are made, let the expression for Φ_1 be
$$\Phi_1 = \rho_0 w_1^5 + \rho_1 w_1^4 + \rho_2 w_1^3 + \rho_3 w_1^2 + \rho_4 w_1 + \rho_5,$$

where the coefficients ρ are polynomial in w', and are rational in z and z'. Then finally, absorbing the rational function of z and z' represented by $-\dfrac{1}{\Theta}$ into the coefficients of Φ_1, we have

$$\frac{1}{w+Z} = -\frac{w'}{J}\left(\frac{\rho_0}{\Theta}w^5 + \frac{\rho_1}{\Theta}w^4 + \frac{\rho_2}{\Theta}w^3 + \frac{\rho_3}{\Theta}w^2 + \frac{\rho_4}{\Theta}w + \frac{\rho_5}{\Theta}\right),$$

which is of the required type.

Equivalent forms are obtained for the numerator by using the equations $f = 0$, $g = 0$.

Integrals of algebraic functions.

103. The development of the theory of integrals, whether single or double, of algebraic functions when there are two independent complex variables, owes its main foundations to Picard[*]. Here I shall only restate one or two of the simplest results for the case when there are two initial fundamental algebraic equations

$$f(w, w', z, z') = 0, \quad g(w, w', z, z') = 0,$$

defining two dependent variables w and w' as algebraic functions of z and z', the quantities f and g being polynomial in all their arguments.

Writing

$$J(w, w') = \frac{\partial f}{\partial w}\frac{\partial g}{\partial w'} - \frac{\partial f}{\partial w'}\frac{\partial g}{\partial w} = J\left(\frac{f, g}{w, w'}\right),$$

we have seen that any rational function of all the variables can be expressed in the form

$$\frac{\Theta(w, w', z, z')}{J(w, w')},$$

where $\Theta(w, w', z, z')$ is a polynomial in w and w' having rational functions of z and z' for its coefficients.

Accordingly, following Picard, we take our most general single integral of algebraic functions in the form

$$\int \frac{Zdz' - Z'dz}{J(w, w')}$$

where Z and Z' possess the same general form as the preceding function Θ.

Integrals of this form are said to be of the first kind when, on the analogy of Abelian integrals, they have no infinities anywhere in the whole field of variation. Picard proves[†] that no integral of the first kind exists in connection with a single equation $F(w, z, z') = 0$, when this single equation is quite general; and he shews[‡] that, when such an integral does exist in connection with a less general single equation $F(w, z, z') = 0$, the form of

---

[*] A full and consecutive account of his researches is contained in his treatise already quoted.
[†] His treatise, vol. i, p. 113.   [‡] Ib., p. 118.

the subject of integration must satisfy special preliminary relations, even though these necessary relations are not of themselves sufficient to secure the existence of the integral. Here I shall proceed only so far as to obtain the corresponding necessary preliminary relations affecting the form of the subject of integration in the foregoing single integral, if it is to exist in connection with the two equations $f = 0$, $g = 0$.

The quantities Z and Z' are polynomial in w and w'; we proceed to shew that, if the integral is everywhere finite, they must be polynomial also in z and z', of limited order. The coefficients of the various combinations of powers of w and w' are certainly rational functions of z and z'; let any such coefficient be

$$\frac{S(z, z')}{R(z, z')},$$

where R and S denote polynomials in z and z', and consider the integral

$$\int \frac{Z dz'}{J}.$$

Assigning any parametric value to z, let $z' = c'$ be a zero of $R(z, z')$ for that value of z. (If there is no such zero, i.e., if R is a function of z only, the zeros of R would make the integral infinite: so that, for our purpose, R would then have to be constant). For that parametric value of z, let the subject of integration be expanded in powers of $z' - c'$; then, whether $z' = c'$ does or does not give a zero value to J, the subject of integration is—for every set of values of w and w'—of the form

$$\frac{A_s}{(z'-c')^s} + \frac{A_{s-1}}{(z'-c')^{s-1}} + \ldots + \frac{A_1}{z'-c'} + \text{regular function of } z'-c',$$

in the immediate vicinity of $z' = c'$, the positive integer s being $\geqslant 1$. The integral would be infinite at $z' = c'$, unless all the quantities $A_1, \ldots, A_s$ vanish. These quantities involve the parametric value of z; they can only vanish for all parametric values by vanishing identically, that is, by having no powers of $z' - c'$ with negative indices. Hence the polynomial $R(z, z')$, for any parametric value of z, can have no zero for a value of z'. It thus cannot involve z'; we have seen that it cannot be a function of z alone; hence $R(z, z')$ is a constant. The coefficient in question is a polynomial in z and z'.

Similarly for every coefficient in either Z or Z' in the integrals

$$\int \frac{Z dz'}{J}, \quad \int \frac{Z' dz}{J}.$$

Consequently the quantities Z and Z' are polynomial in all four arguments w, w', z, z'. And we know that J is polynomial in those four arguments.

Next, as regards the limitations upon the orders of these polynomials Z and Z', we shall assume that $f(w, w', z, z')$ is a quite general polynomial of order m in the four arguments combined, and that $g(w, w', z, z')$ is a similar polynomial of order n. Then J is a polynomial of order $m + n - 2$. It is easy to see, by an argument similar to the preceding argument, that integrals cannot be finite for infinite values of z and of z', if the order of the polynomials Z and Z' in all the four arguments combined is greater than $m + n - 4$.

We therefore infer, as a first condition, that if the integral is to be finite at all places in the whole field of variation, Z and Z' must be polynomial in all the four variables of order $\leqslant m + n - 4$, when f is the most general polynomial of order m and g is the most general polynomial of order n.

104. The independent variables for the integrals have been taken to be z and z'; but any two of the variables may thus be chosen, and the integral must still remain finite. We proceed to give the corresponding and equivalent expressions. We have

$$\frac{\partial f}{\partial w} dw + \frac{\partial f}{\partial w'} dw' + \frac{\partial f}{\partial z} dz + \frac{\partial f}{\partial z'} dz' = 0,$$

$$\frac{\partial g}{\partial w} dw + \frac{\partial g}{\partial w'} dw' + \frac{\partial g}{\partial z} dz + \frac{\partial g}{\partial z'} dz' = 0,$$

so that, on the elimination of dw', dw, dz, dz' in turn,

$$J(w, w') dw + J(z, w') dz + J(z', w') dz' = 0,$$
$$J(w', w) dw' + J(z, w) dz + J(z', w) dz' = 0,$$
$$J(w, z) dw + J(w', z) dw' + J(z', z) dz' = 0,$$
$$J(w, z') dw + J(w', z') dw' + J(z, z') dz = 0.$$

Using the first of these relations to substitute dw for dz' in the differential element, we have

$$\frac{Z dz' - Z' dz}{J(w, w')} = -\frac{Z' dz}{J(w, w')} - \frac{Z}{J(w, w') J(z', w')} \{J(w, w') dw + J(z, w') dz\}$$

$$= \frac{-Z dw}{J(z', w')} - \frac{Z' J(z', w') + Z J(z, w')}{J(w, w') J(z', w')} dz.$$

The differential element now is to be

$$\frac{W dz - Z dw}{J(z', w')},$$

where W is a polynomial in all the four variables; we therefore take

$$Z J(z, w') + Z' J(z', w') + W J(w, w') = 0.$$

Similarly, when we make z and w' the independent variables, the differential element of the integral of the first kind is

$$\frac{Z dw' - W' dz}{J(z', w)},$$

where W' is a polynomial in all the four variables, and

$$ZJ(z, w) + Z'J(z', w) + W'J(w', w) = 0.$$

In the same way, we can take any pair out of the four as the independent variables, and thus obtain six expressions in all for the subject of integration. The six expressions are

$$\frac{Zdz' - Z'dz}{J(w, w')}, \quad \frac{Wdz - Zdw}{J(z', w')}, \quad \frac{Z'dw - Wdz'}{J(z, w')},$$

$$\frac{Zdw' - W'dz}{J(z', w)}, \quad \frac{W'dw - Wdw'}{J(z', z)}, \quad \frac{W'dz - Z'dw}{J(z, w)};$$

and the relations connecting the polynomials are

$$ZJ(z, w') + Z'J(z', w') + WJ(w, w') = 0,$$
$$ZJ(z, w) + Z'J(z', w) + W'J(w', w) = 0,$$
$$Z'J(z', z) + WJ(w, z) + W'J(w', z) = 0,$$
$$ZJ(z, z') + WJ(w, z') + W'J(w', z') = 0,$$

which are always subject to the two fundamental equations

$$f = 0, \quad g = 0,$$

and are equivalent to only two independent equations. Writing

$$M = Z\frac{\partial f}{\partial z} + Z'\frac{\partial f}{\partial z'} + W\frac{\partial f}{\partial w} + W'\frac{\partial f}{\partial w'},$$

$$N = Z\frac{\partial g}{\partial z} + Z'\frac{\partial g}{\partial z'} + W\frac{\partial g}{\partial w} + W'\frac{\partial g}{\partial w'},$$

we can express the first of the four equations in the form

$$\left(M - W'\frac{\partial f}{\partial w'}\right)\frac{\partial g}{\partial w'} - \left(N - W'\frac{\partial g}{\partial w'}\right)\frac{\partial f}{\partial w'} = 0,$$

that is,

$$M\frac{\partial g}{\partial w'} - N\frac{\partial f}{\partial w'} = 0.$$

The others similarly give

$$M\frac{\partial g}{\partial w} - N\frac{\partial f}{\partial w} = 0,$$

$$M\frac{\partial g}{\partial z} - N\frac{\partial f}{\partial z} = 0,$$

$$M\frac{\partial g}{\partial z'} - N\frac{\partial f}{\partial z'} = 0.$$

The fundamental equations $f=0$ and $g=0$ are independent of one another; hence we must have

$$M = 0, \quad N = 0,$$

that is, the polynomials Z, Z', W, W' are such that

$$W\frac{\partial f}{\partial w} + W'\frac{\partial f}{\partial w'} + Z\frac{\partial f}{\partial z} + Z'\frac{\partial f}{\partial z'} = 0,$$

$$W\frac{\partial g}{\partial w} + W'\frac{\partial g}{\partial w'} + Z\frac{\partial g}{\partial z} + Z'\frac{\partial g}{\partial z'} = 0.$$

But these equations are not satisfied necessarily as identities; they need only be satisfied in virtue of the permanent equations

$$f = 0, \quad g = 0.$$

These relations impose limitations upon the forms of the polynomials Z, Z', W, W', which occur in the differential element of an integral of the first kind.

105. Limitations arise from two other causes. The first of these causes lies in the requirement that the condition of exact integrability shall be satisfied. As regards this condition, we shall take it for one of the forms of the integral, and shall reduce it to an expression symmetrical in all the variables.

The condition, that

$$\frac{Z\,dz' - Z'\,dz}{J(w, w')}$$

shall be a perfect differential, is

$$\frac{d}{dz}\left(\frac{Z}{J}\right) + \frac{d}{dz'}\left(\frac{Z'}{J}\right) = 0.$$

Now since

$$\frac{\partial f}{\partial z} + \frac{\partial f}{\partial w}\frac{\partial w}{\partial z} + \frac{\partial f}{\partial w'}\frac{\partial w'}{\partial z} = 0,$$

$$\frac{\partial g}{\partial z} + \frac{\partial g}{\partial w}\frac{\partial w}{\partial z} + \frac{\partial g}{\partial w'}\frac{\partial w'}{\partial z} = 0,$$

we have

$$J(w, w')\frac{\partial w}{\partial z} + J(z, w') = 0, \quad J(w', w)\frac{\partial w'}{\partial z} + J(z, w) = 0;$$

and similarly

$$J(w, w')\frac{\partial w}{\partial z'} + J(z', w') = 0, \quad J(w', w)\frac{\partial w'}{\partial z'} + J(z', w) = 0.$$

The condition of integrability is therefore

$$J(w, w')\left(\frac{\partial Z}{\partial z} + \frac{\partial Z'}{\partial z'}\right) - \left\{\frac{\partial Z}{\partial w} J(z, w') + \frac{\partial Z'}{\partial w} J(z', w')\right\}$$

$$+ \left\{\frac{\partial Z}{\partial w'} J(z, w) + \frac{\partial Z'}{\partial w'} J(z', w)\right\}$$

$$- Z\left\{\frac{\partial J(w, w')}{\partial z} - \frac{J(z, w')}{J(w, w')}\frac{\partial J(w, w')}{\partial w} + \frac{J(z, w)}{J(w, w')}\frac{\partial J(w, w')}{\partial w'}\right\}$$

$$- Z'\left\{\frac{\partial J(w, w')}{\partial z'} - \frac{J(z', w')}{J(w, w')}\frac{\partial J(w, w')}{\partial w} + \frac{J(z', w)}{J(w, w')}\frac{\partial J(w, w')}{\partial w'}\right\} = 0;$$

and it suffices that this condition should be satisfied in virtue of the governing equations $f = 0$ and $g = 0$.

Now, for appropriate polynomials A and B, we have

$$ZJ(z, w') + Z'J(z', w') + WJ(w, w') = Af + Bg,$$

identically; and so for our purpose, where the governing equations persist, we can take

$$\frac{\partial W}{\partial w} = -\frac{\partial Z}{\partial w}\frac{J(z, w')}{J(w, w')} - \frac{\partial Z'}{\partial w}\frac{J(z', w')}{J(w, w')} - \frac{Z}{J(w, w')}\frac{\partial J(z, w')}{\partial w} - \frac{Z'}{J(w, w')}\frac{\partial J(z', w')}{\partial w}$$

$$+ \frac{ZJ(z, w') + Z'J(z', w')}{J^2(w, w')}\frac{\partial J(w, w')}{\partial w} + \frac{A}{J(w, w')}\frac{\partial f}{\partial w} + \frac{B}{J(w, w')}\frac{\partial g}{\partial w},$$

the omitted terms vanishing in virtue of $f = 0$ and $g = 0$.

Similarly, for appropriate polynomials C and D, we have

$$ZJ(z, w) + Z'J(z', w) - W'J(w, w') = Cf + Dg;$$

and we similarly infer the corresponding relation

$$\frac{\partial W'}{\partial w'} = \frac{\partial Z}{\partial w'}\frac{J(z, w)}{J(w, w')} + \frac{\partial Z'}{\partial w'}\frac{J(z', w)}{\partial w'} + \frac{Z}{J(w, w')}\frac{\partial J(z, w)}{\partial w'} + \frac{Z'}{J(w, w')}\frac{\partial J(z', w)}{\partial w'}$$

$$- \frac{ZJ(z, w) + Z'J(z', w)}{J^2(w, w')}\frac{\partial J(w, w')}{\partial w'} - \frac{C}{J(w, w')}\frac{\partial f}{\partial w'} - \frac{D}{J(w, w')}\frac{\partial g}{\partial w'},$$

the omitted terms vanishing for the same reason as before.

Also we have

$$\frac{\partial J(w, w')}{\partial z} + \frac{\partial J(w', z)}{\partial w} + \frac{\partial J(z, w)}{\partial w'} = 0$$

identically, together with three similar relations by omitting z, w, w' in turn from the set of four variables. Moreover

$$J(z, w) J(z', w') + J(z', w) J(w', z) + J(w', w) J(z, z') = 0,$$

also identically. Using the foregoing relations, we have

$$J(w, w')\left\{\frac{\partial Z}{\partial z} + \frac{\partial Z'}{\partial z'} + \frac{\partial W}{\partial w} + \frac{\partial W'}{\partial w'}\right\} - \left\{A\frac{\partial f}{\partial w} + B\frac{\partial g}{\partial w} - C\frac{\partial f}{\partial w'} - D\frac{\partial g}{\partial w'}\right\}$$

$$- Z\left\{\frac{\partial J(w, w')}{\partial z} + \frac{\partial J(z, w)}{\partial w'} + \frac{\partial J(w', z)}{\partial w}\right\}$$

$$- Z'\left\{\frac{\partial J(w, w')}{\partial z'} + \frac{\partial J(z', w)}{\partial w'} + \frac{\partial J(w', z')}{\partial w}\right\} = 0,$$

that is, the relation

$$\frac{\partial Z}{\partial z} + \frac{\partial Z'}{\partial z'} + \frac{\partial W}{\partial w} + \frac{\partial W'}{\partial w'} = \frac{1}{J(w, w')}\left\{A\frac{\partial f}{\partial w} + B\frac{\partial g}{\partial w} - C\frac{\partial f}{\partial w'} - D\frac{\partial g}{\partial w'}\right\}$$

is satisfied in connection with the governing equations

$$f = 0, \quad g = 0.$$

Now we know that, in virtue of the governing equations, the quantities

$$\Sigma Z \frac{\partial f}{\partial z}, \quad \Sigma Z \frac{\partial g}{\partial z}$$

vanish; hence polynomials F, E, H, G (any one or more of which may be zero) exist such that the equations

$$Z\frac{\partial f}{\partial z} + Z'\frac{\partial f}{\partial z'} + W\frac{\partial f}{\partial w} + W'\frac{\partial f}{\partial w'} = Ff + Eg,$$

$$Z\frac{\partial g}{\partial z} + Z'\frac{\partial g}{\partial z'} + W\frac{\partial g}{\partial w} + W'\frac{\partial g}{\partial w'} = Hf + Gg,$$

are satisfied identically. These equations give

$$ZJ(z, w') + Z'J(z', w') + WJ(w, w') = \left(F\frac{\partial g}{\partial w'} - H\frac{\partial f}{\partial w'}\right)f + \left(E\frac{\partial g}{\partial w'} - G\frac{\partial f}{\partial w'}\right)g$$

satisfied identically. But the left-hand side is identically equal to

$$Af + Bg;$$

hence, subject to the governing equations, we must have

$$A = F\frac{\partial g}{\partial w'} - H\frac{\partial f}{\partial w'}, \qquad B = E\frac{\partial g}{\partial w'} - G\frac{\partial f}{\partial w'}.$$

Similarly, subject to the governing equations, we have

$$C = F\frac{\partial g}{\partial w} - H\frac{\partial f}{\partial w}, \qquad D = E\frac{\partial g}{\partial w} - G\frac{\partial f}{\partial w}.$$

Consequently

$$A\frac{\partial f}{\partial w} - C\frac{\partial f}{\partial w'} = FJ(w, w'), \qquad B\frac{\partial g}{\partial w} - D\frac{\partial g}{\partial w'} = GJ(w, w'),$$

always subject to the governing equations $f = 0$, $g = 0$.

Thus the equations become

$$\begin{aligned}
Z\frac{\partial f}{\partial z} + Z'\frac{\partial f}{\partial z'} + W\frac{\partial f}{\partial w} + W'\frac{\partial f}{\partial w'} &= Ff + Eg \\
Z\frac{\partial g}{\partial z} + Z'\frac{\partial g}{\partial z'} + W\frac{\partial g}{\partial w} + W'\frac{\partial g}{\partial w'} &= Hf + Gg \\
\frac{\partial Z}{\partial z} + \frac{\partial Z'}{\partial z'} + \frac{\partial W}{\partial w} + \frac{\partial W'}{\partial w'} &= F + G
\end{aligned}\right\}.$$

The first two of these equations are satisfied identically; the third only needs to be satisfied in connection with $f = 0$, $g = 0$.

They are the extension of Picard's equations* which are given for the case when there is only a single equation

$$f(w, z, z') = 0.$$

Picard's equations are derived from the foregoing set, by taking

$$g = w' = 0$$

as the second of our fundamental equations, together with

$$W' = 0, \quad E = 0, \quad H = 0, \quad G = 0;$$

and then, owing to the order of F, the third of the equations is satisfied identically.

It thus appears that, when there are two equations $f = 0$ and $g = 0$, the exact differential can be presented in six forms; that four quantities Z, Z', W, W', each polynomial in all the four variables, occur in these forms; and that there are other four polynomials E, F, G, H, such that the foregoing three equations exist, the first two being satisfied identically, while the third only needs to be satisfied concurrently with the governing equations $f = 0$ and $g = 0$.

106. It can easily be seen that, when $f = 0$ is a quite general equation of order m and $g = 0$ is a quite general equation of order n, the conditions required cannot be satisfied.

Let $N(p)$ denote the number of terms in the most general polynomial, which is of order p in w, w', z, z', so that

$$N(p) = \tfrac{1}{24}(p+1)(p+2)(p+3)(p+4).$$

We have seen (§ 102) that the polynomial Z, which (§ 103) can be of order $m + n - 4$, is subject to modification by use of the equations $f = 0$ and $g = 0$:

---

* *l. c.*, t. i, ch. v, § 4.

that is, it is subject to an additive quantity $Af + Bg$, where A and B are quite general polynomials of orders $n - 4$ and $m - 4$ respectively. Hence the number of disposable constants in Z effectively is

$$N(m + n - 4) - N(m - 4) - N(n - 4).$$

Similarly as regards Z', W, W'.

Again, E, F, G, H are polynomials of order $\leqslant 2m - 5$, $m + n - 5$, $m + n - 5$, $2n - 5$ respectively. The expression $Ff + Eg$ is unaltered by changing F into $F + Jg$ and E into $E - Jf$, where J is a quite general polynomial of order $m - 5$; hence the number of disposable constants in F and E together is

$$N(m + n - 5) + N(2m - 5) - N(m - 5).$$

Similarly the number of disposable constants in G and H together is

$$N(m + n - 5) + N(2n - 5) - N(n - 5).$$

The modifications in F and G do not affect the third condition, which has to be satisfied only concurrently with $f = 0$ and $g = 0$. Thus the total number of disposable constants is

$$4 \{N(m + n - 4) - N(m - 4) - N(n - 4)\}$$
$$+ N(m + n - 5) + N(2m - 5) - N(m - 5)$$
$$+ N(m + n - 5) + N(2n - 5) - N(n - 5).$$

The number of conditions to be satisfied in connection with the first identity is $N(2m + n - 5)$, and the number in connection with the second identity is $N(m + 2n - 5)$. The third relation, which affects the polynomials F and G, only needs to be satisfied subject to the equations $f = 0$ and $g = 0$; that is, subject to an additive quantity $Cf + Dg$ on the right-hand side, where C and D are quite general polynomials of order $n - 5$ and $m - 5$ respectively; consequently, the third relation requires

$$N(m + n - 5) - N(n - 5) - N(m - 5)$$

conditions. Thus the total number of conditions is

$$N(2m + n - 5) + N(m + 2n - 5) + N(m + n - 5) - N(n - 5) - N(m - 5).$$

The excess of the number of conditions to be satisfied, above the number of disposable constants, is

$$N(2m + n - 5) + N(m + 2n - 5) + N(m + n - 5) - N(n - 5) - N(m - 5)$$
$$- 4 \{N(m + n - 4) - N(m - 4) - N(n - 4)\}$$
$$- \{N(m + n - 5) + N(2m - 5) - N(m - 5)\}$$
$$- \{N(m + n - 5) + N(2n - 5) - N(n - 5)\}.$$

When the values of the different numbers N are inserted, this excess is easily found to be
$$\tfrac{1}{24} mn \{20(m-1)(m-2) + 18(m-1)(n-1) + 20(n-1)(n-2) + 24\} - 1,$$
which manifestly is positive when $m > 1$ and $n > 1$. Accordingly, in general, the relations cannot be satisfied by the disposable constants, and so we infer the result:—

When $f = 0$ and $g = 0$ are quite general equations, no single integral of the first kind connected with them exists: a result which obviously corresponds to the theorem of Picard already (§ 103) mentioned.

It follows that, if an integral of the first kind is to exist in connection with two equations $f = 0$ and $g = 0$, these equations must have special forms.

Ex. Shew that all the preceding conditions for the existence of an integral of the first kind, in connection with the equations
$$f = az + bw + cz^2z' + dwzz' + ew'z^2 + fw^2z' + gww'z + hw^2w' = 0,$$
$$g = a'z' + b'w' + c'zz'^2 + d'w'zz' + e'wz'^2 + f'w'^2z + g'ww'z' + h'ww'^2 = 0,$$
where the coefficients $a, \ldots, h, a', \ldots, h'$ are constants, are satisfied when
$$Z = z, \quad Z' = -z', \quad W = w, \quad W' = -w'.$$

107. The second class of conditions, mentioned at the beginning of § 105 as required to be satisfied in order that the single integral may be everywhere finite, depends upon the places where we have
$$J\left(\frac{f, g}{w, w'}\right) = 0,$$
which is not an identity, simultaneously with
$$f = 0, \quad g = 0.$$

As already indicated (§ 103), I do not propose here to enter upon any discussion of these conditions. The discussion will be difficult, but it is of supreme importance as regards even the existence of these integrals of the first order, as well as for all other single integrals. It can be initiated analytically on the lines of Picard's investigations in his treatise already quoted. It will involve the algebraical singularities of w and w' as algebraic functions defined by the two fundamental equations.

Double Integrals.

108. The discussion of double integrals follows a different trend. There is no limitation corresponding to the condition that must be fulfilled if the element of the integral is to be a complete differential element, as in § 105.

We have seen (§ 102) that, when two algebraic functions of z and z' are simultaneously given by two algebraic equations

$$f = f(w, w', z, z') = 0, \quad g = g(w, w', z, z') = 0,$$

the most general rational function of the variables can be expressed in the form

$$\frac{\Theta(w, w', z, z')}{J\left(\dfrac{f, g}{w, w'}\right)},$$

where Θ is a polynomial in w and w', the coefficients in this polynomial being rational functions of z and z'. Thus the typical double integral, connected with the algebraical equations $f = 0$ and $g = 0$, is of the form

$$\iint \frac{\Theta(w, w', z, z')}{J\left(\dfrac{f, g}{w, w'}\right)} \, dz\, dz';$$

the integration extends over a two-fold continuum. To express the integral more definitely, we take z and z' as functions of two real variables p and q, as in § 95; and then the expression of the integral becomes

$$\iint \frac{\Theta(w, w', z, z')}{J\left(\dfrac{f, g}{w, w'}\right)} J\left(\frac{z, z'}{p, q}\right) dp\, dq,$$

where the integration can be regarded as extending over an area in the p, q plane, limited initially by a fixed curve (or curves) in that plane and finally by a variable curve (or curves) in that plane. The simplest case arises, when we have a single simple closed curve as the fixed initial limit and a single simple closed curve as the variable final limit.

The first form of the preceding definition takes z and z' as the independent variables for integration. As we have already suggested that it may be convenient to take any two of the four variables as the independent variables for integration, we proceed to give the equivalent forms.

For this purpose we assume that, in order to express the quantities w, w', z, z' in terms of real variables p and q, we take two algebraic equations

$$F = F(w, w', z, z', p, q) = 0, \quad G = G(w, w', z, z', p, q) = 0,$$

forms which will prove useful in attempting an extension of Abel's theorem for the sum of any number of algebraic integrals of a single variable. The simultaneous roots of the four equations

$$f = 0, \quad g = 0, \quad F = 0, \quad G = 0,$$

are functions of p and q; so we have

$$0 = \frac{\partial F}{\partial w}\frac{\partial w}{\partial p} + \frac{\partial F}{\partial w'}\frac{\partial w'}{\partial p} + \frac{\partial F}{\partial z}\frac{\partial z}{\partial p} + \frac{\partial F}{\partial z'}\frac{\partial z'}{\partial p} + \frac{\partial F}{\partial p},$$

$$0 = \frac{\partial G}{\partial w}\frac{\partial w}{\partial p} + \frac{\partial G}{\partial w'}\frac{\partial w'}{\partial p} + \frac{\partial G}{\partial z}\frac{\partial z}{\partial p} + \frac{\partial G}{\partial z'}\frac{\partial z'}{\partial p} + \frac{\partial G}{\partial p},$$

$$0 = \frac{\partial f}{\partial w}\frac{\partial w}{\partial p} + \frac{\partial f}{\partial w'}\frac{\partial w'}{\partial p} + \frac{\partial f}{\partial z}\frac{\partial z}{\partial p} + \frac{\partial f}{\partial z'}\frac{\partial z'}{\partial p},$$

$$0 = \frac{\partial g}{\partial w}\frac{\partial w}{\partial p} + \frac{\partial g}{\partial w'}\frac{\partial w'}{\partial p} + \frac{\partial g}{\partial z}\frac{\partial z}{\partial p} + \frac{\partial g}{\partial z'}\frac{\partial z'}{\partial p},$$

and therefore

$$J\left(\frac{F, G, f, g}{z, z', w, w'}\right)\frac{\partial z}{\partial p} + J\left(\frac{F, G, f, g}{p, z', w, w'}\right) = 0,$$

$$J\left(\frac{F, G, f, g}{z, z', w, w'}\right)\frac{\partial z'}{\partial p} - J\left(\frac{F, G, f, g}{p, z, w, w'}\right) = 0.$$

Similarly

$$J\left(\frac{F, G, f, g}{z, z', w, w'}\right)\frac{\partial z}{\partial q} + J\left(\frac{F, G, f, g}{q, z', w, w'}\right) = 0,$$

$$J\left(\frac{F, G, f, g}{z, z', w, w'}\right)\frac{\partial z'}{\partial q} - J\left(\frac{F, G, f, g}{q, z, w, w'}\right) = 0.$$

Now, by the properties of determinants, we have

$$J\left(\frac{F, G, f, g}{p, z', w, w'}\right) J\left(\frac{F, G, f, g}{q, z, w, w'}\right) = J\left(\frac{F, G, f, g}{z, z', w, w'}\right) J\left(\frac{f, g}{w, w'}\right) J\left(\frac{F, G}{p, q}\right);$$

hence

$$J\left(\frac{F, G, f, g}{z, z', w, w'}\right) J\left(\frac{z, z'}{p, q}\right) = -J\left(\frac{f, g}{w, w'}\right) J\left(\frac{F, G}{p, q}\right),$$

and therefore

$$\frac{1}{J\left(\frac{f, g}{w, w'}\right)} J\left(\frac{z, z'}{p, q}\right) = \frac{-1}{J\left(\frac{F, G, f, g}{z, z', w, w'}\right)} J\left(\frac{F, G}{p, q}\right).$$

The right-hand side is symmetrical, save as to signs, for the four variables z, z', w, w'; hence it is equal to each of the six expressions

$$J\left(\frac{z, z'}{p, q}\right) \div J\left(\frac{f, g}{w, w'}\right), \quad -J\left(\frac{z', w}{p, q}\right) \div J\left(\frac{f, g}{w', z}\right), \quad J\left(\frac{w, w'}{p, q}\right) \div J\left(\frac{f, g}{z, z'}\right),$$

$$-J\left(\frac{z, w}{p, q}\right) \div J\left(\frac{f, g}{z', w'}\right), \quad J\left(\frac{z, w'}{p, q}\right) \div J\left(\frac{f, g}{z', w}\right), \quad -J\left(\frac{z'.\, w'}{p, q}\right) \div J\left(\frac{f, g}{z, w}\right).$$

Accordingly, when the variables of integration in the double integral are taken to be p and q, there are six equivalent expressions of the integral; one of them is the form first taken, and the other five are similarly constructed from a comparison of the six foregoing quantities; and each of the six expressions so obtained is (save as to sign) equal to the double integral*

$$\iint \frac{\Theta(w, w', z, z')}{J\left(\begin{array}{c}F, G, f, g\\z, z', w, w'\end{array}\right)} J\left(\frac{F, G}{p, q}\right) dp\, dq.$$

Double integrals of algebraic functions may be divided into various classes, following the analogy of the division of simple integrals of algebraic functions of a single variable; but the analogy is little more than a suggestion, because (as has been seen in Chap. IV) a definite infinity of a function of two variables can be a one-fold continuum in the immediate vicinity of any one definite place of infinite value, and because unessential singularities (when the term is used in the sense defined in § 58) have no limited analogue even in the case of uniform functions of only a single variable. One class, however, survives naturally in spite of the deficiencies in the analogy; it is composed of those integrals of algebraic functions which never acquire an infinite value, no matter how the two-fold continuum of integration is deformed. Such integrals are formally styled *double integrals of the first kind*.

109. The conditions, which must be satisfied by the double integral of an algebraic function connected with two given algebraic functions if it is to be of the first kind, are of four categories, according to the character of a place z, z' in relation to the subject of integration; and the four categories can be grouped in two pairs.

It is manifest that a finite place z, z', which is ordinary for the equations $f = 0$ and $g = 0$, and is also ordinary for the subject of integration, cannot give rise to an infinity of the integral. For near such a place $w = \alpha$, $w' = \alpha'$, $z = a$, $z' = a'$, we have

$$w = \alpha + W, \quad w' = \alpha' + W', \quad z = a + Z, \quad z' = a' + Z';$$

---

* This integral can also be expressed in the form

$$\iint \frac{\Theta(w, w', z, z')}{J\left(\begin{array}{c}F, G, f, g\\z, z', w, w'\end{array}\right)} dF\, dG,$$

which is the natural extension of the single integral

$$\int \frac{R(w, z)}{J\left(\begin{array}{c}\phi, f\\z, w\end{array}\right)} d\phi.$$

The latter integral is fundamental in one of the proofs of Abel's theorem for the sum of a number of integrals

$$\int \frac{R(w, z)}{\frac{\partial f}{\partial w}} dz,$$

when the upper limits of the integrals are given by the simultaneous roots of a permanent algebraic equation $f(w, z) = 0$ and a parametric algebraic equation $\phi(w, z) = 0$.

the equations $f = 0$, $g = 0$, then give relations of the form
$$W = (Z, Z')_1 + (Z, Z')_2 + \dots,$$
$$W' = (Z, Z')_1 + (Z, Z')_2 + \dots,$$
and no one of the quantities
$$\left\| \begin{array}{cccc} \frac{\partial f}{\partial w}, & \frac{\partial f}{\partial w'}, & \frac{\partial f}{\partial z}, & \frac{\partial f}{\partial z'} \\ \frac{\partial g}{\partial w}, & \frac{\partial g}{\partial w'}, & \frac{\partial g}{\partial z}, & \frac{\partial g}{\partial z'} \end{array} \right\|$$
vanishes at α, α', a, a'. As the place is ordinary also for $\Theta(w, w', z, z')$, the form of
$$\frac{\Theta(w, w', z, z')}{J\left(\frac{f, g}{w, w'}\right)}$$
in the vicinity of the place becomes
$$\frac{\Theta_0 + \Theta_1(Z, Z') + \Theta_2(Z, Z') + \dots}{J_0 + J_1(Z, Z') + J_2(Z, Z') + \dots};$$
and so the integral, in the vicinity of the place, becomes equal to
$$\iint \frac{\Theta_0 + \Theta_1(Z, Z') + \Theta_2(Z, Z') + \dots}{J_0 + J_1(Z, Z') + J_2(Z, Z') + \dots} dZ\, dZ',$$
which is finite at the place and in its immediate vicinity*.

In the first category, there are the conditions to be satisfied at a place z, z', which is ordinary for the equations $f = 0$, $g = 0$, but is not ordinary for the subject of integration. In the second category occur the conditions that must be satisfied for infinite values of z and z', when these constitute ordinary places for the equations $f = 0$ and $g = 0$. These two categories form one group, containing all the conditions which arise in connection with all the ordinary places of the two fundamental equations.

In the third category occur the conditions that must be satisfied at a non-ordinary finite place of the two fundamental equations; all such non-ordinary places are such as to satisfy some one or more than one of the six Jacobian equations
$$J\left(\left(\frac{f, g}{w, w', z, z'}\right)\right) = 0,$$
concurrently with the fundamental equations themselves. In the fourth category occur the conditions that must be satisfied for infinite values of z and z' when these constitute non-ordinary places for the equations $f = 0$ and $g = 0$. These two categories form one group, containing all the

---

* The symbols $(Z, Z')_1$, $\Theta_1(Z, Z')$, $J_1(Z, Z')$ denote the aggregate of terms of the first order; the symbols $(Z, Z')_2$, $\Theta_2(Z, Z')$, $J_2(Z, Z')$ denote the aggregate of terms of the second order; and so on.

conditions which arise in connection with all the non-ordinary places of the two fundamental equations.

110. As regards the first of these categories of places which, while ordinary finite places for the equations $f = 0$ and $g = 0$, provide an infinite value for the subject of integration, this infinite value can arise only through the coefficients of the powers of w and w' in the polynomial Θ. These coefficients are rational functions of z and z'. If then the double integral is not to have an infinity, the existence of these rational functions of z and z' must not compel such an infinity. Accordingly, the rational functions of z and z' must be integral functions: that is, they must be polynomials in z and z'. Thus $\Theta(w, w', z, z')$ becomes a polynomial in all its four arguments; consequently, as a first condition that our double integral may be everywhere finite, it follows that *the quantity $\Theta(w, w', z, z')$ must be a polynomial in the four variables w, w', z, z'*.

The similar consideration of the second category of places, constituted of infinite places (supposed ordinary) for $f = 0$ and $g = 0$, leads to a limitation upon the order of the polynomial $\Theta(w, w', z, z')$ if the double integral is to be not infinite for such places. For simplicity, suppose that f and g are quite general polynomials of aggregate orders m and n respectively, so that we may take

$$f = (* \!\!\! \bigcirc \!\!\! w, w', z, z', 1)^m, \quad g = (* \!\!\! \bigcirc \!\!\! w, w', z, z', 1)^n.$$

Then

$$J\left(\frac{f, g}{w, w'}\right) = (* \!\!\! \bigcirc \!\!\! w, w', z, z', 1)^{m+n-2},$$

in the quite general case. In order that the double integral may be not infinite for infinite values of z and z', the order of

$$\frac{\Theta(w, w', z, z')}{J\left(\dfrac{f, g}{w, w'}\right)}$$

must be equal to, or be less than, -3; and therefore the aggregate order of the polynomial $\Theta(w, w', z, z')$ must be not greater than $m + n - 5$. Thus in order that the double integral may remain finite for infinite values of z and z', when these are ordinary places of $f = 0$ and $g = 0$, *the aggregate order of the polynomial $\Theta(w, w', z, z')$ must be $\leqslant m + n - 5$, where m and n denote the respective aggregate orders of f and g*.

As regards the second group of conditions indicated above, they are concerned with the places where the equations

$$f = 0, \quad g = 0, \quad J\left(\frac{f, g}{w, w'}\right) = 0,$$

are simultaneously satisfied. Their discussion will involve the consideration of the singularities of w and w' as algebraic functions of the variables. As before for single integrals (§ 107), so here for double integrals, the whole subject is left for investigation; a beginning can be made on the lines of Picard's discussion of the matter when there is only a single equation $f = 0$ defining a single algebraic function*.

111. It is possible to obtain an extension of Abel's theorem for the sum of a number of integrals of algebraic functions of a single variable, by constructing an expression for the sum of a number of double integrals of the type

$$\iint \frac{\Theta(w, w', z, z')}{J\left(\dfrac{f, g}{w, w'}\right)} dz dz',$$

where f and g are polynomials of aggregate orders m and n respectively. We shall assume that the aggregate order of the polynomial Θ is not greater than $m + n - 5$.

As before (§ 108), we define w, w', z, z' as functions of two real variables p and q by means of the permanent equations

$$f(w, w', z, z') = 0, \quad g(w, w', z, z') = 0,$$

and associated parametric equations

$$F(w, w', z, z', p, q) = 0, \quad G(w, w', z, z', p, q) = 0;$$

and we shall assume that F and G are quite general polynomials in w, w', z, z', of aggregate orders k and l respectively. As these are four algebraical equations in w, w', z, z', of orders m, n, k, l respectively, they determine $klmn$ ($= \mu$) sets of roots, each root in each set of roots being a function of p and q. Denoting any such set by w_r, w_r', z_r, z_r', the double integral can as before be transformed to

$$\iint \frac{\Theta(w_r, w_r', z_r, z_r')}{J\left(\dfrac{F_r, G_r, f_r, g_r}{z_r, z_r', w_r, w_r'}\right)} J\left(\frac{F_r, G_r}{p, q}\right) dp dq,$$

or, if we write

$$\Phi_r = \Theta(w_r, w_r', z_r, z_r') J\left(\frac{F_r, G_r}{p, q}\right) = \Phi(w_r, w_r', z_r, z_r'),$$

$$J_r = J\left(\frac{F_r, G_r, f_r, g_r}{z_r, z_r', w_r, w_r'}\right),$$

so that Φ is a polynomial of aggregate order $\leqslant k + l + m + n - 5$, the integral (for this set of roots) becomes

$$\iint \frac{\Phi_r}{J_r} dp dq.$$

We assume the integral taken over any finite simple closed region in the p, q plane.

* *l.c.*, t. i, ch. vii.

Let W denote the result of eliminating w', z, z' between $f = 0$, $g = 0$, $F = 0$, $G = 0$; the quantities $w_1, \ldots, w_\mu$ are the roots of $W = 0$. The theory of elimination shews that we have a relation of the form

$$W = Kf + Lg + MF + NG.$$

Similarly, eliminating w, z, z', and denoting the eliminant by W', we have a relation of the form

$$W' = K'f + L'g + M'F + N'G,$$

and the quantities $w_1', \ldots, w_\mu'$ are the roots of $W' = 0$. Likewise eliminating w, w', z', and w, w', z in turn, and denoting the respective eliminants by Z and Z', we have relations of the form

$$Z = Pf + Qg + RF + SG,$$
$$Z' = P'f + Q'g + R'F + S'G;$$

the quantities $z_1, \ldots, z_\mu$ are the roots of $Z = 0$, and the quantities $z_1', \ldots, z_\mu'$ are the roots of $Z' = 0$. And the quantities K, L, M, N, K', L', M', N', P, Q, R, S, P', Q', R', S' are polynomials of the respective appropriate orders. In particular, if we write

$$\Delta = \begin{vmatrix} K, & L, & M, & N \\ K', & L', & M', & N' \\ P, & Q, & R, & S \\ P', & Q', & R', & S' \end{vmatrix},$$

Δ is a polynomial of aggregate order

$$(mnpq - m) + (mnpq - n) + (mnpq - k) + (mnpq - l),$$
$$= 4\mu - m - n - k - l.$$

The simultaneous combinations w_r, w_r', z_r, z_r' (for $r = 1, \ldots, \mu$) are the simultaneous roots of

$$f = 0, \quad g = 0, \quad F = 0, \quad G = 0;$$

these we call the congruous roots. All other combinations of the roots of $W = 0$, $W' = 0$, $Z = 0$, $Z' = 0$, are called non-congruous roots; they are not simultaneous roots of $f = 0$, $g = 0$, $F = 0$, $G = 0$; but, for each such combination, we have

$$\Delta = 0.$$

For the sake of simplicity, we shall assume that each of the roots of $W = 0$, $W' = 0$, $Z = 0$, $Z' = 0$, is simple.

Now consider the quantity

$$\frac{\Phi(w, w', z, z')\,\Delta}{W W' Z Z'}.$$

It can be expressed in a partial-fraction series of the form

$$\Sigma\Sigma\Sigma\Sigma \frac{A_{rr'ss'}}{(w-w_r)(w'-w'_{r'})(z-z_s)(z'-z'_{s'})},$$

the summation being for $r, r', s, s', = 1, \ldots, \mu$, independently of one another; and

$$A_{rr'ss'} = \frac{\Phi(w_r, w'_{r'}, z_s, z'_{s'}) \Delta_{rr'ss'}}{\dfrac{\partial W}{\partial w_r} \dfrac{\partial W'}{\partial w'_{r'}} \dfrac{\partial Z}{\partial z_s} \dfrac{\partial Z'}{\partial z'_{s'}}}.$$

When $r = r' = s = s'$, we can denote the coefficient A by A_r; then

$$A_r = \frac{\Phi_r \Delta_r}{\dfrac{\partial W}{\partial w_r} \dfrac{\partial W'}{\partial w_r'} \dfrac{\partial Z}{\partial z_r} \dfrac{\partial Z'}{\partial z_r'}}.$$

Unless all the equalities $r = r' = s = s'$ are satisfied, we have

$$\Delta_{rr'ss'} = 0,$$

so that all the coefficients A other than A_r, for $r = 1, \ldots, \mu$, vanish. Thus we have the identity

$$\frac{\Phi(w, w', z, z') \Delta}{WW'ZZ'} = \sum_{r=1}^{\mu} \frac{A_r}{(w-w_r)(w'-w'_{r'})(z-z_r)(z'-z'_{r'})}.$$

Let both sides be expanded in ascending powers of $1/w, 1/w', 1/z, 1/z'$. On the left-hand side, the index of the term of highest order in w, w', z, z' in the numerator is

$$\leqslant k + l + m + n - 5 + (4\mu - m - n - k - l)$$
$$\leqslant 4\mu - 5;$$

the index of the term of highest order in w, w', z, z' in the denominator is 4μ; hence the index of the first term in the expansion $\leqslant 5$. On the right-hand side, the index of the first term in the expansion is -4, and its coefficient is

$$\sum_{r=1}^{\mu} A_r.$$

No such term can occur in the left-hand side under the assigned conditions; hence

$$\sum_{r=1}^{\mu} A_r = 0,$$

that is,

$$\sum_{r=1}^{\mu} \frac{\Phi_r \Delta_r}{\dfrac{\partial W}{\partial w_r} \dfrac{\partial W'}{\partial w_r'} \dfrac{\partial Z}{\partial z_r} \dfrac{\partial Z'}{\partial z_r'}} = 0.$$

From the expression for W, we have

$$\frac{\partial W}{\partial w_r} = K_r \frac{\partial f}{\partial w_r} + L_r \frac{\partial g}{\partial w_r} + M_r \frac{\partial F}{\partial w_r} + N_r \frac{\partial G}{\partial w_r},$$

$$0 = K_r \frac{\partial f}{\partial w_r'} + L_r \frac{\partial g}{\partial w_r'} + M_r \frac{\partial F}{\partial w_r'} + N_r \frac{\partial G}{\partial w_r'},$$

$$0 = K_r \frac{\partial f}{\partial z_r} + L_r \frac{\partial g}{\partial z_r} + M_r \frac{\partial F}{\partial z_r} + N_r \frac{\partial G}{\partial z_r},$$

$$0 = K_r \frac{\partial f}{\partial z_r'} + L_r \frac{\partial g}{\partial z_r'} + M_r \frac{\partial F}{\partial z_r'} + N_r \frac{\partial G}{\partial z_r'};$$

and similarly from the expressions for W', Z, Z'. Thus

$$\begin{vmatrix} \frac{\partial W}{\partial w_r}, & 0, & 0, & 0 \\ 0, & \frac{\partial W'}{\partial w_r'}, & 0, & 0 \\ 0, & 0, & \frac{\partial Z}{\partial z_r}, & 0 \\ 0, & 0, & 0, & \frac{\partial Z'}{\partial z_r'} \end{vmatrix}$$

$$= \begin{vmatrix} K_r, & L_r, & M_r, & N_r \\ K_r', & L_r', & M_r', & N_r' \\ P_r, & Q_r, & R_r, & S_r \\ P_r', & Q_r', & R_r', & S_r' \end{vmatrix} \begin{vmatrix} \frac{\partial f}{\partial w_r}, & \frac{\partial g}{\partial w_r}, & \frac{\partial F}{\partial w_r}, & \frac{\partial G}{\partial w_r} \\ \frac{\partial f}{\partial w_r'}, & \frac{\partial g}{\partial w_r'}, & \frac{\partial F}{\partial w_r'}, & \frac{\partial G}{\partial w_r'} \\ \frac{\partial f}{\partial z_r}, & \frac{\partial g}{\partial z_r}, & \frac{\partial F}{\partial z_r}, & \frac{\partial G}{\partial z_r} \\ \frac{\partial f}{\partial z_r'}, & \frac{\partial g}{\partial z_r'}, & \frac{\partial F}{\partial z_r'}, & \frac{\partial G}{\partial z_r'} \end{vmatrix},$$

that is,

$$\frac{\partial W}{\partial w_r} \frac{\partial W'}{\partial w_r'} \frac{\partial Z}{\partial z_r} \frac{\partial Z'}{\partial z_r'} = \Delta_r J_r.$$

Consequently, we have

$$\sum_{r=1}^{\mu} \frac{\Phi_r}{J_r} = 0,$$

and therefore

$$\sum_{r=1}^{\mu} \iint \frac{\Phi_r}{J_r} dp\,dq = 0,$$

when the double integration is taken over any simple closed region in the plane of the real variables p, q.

This is a restricted extension of a part of Abel's general theorem on the sum of integrals. The result is true, even if the integral

$$\iint \frac{\Phi}{J} \, dp \, dq$$

is not everywhere finite, that is, if the integral is not of the first kind*. The conditions, which have been imposed upon the integral, are that it is to be finite for all places which are ordinary for the equations $f = 0$, $g = 0$, all infinite places being supposed included among these ordinary places.

---

* It should be added that, by a different method, Picard (*l. c.*, t. i, p. 190) obtains this extension for double integrals of the first kind (that is, integrals which are everywhere finite) when there is a single fundamental equation $f(w, z, z') = 0$.

CHAPTER VII

Level Places of Two Uniform Functions

112. Hitherto, save for rare exceptions, only individual functions of two variables have been considered at any one time; and we have seen that there exist continuous aggregates of places where a function has an assigned level value or a zero value. This property precludes us from establishing definite relations of inversion between a single function of more than one variable and the variables of that function. Such relations are highly important in various branches of the theory of functions of a single variable; they are no less important when functions involve several independent variables. To establish them, it is necessary to have as many functions, independent of one another, as there are variables; and therefore, for the present purpose, we shall consider two independent functions of z and z'. Moreover, quite apart from reasons that make inversion a possible necessity, we have seen that it is desirable to consider simultaneously two independent functions of z and z'.

We still shall limit ourselves throughout to uniform analytic functions; and we shall begin with the discussion of the relations between two functions that are regular everywhere in the finite part of the field of variation. As we know, every such function can be expressed as a series of positive integral powers of z and z', which (if an infinite series) converges absolutely for finite values of $|z|$ and $|z'|$, and has all its essential singularities outside the finite part of the field of variation. We know (§ 53) that such a function must possess zeros somewhere in the field of variation; but it may happen that the zeros do not occur in the finite part of the field[*], and then they occur at the essential singularities.

We proceed to establish the following theorem:—

Two independent functions, regular throughout the finite part of the field of variation, vanish simultaneously at some place or places within the whole field.

---

[*] For example, the function $e^{z+z'}$ cannot vanish for finite values of z and of z'; all its zeros, a continuous aggregate, occur for those values of z and z' which make the real part of $z+z'$ negative and infinite.

113. Let the two functions, everywhere regular, be denoted by $f(z, z')$ and $g(z, z')$; and let a, a' be any place in the finite part of the whole field of variation for z and z'. In view of the proposition to be established, it is reasonable to assume that neither $f(z, z')$ nor $g(z, z')$ vanishes at a, a'; if both should vanish at a, a', the proposition needs no proof; if one of them should vanish at a, a', but not the other, the following proof will be found to cover the case.

We consider the immediate vicinity of a, a', and take
$$z = a + u, \quad z' = a' + u'.$$
Because $f(z, z')$ and $g(z, z')$ are regular everywhere in the finite part of the field of variation, we have expressions for them in the form
$$f(z, z') = f(a, a') + {}_f(u, u')_m + {}_f(u, u')_{m+1} + \ldots,$$
$$g(z, z') = g(a, a') + {}_g(u, u')_n + {}_g(u, u')_{n+1} + \ldots,$$
where ${}_f(u, u')_m$ represents the aggregate of terms of combined dimension m in u and u' as contained in the power-series for f; and similarly for the other homogeneous sets of terms in f, and for the homogeneous sets of terms in g. In the simplest cases, the integer m is unity and the integer n is unity; in all cases, both the positive integers m and n are finite.

When $m = 1$ and $n = 1$, the quantities
$$_f(u, u')_1, \quad {}_g(u, u')_1,$$
are usually independent linear combinations of u and u'; their determinant is the value, at a, a', of
$$J\left(\frac{f, g}{z, z'}\right),$$
which does not vanish everywhere, because the functions f and g are independent. If it should happen that J vanishes at a, a', so that there
$$\frac{\partial f}{\partial a} \div \frac{\partial g}{\partial a} = \frac{\partial f}{\partial a'} \div \frac{\partial g}{\partial a'} = \kappa,$$
then we have
$$f(a + u, a' + u') - f(a, a') = {}_f(u, u')_1 + \ldots,$$
$$f(a + u, a' + u') - f(a, a') - \kappa \{g(a + u, a' + u') - g(a, a')\} = {}_g(u, u')_2 + \ldots,$$
where the first set of terms ${}_g(u, u')_2$ is of order higher than the first set ${}_f(u, u')_1$ and usually is not the square of ${}_f(u, u')_1$. If, however,
$$\lambda \{{}_g(u, u')_2\} = \{{}_f(u, u')_1\}^2,$$
where λ is a constant, then we should take a new combination
$$f(a + u, a' + u') - f(a, a') - \kappa \{g(a + u, a' + u') - g(a, a')\}$$
$$- \lambda \{f(a + u, a' + u') - f(a, a')\}^2.$$

Similarly for other cases.

We proceed until, at some stage, we obtain two series in u and u', such that the lowest set of terms in one series cannot be expressed solely by means of the lowest set of terms in the other series; and this stage is attained after steps that are finite in number, because

$$J\left(\begin{matrix}f, g \\ z, z'\end{matrix}\right)$$

does not vanish identically.

Similarly, if m is greater than unity and $n = 1$; and if $m = 1$, while n is greater than unity; and if both m and n are greater than unity. In each case, we obtain a couple of series, the aggregate of terms of lowest dimensions in the two series not being expressible solely in terms of one another. And then, because of this independence, the equations

$$A = {}_f(u, u')_m, \quad B = {}_g(u, u')_n,$$

where A and B are assigned quantities independent of u and u', determine a limited number of values of u and u'. In particular, let l be the greatest common measure of m and n, and write

$$m = \mu l, \quad n = \nu l;$$

and let E be the eliminant of ${}_f(u, u')_m$ and ${}_g(u, u')_n$, so that

$$E = a_{m0}{}^n c_{0n}{}^m + \dots.$$

Then the equation giving values of u is

$$(a_{m0}{}^n c_{0n}{}^m + \dots) u^{mn} + \dots + \{(-Ac_{0n})^\nu - (-Ba_{m0})^\mu\}^l = 0,$$

and therefore, if

$$A = \kappa P^m = \kappa P^{\mu l}, \quad B = \lambda P^n = \lambda P^{\nu l},$$

each value of u is of the type

$$u = kP;$$

or, for sufficiently small values of $|u|, |A|, |u'|, |B|$, and so of $|P|$, we have

$$u = kP, \quad u' = k'P,$$

where $|k|$ and $|k'|$ are finite, while some of the quantities k and k' can be zero. Manifestly,

$$\kappa = {}_f(k, k')_m, \quad \lambda = {}_g(k, k')_n;$$

and, in general, we shall have

$$\left. \begin{matrix} u = kP + k_1 P^2 + \dots \\ u' = k'P + k_1' P^2 + \dots \end{matrix} \right\},$$

from the relations

$$\left. \begin{matrix} A = {}_f(u, u')_m + {}_f(u, u')_{m+1} + \dots \\ B = {}_g(u, u')_n + {}_g(u, u')_{n+1} + \dots \end{matrix} \right\}.$$

After these explanations and inferences, we proceed to shew that it is possible to choose quantities u and u' of small moduli, so that the place $a + u$, $a' + u'$ is in a small domain of a, a', and so also that

$$|f(a+u, a'+u')| < |f(a, a')|,$$
$$|g(a+u, a'+u')| < |g(a, a')|,$$

simultaneously. Let

$$f(a, a') = Q + iR, \quad g(a, a') = S + iT,$$

where Q, R, S, T are real quantities, and neither $|Q+iR|$ nor $|S+iT|$ vanishes. Now choose M a small positive quantity, in every case less than $|Q+iR|$, unless $|Q+iR|$ happens to be zero and then we take M zero; and choose an argument ψ such that Q and $M\cos\psi$ have opposite signs and, at the same time, R and $M\sin\psi$ have opposite signs. (If R be zero, we can take ψ equal to either 0 or π and should choose the value giving opposite signs to Q and $M\cos\psi$. Similarly, if Q be zero, with a choice of $\frac{1}{2}\pi$ or $\frac{3}{2}\pi$ for ψ). Again, choose N a small positive quantity, in every case less than $|S+iT|$, unless $|S+iT|$ happens to be zero and then we take N zero; and choose an argument χ such that S and $N\cos\chi$ have opposite signs and, at the same time, T and $N\sin\chi$ have opposite signs. (Arrangements as to choice of χ can be made similar to those for ψ, if either S or T should vanish). Then evidently

$$|f(a, a') + Me^{\psi i}| < |f(a, a')|,$$
$$|g(a, a') + Ne^{\chi i}| < |g(a, a')|.$$

Now we have seen that, for sufficiently small values of M and of N, the relations

$$Me^{\psi i} = {}_f(u, u')_m + {}_f(u, u')_{m+1} + \ldots,$$
$$Ne^{\chi i} = {}_g(u, u')_n + {}_g(u, u')_{n+1} + \ldots,$$

give a limited number of sets of values of the form

$$\left. \begin{array}{l} u = kP + k_1 P^2 + \ldots \\ u' = k'P + k_1' P^2 + \ldots \end{array} \right\},$$

where $|P|$ is a small magnitude such that

$$Me^{\psi i} = \kappa P^n, \quad Ne^{\chi i} = \lambda P^m;$$

thus $|u|$ and $|u'|$ are small, of the same magnitude as $|P|$, while $|k_1 P^2 + \ldots|$, $|k_1' P^2 + \ldots|$, are small compared with $|P|$. For such values, we have

$$|f(a+u, a'+u')| < |f(a, a')|,$$
$$|g(a+u, a'+u')| < |g(a, a')|,$$

which was to be proved.

Accordingly, we infer that it is possible to pass from a place a, a' to a place z, z', which may be called a place adjacent to a, a', and which is such as to give the relations
$$|f(z, z')| < |f(a, a')|,$$
$$|g(z, z')| < |g(a, a')|,$$
simultaneously.

Within the finite part of the field of variation, the functions $f(z, z')$ and $g(z, z')$ are everywhere regular, so that no singularities are encountered in transitions from a place to an adjacent place. We therefore can pass from place to place within the finite part of the field of variation, always choosing the passage so as to give successively decreasing values of $|f(z, z')|$ and $|g(z, z')|$.

If at any place c, c', one of the two functions (but not both of them) should vanish—say $f(c, c') = 0$—then we choose the next place $c + u, c' + u'$, so that M is zero, that is, so that κ is zero, and such that
$$f(c+u, c'+u') = 0, \quad |g(c+u, c'+u')| < |g(c, c')|.$$
The choice is always possible for finite values of z and z', because the functions $f(z, z')$ and $g(z, z')$ are regular for those finite values and consequently can be expressed as regular power-series.

114. It thus follows that, by an appropriately determinate choice of successive places at every stage, each place being adjacent to its predecessor, the moduli of $f(z, z')$ and $g(z, z')$ can be continually decreased so long as they differ, either or both, from zero. Thus they tend to zero in value, as the successive places are chosen; and continued decrease can be effected, so long as they are not zero.

Moreover, we know that every regular function possesses a zero value or zero values somewhere within the whole field of variation. If the zero value does not occur at some ordinary place, then (§ 53) it occurs at the essential singularity or singularities, as e.g. for the function $e^{P(z, z')}$, where $P(z, z')$ is a polynomial in z and z', when the places for the zero values belong to the non-finite part of the field.

Hence ultimately, either for finite values of z and z', or for infinite values of either of them or of both of them, a place will be attained at which both the moduli $|f(z, z')|$ and $|g(z, z')|$ are zero. Such a place is a common zero of $f(z, z')$ and $g(z, z')$; and therefore our theorem—that two functions $f(z, z')$ and $g(z, z')$, regular everywhere in the finite part of the field of variation, vanish simultaneously somewhere in the whole field—is established.

Ex. Consider the functions
$$f(z, z') = e^{z+z'}, \quad g(z, z') = ze^{-(z+z')},$$
both of which are regular for all finite values of z and z'.

Let
$$z + z' = \log(r^n e^{m\theta i}),$$
$$z = re^{\theta i},$$

where r, θ, m, n are real constants; then
$$f(z, z') = r^n e^{m\theta i},$$
$$g(z, z') = r^{(1-n)} e^{(1-m)\theta i}.$$

When $0 < n < 1$, we manifestly have
$$f(z, z') = 0, \quad g(z, z') = 0,$$

when r is zero: that is, the two suggested functions acquire zero values for some specified values of z' (even when $z=0$) which do not lie in the finite part of the field of variation of the two variables.

115. Next, consider the case of two uniform analytic functions, each of them devoid of essential singularities in the finite part of the field of variation, and each of them possessing continuous aggregates of poles and isolated unessential singularities. We know, from an earlier proposition (§ 90), that the functions can be expressed in the forms

$$f(z, z') = \frac{P(z, z')}{Q(z, z')}, \qquad g(z, z') = \frac{R(z, z')}{S(z, z')},$$

where $P(z, z')$, $Q(z, z')$, $R(z, z')$, $S(z, z')$ are functions of z and z', which are regular everywhere in the finite part of the field of variation.

The zero-places of $f(z, z')$ are those of $P(z, z')$; it may happen that a zero-place of $P(z, z')$ is also a zero-place of $Q(z, z')$, and then the place is an unessential singularity of $f(z, z')$ which, among its unlimited set of values there, can acquire the value zero: that is, the zeros of $f(z, z')$ are given by the zeros of $P(z, z')$. Similarly for $g(z, z')$ and $R(z, z')$. Hence $f(z, z')$ and $g(z, z')$ will vanish simultaneously somewhere in the field of variation, if the functions $P(z, z')$ and $R(z, z')$, everywhere regular in the finite part of the field, vanish simultaneously somewhere in the whole field. But we have proved that these regular functions $P(z, z')$ and $R(z, z')$ must vanish simultaneously at some place or at some places in the whole field. Hence we infer the following theorem:—

Two independent functions $f(z, z')$ and $g(z, z')$, which are uniform and analytic, and all the essential singularities of which occur only in the non-finite part of the field of variation, must vanish together at some place or some places in the whole field of variation.

We infer also, as an immediate corollary, the following further theorem:—

Two independent functions $f(z, z')$ and $g(z, z')$, which are uniform and analytic, and all the essential singularities of which occur only in the non-finite part of the field of variation, must acquire assigned level values at some place or some places in the whole field of variation.

For if the assigned level values be α for $f(z, z')$ and β for $g(z, z')$, the functions $f(z, z') - \alpha$ and $g(z, z') - \beta$ satisfy all the conditions imposed upon the functions $f(z, z')$ and $g(z, z')$ in the earlier theorem; the application of that earlier theorem leads to the result just stated.

A corresponding result holds as regards simultaneous poles for $f(z, z')$ and $g(z, z')$.

In general, a corresponding result does not hold as regards the occurrence of simultaneous unessential singularities of $f(z, z')$ and $g(z, z')$.

116. When two functions $f(z, z')$ and $g(z, z')$ have a common zero-place, we need to consider their relations to one another in its immediate vicinity; we need also, if possible, to assign an integer which shall represent its multiplicity as a common zero-place. Let a, a' be such a place, so that

$$f(a, a') = 0, \quad g(a, a') = 0;$$

for places in its immediate vicinity, represented by $a + u, a' + u'$, we have

$$\left.\begin{aligned} f(z, z') &= K u^s u'^t P(u, u') e^{\bar{P}(u, u')} \\ &= L u^s u'^t Q(u, u') e^{\bar{Q}(u, u')} \\ g(z, z') &= K' u^{s'} u'^{t'} R(u, u') e^{\bar{R}(u, u')} \\ &= L' u^{s'} u'^{t'} S(u, u') e^{\bar{S}(u, u')} \end{aligned}\right\}.$$

Here K, L, K', L' are constants; s, t, s', t' are positive integers which can be zero separately or together; $\bar{P}(u, u'), \bar{Q}(u, u'), \bar{R}(u, u'), \bar{S}(u, u')$ are regular functions of u and u', which vanish with u and u'. The functions $P(u, u')$ and $R(u, u')$ are polynomials in u, having as their coefficients regular functions of u' which vanish with u'; the functions $Q(u, u')$ and $S(u, u')$ are polynomials in u', having as their coefficients regular functions of u which vanish with u. When $u^{-s} u'^{-t} f(z, z')$ does not vanish with u and u', we substitute unity for each of the functions P and Q; and similarly when $u^{-s} u'^{-t} g(z, z')$ does not vanish with u and u', we substitute unity for each of the functions R and S.

The order of a zero-place for a single function in each variable has already been defined. For the function $f(z, z')$, it is

$$s + m \text{ in } z, \quad t + n \text{ in } z',$$

where m and n are the positive integers, which are the degrees of P and Q regarded respectively as polynomials in u and in u'; and m and n are zero, only when $u^{-s} u'^{-t} f(z, z')$ does not vanish with u and u'. For the function $g(z, z')$, it is similarly

$$s' + m' \text{ in } z, \quad t' + n' \text{ in } z',$$

where m' and n' are the positive integers, which are the degrees of R and S regarded respectively as polynomials in u and in u'; and m' and n' are zero, only when $u^{-s'} u'^{-t'} g(z, z')$ does not vanish with u and u'.

Beyond the factors $u^s u'^t$ and $u^{s'} u'^{t'}$, the relations of $f(z, z')$ and $g(z, z')$ in the vicinity of a, a' depend upon the relations of the functions P or Q (as representative of f) and the functions R or S (as representative of g) to one another. Consider, in particular, the functions

$$P(u, u') = u^m + u^{m-1} p_1(u') + \ldots + p_m(u'),$$

where $p_1, \ldots, p_m$ are regular functions of u', vanishing with u', and

$$R(u, u') = u^{m'} + u^{m'-1} r_1(u') + \ldots + r_{m'}(u'),$$

where $r_1, \ldots, r_{m'}$ are regular functions of u', vanishing with u'. To determine whether there are common sets of values of u and u', in the vicinity of $u = 0$ and $u' = 0$, where P and R vanish together, we take

$$P = 0, \quad R = 0,$$

as simultaneous equations, algebraical in u. Eliminating u between them, we have (save in one case) a resultant which is a function of u' only; also, as each of the quantities $p_1, \ldots, p_m, r_1, \ldots, r_{m'}$ is a regular function of u' vanishing with u', this resultant is of the form

$$u'^M \phi(u'),$$

where M is a positive integer, chosen so that $\phi(u')$, a regular function of u', does not vanish when $u' = 0$. To the exact determination of M we shall return later.

The excepted case arises when the resultant vanishes identically. When the resultant does not vanish identically, the necessary values of u', making P and R vanish together, are given by

$$u'^M \phi(u') = 0,$$

where $\phi(0)$ is not zero and $\phi(u')$ is a regular function. We at once have $u' = 0$, as a possibility; the associated value of u is $u = 0$. The alternative possibilities would arise through zeros of the regular function $\phi(u')$: but as $\phi(0)$ is not zero, it is possible to assign a finite positive quantity ϵ, less than the smallest among the moduli of the zeros of $\phi(u')$. In that case, there is no value of u' within the range $|u'| \leq \epsilon$ such that $\phi(u')$ vanishes; and then the resultant vanishes for no value of u' other than $u' = 0$: that is to say, there is no zero-place for f and g in the immediate vicinity of a, a', other than a, a' itself.

117. When the resultant of the two equations $P = 0$ and $R = 0$, which are algebraical in u, vanishes identically, the inference is that these two equations in u have common roots, one or more. Let the number of these common roots be l, and let them be the roots of an equation

$$U = u^l + u^{l-1} k_1(u') + \ldots + k_l(u') = 0,$$

where $k_1, \ldots, k_l$ manifestly are regular functions of u' vanishing with u'. Then U is a factor of P save as to possible multiplication by a factor $e^{a(u')}$, where $a(u')$ is a regular function of u' that vanishes with u'; and similarly U

is a factor of R, save as to a similar possible limitation. Let the quotient of P by U be

$$u^{m-l} + u^{m-l-1} f_1(u') + \ldots + f_{m-l}(u');$$

and let the quotient of R by U be

$$u^{m'-l} + u^{m'-l-1} g_1(u') + \ldots + g_{m'-l}(u'),$$

where all the quantities $f_1, \ldots, f_{m-l}, g_1, \ldots, g_{m'-l}$ are regular functions of u', vanishing with u'. The conditions, necessary and sufficient to secure this result, are those which render the relation

$$(u^{m-l} + u^{m-l-1} f_1 + \ldots + f_{m-l})(u^{m'} + u^{m'-1} q_1 + \ldots + q_{m'})$$
$$= (u^{m'-l} + u^{m'-l-1} g_1 + \ldots + g_{m'-l})(u^m + u^{m-1} p_1 + \ldots + p_m),$$

an identity: viz. we must have the l independent determinants, each of $m + m' - 2l - 1$ rows and $m + m' - 2l - 1$ columns (we assume $m \geqslant m'$ for purposes of statement), which can be formed out of the array

$$\begin{Vmatrix} p_1-r_1, & p_2-r_2, & p_3-r_3, & \ldots, & p_{m'}-r_{m'}, & p_{m'+1}, & \ldots\ldots, & p_m, & 0, & 0, & \ldots, & 0 \\ 1, & r_1, & r_2, & \ldots, & r_{m'-1}, & r_{m'}, & \ldots\ldots, & 0, & 0, & 0, & \ldots\ldots \\ 0, & 1, & r_1, & \ldots, & r_{m'-2}, & r_{m'-1}, & r_{m'}, \ldots, & 0, & 0, & 0, & \ldots\ldots \\ \cdots\cdots\cdots\cdots\cdots\cdots\cdots\cdots\cdots\cdots\cdots\cdots\cdots\cdots\cdots\cdots \\ 0, & 0, & 0, & \ldots\ldots\ldots\ldots\ldots\ldots\ldots\ldots\ldots\ldots\ldots\ldots, & q_{m'} \\ 1, & p_1, & p_2, & \ldots, & p_{m'-1}, & p_{m'}, & \ldots\ldots, & p_{m-1}, & p_m, & 0, & \ldots, & 0 \\ 0, & 1, & p_1, & \ldots\ldots\ldots\ldots\ldots\ldots\ldots\ldots\ldots, & p_{m-2}, p_{m-1}, p_m, & \ldots, & 0 \\ \cdots\cdots\cdots\cdots\cdots\cdots\cdots\cdots\cdots\cdots\cdots\cdots\cdots\cdots\cdots\cdots \\ 0, & 0, & 0, & \ldots\ldots\ldots\ldots\ldots\ldots\ldots\ldots\ldots\ldots\ldots\ldots, & p_m \end{Vmatrix}$$

vanishing identically for all values of u'.

In actual practice with two given functions, we should in general experience the same arithmetical difficulty as before (§§ 70, 71). Here we are concerned with the effect of the relative reducibility of the functions; the foregoing are the l analytical conditions for this reducibility.

When all the conditions for the identical evanescence of these l determinants are satisfied, P and R have a common factor U: and then all the zeros of U within the domain are also zeros of P and R. Now these zeros of U form a continuous aggregate, since U is a regular function; for l values of u can be associated with any value of u' in the domain so as to make U vanish.

118. It thus appears on the one hand that, when the resultant of P and R, regarded as polynomials in u, does not vanish identically, the zero-place a, a' is isolated: that is to say, simultaneous zero-values of P and R cannot be found, except at a, a', in a region given by

$$|z - a| \leqslant \epsilon, \quad |z' - a'| \leqslant \epsilon',$$

where ϵ and ϵ' are assigned positive quantities made as small as we please. And it appears on the other hand that, when the resultant of P and R, regarded as polynomials in u, does vanish identically, the zero-place a, a' is not isolated.

Moreover, in the case when P and R have a common factor U, we can write
$$P = Up(u, u'), \quad R = Uq(u, u'),$$
where all the functions P, R, U, p, q are regular functions of u and u'; each of them vanishes when $u = 0$ and $u' = 0$; and each of them is a polynomial in u, having unity as the coefficient of the highest power of u and, as coefficients of the succeeding powers of u, regular functions of u' which vanish when $u' = 0$. From the construction of U, we may assume that p and q have no common factor; so that the zero-place of p and q at $u = 0$ and $u' = 0$ is isolated. Now

$$J\left(\frac{P, R}{u, u'}\right) = RJ\left(\frac{p, U}{u, u'}\right) + PJ\left(\frac{U, q}{u, u'}\right) + U^2 J\left(\frac{p, q}{u, u'}\right).$$

Hence the Jacobian of P and R vanishes for all the aggregate of places making U vanish, because all these places make P and R vanish. But this Jacobian does not vanish (except at a, a') for places in the domain of a, a', which make P and R vanish but leave U different from zero. Also, as

$$\left.\begin{array}{l} f(z, z') = K u^s u'^t P(u, u') e^{\overline{P}(u, u')} \\ g(z, z') = L u^{s'} u'^{t'} R(u, u') e^{\overline{R}(u, u')} \end{array}\right\},$$

it follows that the Jacobian of the independent regular functions f and g vanishes for all the aggregate of places making U vanish, while it does not vanish (except at a, a') for places in the domain of a, a' that make f and g vanish but leave U different from zero.

These results have followed upon the selection of $P(u, u')$ as the significant factor of f in the immediate domain of a, a', and of $R(u, u')$ as the significant factor of g in the same domain. The same results follow upon a selection of $Q(u, u')$ and $R(u, u')$ as the significant factors of f and g; likewise upon a selection of $P(u, u')$ and $S(u, u')$ as these factors, and upon a selection of $Q(u, u')$ and $S(u, u')$ as these factors.

Gathering together all the results, we can summarise them as follows:—

(i) *Any two independent functions, uniform, analytic, and devoid of essential singularities in the finite part of the field of variation of the two variables z and z', possess common zero-places somewhere within the field of variation:—*

(ii) *In general, each common zero-place of two independent functions, which are uniform, analytic, and devoid of essential singularities in the finite part of the field of variation of z and z', is an isolated place, so far as concerns the vanishing of the two functions:—*

(iii) *Less generally, when two such independent functions possess a common factor, which is necessarily of the same character throughout the finite part of the field of variation and which itself vanishes at the common zero-place of the two functions, then the common zero-place of the two functions is not isolated; in its immediate vicinity, the two functions possess a continuous aggregate of zero-places which belong to the common factor:—*

(iv) *The Jacobian J, of two independent functions f and g, does not vanish identically. It may vanish at a zero-place common to the two functions. When the common zero-place is isolated, then f, g, and J do not simultaneously vanish at any other place in the immediate vicinity of that place. When the common zero-place is not isolated, then f, g, and J vanish simultaneously at a continuous aggregate of places in the immediate vicinity of the common zero-place.*

119. In the preceding consideration of two functions $f(z, z')$ and $g(z, z')$ discussed simultaneously, there has been the fundamental assumption that the two functions are analytically independent of one another in the sense that neither of them can be expressed, either implicitly or explicitly, by any functional relation which, save for the occurrence of f and g, is otherwise free from variable quantities. Were the assumption not justified, the Jacobian of the two functions would vanish identically; we then should not possess sufficient material for the consideration of the common characteristic properties of f and g as simultaneous functions of two variables.

But, after the preceding explanations, two limitations can be introduced as regards a couple of functions. One of these affects them simultaneously: the other affects them individually: yet neither of them imposes limitations upon generality, for the purposes of this investigation.

Our discussions will deal with any pair of regular functions, which are not merely independent in the general sense, but which possess the further quality that they have no common factor, itself a regular function and vanishing at places within the domain considered. For any such pair of regular functions, each simultaneous zero-place is isolated. The zero-place may be simple or it may be multiple; when it is multiple, the multiplicity is represented by a definite positive integer.

It will be convenient to use some epithet to imply that two independent regular functions, existing together in the domain of a place where they vanish, do not possess a common factor, which is itself a regular function in that domain and vanishes at the centre of the domain. When a common factor of that type is not possessed by a couple of such functions, they will be called *free*. If on the contrary they do possess a common factor of that type, they will be called *tied*. Accordingly, when we deal with a couple of regular functions simultaneously, they will be assumed to be both independent and free.

The other limitation aims at the exclusion of unessential complications, and is suggested by the most general form of a function $f(z, z')$ in the immediate vicinity of a zero a, a', viz.

$$f(z, z') = K(z-a)^s (z'-a')^t P(z-a, z'-a') e^{\bar{P}(z-a, z'-a')}.$$

Thus $(z-a)^s$ is a factor of $f(z, z')$: at another zero c, c', it could have another factor $(z-c)^\sigma$; that is, it would have a factor $(z-a)^s(z-c)^\sigma$. And so on, for other zeros. We shall assume that, if $f(z, z')$ initially possesses a factor which is a function of z alone, then $f(z, z')$ is modified by the removal of that factor in z alone. Similarly, of course, if it initially possesses a factor which is a function of z' alone, then we shall assume it to be modified by the removal of that factor also. Any such factor of either variable alone can only contribute properties characteristic of a function of a single variable. Thus, for instance, we should not consider $\wp(z)\wp(z')$, where the periods of $\wp(z)$ are unaffected by the periods of $\wp(z')$, as a proper quadruply-periodic function; we should not consider $\wp(z)\sin z'$ as a proper triply-periodic function; we should not consider $\sin z \sin z'$ as a proper doubly-periodic function.

It seems unnecessary to introduce an epithet to indicate the non-composite character of a function $f(z, z')$; in what follows, we shall assume that we are dealing with functions which are of this non-composite character.

Accordingly we can enunciate the theorem:—

The common zero-places of two functions of z and z', which are uniform, analytic, and devoid of essential singularities in the finite part of the field of variation, and which are independent and free, are isolated places in the field of variation.

120. An indication has been given of the determination of the integer which shall represent the multiplicity of an isolated simultaneous zero-place of two regular functions. In the vicinity of such a place a, a', we take

$$z = a + u, \quad z' = a' + u';$$

and then, after the preceding explanations, we can assume that the integers s and t are zero for $f(z, z')$, and that the integers s' and t' are zero for $g(z, z')$. Thus

$$f(z, z') = KP(u, u') e^{\bar{P}(u, u')}, \quad g(z, z') = LR(u, u') e^{\bar{R}(u, u')},$$

in the immediate vicinity of $u = 0, u' = 0$; and

$$P(u, u') = u^m + u^{m-1} p_1(u') + \ldots + p_m(u'),$$
$$R(u, u') = u^{m'} + u^{m'-1} r_1(u') + \ldots + r_{m'}(u'),$$

where all the coefficients $p_1, \ldots, p_m, r_1, \ldots, r_{m'}$ are regular functions of u' and vanish when $u' = 0$. When the eliminant of $P(u, u')$ and $R(u, u')$, regarded as polynomials in u, is formed, it is a regular function of u' which vanishes when $u' = 0$; and so it can be expressed in a form

$$u'^M \phi(u'),$$

where $\phi(0)$ does not vanish, and where M is a positive integer. This integer M measures the multiplicity of a, a', as a simultaneous zero of f and g.

The detailed determination of M can be effected as follows. Let
$$P(u, u') = (u - \rho_1)(u - \rho_2) \ldots (u - \rho_m),$$
$$R(u, u') = (u - \sigma_1)(u - \sigma_2) \ldots (u - \sigma_{m'}),$$
where $\rho_1, \ldots, \rho_m, \sigma_1, \ldots, \sigma_{m'}$ are functions of u' (regular functions of fractional or integer powers of u') all vanishing when $u' = 0$. Their governing terms—that is, the lowest power of u' in each of them, with its appropriate coefficient—can be determined as in Puiseux's treatment of algebraic functions. Now, except as to a constant factor that is of no importance here, the eliminant of P and R is
$$\prod_{r=1}^{m} \prod_{s=1}^{m'} (\rho_r - \sigma_s).$$

When $\rho_r - \sigma_s$ is expressed in terms of u', every occurring power having a positive index, let μ_{rs} be the index of the lowest power it contains; then we see that
$$M = \sum_{r=1}^{m} \sum_{s=1}^{m'} \mu_{rs},$$
which thus gives an expression for the multiplicity M. It is easily established that the quantity M, thus obtained, is an integer.

The simplest case occurs when, in the expansions
$$\left. \begin{array}{l} f(z, z') = a_{10}(z - a) + a_{01}(z' - a') + \ldots \\ g(z, z') = c_{10}(z - a) + c_{01}(z' - a') + \ldots \end{array} \right\},$$
no one of the quantities $a_{10}, a_{01}, c_{10}, c_{01}, a_{10}c_{01} - c_{10}a_{01}$ vanishes: the value of M, for the zero a, a', is unity in this case.

Note. If, instead of the functions P and R, we take Q and S, as representative of f and g, and construct the eliminant of Q and S regarded as polynomials in u', the eliminant is
$$u^M \psi(u),$$
where ψ is a regular function of u such that $\psi(0)$ is not zero, and M is the same integer as before. The proof is a simple matter of pure algebra.

121. All the preceding remarks apply to the simultaneous zero-places of two regular functions $f(z, z')$ and $g(z, z')$. It applies equally to the level values of two regular functions $f(z, z')$ and $g(z, z')$, say α and β respectively, where $|\alpha|$ and $|\beta|$ are finite. The functions $f(z, z')$ and $g(z, z')$ are independent, as before. The functions $f(z, z') - \alpha$ and $g(z, z') - \beta$ will be supposed free, that is, we shall extend the significance of the epithet 'free,' as applied to $f(z, z')$ and $g(z, z')$, so that it applies to this case also. The functions $f(z, z') - \alpha$ and $g(z, z') - \beta$ will also be supposed non-composite as regards factors which are functions of z alone or functions of z' alone, as was the case with $f(z, z')$ and $g(z, z')$. And, now, we can enunciate the theorem:—

The common level places of two regular functions, which exist together in a domain of the variables, and which are independent and free, are isolated; and the multiplicity of any level place, giving values α and β to $f(z, z')$ and $g(z, z')$ respectively, is the multiplicity of the place, as a simultaneous zero of the functions $f(z, z') - \alpha$, $g(z, z') - \beta$.

122. Further, consider two functions $f(z, z')$ and $g(z, z')$, independent of one another, not tied, and existing in a common domain; and suppose that $f(z, z')$ has a pole at a place p, p', which is an ordinary place for $g(z, z')$, say a level place for $g(z, z')$, (zero being a possible level value there). Then the place is a common level place for the functions $\phi(z, z')$ and $g(z, z')$; and we know that, if $\phi(z, z')$ and $g(z, z')$ are free, that is, if $\phi(z, z')$ and $g(z, z') - g(p, p')$ possess no common factor which is a regular function of z, z' vanishing at p, p', then the common level place at p, p' for $\phi(z, z')$ and $g(z, z')$ is isolated, and its multiplicity is the index of the lowest power of z' in the z'-eliminant of $\phi(z, z')$ and $g(z, z') - g(p, p')$.

It is convenient to extend the significance of the terms *tied* and *free* as applied to a couple of independent uniform functions f and g. We shall say that they are tied if, for any constant quantities α and β, either $f - \alpha$ and $g - \beta$; or $f - \alpha$ and $(g - \beta)^{-1}$; or $(f - \alpha)^{-1}$ and $g - \beta$; or $(f - \alpha)^{-1}$ and $(g - \beta)^{-1}$ (being really two alternatives) possess a common factor which is a regular function of z and z' having a zero (and so an infinitude of zeros) in the domain; and we shall say that the two independent functions f and g are free, when no common factor of that type exists for any one of the combinations. Moreover, we shall also assume that neither $f - \alpha$ nor $(f - \alpha)^{-1}$ nor $g - \beta$ nor $(g - \beta)^{-1}$ contains any factor, which is a regular function of z alone or of z' alone and vanishes for one (or for more than one) finite value of the variable.

On the basis of earlier results, we can now enunciate the following theorems:—

(i) *Let $f(z, z')$ and $g(z, z')$ be two functions, which are uniform, analytic, and devoid of essential singularities in the finite part of the field of variation of z and z', and which are independent and free. The places where one of the functions acquires a level value and where the other has a pole, are isolated; and the multiplicity of the place for the two functions conjointly is the multiplicity of the place as a level-and-zero place for one of the functions and the reciprocal of the other.*

(ii) *The common poles of two uniform functions, which exist together in a domain of the variables, and which are independent and free, are isolated; and the multiplicity of the common pole for the two functions conjointly is the*

14—2

multiplicity of the place as a common zero for the reciprocals of the two functions jointly.

The theorems follow at once from an earlier theorem by considering the behaviour of the reciprocal of a function in the immediate vicinity of any pole of the function.

When we extend the term *level value* of a uniform function to include

(i) a zero value of the function, this being a unique zero, independent of the way in which the variables reach the place giving the zero value:

(ii) a level value α of the function, where $|\alpha|$ is finite, this being a similarly unique level value of the function:

(iii) an infinite value of the function, this being a unique infinity of the function arising at a pole:

then all the theorems, already enunciated concerning two functions, can be summarised in the one theorem :—

The common level places of two uniform functions, which are uniform, analytic, and devoid of essential singularities in the finite part of the field of variation of z and z', and which are independent and free, are isolated; and the multiplicity of the level place for the two functions conjointly is the index of the lowest term in the eliminant of the two functions or of their reciprocals or of either with the reciprocal of the other, expressed in the vicinity of the place.

Combining this result with the investigation, which settled the order of multiplicity of the place a, a' as a level place of the functions f and g and therefore as a zero of the functions

$$f(z, z') - \alpha, \quad g(z, z') - \beta,$$

we have the following corollary :—

Let a, a' be an isolated common zero of multiplicity M of the functions

$$f(z, z') - \alpha, \quad g(z, z') - \beta:$$

then, for values of $|\alpha'|$ and $|\beta'|$ sufficiently small, there are common zeros, simple or multiple, of aggregate multiplicity M, of the functions

$$f(z, z') - \alpha - \alpha', \quad g(z, z') - \beta - \beta',$$

which coalesce into the single common zero of multiplicity M of

$$f(z, z') - \alpha, \quad g(z, z') - \beta,$$

when α' and β' vanish.

CHAPTER VIII

Uniform Periodic Functions

123. We now proceed to consider the property, of such functions as possess the property, which customarily is called periodicity. Limitation will be made at this stage to periodicity of the type that is linear and additive, though the type is only a very particular form of the general automorphic property, mentioned in Chapter II.

In conformity with general usage, we say that two constant quantities ω and ω' are periods, or a period-pair, or a period, of a function $f(z, z')$ of two complex variables, when the relation

$$f(z + \omega, z' + \omega') = f(z, z')$$

is satisfied for all values of z and of z'. In such an event, the relation

$$f(z + s\omega, z' + s\omega') = f(z, z')$$

is satisfied for all integer values, positive and negative, of s. Moreover, it is assumed implicitly that ω and ω' constitute a proper period-pair; that is to say, a relation

$$f(z + k\omega, z' + k'\omega') = f(z, z')$$

is not satisfied for all values of z and z' except when $k = k'$, both k and k' being integers, and that the same relation is not satisfied, even if $k = k'$, when the common value of k and k' is the reciprocal of an integer.

In dealing with periodic functions of a single complex variable, infinitesimal periods are excluded. Speaking generally, we could say* that, if a uniform function of a single variable possessed an infinitesimal period, then within any finite region, however small, round any point, however arbitrary, the function would acquire the same value an unlimited number of times. The possibility of the existence of such functions may not be denied; but they cannot belong to the class of analytic functions. In the case of analytic functions which are not mere constants, the result of the possession of infinitesimal periods would be to make practically any point and every point an essential singularity. Accordingly, so far as concerns functions of a single variable, the possibility of infinitesimal periods is excluded.

124. We likewise exclude the possibility of infinitesimal periods for functions of two variables; but the exclusion can be based on different

* See my *Theory of Functions*, § 105.

grounds also. For the present purpose, we shall limit ourselves to uniform analytic functions* of two variables; and we then have a theorem†, due to Weierstrass, as follows:—

A uniform analytic function of two independent complex variables z and z' possesses infinitesimal periods only if it can be expressed as a function of $az + a'z'$, where a and a' are any constants.

First, suppose that our function $f(z, z')$ can be expressed in a form
$$f(z, z') = F(az + a'z').$$
Then if we take any two quantities P and P' such that
$$aP + a'P' = 0,$$
we have
$$f(z + P, z' + P') = F(az + a'z' + aP + a'P')$$
$$= F(az + a'z')$$
$$= f(z, z');$$
and therefore when P and P' are constants, we may regard P and P' as a period-pair for $f(z, z')$, supposed expressible in the given form. The only relation between P and P' is $aP + a'P' = 0$; hence either of them can be taken infinitesimally small, and the other then is infinitesimally small also. It follows that, when a function of z and z' can be expressed in the form of a function of $az + a'z'$ alone, where a and a' are any constants, then it possesses infinitesimal periods.

Further, writing $az + a'z' = v$, we have
$$\frac{\partial f}{\partial z} = a \frac{\partial F}{\partial v}, \quad \frac{\partial f}{\partial z'} = a' \frac{\partial F}{\partial v},$$
and therefore
$$a' \frac{\partial f}{\partial z} - a \frac{\partial f}{\partial z'} = 0.$$

Hence when the function is of the form $f(az + a'z')$, so that it possesses infinitesimal periods, the foregoing relation is satisfied. Conversely, by the theory of equations of this form, the most general integral equation equivalent to this differential equation is
$$f(z, z') = F(az + a'z'),$$
where F is any function whatever of its single argument; and therefore, when a function $f(z, z')$ satisfies the relation
$$a' \frac{\partial f}{\partial z} - a \frac{\partial f}{\partial z'} = 0$$
in general (and not merely for an arithmetical pair, or for sets of arithmetical pairs, of values for z and z'), it possesses infinitesimal periods.

* The result holds for multiform functions and, under conditions not yet established, possibly even for functions that have an unlimited number of values for any assigned values of the variables; see Weierstrass, *Ges. Werke*, t. ii, p. 69, p. 70.

† It is established for the case of n variables, Weierstrass, *Ges. Werke*, t. ii, pp. 62—64.

Next, suppose that our uniform analytic function is not expressible in a form $F(az + a'z')$ for any constants a and a' whatever; and consider a region in the field of variation where the function $f(z, z')$ is regular. No relation

$$a' \frac{\partial f}{\partial z} - a \frac{\partial f}{\partial z'} = 0,$$

for non-vanishing values of a and a', is satisfied over the whole of this region; hence we can take places z_1 and z_1', z_2 and z_2' within the region, such that $|J_{12}|$, where

$$J_{12} = \begin{vmatrix} \dfrac{\partial f(z_1, z_1')}{\partial z_1}, & \dfrac{\partial f(z_1, z_1')}{\partial z_1'} \\ \dfrac{\partial f(z_2, z_2')}{\partial z_2}, & \dfrac{\partial f(z_2, z_2')}{\partial z_2'} \end{vmatrix},$$

is finite and not zero. Also when we take places $z_1 + u_1$ and $z_1' + u_1'$, $z_2 + u_2$ and $z_2' + u_2'$, $z_1 + v_1$ and $z_1' + v_1'$, $z_2 + v_2$ and $z_2' + v_2'$, where all the quantities $|u_1|, |u_1'|, |u_2|, |u_2'|, |v_1|, |v_1'|, |v_2|, |v_2'|$ are infinitesimally small, the quantity $|J_{12}'|$, where

$$J_{12}' = \begin{vmatrix} \dfrac{\partial f(z_1 + u_1, z_1' + u_1')}{\partial z_1}, & \dfrac{\partial f(z_1 + v_1, z_1' + v_1')}{\partial z_1'} \\ \dfrac{\partial f(z_2 + u_2, z_2' + u_2')}{\partial z_2}, & \dfrac{\partial f(z_2 + v_2, z_2' + v_2')}{\partial z_2'} \end{vmatrix},$$

differs from $|J_{12}|$ only infinitesimally, and therefore its modulus is finite and not zero.

Consider the possibility of the existence of two periods h and h'. Whatever these quantities may be, we have generally

$$f(z + h, z' + h') - f(z, z') = \int_{z, z'}^{z+h, z'+h'} \left(\frac{\partial f}{\partial \zeta} d\zeta + \frac{\partial f}{\partial \zeta'} d\zeta' \right),$$

because the subject of integration is a perfect differential. Take a combined ζ-path from z to $z + h$ and a ζ'-path from z' to $z' + h'$, and let

$$\zeta = z + ht, \quad \zeta' = z' + h't,$$

so that the range of integration is represented by variations of t from 0 to 1; and then generally

$$f(z + h, z' + h') - f(z, z') = h \int_0^1 \frac{\partial f(z + ht, z' + h't)}{\partial z} dt + h' \int_0^1 \frac{\partial f(z + ht, z' + h't)}{\partial z'} dt.$$

Suppose now that h and h' are infinitesimal, so that the derivatives of $f(z, z')$ differ only infinitesimally in the t-range from 0 to 1 from their values at $t = 0$; then we have a relation of the form

$$f(z + h, z' + h') - f(z, z') = h \frac{\partial f(z + u, z' + u')}{\partial z} + h' \frac{\partial f(z + v, z' + v')}{\partial z'},$$

where $|u|, |u'|, |v|, |v'|$ are infinitesimal of the same order as $|h|$ and $|h'|$, and may depend upon z and z'. Accordingly, returning in particular to our two places z_1 and z_1', z_2 and z_2', we have

$$f(z_1 + h, z_1' + h') - f(z_1, z_1') = h \frac{\partial f(z_1 + u_1, z_1' + u_1')}{\partial z_1} + h' \frac{\partial f(z_1 + v_1, z_1' + v_1')}{\partial z_1'},$$

$$f(z_2 + h, z_2' + h') - f(z_2, z_2') = h \frac{\partial f(z_2 + u_2, z_2' + u_2')}{\partial z_2} + h' \frac{\partial f(z_2 + v_2, z_2' + v_2')}{\partial z_2'},$$

and so on for any number of places; two will suffice for our purpose.

When h and h' are periods (whether infinitesimal or not), the left-hand sides vanish. As the equations are valid, when the periods are infinitesimal, the right-hand sides also vanish; so that we have

$$h J_{12}' = 0, \quad h' J_{12}' = 0.$$

Now J_{12}' is not zero; hence both h and h' are zero. In other words, our uniform analytic function of two variables cannot have infinitesimal periods, unless it is expressible as a function of a single argument $az + a'z'$, where a and a' are two constants.

125. Next, let ω_1 and ω_1', ω_2 and ω_2', ω_3 and ω_3', ... be period-pairs for a uniform analytic function $f(z, z')$; then we have

$$f(z + r_1\omega_1 + r_2\omega_2 + r_3\omega_3 + ..., z' + r_1\omega_1' + r_2\omega_2' + r_3\omega_3' + ...) = f(z, z'),$$

where $r_1, r_2, r_3, ...$ are any integers, positive or negative, and independent of one another.

In the case of a uniform analytic function of one variable, it is known that there are not more than two independent periods and that the ratio of these periods for a doubly periodic function cannot be real[*]; the last property can be expressed by saying that if the periods are $\omega, = \alpha + i\beta$, and $\omega', = \alpha' + i\beta'$, the determinant

$$\begin{vmatrix} \alpha, & \beta \\ \alpha', & \beta' \end{vmatrix}$$

is not zero.

The corresponding theorem[†] in the case of uniform analytic functions of two variables is as follows:—

A uniform analytic function of two variables z and z' cannot possess more than four independent period-pairs ω_1 and ω_1', ω_2 and ω_2', ω_3 and ω_3', ω_4 and ω_4'; and if

$$\omega_s = \alpha_s + i\beta_s, \quad \omega_s' = \alpha_s' + i\beta_s',$$

---

[*] When the ratio is real and commensurable, both periods are integer multiples of one and the same period; when the ratio is real and incommensurable, there are infinitesimal periods.

[†] It is partly due to Jacobi, *Ges. Werke*, t. ii, pp. 25—50.

for all four values of s (the parts α, β, α', β' being real), the determinant

$$\begin{vmatrix} \alpha_1, & \alpha_2, & \alpha_3, & \alpha_4 \\ \beta_1, & \beta_2, & \beta_3, & \beta_4 \\ \alpha_1', & \alpha_2', & \alpha_3', & \alpha_4' \\ \beta_1', & \beta_2', & \beta_3', & \beta_4' \end{vmatrix}$$

must not vanish.

126. As a preliminary lemma, we require the following proposition: if relations

$$\begin{aligned} \omega_4 &= k\omega_1 + l\omega_2 + m\omega_3 \\ \omega_4' &= k\omega_1' + l\omega_2' + m\omega_3' \end{aligned}$$

are satisfied among four period-pairs, where k, l, m are real quantities, then either there are not more than three linearly independent period-pairs or there are infinitesimal periods.

First, suppose that k, l, m are commensurable, and that then each of them is expressed in its lowest terms. Let d denote the highest common factor of their numerators, and let M denote the least common multiple of their denominators; and write

$$k = \frac{d}{M} k', \quad l = \frac{d}{M} l', \quad m = \frac{d}{M} m',$$

where k', l', m' are integers; then we have

$$\frac{M}{d} \omega_4 = k'\omega_1 + l'\omega_2 + m'\omega_3,$$

$$\frac{M}{d} \omega_4' = k'\omega_1' + l'\omega_2' + m'\omega_3'.$$

Now M/d is a fraction in its lowest terms, being an integer only if d is unity; change M/d into a continued fraction and let p/q be the last convergent before the final value; then

$$\frac{M}{d} - \frac{p}{q} = \pm \frac{1}{dq},$$

so that

$$q \frac{M}{d} - p = \pm \frac{1}{d}.$$

Now $\frac{M}{d} \omega_4$ and $\frac{M}{d} \omega_4'$ manifestly are a period-pair, and therefore also $q \frac{M}{d} \omega_4$ and $q \frac{M}{d} \omega_4'$; consequently

$$\left(q \frac{M}{d} - p \right) \omega_4 \quad \text{and} \quad \left(q \frac{M}{d} - p \right) \omega_4'$$

also are a period-pair, that is, ω_4/d and ω_4'/d are a period-pair. Let*

$$\frac{\omega_4}{d} = \Omega_4, \quad \frac{\omega_4'}{d} = \Omega_4';$$

then

$$M\Omega_4 = k'\omega_1 + l'\omega_2 + m'\omega_3, \quad M\Omega_4' = k'\omega_1' + l'\omega_2' + m'\omega_3',$$

where the integers M, k', l', m' have no factor common to all.

Moreover, we can assume that any two of the four quantities have no common factor. For if two of them, say k' and l' had a common factor μ, the quantities

$$\frac{k'}{\mu}\omega_1 + \frac{l'}{\mu}\omega_2, \quad \frac{k'}{\mu}\omega_1' + \frac{l'}{\mu}\omega_2'$$

are period-pairs, integral in ω_1 and ω_1', ω_2 and ω_2'; hence

$$\frac{M}{\mu}\Omega_4 - \frac{m'}{\mu}\omega_3, \quad \frac{M}{\mu}\Omega_4' - \frac{m'}{\mu}\omega_3',$$

are a period-pair, say ω_5 and ω_5'; then as

$$\frac{M}{\mu}\Omega_4 - \frac{m'}{\mu}\omega_3 = \omega_5, \quad \frac{M}{\mu}\Omega_4' - \frac{m'}{\mu}\omega_3' = \omega_5',$$

where M, m', μ are integers and Ω_4, ω_3, ω_5, Ω_4', ω_3', ω_5' are constituents of pairs. But we know† that, in such an event there are two integral combinations of ω_3, ω_5, Ω_4, and the same two integral combinations of ω_3', ω_5', Ω_4', because the coefficients $\dfrac{M}{\mu}$ and $\dfrac{m'}{\mu}$ are the same in the two relations, such that ω_3, ω_5, Ω_4 are expressible as integral combinations of the first and ω_3', ω_5', Ω_4' are integral combinations of the second; that is, we have

$$\frac{k'}{\mu}\omega_1 + \frac{l'}{\mu}\omega_2 = \text{linear function of two periods } \Omega_1 \text{ and } \Omega_2,$$

$$\frac{k'}{\mu}\omega_1' + \frac{l'}{\mu}\omega_2' = \text{same} \dots\dots\dots\dots\dots\dots\dots\dots \Omega_1' \text{ and } \Omega_2',$$

and now, in our equations, the integral coefficients $\dfrac{k'}{\mu}$ and $\dfrac{l'}{\mu}$ have no common factor.

Similarly for the other cases; we can assume, in our relations

$$M\Omega_4 = k'\omega_1 + l'\omega_2 + m'\omega_3, \quad M\Omega_4' = k'\omega_1' + l'\omega_2' + m'\omega_3',$$

that no two of the integers M, k', l', m' have a common factor.

Accordingly, we have k'/l' a fraction in its lowest terms. Expressing it as a continued fraction, and denoting by r/s the last convergent before the final value, we have

$$\frac{k'}{l'} - \frac{r}{s} = \pm\frac{1}{sl'}.$$

---

* Obviously, if $d=1$, the period-pair ω_4 and ω_4' is unchanged.
† See my *Theory of Functions*, § 107.

Then
$$\pm \omega_1 = \omega_1(sk' - rl') = sM\Omega_4 - l'(r\omega_1 + s\omega_2) - sm'\omega_3,$$
$$\pm \omega_1' = sM\Omega_4' - l'(r\omega_1' + s\omega_2') - sm'\omega_3',$$
$$\pm \omega_2 = \omega_2(sk' - rl') = -rM\Omega_4 + k'(r\omega_1 + s\omega_2) + rm'\omega_3,$$
$$\pm \omega_2' = -rM\Omega_4' + k'(r\omega_1' + s\omega_2') + rm'\omega_3';$$

and so the four period-pairs are expressible in terms of three period-pairs
$$\Omega_4, \Omega_4'; \quad \omega_3, \omega_3'; \quad r\omega_1 + s\omega_2, r\omega_1' + s\omega_2'.$$

Thus there are not more than three linearly independent period-pairs.

Next, suppose that one of the three quantities k, l, m, say k, is incommensurable, while the other two are commensurable. When l, m are expressed in their lowest terms, let the integer D be the least common multiple of their denominators, so that we can write
$$l = \frac{l'}{D}, \quad m = \frac{m'}{D}.$$

Then
$$D\omega_4 - l'\omega_2 - m'\omega_3 = kD\omega_1,$$
$$D\omega_4' - l'\omega_2' - m'\omega_3' = kD\omega_1'.$$

Now kD, like k, is incommensurable; hence, expressing it as an infinite continued fraction, and denoting two consecutive convergents by p/q and p'/q', we have
$$kD = \frac{p}{q} + \frac{\theta}{qq'},$$
where the real quantity θ is such that $1 > \theta > -1$. Thus
$$\left(\frac{p}{q} + \frac{\theta}{qq'}\right)\omega_1 \quad \text{and} \quad \left(\frac{p}{q} + \frac{\theta}{qq'}\right)\omega_1'$$
are a period-pair, and therefore also
$$q\left(\frac{p}{q} + \frac{\theta}{qq'}\right)\omega_1 - p\omega_1, \quad q\left(\frac{p}{q} + \frac{\theta}{qq'}\right)\omega_1' - p\omega_1',$$
that is,
$$\frac{\theta}{q'}\omega_1 \quad \text{and} \quad \frac{\theta}{q'}\omega_1'$$
are a period-pair. We may take q' as large as we please, for the continued fraction is infinite; and the circumstances thus give rise to infinitesimal periods.

Next, suppose that two of the three quantities k, l, m are incommensurable, say k and l, and that m is commensurable, equal to λ/μ, where λ and μ are integers. Then our relations can be taken in the form
$$\mu\omega_4 - \lambda\omega_3 = k\mu\omega_1 + l\mu\omega_2, \quad \mu\omega_4' - \lambda\omega_3' = k\mu\omega_1' + l\mu\omega_2'.$$

But, writing
$$\omega_5 = \mu\omega_4 - \lambda\omega_3, \quad \omega_5' = \mu\omega_4' - \lambda\omega_3',$$
and denoting $k\mu$ and $l\mu$ by k' and l' respectively, we have
$$\omega_5 = k'\omega_1 + l'\omega_2, \quad \omega_5' = k'\omega_1' + l'\omega_2',$$
where k' and l' are incommensurable, while ω_5 and ω_5' are a period-pair. Again it is known* that, by successive linear combinations of the period so always as to give a period, we can change ω_2 into Ω_2 (and ω_2' into Ω_2' by the same algebraic relations) so that
$$|\omega_2| < \tfrac{1}{2}|\Omega_2|, \quad |\omega_2'| < \tfrac{1}{2}|\Omega_2'|,$$
and at the same time have relations
$$\omega_5 = k''\omega_1 + l''\Omega_2, \quad \omega_5' = k''\omega_1' + l''\Omega_2',$$
where both k'' and l'' are incommensurable. The process can be continued to any extent, by successive combinations of the period-pairs; so ultimately, we can construct an infinitesimal period-pair.

Lastly, we have the case when all the quantities k, l, m are incommensurable; and we assume that the ratios $k:l:m$ also are incommensurable†. Then we express k as a continued fraction, which of course will be infinite; taking any convergent r/s, we have
$$k = \frac{r}{s} + \frac{x}{s^2},$$
where always r and s are integers, and x is a real quantity such that $1 > x > -1$. Also let t_1 be the integer nearest to the incommensurable quantity sl, and t_2 be the integer nearest to the incommensurable quantity sm; then we have
$$sl - t_1 = \Delta_2, \quad sm - t_2 = \Delta_3,$$
where Δ_2 and Δ_3 are incommensurable quantities, each in numerical value being less than $\tfrac{1}{2}$. Thus
$$s\omega_4 - r\omega_1 - t_1\omega_2 - t_2\omega_3 = \frac{x}{s}\omega_1 + \Delta_2\omega_2 + \Delta_3\omega_3,$$
$$s\omega_4' - r\omega_1' - t_1\omega_2' - t_2\omega_3' = \frac{x}{s}\omega_1' + \Delta_2\omega_2' + \Delta_3\omega_3'.$$

Again, as Δ_2 is an incommensurable quantity, let it be expressed as a continued fraction; taking any convergent ρ/σ, where always ρ and σ are integers, we have
$$\Delta_1 = \frac{\rho}{\sigma} + \frac{y}{\sigma^2},$$

---
* See my *Theory of Functions*, § 108.

† The alternative suppositions, for the last case, and for the present case, are left as an exercise.

where y is a real quantity such that $1 > y > -1$. Also let t_3 be the integer nearest to the value of $\sigma\Delta_3$, and write

$$\sigma\Delta_3 = t_3 + \nabla,$$

where ∇ is an incommensurable real quantity less than $\frac{1}{2}$. We then have

$$\sigma(s\omega_4 - r\omega_1 - t_1\omega_2 - t_2\omega_3) - \rho\omega_2 - t_3\omega_3 = \sigma\frac{x}{s}\omega_1 + \frac{y}{\sigma}\omega_2 + \nabla\omega_3,$$

$$\sigma(s\omega_4' - r\omega_1' - t_1\omega_2' - t_2\omega_3') - \rho\omega_2' - t_3\omega_3' = \sigma\frac{x}{s}\omega_1' + \frac{y}{\sigma}\omega_2' + \nabla\omega_3';$$

the quantities on the left-hand side are a period-pair, which can be denoted by Ω_3 and Ω_3'.

Now take an advanced convergent for Δ_1; we have σ very large, and so the values of $y\omega_2/\sigma$ and $y\omega_2'/\sigma$ are infinitesimal. Take a much more advanced convergent for k, so that s is very large compared with σ; the values of $\sigma x\omega_1/s$ and $\sigma x\omega_1'/s$ are infinitesimal. We thus have a new period-pair Ω_3 and Ω_3', such that

$$|\Omega_3| = \left|\sigma\frac{x}{s}\omega_1 + \frac{y}{\sigma}\omega_2 + \nabla\omega_3\right| < \tfrac{1}{2}|\omega_3|,$$

$$|\Omega_3'| = \left|\sigma\frac{x}{s}\omega_1' + \frac{y}{\sigma}\omega_2' + \nabla\omega_3'\right| < \tfrac{1}{2}|\omega_3'|.$$

Our relations now have the form

$$\omega_4 = k'\omega_1 + l'\omega_2 + m'\Omega_3, \quad \omega_4' = k'\omega_1' + l'\omega_2' + m'\Omega_3',$$

where the quantities k', l', m' fall under one or other of the cases already considered. Either we have not more than three period-pairs; or we have infinitesimal periods; or all the quantities k', l', m' are incommensurable, while

$$|\Omega_3| < \tfrac{1}{2}|\omega_3|, \quad |\Omega_3'| < \tfrac{1}{2}|\omega_3'|.$$

In the last event, the same kind of transformation can be adopted; and by appropriate choice, we can form a new period-pair $\bar{\Omega}_3$, $\bar{\Omega}_3'$, such that

$$|\bar{\Omega}_3| < \tfrac{1}{2}|\Omega_3|, \quad |\bar{\Omega}_3'| < \tfrac{1}{2}|\Omega_3'|.$$

And so on, in succession. By taking a sufficient number n of transformations, each of the preceding type, we ultimately can construct a period-pair Φ_3 and Φ_3', such that

$$|\Phi_3| < \frac{1}{2^n}|\omega_3|, \quad |\Phi_3'| < \frac{1}{2^n}|\omega_3'|:$$

that is, by taking n sufficiently large, we should have an infinitesimal period.

It therefore follows that, if we have two relations

$$A\omega_1 + B\omega_2 + C\omega_3 + D\omega_4 = 0,$$
$$A\omega_1' + B\omega_2' + C\omega_3' + D\omega_4' = 0,$$

between four period-pairs, where the coefficients A, B, C, D are real quantities, either there are not more than three period-pairs, or there are infinitesimal periods for the variables.

Accordingly, when we have to deal with uniform analytic functions of two variables, there is nothing in the preceding analysis to exclude the possession of even four period-pairs, when these pairs are linearly independent in respect of combinations between their respective members.

127. For the remainder of the proposition in § 125, it is necessary to consider the possibility of the existence of five period-pairs: if this be excluded, then *a fortiori* we need not consider the existence of more than four period-pairs.

For this purpose, let there be four period-pairs of the kind postulated in the theorem such that, if
$$\omega_s = \alpha_s + i\beta_s, \quad \omega_s' = \alpha_s' + i\beta_s',$$
(for $s = 1, 2, 3, 4$), the determinant
$$\begin{vmatrix} \alpha_1, & \alpha_2, & \alpha_3, & \alpha_4 \\ \beta_1, & \beta_2, & \beta_3, & \beta_4 \\ \alpha_1', & \alpha_2', & \alpha_3', & \alpha_4' \\ \beta_1', & \beta_2', & \beta_3', & \beta_4' \end{vmatrix}$$
does not vanish. When this last condition is satisfied, we cannot have relations
$$m_1 \alpha_1 + m_2 \alpha_2 + m_3 \alpha_3 + m_4 \alpha_4 = 0,$$
$$m_1 \beta_1 + m_2 \beta_2 + m_3 \beta_3 + m_4 \beta_4 = 0,$$
$$m_1 \alpha_1' + m_2 \alpha_2' + m_3 \alpha_3' + m_4 \alpha_4' = 0,$$
$$m_1 \beta_1' + m_2 \beta_2' + m_3 \beta_3' + m_4 \beta_4' = 0,$$
for any set of real quantities m_1, m_2, m_3, m_4 other than simultaneous zeros. The exclusion of the first pair of these relations excludes a relation
$$m_1 \omega_1 + m_2 \omega_2 + m_3 \omega_3 + m_4 \omega_4 = 0,$$
and conversely; and the exclusion of the second pair excludes a relation
$$m_1 \omega_1' + m_2 \omega_2' + m_3 \omega_3' + m_4 \omega_4' = 0,$$
and conversely. Hence, after the preceding lemma, we infer that our uniform analytic functions may possess four periods, or fewer than four periods; and they do not possess, as they cannot be allowed to possess, infinitesimal periods.

Now suppose that a uniform analytic function $f(z, z')$ possesses, in addition to four given linearly independent period-pairs ω_1, ω_1'; ω_2, ω_2'; ω_3, ω_3'; ω_4, ω_4'; also a fifth period-pair, say ω_5, ω_5'. Let
$$\omega_5 = \alpha_5 + i\beta_5, \quad \omega_5' = \alpha_5' + i\beta_5'.$$

Then, with the preceding hypothesis of the non-evanescence of the determinant $(\alpha_1, \beta_2, \alpha_3', \beta_4')$ in the customary notation, the equations

$$\alpha_5 = n_1 \alpha_1 + n_2 \alpha_2 + n_3 \alpha_3 + n_4 \alpha_4,$$
$$\beta_5 = n_1 \beta_1 + n_2 \beta_2 + n_3 \beta_3 + n_4 \beta_4,$$
$$\alpha_5' = n_1 \alpha_1' + n_2 \alpha_2' + n_3 \alpha_3' + n_4 \alpha_4',$$
$$\beta_5' = n_1 \beta_1' + n_2 \beta_2' + n_3 \beta_3' + n_4 \beta_4',$$

determine uniquely four real finite quantities n_1, n_2, n_3, n_4; and they are such as to secure and to require the equations

$$\left. \begin{array}{l} \omega_5 = n_1 \omega_1 + n_2 \omega_2 + n_3 \omega_3 + n_4 \omega_4 \\ \omega_5' = n_1 \omega_1' + n_2 \omega_2' + n_3 \omega_3' + n_4 \omega_4' \end{array} \right\}.$$

It therefore is necessary to consider the conditions, under which these equations are possible.

The analytical consideration of the conditions follows a general march similar to that followed in the establishment of the preceding lemma. The results therefore will only be stated, without further proof. They will relate only to the most general case when no one of the six ratios $n_1 : n_2 : n_3 : n_4$, as determined by the elements of the four period-pairs is an integer; the alternative is to provide only less general cases. We find

(i) when all the real quantities n_1, n_2, n_3, n_4 are commensurable, the formally five period-pairs can be expressed in terms of not more than four period-pairs:—

(ii) when one (and only one) of these quantities is incommensurable, then an infinitesimal period-pair exists:—

(iii) when two of these quantities are incommensurable, then certainly one infinitesimal period-pair exists, and possibly two such pairs exist:—

(iv) when three of these quantities are incommensurable, then one infinitesimal period-pair certainly exists, and three such pairs may exist:—

(v) when four of these quantities are incommensurable, then one infinitesimal period-pair certainly exists, and four such pairs may exist.

It therefore follows that for any uniform analytic function, which is really a function of two (and only two) independent complex variables so that it cannot possess infinitesimal periods, there may be four period-pairs, and there cannot be more than four linearly independent period-pairs[*].

[*] It is a tacit assumption, throughout the preceding investigation, that an infinitesimal period-pair $\bar{\omega}$ and $\bar{\omega}'$ for z and z' means a period-pair for which both $|\omega|$ and $|\omega'|$ are infinitesimal.

128. Now that we have established the result that a uniform analytic function of two complex variables cannot possess more than four linearly independent pairs of periods, so that we should have

$$f(z + m_1\omega_1 + m_2\omega_2 + m_3\omega_3 + m_4\omega_4, \; z' + m_1\omega_1' + m_2\omega_2' + m_3\omega_3' + m_4\omega_4') = f(z, z'),$$

for all integer values of m_1, m_2, m_3, m_4, positive or negative, we proceed to consider the various possible cases that can arise, under the significance of the result and within the alternatives admitted by the analysis leading to the result.

For the present purpose, the case when there are no periods needs only to be mentioned. We then have the customary theory of the uniform analytic functions of two variables, which has been previously discussed in some detail.

The remaining cases will be considered in succession.

One pair of periods.

129. Let the variables z and z' have the periods α and α', and no other periods. Take new variables u and u', where

$$z = \alpha u, \quad \alpha z' - \alpha' z = \alpha \alpha' u',$$

which is an effective transformation of variables unless (i) both α and α' vanish—a possibility that can be excluded—or (ii) either α or α' vanishes.

If α' vanishes, we take u and z' as new variables. If α vanishes, we take z and v as the variables, where $z' = \alpha' v$. In all the cases, denoting the variables by u and u', we can now take $1, 0$ as the pair of periods. Hence the field of variation of the variables is composed of a strip in the u-plane of breadth unity, measured parallel to the axis of real variables, and the whole of the u'-plane; and the uniform function in question can be expressed as a uniform function of $e^{\pi i u}$ and u'.

Two pairs of periods.

130. Let the periods be

$$\text{for } \begin{array}{l} z, \\ z', \end{array} \begin{array}{l} = \alpha \\ = \alpha' \end{array} \Big\}, \quad \begin{array}{l} = \beta \\ = \beta' \end{array} \Big\},$$

respectively, in bracketted pairs; manifestly it may be assumed that α and α' do not simultaneously vanish, and likewise that β and β' do not simultaneously vanish.

Choose quantities k, l, m, n, such that

$$k\alpha + l\alpha' = 1, \quad k\beta + l\beta' = 0,$$
$$m\alpha + n\alpha' = 0, \quad m\beta + n\beta' = 1.$$

When one of the two quantities α and α' vanishes, say α', and neither of the two quantities β and β' vanishes, we take $m = 0$; and when one of the two quantities β and β' vanishes, say β', and neither of the two quantities α and α' vanishes, we take $k = 0$. As will be seen, all the other possible special cases are included in the one special case that is to be considered.

The values of k, l, m, n are given by
$$k(\alpha\beta' - \alpha'\beta) = \beta', \quad m(\alpha\beta' - \alpha'\beta) = -\alpha',$$
$$l(\alpha\beta' - \alpha'\beta) = -\beta, \quad n(\alpha\beta' - \alpha'\beta) = \alpha;$$
and these values are determinate and finite unless
$$\alpha\beta' - \alpha'\beta = 0.$$

First, suppose that $\alpha\beta' - \alpha'\beta$ is not zero—which, of course, is the more general case. Introduce new variables u and u', such that
$$u = kz + lz', \quad u' = mz + nz';$$
and then the period-pairs of these new variables are

$$\text{for } \begin{matrix} u, & = 1 \\ u', & = 0 \end{matrix} \bigg\}, \quad \begin{matrix} = 0 \\ = 1 \end{matrix} \bigg\},$$

respectively, in bracketted pairs. The field of variation of the variables is composed of a strip of unit breadth in the u-plane and of a strip of unit breadth in the u'-plane, the breadth of each of the strips being measured parallel to the axes of real quantities in the planes. The uniform function in question can be expressed as a uniform function of $e^{\pi i u}$ and $e^{\pi i u'}$.

Next, suppose that $\alpha\beta' - \alpha'\beta$ is zero—which, of course, is a special case. As α and α' may not be zero simultaneously, let α be different from zero; and as β and β' may not be zero simultaneously, let β be different from zero. Then there are two alternatives

(i) when both α' and β' vanish:

(ii) when neither α' nor β' vanishes, and then we have
$$\frac{\alpha'}{\alpha} = \frac{\beta'}{\beta}, \quad = c,$$
say, where c is not zero nor infinite.

As regards (i), the variable z has periods α and β, while the variable z' is devoid of periods: and in order that α and β may be effective distinct periods for z, we must as usual have the real part of $i\alpha/\beta$ distinct from zero. The field of variation of the variables is composed of the customary α-β parallelogram in the z-plane, and of the whole of the z'-plane; and the uniform function in question can be expressed as a uniform function of $\wp(z)$, $\wp'(z)$, and z', where $\wp(z)$ is the customary Weierstrassian doubly-periodic function with periods α and β.

F.   15

As regards (ii), we keep the original variable z; and we introduce a variable v such that

$$v = z' - cz.$$

When z and z' have the periods α and α', then v has zero for its period; and when z and z' have the periods β and β', then again v has zero for its period. Accordingly, when we take z and v for variables, the periods of z are α and β, while the variable v is devoid of periods. The uniform function in question can be expressed as a uniform function of $\wp(z)$, $\wp'(z)$, and v, with the same significance as before for $\wp(z)$ and the same requirement as to the real part of $i\alpha/\beta$.

Should the requirement as to the real part of $i\alpha/\beta$ not be satisfied, either there is an infinitesimal period, or the two pairs are equivalent to one pair only. In the former case, there is no proper uniform function with the periods; in the latter, the periods are not effectively two pairs of periods.

Three pairs of periods.

131. Taking the variables to be z and z' as before, let the periods be

$$\text{for } \begin{matrix} z, \\ z', \end{matrix} \begin{matrix} =\alpha \\ =\alpha' \end{matrix}\bigg\}, \quad \begin{matrix} =\beta \\ =\beta' \end{matrix}\bigg\}, \quad \begin{matrix} =\gamma \\ =\gamma' \end{matrix}\bigg\},$$

where manifestly no pair of quantities in a column can vanish simultaneously. Thus α can vanish, and α' can vanish; as they may not vanish together, there are three possibilities for the α, α' pair. Similarly for each of the other two pairs; so that there are twenty-seven possibilities in all. They can be set out as follows.

A. When all the quantities α', β', γ' vanish, the period-tableau is

$$\begin{pmatrix} \alpha, & \beta, & \gamma \\ 0, & 0, & 0 \end{pmatrix}, \quad (A);$$

no one of the quantities α, β, γ can vanish: there is one case.

B. Let two of the three quantities α', β', γ' vanish, but not the third of them; there are three possibilities. When γ' is the one which does not vanish, then neither α nor β can vanish; and we can have two alternatives, viz. γ vanishing, or γ not vanishing. The period-tableaux are

$$\begin{pmatrix} \alpha, & \beta, & 0 \\ 0, & 0, & \gamma' \end{pmatrix}, (B_1); \quad \begin{pmatrix} \alpha, & \beta, & \gamma \\ 0, & 0, & \gamma' \end{pmatrix}, (B_2);$$

each is typical of three cases.

C. Let one of the three quantities α', β', γ' vanish, but not the other two; there are three possibilities. When α' vanishes, then α cannot vanish: and as β' and γ' do not vanish in that event, we can have four alternatives, viz., β and γ, either vanishing or not vanishing, independently of one another. The period-tableaux are

$$\begin{pmatrix} \alpha, & \beta, & \gamma \\ 0, & \beta', & \gamma' \end{pmatrix}, (C_1); \quad \begin{pmatrix} \alpha, & 0, & \gamma \\ 0, & \beta', & \gamma' \end{pmatrix}, (C_2);$$

$$\begin{pmatrix} \alpha, & \beta, & 0 \\ 0, & \beta', & \gamma' \end{pmatrix}, (C_3); \quad \begin{pmatrix} \alpha, & 0, & 0 \\ 0, & \beta', & \gamma' \end{pmatrix}, (C_4);$$

each is typical of three cases.

D. Let no one of the three quantities α', β', γ' vanish; there is only a single possibility. But as regards α, β, γ, there are eight alternatives, viz., they may either vanish or not vanish, independently of one another. The period-tableaux are

$$\begin{pmatrix} \alpha, & \beta, & \gamma \\ \alpha', & \beta', & \gamma' \end{pmatrix}, (D_1); \quad \begin{pmatrix} 0, & \beta, & \gamma \\ \alpha', & \beta', & \gamma' \end{pmatrix}, (D_2);$$

$$\begin{pmatrix} 0, & 0, & \gamma \\ \alpha', & \beta', & \gamma' \end{pmatrix}, (D_3); \quad \begin{pmatrix} 0, & 0, & 0 \\ \alpha', & \beta', & \gamma' \end{pmatrix}, (D_4).$$

Among these, (D_1) and (D_4) are one case each; (D_2) and (D_3) are, each of them, typical of three cases.

132. As regards the kinds of functions considered, no generality can be lost by assuming that a function is substantially unaltered

(i) when one period-pair is interchanged with another period-pair: or

(ii) when linear transformations are effected upon the variables, coupled with corresponding linear transformations upon the period-pairs: and, in particular, when the variables are interchanged provided that the periods are interchanged at the same time, each combined period-pair being conserved.

Under the first of these assumptions, the three cases typified by (B_1) become one case only, of which (B_1) will be taken as the tableau of periods. The same applies to (B_2), (C_1), (C_2), (C_3), (C_4), (D_2), and (D_3), in succession.

As regards (B_2), when we replace the variable z by u, where

$$u = z - \frac{\gamma}{\gamma'} z',$$

the periods for u and z' are

$$\begin{pmatrix} \alpha, & \beta, & 0 \\ 0, & 0, & \gamma' \end{pmatrix};$$

the case becomes (B_1), and therefore needs no separate discussion.

It is convenient to consider next the case (D_1). Let four quantities k, l, m, n be chosen so that

$$\left.\begin{array}{ll} k\alpha + l\alpha' = 1, & k\beta + l\beta' = 0 \\ m\alpha + n\alpha' = 0, & m\beta + n\beta' = 1 \end{array}\right\};$$

their values are given by

$$\left.\begin{array}{ll} k(\alpha\beta' - \alpha'\beta) = \beta', & m(\alpha\beta' - \alpha'\beta) = -\alpha' \\ l(\alpha\beta' - \alpha'\beta) = -\beta, & n(\alpha\beta' - \alpha'\beta) = \alpha \end{array}\right\}.$$

When $\alpha\beta' - \alpha'\beta$ does not vanish, the values of k, l, m, n are determinate and finite; when it does vanish, the selection cannot be made.

Accordingly, in the first place, suppose that $\alpha\beta' - \alpha'\beta$ does not vanish. No generality is then lost by assuming that $\gamma\beta' - \gamma'\beta$ does not vanish and also that $\alpha\gamma' - \alpha'\gamma$ does not vanish; for the alternative hypothesis as to each of these magnitudes leads, by the permissible interchange of period-pairs, to the case when $\alpha\beta' - \alpha'\beta$ vanishes—a case yet to be considered. Now write

$$u = kz + lz', \quad u' = mz + nz',$$
$$\mu = k\gamma + l\gamma' = (\gamma\beta' - \gamma'\beta) \div (\alpha\beta' - \alpha'\beta),$$
$$\mu' = m\gamma + n\gamma' = (\alpha\gamma' - \alpha'\gamma) \div (\alpha\beta' - \alpha'\beta),$$

where the new variables u and u' are independent of one another because $kn - lm, = (\alpha\beta' - \alpha'\beta)^{-1}$, is not zero. Thus the uniform function in question becomes a uniform function of u and u', with the tableau of periods

$$\begin{pmatrix} 1, & 0, & \mu \\ 0, & 1, & \mu' \end{pmatrix}.$$

In the second place, suppose that $\alpha\beta' - \alpha'\beta$ does vanish. Then

$$\frac{\alpha'}{\alpha} = \frac{\beta'}{\beta} = c,$$

say. Introduce two new variables u and u', defined by the relations

$$u = \frac{\gamma'z - \gamma z'}{\gamma' - c\gamma}, \quad u' = z' - cz,$$

which are definite and provide independent variables when $\gamma' - c\gamma$ does not vanish. The period-tableau for u and u' is

$$\begin{pmatrix} \alpha, & \beta, & 0 \\ 0, & 0, & \gamma' - c\gamma \end{pmatrix};$$

and so the case is inclusible in (B_1), provided $\gamma' - c\gamma$ does not vanish. If however $\gamma' - c\gamma$ does vanish, so that

$$\frac{\alpha'}{\alpha} = \frac{\beta'}{\beta} = \frac{\gamma'}{\gamma} = c,$$

we retain the variable z and take a new independent variable v, where $v = u' - cu$; the period-tableau for z and v is

$$\begin{pmatrix} \alpha, & \beta, & \gamma \\ 0, & 0, & 0 \end{pmatrix},$$

and so the case is inclusible in (A). Thus no new kind of function, other than those already retained, arises out of (D_1) when $\alpha\beta' - \alpha'\beta = 0$.

Now consider the cases under (C). The case (C_1) is included in (D_1) unless $\beta\gamma' - \beta'\gamma$ vanishes. When this quantity does vanish, we have

$$\frac{\beta}{\beta'} = \frac{\gamma}{\gamma'} = k,$$

say; we take a new variable u, where $u = z - kz'$, and then the period-tableau for u and z' is

$$\begin{pmatrix} \alpha, & 0, & 0 \\ 0, & \beta', & \gamma' \end{pmatrix},$$

that is, the case is inclusible in (B_1). Thus no new kind of function, other than those already retained, arises out of (C_1).

The case (C_2) is inclusible in (D_1).

The case (C_3), by interchange of period-pairs, becomes (C_2) and so is inclusible in (D_1).

The case (C_4), by interchange of variables together with the proper interchange of periods, becomes (B_1).

Similarly for the cases under (D). The case (D_2), by interchange of variables together with the proper interchange of periods, becomes (C_1) and so provides no new kind of function. In the same way, the case (D_3) becomes (B_2), which is inclusible in (B_1); it therefore provides no new kind of function. And, in the same way also, the case (D_4) becomes (A).

Hence the surviving independent cases are (A); (B_1); and the case which has emerged from (D_1). These will be considered now in succession.

133. We can dismiss the case (A) very briefly. There are no periods for z'. There are three periods for z; so that, in effect, the uniform function is periodic in a single variable only. But, in such an event, there cannot be more than two periods at the utmost*; hence the case either is impossible, or is degenerate by falling into a class of doubly periodic functions of two variables already considered.

The case (B_1) can also be dismissed briefly. In all the functions which it provides, the double periodicity in z alone and the single periodicity in z' alone are independent of one another. Even when the double periodicity

---

* *Theory of Functions*, § 108.

does not degenerate, the function in question is a uniform function of $\wp(z, \alpha, \beta)$—with $\wp'(z, \alpha, \beta)$—and $e^{\pi i z'/\gamma'}$; its triple periodicity in the two variables combined is not a proper triple periodicity, for it is resoluble into the double periodicity in one variable alone and the independent single periodicity in the other variable alone.

It remains to consider the case which has emerged from (D_1). This case provides uniform triply periodic functions, for which the triple periodicity is proper and not resoluble as it is in the case (B_1). We have seen that, without any loss of substantial generality, the tableau of periods for the variables z and z' can be taken in the form

$$\begin{pmatrix} 1, & 0, & \mu \\ 0, & 1, & \mu' \end{pmatrix},$$

where neither μ nor μ' vanishes.

Further, both μ and μ' cannot be purely real. If, for instance, μ were real and commensurable (equal to p/q, say, where p and q are integers), then a set of periods is

$$\begin{pmatrix} 1, & 0, & q\mu - p \\ 0, & 1, & q\mu' \end{pmatrix},$$

that is,

$$\begin{pmatrix} 1, & 0, & 0 \\ 0, & 1, & q\mu' \end{pmatrix},$$

which is an instance of (B_1). Similarly, if μ' were real and commensurable.

If μ and μ' were real and, after the foregoing cases, were incommensurable, then the function would have infinitesimal periods. Thus let the supposed incommensurable quantity μ be expressed as a continued fraction and take an advanced convergent to its value, say p/q; then

$$\mu = \frac{p}{q} + \frac{\epsilon}{q^2},$$

where $0 < |\epsilon| < 1$, so that

$$q\mu - p = \frac{\epsilon}{q}.$$

Thus a set of periods is

$$\begin{pmatrix} 1, & 0, & \dfrac{\epsilon}{q} \\ 0, & 1, & q\mu' \end{pmatrix}.$$

As μ' is incommensurable, so also is $q\mu'$; let it be expressed as a continued fraction and take a convergent r/s to its value, so that

$$q\mu' = \frac{r}{s} + \frac{\eta}{s^2},$$

where $0 < |\eta| < 1$; thus

$$sq\mu' - r = \frac{\eta}{s}.$$

Accordingly, a set of periods is

$$\begin{pmatrix} 1, & 0, & \epsilon\dfrac{s}{q} \\ 0, & 1, & \eta\dfrac{1}{s} \end{pmatrix}.$$

When we take s very large and q/s also very large, the quantities

$$\epsilon\frac{s}{q}, \text{ and } \eta\frac{1}{s},$$

are infinitesimal: that is, we should have an infinitesimal period-pair—a possibility that is excluded. Thus μ and μ' cannot be simultaneously real.

The most general case arises when neither μ nor μ' is real: and we shall assume that, henceforward, we are dealing with this case. It is to be remembered that, in effecting the linear transformation upon the variables so that 1, 0; and 0, 1; are two period-pairs, we have used the constants of relation.

Moreover, as the periods in the tableau can be linearly combined in simultaneous pairs, we have

that is,
$$\mu + p \cdot 1 + q \cdot 0, \quad \mu' + p \cdot 0 + q \cdot 1,$$
$$\mu + p, \quad \mu' + q,$$

as a period-pair, p and q being any independent integers; and this period-pair can replace μ and μ' in the tableau, for any values of p and q. Let these integers be chosen so that the real parts of $\mu + p$ and $\mu' + q$, say $R(\mu + p)$ and $R(\mu' + q)$, satisfy the conditions

$$0 \leqslant R(\mu + p) < 1, \quad 0 \leqslant R(\mu' + q) < 1.$$

Assuming this done it follows that, *without any loss of generality in the period-tableau*

$$\begin{pmatrix} 1, & 0, & \mu \\ 0, & 1, & \mu' \end{pmatrix},$$

we can assume that

$$0 \leqslant R(\mu) < 1, \quad 0 \leqslant R(\mu') < 1,$$

while neither of the quantities μ and μ' is purely real; moreover, this is effectively the general tableau for the proper triple periodicity of uniform functions of two variables.

134. The field of variation of the two independent variables occurring in uniform triply periodic functions can be assigned in two ways, which can be used in complementary fashion and will leave open an element of arbitrary choice. Let c and c' denote simultaneous values of the variables z and z'; for purposes of convenience we shall assume that they are a pair of ordinary non-zero places of two uniform triply periodic functions with which we may have to deal. Moreover, we shall assume at once that the functions in question possess no essential singularities for finite values of the variables; and we shall take

$$\begin{pmatrix} 1, & 0, & \mu \\ 0, & 1, & \mu' \end{pmatrix}$$

as the tableau of the periods, with the due restrictions on μ and μ'.

Owing to the period-pair 1, 0, we can reduce any point in the z-plane to a point in, or upon the boundary of, a strip enclosing c, without thereby affecting the position of z' in its plane. Similarly owing to the period-pair 0, 1, we can reduce any point in the z'-plane to a point in, or upon the boundary of, a strip enclosing c', without thereby affecting the position of z in its plane. Accordingly construct in the z-plane a parallelogram having c, $c+1$, $c+\mu$, $c+1+\mu$ as its angular points; and produce, to infinity in both directions, the side joining c to $c+\mu$ and the side joining $c+1$ to $c+1+\mu$. Similarly construct in the z'-plane a parallelogram having c', $c'+1$, $c'+\mu'$, $c'+1+\mu'$ as its angular points: and produce, to infinity in both directions, the side joining c' to $c'+\mu'$ and the side joining $c'+1$ to $c'+1+\mu'$.

Then, for our triply periodic functions, we can choose a complete field of variation in two ways. By the first choice, we allow z to vary over the parallelogram constructed in its plane, while we allow z' to vary over the strip between the two infinite lines drawn in its plane. By the second choice, we allow z' to vary over the parallelogram constructed in its plane, while we allow z to vary over the strip between the two infinite lines drawn in its plane. For special purposes, it may prove convenient to contemplate both the fields simultaneously, even though each field by itself is complete for the triply periodic functions.

But we do not obtain a complete field if we limit the simultaneous variations of z and z' to the two parallelograms drawn in the two planes. For, in effect, such a field would give

$$\begin{pmatrix} 1, & \mu, & 0, & 0 \\ 0, & 0, & 1, & \mu' \end{pmatrix}$$

as the period-tableau; and then there would emerge a repeated double periodicity, one in z alone, the other in z' alone; that is, we should have a degenerate quadruply periodic function, instead of a triply periodic function.

Four pairs of periods.

135. Again denoting the variables by z and z', let the periods be

$$\text{for } \begin{matrix} z, \\ z', \end{matrix} \begin{matrix} =\alpha \\ =\alpha' \end{matrix} \Bigg\}, \begin{matrix} =\beta \\ =\beta' \end{matrix} \Bigg\}, \begin{matrix} =\gamma \\ =\gamma' \end{matrix} \Bigg\}, \begin{matrix} =\delta \\ =\delta' \end{matrix} \Bigg\},$$

where manifestly no pair of quantities in a column can vanish simultaneously. Thus there are three possibilities for each pair of periods; and each possibility for a pair is unaffected by the possibilities for any other pair. Hence there are eighty-one possibilities in all; they can be set out in a scheme, as follows.

A. When all the quantities α', β', γ', δ' vanish, the period-tableau is

$$\begin{pmatrix} \alpha, & \beta, & \gamma, & \delta \\ 0, & 0, & 0, & 0 \end{pmatrix}, \ (A);$$

no one of the quantities α, β, γ, δ can vanish; there is one case.

B. Let three of the quantities α', β', γ', δ' vanish, but not the fourth; there are four possibilities. When δ' is the one which does not vanish, then neither α nor β nor γ can vanish; while δ may or may not vanish. Thus the period-tableaux are

$$\begin{pmatrix} \alpha, & \beta, & \gamma, & 0 \\ 0, & 0, & 0, & \delta' \end{pmatrix}, \ (B_1); \quad \begin{pmatrix} \alpha, & \beta, & \gamma, & \delta \\ 0, & 0, & 0, & \delta' \end{pmatrix}, \ (B_2);$$

each is typical of four cases.

C. Let two of the quantities α', β', γ', δ' vanish, but not the other two. The period-tableaux are

$$\begin{pmatrix} \alpha, & \beta, & \gamma, & \delta \\ 0, & 0, & \gamma', & \delta' \end{pmatrix}, \ (C_1); \quad \begin{pmatrix} \alpha, & \beta, & \gamma, & 0 \\ 0, & 0, & \gamma', & \delta' \end{pmatrix}, \ (C_2);$$

$$\begin{pmatrix} \alpha, & \beta, & 0, & \delta \\ 0, & 0, & \gamma', & \delta' \end{pmatrix}, \ (C_3); \quad \begin{pmatrix} \alpha, & \beta, & 0, & 0 \\ 0, & 0, & \gamma', & \delta' \end{pmatrix}, \ (C_4);$$

each is typical of six cases.

D. Let one, but only one, of the quantities α', β', γ', δ' vanish. The period-tableaux are

$$\begin{pmatrix} \alpha, & \beta, & \gamma, & \delta \\ 0, & \beta', & \gamma', & \delta' \end{pmatrix}, \ (D_1); \quad \begin{pmatrix} \alpha, & \beta, & \gamma, & 0 \\ 0, & \beta', & \gamma', & \delta' \end{pmatrix}, \ (D_2);$$

$$\begin{pmatrix} \alpha, & \beta, & 0, & \delta \\ 0, & \beta', & \gamma', & \delta' \end{pmatrix}, \ (D_3); \quad \begin{pmatrix} \alpha, & 0, & \gamma, & \delta \\ 0, & \beta', & \gamma', & \delta' \end{pmatrix}, \ (D_4);$$

$$\begin{pmatrix} \alpha, & \beta, & 0, & 0 \\ 0, & \beta', & \gamma', & \delta' \end{pmatrix}, \ (D_5); \quad \begin{pmatrix} \alpha, & 0, & \gamma, & 0 \\ 0, & \beta', & \gamma', & \delta' \end{pmatrix}, \ (D_6);$$

$$\begin{pmatrix} \alpha, & 0, & 0, & \delta \\ 0, & \beta', & \gamma', & \delta' \end{pmatrix}, \ (D_7); \quad \begin{pmatrix} \alpha, & 0, & 0, & 0 \\ 0, & \beta', & \gamma', & \delta' \end{pmatrix}, \ (D_8);$$

each is typical of four cases.

E. Let no one of the quantities $\alpha', \beta', \gamma', \delta'$ vanish. The period-tableaux are

$$\begin{pmatrix} \alpha, & \beta, & \gamma, & \delta \\ \alpha', & \beta', & \gamma', & \delta' \end{pmatrix}, (E_1); \quad \begin{pmatrix} 0, & \beta, & \gamma, & \delta \\ \alpha', & \beta', & \gamma', & \delta' \end{pmatrix}, (E_2); \quad \begin{pmatrix} 0, & 0, & \gamma, & \delta \\ \alpha', & \beta', & \gamma', & \delta' \end{pmatrix}, (E_3);$$

$$\begin{pmatrix} 0, & 0, & 0, & \delta \\ \alpha', & \beta', & \gamma', & \delta' \end{pmatrix}, (E_4); \quad \begin{pmatrix} 0, & 0, & 0, & 0 \\ \alpha', & \beta', & \gamma', & \delta' \end{pmatrix}, (E_5);$$

of these, (E_1) and (E_5) are each one case; (E_2) and (E_4) are each typical of four cases; and (E_3) is typical of six cases.

136. As regards the kinds of functions considered, the same assumptions, as to the interchangeability of period-pairs and as to the linear transformations of the variables without detriment to the generality of the functions, will be made as were made (§ 132) in the discussion of the triple periodicity.

Consequently all the cases, of which each tableau is typical, become merged into a single case.

The cases (A) and (E_5) are impossible, or else the periods degenerate; there cannot be uniform functions, periodic in a single variable and having four distinct periods for that variable.

The cases (B_1), (B_2), (D_8), (E_4) are impossible, or else the periods degenerate; there cannot be uniform functions, periodic in a single variable and having three distinct periods in that variable.

By taking a variable u instead of z, where

$$u = z - \frac{\gamma}{\gamma'} z',$$

the tableau of periods in (C_1) is changed to a tableau of periods for u and z' represented by (C_3) or (C_4). Also by interchange of period-pairs, (C_3) becomes (C_2); hence (C_2) and (C_4) are the only cases under (C) that require consideration.

By interchange of variables and the proper interchange of periods, (D_5), (D_6), (D_7) become (C_2), and so require no separate discussion; and similarly (E_3) becomes (C_1), and can therefore be omitted.

By interchange of period-pairs, (D_2) and (D_3) become (D_4) and so they require no separate discussion.

By interchange of variables and the proper interchange of periods, (E_2) becomes (D_1) and can therefore be omitted.

Consequently, the cases that survive for further consideration are (C_2), (C_4), (D_1), (D_4), (E_1).

As regards (D_4), change the variables to u and u' by the relations

$$z = \alpha u, \quad z' = \beta' u',$$

and write $\beta = \alpha\lambda$, $\delta = \alpha\mu$, $\gamma' = \beta'\lambda'$, $\delta' = \beta'\mu'$; the period-tableau for the variables u and u' is
$$\begin{pmatrix} 1, & 0, & \lambda, & \mu \\ 0, & 1, & \lambda', & \mu' \end{pmatrix},$$
which temporarily will be called (F).

As regards (C_2), a similar change of variables, viz.,
$$z = \alpha u, \quad z' = \delta' u',$$
leads to a special form of the period-tableau (F) in which λ' is zero. Assuming this included in (F), we have no new case out of (C_2).

As regards (C_4), we have a function, which is doubly periodic in z alone with periods α and β, and is also doubly periodic in z' alone with periods γ' and δ'. The functions thus provided are undoubtedly quadruply periodic, but the periodicity has an isolated distribution; they will therefore be omitted, as not belonging to the class of functions having proper quadruple periodicity.

As regards (D_1) and (E_1), we effect linear transformations of the variables of the type
$$u = kz + lz', \quad u' = mz + nz',$$
where the quantities k, l, m, n are determined by relations
$$k\gamma + l\gamma' = 1, \quad m\gamma + n\gamma' = 0,$$
$$k\delta + l\delta' = 0, \quad m\delta + n\delta' = 1.$$
Different cases arise as under (D_1) in the discussion of triple periodicity: and we find either

(i) a period-tableau, with new variables, represented by (F); or

(ii) cases already decided; or

(iii) cases that are impossible or degenerate.

Consequently it follows that properly quadruply periodic functions, which are uniform and involve only two variables, can be modified as to their variables so that they have
$$\begin{pmatrix} 1, & 0, & \lambda, & \mu \\ 0, & 1, & \lambda', & \mu' \end{pmatrix}$$
for their period-tableau.

137. Now it is a property of quadruply periodic uniform functions, on the Riemann theory, that (for this tableau) the relation
$$\lambda' = \mu$$
(or else $\lambda = \mu'$) holds. Further, Appell[*] has proved, by analysis and reasoning quite different from those adopted for the discussion of functions on a Riemann

---
[*] *Liouville*, 4me Sér., t. vii (1891), pp. 157 sqq.

surface, that this relation holds in general for a properly quadruply periodic uniform function, that is, by change of the variables and by the association of appropriate factors, the function can be made to depend upon others which possess this property. But under both theories, the property emerges from the discussion of the functions themselves, whereas the preceding investigation deals only (or mainly) with the mere transformation of the periods; the property apparently cannot be deduced at this stage solely from the preceding considerations.

Just as was the case with the triple periodicity when the period-tableau had been rendered canonical, so here also we can infer (without any reference to a property $\lambda' = \mu$ or $\lambda = \mu'$) that all the quantities $\lambda, \lambda', \mu, \mu'$ cannot be wholly real; and in the most general case they will be complex and such that neither of the quantities $\lambda'/\mu, \lambda/\mu'$, is real. The course of the argument for the inference and its details are so similar to those in the earlier discussion that no formal exposition will be made. Moreover, the quantity λ/μ is not real, nor is the quantity λ'/μ'; both statements can be established by shewing that the contrary event would lead to a zero-period for commensurable reality and to an infinitesimal period for incommensurable reality.

138. One difficulty, however, now arises; it is connected with the geometrical representation of two independent complex variables, which has already been discussed. Putting aside for the moment the method of representation in four-dimensional space, partly because of the difficulty of framing mental pictures in such a region, and partly because the representation does not by itself seem to retain sufficiently the individuality of the variables, we have the representation by means of the combined points in the z-plane and the z'-plane.

But we cannot construct a region in the z-plane and a region in the z'-plane that shall suffice for the field of variation of z and z' within their

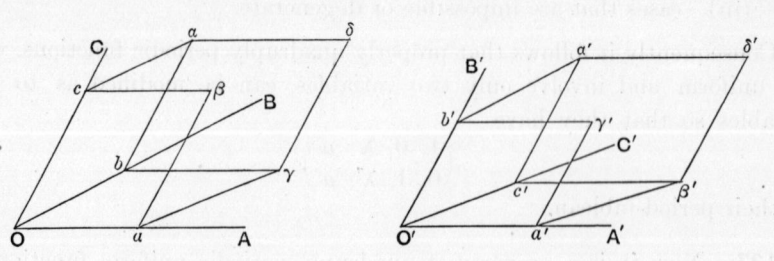

periods. Take any origins in those planes; in the z-plane, let the points a, b, c represent the values $1, \lambda, \mu$; and in the z'-plane, let the points a', b', c' represent the values $1, \lambda', \mu'$; and complete the parallelograms as in the figures, so that the points $\alpha, \beta, \gamma, \delta$ respectively represent the values $\lambda + \mu$, $1 + \mu, 1 + \lambda, 1 + \lambda + \mu$, and similarly in the z'-plane. No one parallelogram such as $Oa\beta cO$ is sufficient for the representation of z; for there is a portion of the parallelogram $ObacO$ not included, and there is a portion of the parallelogram $Oa\gamma bO$ not included. The double parallelogram $Oa\gamma bacO$ is not sufficient, because there is a portion of the parallelogram $Oa\beta cO$ not included; moreover, the whole plane could not be covered once and once only by repetitions of the double parallelogram keeping unchanged the orientations of the sides. In the figure, the parallelogram $Oa\beta cO$ is partly excessive and partly deficient; for the interior of the small parallelogram between ab, $b\gamma$, $a\beta$, βc is reducible to another part of $Oa\beta cO$. The triple parallelogram $Oa\gamma\delta acO$ is excessive; for much of its area (the part outside the parallelogram $Oa\beta cO$) is "reducible" to the area within that parallelogram, and also the whole plane could not be covered, once and once only, by repetitions of the triple parallelogram keeping unchanged the orientations of its sides.

The same remarks apply to the z'-plane, in connection with the figure as drawn.

Thus, neither by means of parallelograms, nor by means of strips in the two planes of reference, is it possible to obtain definite unique and complete limited fields of variation for z and z', that shall discharge for quadruply periodic functions of two variables the same duty as is discharged for doubly periodic functions of a single variable by the customary period-parallelogram.

But by taking an associated two-plane variation of the real variables x, y, x', y', the deficiency can be supplied for one purpose. This representation is as follows*. For a quadruply periodic function, with the period-tableau

$$\begin{pmatrix} 1, & 0, & \lambda, & \mu \\ 0, & 1, & \lambda', & \mu' \end{pmatrix},$$

we resolve $\lambda, \mu, \lambda', \mu'$ into their real and imaginary parts, say

$$\lambda = a + ib, \quad \mu = c + id, \quad \lambda' = a' + ib', \quad \mu' = c' + id';$$

then every place, differing from z, z' only by multiples of the periods, can be represented by

$$x + iy + p + r(a + ib) + s(c + id),$$
$$x' + iy' + q + r(a' + ib') + s(c' + id').$$

Take two planes, one of them to represent the variations of y and y' with reference to $O'y$ and $O'y'$ as rectangular axes, the other of them to represent the variations of x and x' with reference to Ox and Ox' as rectangular axes. In the y, y' plane, let B be the point b, b' and D the point d, d'; and complete the parallelogram $DO'BF$. In the x, x' plane, let $OA = 1$ and $OC = 1$; and complete the square $COAE$.

Then the integers r and s can be chosen, say equal to r' and s', so that the point

$$y + r'b + s'd, \quad y' + r'b' + s'd',$$

* For this suggestion I am indebted to Professor W. Burnside, who communicated it to me in a letter dated 14 January 1914.

lies within or on the boundary of the parallelogram $O'BFD$; let this point be Q. Then every point, which is equivalent to y, y', in the sense that its coordinates are $y + rb + sd$, $y' + rb' + sd'$, is equivalent to Q and lies outside the selected parallelogram.

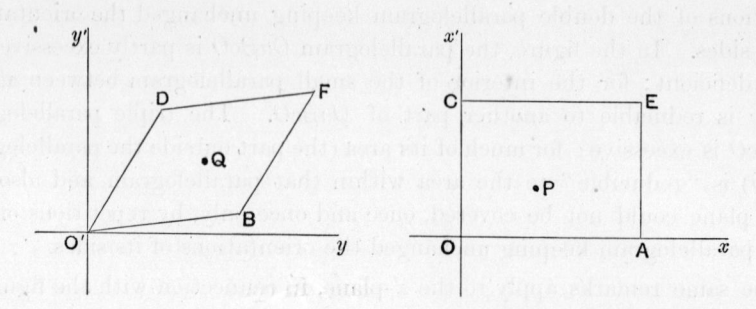

Again the integers p and q can be chosen, say equal to p' and q', so that the point
$$x + p' + r'a + s'c, \quad y + q' + r'a' + s'c'$$
lies within or on the boundary of the square $OAEC$; let this point be P. Then every point, which is equivalent to $x + r'a + s'c$, $y + r'a' + s'c'$, in the sense that its coordinates are $x + p + r'a + s'c$, $y + q + r'a' + s'c'$, is equivalent to P, and lies outside the selected square.

It follows that, in connection with a place z, z', and with all places equivalent to it in the form
$$z + p + r\lambda + s\mu, \quad z' + q + r\lambda' + s\mu',$$
we can select a unique point Q within the y, y' parallelogram, and then associate with it another unique point P within the x, x' square. We take the point-pair QP as representative of the whole set of places that, in the foregoing sense, are equivalent to z, z'; it is given by the specially selected place
$$z + p' + r'\lambda + s'\mu, \quad z' + q' + r'\lambda' + s'\mu'.$$

Uniform triply periodic functions in general.

139. It is known (Chap. V) that a uniform function $f(z, z')$, which can have poles and unessential singularities but which has no essential singularity lying within the finite part of the field of variation, can be expressed in the form
$$f(z, z') = \frac{\phi(z, z')}{\psi(z, z')},$$
where $\phi(z, z')$ and $\psi(z, z')$ are everywhere regular within the finite part of the field of variation.

We shall therefore proceed from this result, specially for the purpose of deducing* some initial properties of triply periodic functions that are uniform. We denote the period-pairs by the tableau

$$\begin{pmatrix} 1, & 0, & \mu \\ 0, & 1, & \mu' \end{pmatrix}.$$

Now because
$$f(z+1, z') = f(z, z'),$$
and because the functions $\phi(z, z')$ and $\psi(z, z')$ are regular, each of the equal fractions
$$\frac{\phi(z+1, z')}{\phi(z, z')} = \frac{\psi(z+1, z')}{\psi(z, z')},$$
derived from the equation expressing the 1, 0 periodicity of f, is devoid of zeros and of poles and of unessential singularities for finite values of the variables: hence, as in § 79, the common value of the fractions is of the form
$$e^{g(z, z')},$$
where $g(z, z')$ is a regular function of the variables. Consequently
$$\left.\begin{array}{l}\phi(z+1, z') = \phi(z, z') e^{g(z, z')} \\ \psi(z+1, z') = \psi(z, z') e^{g(z, z')}\end{array}\right\}.$$

Similarly, through the 0, 1 periodicity of f, we have the relations
$$\left.\begin{array}{l}\phi(z, z'+1) = \phi(z, z') e^{h(z, z')} \\ \psi(z, z'+1) = \psi(z, z') e^{h(z, z')}\end{array}\right\},$$
where also $h(z, z')$ is a regular function of the variables.

In order that the two sets of relations may coexist, we must have
$$\phi(z+1, z'+1) = \phi(z, z') e^{g(z, z'+1) + h(z, z')},$$
$$\phi(z+1, z'+1) = \phi(z, z') e^{g(z, z') + h(z+1, z')},$$
and similarly for $\psi(z, z')$; therefore
$$g(z, z'+1) - g(z, z') \equiv h(z+1, z') - h(z, z'), \quad (\text{mod. } 2\pi i).$$
Let
$$g(z, z'+1) - g(z, z') - 2k\pi i = h(z+1, z') - h(z, z') - 2l\pi i,$$
where $k - l$ is an integer: manifestly, either k or l could be taken equal to zero without loss of generality. Now suppose a function $\lambda(z, z')$ determined such that
$$\left.\begin{array}{l}\lambda(z+1, z') - \lambda(z, z') = g(z, z') - 2k\pi i z' \\ \lambda(z, z'+1) - \lambda(z, z') = h(z, z') - 2l\pi i z\end{array}\right\},$$
which two equations are consistent because of the foregoing relation between g and h. If then
$$\phi_1(z, z') = \phi(z, z') e^{-\lambda(z, z')}, \quad \psi_1(z, z') = \psi(z, z') e^{-\lambda(z, z')},$$

---

* This particular investigation follows the earlier sections of Appell's memoir already quoted, § 137.

we have
$$f(z, z') = \frac{\phi_1(z, z')}{\psi_1(z, z')},$$
where the functions ϕ_1 and ψ_1 satisfy the relations
$$\left.\begin{array}{l}\phi_1(z+1, z') = \phi_1(z, z') e^{2k\pi i z'} \\ \phi_1(z, z'+1) = \phi_1(z, z') e^{2l\pi i z}\end{array}\right\}, \quad \left.\begin{array}{l}\psi_1(z+1, z') = \psi_1(z, z') e^{2k\pi i z'} \\ \psi_1(z, z'+1) = \psi_1(z, z') e^{2l\pi i z}\end{array}\right\}.$$

The function $f(z, z')$ under consideration has μ and μ' for a third pair of periods. Proceeding as with the other pairs 1, 0 and 0, 1, we have
$$\frac{\phi_1(z+\mu, z'+\mu')}{\phi_1(z, z')} = \frac{\psi_1(z+\mu, z'+\mu')}{\psi_1(z, z')} = e^{m(z,z')},$$
where $m(z, z')$ is a regular function throughout the domain. By the earlier relations which are satisfied by ϕ_1 and ψ_1, and from the relation
$$\frac{\phi_1(z+1+\mu, z'+\mu')}{\phi_1(z+1, z')} = e^{m(z+1,z')},$$
we find
$$m(z+1, z') = m(z, z') + 2\pi i (\alpha + k\mu');$$
and similarly
$$m(z, z'+1) = m(z, z') + 2\pi i (\beta + l\mu);$$
where α and β are integers. Let
$$m(z, z') = M(z, z') + 2\pi i (\alpha + k\mu') z + 2\pi i (\beta + l\mu) z',$$
so that
$$M(z+1, z') = M(z, z'), \quad M(z, z'+1) = M(z, z');$$
then both ϕ_1 and ψ_1 satisfy the relations
$$\left.\begin{array}{l}\vartheta(z+1, z') = \vartheta(z, z') e^{2k\pi i z'} \\ \vartheta(z, z'+1) = \vartheta(z, z') e^{2l\pi i z} \\ \vartheta(z+\mu, z'+\mu') = \vartheta(z, z') e^{2\pi i (\alpha + k\mu') z + 2\pi i (\beta + l\mu) z' + M(z, z')}\end{array}\right\},$$
where $M(z, z')$ is periodic with 1, 0 and 0, 1 for period-pairs, and α, β, $k-l$ are integers.

The triple theta-functions.

140. The formally simplest cases arise when we take
$$k = 0, \quad l = 0, \quad \alpha = -2, \quad \beta = -2, \quad M(z, z') = -2\pi i (\mu + \mu'),$$
and when we require that the functions shall be only triply periodic and must not be quadruply periodic. Then
$$\vartheta(z+1, z') = \vartheta(z, z'),$$
$$\vartheta(z, z'+1) = \vartheta(z, z'),$$
$$\vartheta(z+\mu, z'+\mu') = \vartheta(z, z') e^{-2\pi i (2z+2z') - 2\pi i (\mu+\mu')},$$
which (as will appear presently) are equations characteristic of functions that are triply periodic actually (or save as to a factor).

Without enquiring into the comprehensiveness of this set of functions $\vartheta(z, z')$, we see that a large class of functions, which are strictly periodic in three pairs of periods, can be expressed as quotients of these pseudo-periodic functions. Even at the risk of a little confusion (because the title "triple theta-function" has hitherto been assigned to uniform functions of three variables which are similarly pseudo-periodic in six period-pairs), it will be convenient to call certain functions, satisfying relations similar to those satisfied by $\vartheta(z, z')$, *triple theta-functions*.

We now proceed to a more detailed consideration of their simplest properties, obtaining the above characteristic equations in a different manner.

141. We denote by 1, 0; 0, 1; μ, μ'; the period-pairs in the variables z, z'. Owing specially to the first two period-pairs, we are led to consider functions expressible in extended Fourier-series in the form

$$\theta(z, z') = \sum_{-\infty}^{\infty} \sum_{-\infty}^{\infty} a_{mn} e^{(2m+\sigma)\pi i z + (2n+\sigma')\pi i z'}.$$

Here σ and σ' are constants, taken to be integers; m and n are integers, ranging from $-\infty$ to $+\infty$ independently of one another; and the constant coefficients a_{mn} are supposed to be such as to secure the absolute convergence of the double series.

We cannot at once declare, from the indices, that σ and σ' are 0 or 1, each of them. Thus, if σ were 2, we could substitute zero for it by changing m into $m-1$, so far as the variable part of the term is concerned; but the change could not necessarily be made in the coefficient, for there is no knowledge of the way (if any) in which a_{mn} contains σ or σ'. But we have

$$\theta(z+1, z') = (-1)^\sigma \theta(z, z'),$$
$$\theta(z, z'+1) = (-1)^{\sigma'} \theta(z, z');$$

and so we can infer that, so far as σ and σ' are concerned, all the possibilities are covered by taking $\sigma, \sigma' = 0, 1$ in any combination: that is, four cases arise through this source alone.

142. Our function $\theta(z, z')$ is to have μ and μ' as periods or pseudo-periods; so we form $\theta(z+\mu, z'+\mu')$, which is

$$\sum_{-\infty}^{\infty} \sum_{-\infty}^{\infty} a_{mn} e^{(2m+\sigma)\pi i \mu + (2n+\sigma')\pi i \mu' + (2m+\sigma)\pi i z + (2n+\sigma')\pi i z'}.$$

Adopting the usual process for dealing with the periodicity (actual, or save as to a factor) of a uniform function, we compare the coefficients of terms in $\theta(z, z')$ and $\theta(z+\mu, z'+\mu')$; and different possibilities occur, according to the different methods of grouping the terms. We definitely choose (for reasons that will appear very soon) to group the term in $\theta(z+\mu, z'+\mu')$, which involves a_{mn}, with the term in $\theta(z, z')$, which involves $a_{m+1, n+1}$. As

$$\theta(z, z') = \Sigma\Sigma a_{m+1, n+1} e^{(2m+\sigma)\pi i z + (2n+\sigma')\pi i z' + 2\pi i(z+z')},$$

we have
$$\theta(z+\mu, z'+\mu') = Be^{-2\pi i(z+z')}\,\theta(z, z'),$$
if
$$a_{mn}\, e^{(2m+\sigma)\pi i\mu + (2n+\sigma')\pi i\mu'} = B a_{m+1, n+1},$$
where B is taken to be a constant, independent of m and n. Let
$$q = e^{\frac{1}{2}\pi i \mu},\quad q' = e^{\frac{1}{2}\pi i \mu'};$$
and take new quantities c_{mn}, connected with the quantities a_{mn} by the relation
$$a_{mn} = c_{mn}\, q^{(2m+\sigma)^2} q'^{(2n+\sigma')^2};$$
then
$$c_{mn} = B q^4 q'^4\, c_{m+1, n+1}$$
$$= A c_{m+1, n+1},$$
say. The pseudo-periodicity of $\theta(z, z')$ is now exhibited in the property
$$\theta(z+\mu, z'+\mu') = A e^{-2\pi i(z+z') - \pi i(\mu+\mu')}\,\theta(z, z').$$
Further, let
$$A = e^{-\pi i \lambda} = (-1)^{-\lambda};$$
the difference-equation for the quantities c_{mn} becomes
$$c_{mn} = e^{-\pi i \lambda}\, c_{m+1, n+1}.$$
Having regard to the form of this relation, we take
$$c_{mn} = e^{a + \pi i (\rho m + \rho' n) + a_2(m-n)^2 + a_3(m-n)^3 + \ldots}$$
$$= e^{\pi i (\rho m + \rho' n)}\, \phi(m-n);$$
the difference-equation then is satisfied if
$$\rho + \rho' = \lambda,$$
and there is no restriction, beyond the requirements that secure the convergence of $\theta(z, z')$, upon the function ϕ. Accordingly, the form of $\theta(z, z')$ is
$$\theta(z, z') = \Sigma\Sigma\, (-1)^{m\rho + n\rho'}\, q^{(2m+\sigma)^2} q'^{(2n+\sigma')^2}\, \phi(m-n)\, e^{(2m+\sigma)\pi i z + (2n+\sigma')\pi i z'}.$$
Also, ρ and ρ' always will be made integers—either 0 or 1; hence
$$A = (-1)^{-\lambda} = (-1)^{-(\rho+\rho')} = (-1)^{\rho+\rho'};$$
and so the characteristic equations, connected with period-increments of the variables, are
$$\left.\begin{aligned}\theta(z+1, z') &= (-1)^\sigma\, \theta(z, z')\\ \theta(z, z'+1) &= (-1)^{\sigma'}\, \theta(z, z')\\ \theta(z+\mu, z'+\mu') &= (-1)^{\rho+\rho'}\, e^{-2\pi i(z+z') - \pi i(\mu+\mu')}\, \theta(z, z')\end{aligned}\right\}.$$
These results, and *all results connected with period-increments of the variables, are included in the formula*
$$\theta(z + \alpha\mu + \beta, z' + \alpha\mu' + \gamma)$$
$$= (-1)^{\beta\sigma + \gamma\sigma' + \alpha(\rho+\rho')}\, e^{-2\pi i \alpha(z+z') - \pi i \alpha^2(\mu+\mu')}\, \theta(z, z'),$$
where α, β, γ are independent integers.

Manifestly, the integers ρ and ρ' can be restricted to the values 0 and 1 independently of one another. When it is necessary to put ρ, ρ', σ, σ' in evidence as magnitudes occurring in $\theta(z, z')$, we shall denote the function by

$$\theta \begin{pmatrix} \rho, & \rho', & z \\ \sigma, & \sigma', & z' \end{pmatrix}.$$

143. Before proceeding with any development of the properties of these functions θ, it is convenient to indicate the reason for the selected grouping of the terms in the comparison of $\theta(z + \mu, z' + \mu')$ and $\theta(z, z')$. As already stated, some grouping of terms has to be made under the method adopted; and the simplest grouping would compare the term in $\theta(z + \mu, z' + \mu')$, which involves a_{mn}, with either one or other of the terms in $\theta(z, z')$, which involve $a_{m+1, n}$ or $a_{m, n+1}$.

Suppose that a difference-equation is established between a_{mn} and $a_{m+1, n}$: all the following argument, *mutatis mutandis*, holds for the alternative supposition of a difference-equation between a_{mn} and $a_{m, n+1}$. Let it be

$$B a_{mn} e^{(2m+\sigma)\pi i \mu + (2n+\sigma')\pi i \mu'} = a_{m+1, n}.$$

When there is no other difference-equation between the coefficients, (in particular, when there is no relation between a_{mn} and $a_{m, n+1}$), we take

$$a_{mn} = c_{mn} e^{\frac{1}{4}(2m+\sigma)^2 \pi i \mu + m(2n+\sigma')\pi i \mu'};$$

and then

$$c_{m+1, n} = c_{mn} B e^{-\frac{1}{4}\sigma^2 \pi i \mu} = C c_{mn},$$

so that

$$c_{mn} = C^m \psi(n).$$

The function becomes

$$\Sigma\Sigma (-1)^{m\rho + n\rho'} \psi(n) C^m e^{\frac{1}{4}(2m+\sigma)^2 \pi i \mu + m(2n+\sigma')\pi i \mu' + (2m+\sigma)\pi i z + (2n+\sigma')\pi i z'}.$$

The aggregate of all the terms in the double series for one and the same value of n is (with the restrictions as to integer values of ρ and σ) a single theta-function of z alone: and so it becomes

$$\theta_0(z) f_0(z') + \theta_1(z) f_1(z') + \theta_2(z) f_2(z') + \theta_3(z) f_3(z'),$$

where $f_0(z'), f_1(z'), f_2(z'), f_3(z')$ are functions of z' alone. It thus becomes the sum of four resoluble products, each of two factors: and each factor involves only one variable. The case is limited in generality.

A similar result ensues when we assume a grouping which compares a_{mn} with $a_{m+r, n}$ and excludes at the same time a grouping which compares a_{mn} with $a_{m, n+s}$, where r and s are any integers.

Further, we cannot have two distinct sets of periods for the case when there is only a single grouping of terms. For otherwise, we should have

$$B a_{mn} e^{(2m+\sigma)\pi i \mu + (2n+\sigma')\pi i \mu'} = a_{m+1, n}$$
$$= B' a_{mn} e^{(2m+\sigma)\pi i \lambda + (2n+\sigma')\pi i \lambda'},$$

for all values of m and n: hence

$$\lambda \equiv \mu \,(\text{mod. } 1), \quad \lambda' \equiv \mu' \,(\text{mod. } 1),$$

so that, when account is taken of 1, 0 and 0, 1 as period-pairs, λ and λ' are effectively the same as μ and μ'.

On the other hand, when there is a double grouping of terms, so that a_{mn} is compared with $a_{m+1,n}$ in one of the groupings and with $a_{m,n+1}$ in the other, we have one period-pair for the first and another period-pair for the second: this is the case with the double theta-functions, which are quadruply periodic (actually so, or save as to a period). Let the difference-equations be

$$Ba_{mn} e^{(2m+\sigma)\pi i\mu + (2n+\sigma')\pi i\mu'} = a_{m+1,n},$$

$$Ca_{mn} e^{(2m+\sigma)\pi i\lambda + (2n+\sigma')\pi i\lambda'} = a_{m,n+1},$$

for all values of m and n. Then

$$a_{m+1,n+1} = Ba_{m,n+1} e^{(2m+\sigma)\pi i\mu + (2n+2+\sigma')\pi i\mu'}$$
$$= BCa_{mn} e^{(2m+\sigma)\pi i(\mu+\lambda) + (2n+\sigma')\pi i(\mu'+\lambda') + 2\pi i\mu'},$$

and

$$a_{m+1,n+1} = Ca_{m+1,n} e^{(2m+2+\sigma)\pi i\lambda + (2n+\sigma')\pi i\lambda'}$$
$$= BCa_{mn} e^{(2m+\sigma)\pi i(\lambda+\mu) + (2n+\sigma')\pi i(\lambda'+\mu') + 2\pi i\lambda},$$

for all values of m and n; hence

$$2\pi i\lambda \equiv 2\pi i\mu' \,(\text{mod. } 2\pi i),$$

or, having regard to the existence of the period-pairs 1, 0 and 0, 1, we infer the relation

$$\lambda = \mu',$$

the well-known condition in the Riemann theory.

Any other double grouping of terms gives rise to quadruply periodic functions. Consequently when there is a question of dealing only with triply periodic functions, there can be only a single grouping. When the grouping is such as to affect only one of the suffixes in a_{mn}, we have seen that the resulting function is composite and can be resolved into a finite number of sums of products of simpler functions. Accordingly the grouping must be such as to affect both the suffixes in a_{mn}. The simplest difference-equation of this kind connects $a_{m+1,n+1}$ with $a_{m,n}$: and so this is the grouping which has been chosen.

144. We have taken our triply periodic function in the form

$$\theta(z, z') = \sum\sum (-1)^{m\rho + n\rho'} q^{(2m+\sigma)^2} q'^{(2n+\sigma')^2} \phi(m-n) e^{(2m+\sigma)\pi iz + (2n+\sigma')\pi iz'};$$

and we know that, save as to a simple factor, at the utmost, $\theta(z, z')$ has 1, 0; 0, 1; μ, μ'; for its period-pairs, whatever be the form of the coefficient $\phi(m-n)$. The preceding discussion has indicated the reason for the choice that ultimately leads to the construction of the coefficient: but some special cases have to be noted and rejected from the class of triply (and only triply) periodic functions.

I. Let $\phi(m-n) = 1$. Then
$$\theta(z, z') = \{\Sigma(-1)^{m\rho} q^{(2m+\sigma)^2} e^{(2m+\sigma)\pi i z}\} \{\Sigma(-1)^{n\rho'} q'^{(2n+\sigma')^2} e^{(2n+\sigma')\pi i z'}\},$$
that is, $\theta(z, z')$ is the product of two single theta-functions; and the period-pairs are
$$\text{for } z, \quad 1, \ \mu, \ 0, \ 0 \atop z', \quad 0, \ 0, \ 1, \ \mu' \Big\},$$
that is, $\theta(z, z')$ becomes a resoluble, but quadruply periodic, function.

II. Let $\phi(m-n) = e^{\pi i a(m-n)}$. Then
$$\theta(z, z') = \{\Sigma(-1)^{m(\rho+a)} q^{(2m+\sigma)^2} e^{(2m+\sigma)\pi i z}\} \{\Sigma(-1)^{n(\rho'-a)} q'^{(2n+\sigma')^2} e^{(2n+\sigma')\pi i z'}\};$$
we have the same conclusion as in the preceding case. The function $\theta(z, z')$ is not a proper triply periodic function.

III. Let
$$\phi(m-n) = e^{\frac{1}{4}\kappa\pi i(2m+\sigma-2n-\sigma')^2},$$
where κ is independent of m and n. Then it is easy to prove that, save as to a factor, $\theta(z, z')$ has four period-pairs, viz.
$$\text{for } z, \quad 1, \ 0, \ \mu+\kappa, \ -\kappa \atop z', \quad 0, \ 1, \ -\kappa, \ \mu'+\kappa \Big\},$$
the addition of the third and the fourth of the pairs giving the period-pair μ, μ'. In that case, $\theta(z, z')$ is a proper quadruply periodic function, being a non-degenerate, double theta-function; it is not a function which is triply (but only triply) periodic.

Accordingly, $\phi(m-n)$ may not have any one of the three preceding forms, nor any combination such as
$$e^{\pi i a(m-n) + \frac{1}{4}\kappa\pi i(2m+\sigma-2n-\sigma')^2},$$
in order that the function may be only triply periodic. But any other form of $\phi(m-n)$ is admissible provided, of course, that it is such as to secure the absolute convergence of $\theta(z, z')$.

If, in particular, for any one of these admissible forms, ϕ involves σ and σ' so that
$$\phi(m-n) = \text{a function of } 2m + \sigma - (2n + \sigma'),$$
then it is easy to prove that
$$\theta\begin{pmatrix}\rho, & \rho', & z \\ \sigma+2, & \sigma', & z'\end{pmatrix} = (-1)^\rho \theta\begin{pmatrix}\rho, & \rho', & z \\ \sigma, & \sigma', & z'\end{pmatrix},$$
$$\theta\begin{pmatrix}\rho, & \rho', & z \\ \sigma, & \sigma'+2, & z'\end{pmatrix} = (-1)^{\rho'} \theta\begin{pmatrix}\rho, & \rho', & z \\ \sigma, & \sigma', & z'\end{pmatrix},$$
thus furnishing an additional reason for restricting the values of σ and σ' to 0 and 1, independently of each other.

145. One remark may be made at this stage as to the so-called addition-theorem for the theta-functions. Thus it is possible to express the product of four double theta-functions in terms of sums of products of four double theta-functions of other arguments: and it is possible to express the product of a double theta-function of $z_1 + z_2$, $z_1' + z_2'$ and a double theta-function of $z_1 - z_2$, $z_1' - z_2'$, in terms of double theta-functions of z_1, z_1' and of z_2, z_2'. In the purely arithmetical establishment of this theorem, relations

$$\left. \begin{array}{l} \mu_r' = \tfrac{1}{2}(\mu_1 + \mu_2 + \mu_3 + \mu_4) - \mu_r \\ \nu_r' = \tfrac{1}{2}(\nu_1 + \nu_2 + \nu_3 + \nu_4) - \nu_r \end{array} \right\}, \qquad (r = 1, 2, 3, 4),$$

for arguments, parameters, and integer-indices of terms, are adopted (requiring that, for parameters, $\sigma_1 + \sigma_2 + \sigma_3 + \sigma_4$ is an even integer, and so on): and then

$$\Sigma\mu' = \Sigma\mu, \quad \Sigma\nu' = \Sigma\nu,$$
$$\Sigma\mu'^2 = \Sigma\mu^2, \quad \Sigma\mu'\nu' = \Sigma\mu\nu, \quad \Sigma\nu'^2 = \Sigma\nu^2.$$

The last equations allow the transformation of a product of four coefficients such as

$$e^{\kappa(m-n+c)^2}$$

into the product of other four like coefficients: and so renders the addition-theorem possible. But except for coefficients that have this quadratic index, the transformation cannot be effected: for instance, it could not be effected for coefficients such as

$$e^{\kappa(m-n+c)^4}.$$

Consequently, we are not to expect an addition-theorem for our triply periodic function similar to that possessed by the double theta-functions.

The sixteen triple theta-functions.

146. Coming now more specially to the detailed properties of the functions denoted by

$$\theta \begin{pmatrix} \rho, & \rho', & z \\ \sigma, & \sigma', & z' \end{pmatrix},$$

we have seen that, when ρ and ρ' are restricted to be integers, it is sufficient to take for each of them either 0 or 1. Further, the actual values of σ and σ' in the coefficients of the variable parts of the exponential terms would not be of importance as, owing to their linear occurrence, they would (if changed) affect only a factor common to the whole series; but they occur in the coefficient in each term and the occurrence is not linear. We have seen that a large class of these functions θ is selected from the whole body, by assigning to σ and σ' the values 0 or 1 independently of one another; but it must be noted that such an assignment of value is a distinct limitation upon the full generality of the functions.

Suppose then that the values indicated are assigned to $\rho, \rho', \sigma, \sigma'$; as there are two possibilities for each of the four parameters, there are sixteen functions in all. It is convenient to shorten the symbols of the functions: and so we write*

$$\theta\begin{pmatrix}0, & 0, & z \\ 0, & 0, & z'\end{pmatrix} = \theta_0 = \Sigma\Sigma\, a_r\, q^{4m^2}\, q'^{4n^2}\, e^{2m\pi i z + 2n\pi i z'}$$

$$\theta\begin{pmatrix}0, & 0, & z \\ 1, & 0, & z'\end{pmatrix} = \theta_1 = \Sigma\Sigma\, a_r\, q^{(2m+1)^2}\, q'^{4n^2}\, e^{(2m+1)\pi i z + 2n\pi i z'}$$

$$\theta\begin{pmatrix}0, & 0, & z \\ 0, & 1, & z'\end{pmatrix} = \theta_2 = \Sigma\Sigma\, a_r\, q^{4m^2}\, q'^{(2n+1)^2}\, e^{2m\pi i z + (2n+1)\pi i z'}$$

$$\theta\begin{pmatrix}0, & 0, & z \\ 1, & 1, & z'\end{pmatrix} = \theta_3 = \Sigma\Sigma\, a_r\, q^{(2m+1)^2}\, q'^{(2n+1)^2}\, e^{(2m+1)\pi i z + (2n+1)\pi i z'}$$

$$\theta\begin{pmatrix}1, & 0, & z \\ 0, & 0, & z'\end{pmatrix} = \theta_4 = \Sigma\Sigma\, (-1)^m\, a_r\, q^{4m^2}\, q'^{4n^2}\, e^{2m\pi i z + 2n\pi i z'}$$

$$\theta\begin{pmatrix}1, & 0, & z \\ 1, & 0, & z'\end{pmatrix} = \theta_5 = \Sigma\Sigma\, (-1)^m\, a_r\, q^{(2m+1)^2}\, q'^{4n^2}\, e^{(2m+1)\pi i z + 2n\pi i z'}$$

$$\theta\begin{pmatrix}1, & 0, & z \\ 0, & 1, & z'\end{pmatrix} = \theta_6 = \Sigma\Sigma\, (-1)^m\, a_r\, q^{4m^2}\, q'^{(2n+1)^2}\, e^{2m\pi i z + (2n+1)\pi i z'}$$

$$\theta\begin{pmatrix}1, & 0, & z \\ 1, & 1, & z'\end{pmatrix} = \theta_7 = \Sigma\Sigma\, (-1)^m\, a_r\, q^{(2m+1)^2}\, q'^{(2n+1)^2}\, e^{(2m+1)\pi i z + (2n+1)\pi i z'}$$

$$\theta\begin{pmatrix}0, & 1, & z \\ 0, & 0, & z'\end{pmatrix} = \theta_8 = \Sigma\Sigma\, (-1)^n\, a_r\, q^{4m^2}\, q'^{4n^2}\, e^{2m\pi i z + 2n\pi i z'}$$

$$\theta\begin{pmatrix}0, & 1, & z \\ 1, & 0, & z'\end{pmatrix} = \theta_9 = \Sigma\Sigma\, (-1)^n\, a_r\, q^{(2m+1)^2}\, q'^{4n^2}\, e^{(2m+1)\pi i z + 2n\pi i z'}$$

$$\theta\begin{pmatrix}0, & 1, & z \\ 0, & 1, & z'\end{pmatrix} = \theta_{10} = \Sigma\Sigma\, (-1)^n\, a_r\, q^{4m^2}\, q'^{(2n+1)^2}\, e^{2m\pi i z + (2n+1)\pi i z'}$$

$$\theta\begin{pmatrix}0, & 1, & z \\ 1, & 1, & z'\end{pmatrix} = \theta_{11} = \Sigma\Sigma\, (-1)^n\, a_r\, q^{(2m+1)^2}\, q'^{(2n+1)^2}\, e^{(2m+1)\pi i z + (2n+1)\pi i z'}$$

$$\theta\begin{pmatrix}1, & 1, & z \\ 0, & 0, & z'\end{pmatrix} = \theta_{12} = \Sigma\Sigma\, (-1)^{m+n}\, a_r\, q^{4m^2}\, q'^{4n^2}\, e^{2m\pi i z + 2n\pi i z'}$$

$$\theta\begin{pmatrix}1, & 1, & z \\ 1, & 0, & z'\end{pmatrix} = \theta_{13} = \Sigma\Sigma\, (-1)^{m+n}\, a_r\, q^{(2m+1)^2}\, q'^{4n^2}\, e^{(2m+1)\pi i z + 2n\pi i z'}$$

$$\theta\begin{pmatrix}1, & 1, & z \\ 0, & 1, & z'\end{pmatrix} = \theta_{14} = \Sigma\Sigma\, (-1)^{m+n}\, a_r\, q^{4m^2}\, q'^{(2n+1)^2}\, e^{2m\pi i z + (2n+1)\pi i z'}$$

$$\theta\begin{pmatrix}1, & 1, & z \\ 1, & 1, & z'\end{pmatrix} = \theta_{15} = \Sigma\Sigma\, (-1)^{m+n}\, a_r\, q^{(2m+1)^2}\, q'^{(2n+1)^2}\, e^{(2m+1)\pi i z + (2n+1)\pi i z'}$$

---

* The symbols adopted agree with the symbols used for the double theta-functions in a memoir by the author, *Phil. Trans.* (1882), pp. 783—862; the reason is that, as indicated above, the functions actually become double theta-functions when the proper value is assigned to the coefficients a_r.

where, throughout, r denotes $m - n$, and the coefficient a_r is an abbreviation for $\phi(m - n, \sigma, \sigma')$ in the respective cases.

The law that m and n, when they occur in the coefficients, must occur in the combination $m - n$, secures the periodicity (actual, or save as to a factor) of the functions: thus it is essential. As will be seen later, another limitation will be imposed so as to secure the oddness or the evenness of each of the sixteen functions; but the limitation is conventional, not essential. In the meanwhile, we note that σ and σ' are the same for the set $\theta_0, \theta_4, \theta_8, \theta_{12}$; likewise for the set $\theta_1, \theta_5, \theta_9, \theta_{13}$; for the set $\theta_2, \theta_6, \theta_{10}, \theta_{14}$; and for the set $\theta_3, \theta_7, \theta_{11}, \theta_{15}$. Let

$$\left.\begin{aligned}\phi(m - n, 0, 0) &= f(m - n) = f(r) \\ \phi(m - n, 1, 0) &= g(m - n) = g(r) \\ \phi(m - n, 0, 1) &= h(m - n) = h(r) \\ \phi(m - n, 1, 1) &= k(m - n) = k(r)\end{aligned}\right\};$$

then the typical coefficient a_r is

$$\left.\begin{aligned}f(r), &\text{ for } \theta_0, \theta_4, \theta_8, \theta_{12} \\ g(r), &\ldots \theta_1, \theta_5, \theta_9, \theta_{13} \\ h(r), &\ldots \theta_2, \theta_6, \theta_{10}, \theta_{14} \\ k(r), &\ldots \theta_3, \theta_7, \theta_{11}, \theta_{15}\end{aligned}\right\}.$$

Even functions: Odd functions.

147. It is important to know the conditions that will allow any (and, if so, which) of these functions to be either odd or even in their arguments. We have

$$\theta(-z, -z') = \Sigma\Sigma(-1)^{m\rho + n\rho'} a_r q^{(2m+\sigma)^2} q'^{(2n+\sigma')^2} e^{-(2m+\sigma)\pi i z - (2n+\sigma')\pi i z'},$$

where

$$a_r = \phi(m - n, \sigma, \sigma').$$

Let new integers m' and n' be chosen so that

$$m + m' + \sigma = 0, \quad n + n' + \sigma' = 0;$$

then

$$\theta(-z, -z') = (-1)^{\rho\sigma + \rho'\sigma'} \Sigma\Sigma(-1)^{m'\rho + n'\rho'} a_r q^{(2m'+\sigma)^2} q'^{(2n'+\sigma')^2} e^{(2m'+\sigma)\pi i z + (2n'+\sigma')\pi i z'}.$$

But

$$\theta(z, z') = \Sigma\Sigma(-1)^{m'\rho + n'\rho'} c_r q^{(2m'+\sigma)^2} q'^{(2n'+\sigma')^2} e^{(2m'+\sigma)\pi i z + (2n'+\sigma')\pi i z'},$$

where

$$c_r = \phi(m' - n', \sigma, \sigma').$$

In order to compare $\theta(-z, -z')$ with $\theta(z, z')$, we take

$$\phi(m' - n', \sigma, \sigma') = \phi(m - n, \sigma, \sigma');$$

and then
$$\theta(-z, -z') = (-1)^{\rho\sigma+\rho'\sigma'}\theta(z, z'),$$
that is, $\theta(z, z')$ then is even when $\rho\sigma + \rho'\sigma'$ is even, and $\theta(z, z')$ then is odd when $\rho\sigma + \rho'\sigma'$ is odd.

Thus the imposition of the condition upon ϕ secures the evenness or the oddness of the functions. As regards the expression of the condition, let
$$m' - n' = -r,$$
so that
$$m - n = r - \sigma + \sigma';$$
the condition is
$$\phi(-r, \sigma, \sigma') = \phi(r - \sigma + \sigma', \sigma, \sigma').$$
To modify the expression of the condition, let
$$\phi(t, \sigma, \sigma') = \psi(2t + \sigma - \sigma', \sigma, \sigma'),$$
where ψ is a new form of coefficient; then the condition is
$$\psi(-2r + \sigma - \sigma', \sigma, \sigma') = \psi(2r - \sigma + \sigma', \sigma, \sigma')$$
shewing that ψ is an even function of the first of its three arguments. This is the necessary and sufficient condition, that each of the functions $\theta(z, z')$ should be either odd or even.

One very important class of functions is provided by limiting the coefficients ψ still further. Let it be assumed that the function ψ is a function of its first argument only, so that the typical coefficient, which was $\phi(m - n, \sigma, \sigma')$, is
$$\psi(2m - 2n + \sigma - \sigma'),$$
where ψ is now an even function of its only argument $2m - 2n + \sigma - \sigma'$: the parameters σ and σ' enter into the coefficient solely through their occurrence in this argument. If then by any change in the function $\theta(z, z')$, such as an increment of the arguments, the parameters σ and σ' are increased or are decreased by the same integer, the coefficient ψ is unaltered.

It may be noted that the double theta-functions arise from one particular case of this last law, viz.
$$\psi = p^{(2m-2n+\sigma-\sigma')^2}.$$
Other simple laws can be constructed, subject always to the requirement of convergence; for our immediate purpose, we have also the requirement of merely triple periodicity.

148. Before the final postulation of the aggregate of conditions and limitations upon the coefficients, consider any function $\theta(z, z')$, which is triply periodic but not otherwise limited, so that it is mixed as to a quality of oddness or evenness. Let
$$E(z, z') = \theta(z, z') + \theta(-z, -z'), \quad O(z, z') = \theta(z, z') - \theta(-z, -z'),$$

so that $E(z, z')$ is certainly an even function, and $O(z, z')$ is certainly an odd function; and let the series-expressions for E and O be

$$E(z, z') = \Sigma\Sigma (-1)^{m\rho+n\rho'} k_{m,n} q^{(2m+\sigma)^2} q'^{(2n+\sigma')^2} e^{(2m+\sigma)\pi i z + (2n+\sigma')\pi i z'}$$
$$O(z, z') = \Sigma\Sigma (-1)^{m\rho+n\rho'} l_{m,n} q^{(2m+\sigma)^2} q'^{(2n+\sigma')^2} e^{(2m+\sigma)\pi i z + (2n+\sigma')\pi i z'}$$

Then substituting for θ in the definition of the function E, and denoting by $a_{m,n}$ (as at first) the customary part of the coefficient of the typical term in θ, we find

$$k_{m,n} = a_{m,n} + (-1)^{\rho\sigma+\rho'\sigma'} a_{-m-\sigma, -n-\sigma'}.$$

Consequently

$$k_{m-\sigma, n-\sigma'} = a_{m-\sigma, n-\sigma'} + (-1)^{\rho\sigma+\rho'\sigma'} a_{-m,-n},$$
$$k_{-m,-n} = a_{-m,-n} + (-1)^{\rho\sigma+\rho'\sigma'} a_{m-\sigma, n-\sigma'};$$

and therefore
$$k_{-m,-n} = (-1)^{\rho\sigma+\rho'\sigma'} k_{m-\sigma, n-\sigma'}.$$

Similarly, we have
$$l_{-m,-n} = -(-1)^{\rho\sigma+\rho'\sigma'} l_{m-\sigma, n-\sigma'}.$$

Moreover, by analysis that is similar to the analysis used in establishing the earlier condition that a function should be odd or even (and not mixed), we have

$$E(-z, -z')$$
$$= (-1)^{\rho\sigma+\rho'\sigma'} \Sigma\Sigma (-1)^{m'\rho+n'\rho'} k_{-m'-\sigma, -n'-\sigma'} q^{(2m'+\sigma)^2} q'^{(2n'+\sigma')^2} e^{(2m'+\sigma)\pi i z + (2n'+\sigma')\pi i z'}$$
$$= \Sigma\Sigma (-1)^{m'\rho+n'\rho'} k_{m',n'} q^{(2m'+\sigma)^2} q'^{(2n'+\sigma')^2} e^{(2m'+\sigma)\pi i z + (2n'+\sigma')\pi i z'}$$
$$= E(z, z').$$

Similarly, we have
$$O(-z, -z') = -O(z, z').$$

Consequently, even when the initial function $\theta(z, z')$ is mixed as regards its quality of oddness or evenness, we can deduce (by appropriate combinations) triply periodic functions which definitely are odd or definitely are even. We therefore have said that the limitations imposed upon the coefficients in θ, to secure the oddness or the evenness of the function, are conventional and are not essential.

Effect of half-period increments of variables.

149. The law of reproduction of the general function $\theta(z, z')$, when the arguments are increased by any combination of integer multiples of the periods, has already been given. We proceed to consider the laws of changes among the functions $\theta(z, z')$, when the arguments are increased by linear combinations of half-periods: and these have two forms according as the typical coefficients in the series are taken to be $\phi(m-n, \sigma, \sigma')$ in general or $\psi(2m+\sigma-2n-\sigma')$ less generally, excepting from the latter the single case when the expression for ψ gives quadruply periodic functions.

I. Let the coefficient in θ be $\phi(m-n, \sigma, \sigma')$. We have

$$\theta\begin{pmatrix}\rho, & \rho', & z+\frac{1}{2}\\ \sigma, & \sigma', & z'\end{pmatrix} = i^\sigma \theta\begin{pmatrix}\rho+1, & \rho', & z\\ \sigma, & \sigma', & z'\end{pmatrix},$$

$$\theta\begin{pmatrix}\rho, & \rho', & z\\ \sigma, & \sigma', & z'+\frac{1}{2}\end{pmatrix} = i^{\sigma'} \theta\begin{pmatrix}\rho, & \rho'+1, & z\\ \sigma, & \sigma', & z'\end{pmatrix},$$

$$\theta\begin{pmatrix}\rho, & \rho', & z+\frac{1}{2}\\ \sigma, & \sigma', & z'+\frac{1}{2}\end{pmatrix} = i^{\sigma+\sigma'} \theta\begin{pmatrix}\rho+1, & \rho'+1, & z\\ \sigma, & \sigma', & z'\end{pmatrix}.$$

With these half-period increments, the members of the set

$$\theta_0, \quad \theta_4, \quad \theta_8, \quad \theta_{12}$$

are interchanged among one another, as also are the members of each of the sets

$$\theta_1, \quad \theta_5, \quad \theta_9, \quad \theta_{13};$$
$$\theta_2, \quad \theta_6, \quad \theta_{10}, \quad \theta_{14};$$
$$\theta_3, \quad \theta_7, \quad \theta_{11}, \quad \theta_{15};$$

the law of interchange being the same as that given in the first four columns of the table on p. 254.

Further, let $\Im\begin{pmatrix}\rho, & \rho', & z\\ \sigma, & \sigma', & z'\end{pmatrix}$ denote the value of $\theta\begin{pmatrix}\rho, & \rho', & z\\ \sigma, & \sigma', & z'\end{pmatrix}$ when, in the latter, we take $\phi(m-n, \sigma-1, \sigma'-1)$ as the typical coefficient in place of $\phi(m-n, \sigma, \sigma')$. Also, let

$$N = \pi i (z+z') + \tfrac{1}{4}\pi i (\mu+\mu').$$

Then we have

$$\left.\begin{aligned}\theta\begin{pmatrix}\rho, & \rho', & z+\tfrac{1}{2}\mu\\ \sigma, & \sigma', & z'+\tfrac{1}{2}\mu'\end{pmatrix} &= \; e^{-N}\Im\begin{pmatrix}\rho, & \rho', & z\\ \sigma+1, & \sigma'+1, & z'\end{pmatrix}\\ \theta\begin{pmatrix}\rho, & \rho', & z+\tfrac{1}{2}\mu+\tfrac{1}{2}\\ \sigma, & \sigma', & z'+\tfrac{1}{2}\mu'\end{pmatrix} &= i^\sigma\; e^{-N}\Im\begin{pmatrix}\rho+1, & \rho', & z\\ \sigma+1, & \sigma'+1, & z'\end{pmatrix}\\ \theta\begin{pmatrix}\rho, & \rho', & z+\tfrac{1}{2}\mu\\ \sigma, & \sigma', & z'+\tfrac{1}{2}\mu'+\tfrac{1}{2}\end{pmatrix} &= i^{\sigma'}\; e^{-N}\Im\begin{pmatrix}\rho, & \rho'+1, & z\\ \sigma+1, & \sigma'+1, & z'\end{pmatrix}\\ \theta\begin{pmatrix}\rho, & \rho', & z+\tfrac{1}{2}\mu+\tfrac{1}{2}\\ \sigma, & \sigma', & z'+\tfrac{1}{2}\mu'+\tfrac{1}{2}\end{pmatrix} &= i^{\sigma+\sigma'} e^{-N}\Im\begin{pmatrix}\rho+1, & \rho'+1, & z\\ \sigma+1, & \sigma'+1, & z'\end{pmatrix}\end{aligned}\right\}.$$

It therefore follows that, with the general coefficients adopted, there is no interchange of the functions $\theta(z, z')$ among one another; they change into other triply periodic functions $\Im(z, z')$ with different general coefficients.

There are corresponding laws of change for the functions $\Im(z, z')$, when the arguments are increased by linear combinations of half-periods, into the functions $\theta(z, z')$: this reciprocal property being, of course, due to the periodicity of $\theta(z, z')$ and of $\Im(z, z')$.

It is to be noted that, in all these changes, the quantity $\sigma - \sigma'$ is unchanged: so that, when the coefficient $\phi(m-n, \sigma, \sigma')$ is specialised into $\psi(2m + \sigma - 2n - \sigma')$, the functions $\vartheta(z, z')$ are the same as the functions $\theta(z, z')$. The functions $\theta(z, z')$ would then interchange for all these half-period combinations; these laws of interchange will be given in the table (p. 254).

Again, we have

$$\left.\begin{aligned}\theta\begin{pmatrix}\rho, & \rho', & z+\tfrac{1}{2}\mu\\ \sigma, & \sigma', & z'\end{pmatrix} &= e^{-\pi i z - \tfrac{1}{4}\pi i \mu}\,\theta^+\begin{pmatrix}\rho, & \rho', & z\\ \sigma+1, & \sigma', & z'\end{pmatrix}\\[2pt]\theta\begin{pmatrix}\rho, & \rho', & z\\ \sigma, & \sigma', & z'+\tfrac{1}{2}\mu'\end{pmatrix} &= e^{-\pi i z' - \tfrac{1}{4}\pi i \mu'}\,\theta^-\begin{pmatrix}\rho, & \rho', & z\\ \sigma, & \sigma'+1, & z'\end{pmatrix}\\[2pt]\theta\begin{pmatrix}\rho, & \rho', & z\\ \sigma+2, & \sigma', & z'\end{pmatrix} &= (-1)^\rho\,\Theta^-\begin{pmatrix}\rho, & \rho', & z\\ \sigma, & \sigma', & z'\end{pmatrix}\\[2pt]\theta\begin{pmatrix}\rho, & \rho'+2, & z\\ \sigma, & \sigma', & z'\end{pmatrix} &= (-1)^{\rho'}\,\Theta^+\begin{pmatrix}\rho, & \rho', & z\\ \sigma, & \sigma', & z'\end{pmatrix}\\[2pt]\theta\begin{pmatrix}\rho, & \rho', & z\\ \sigma+2, & \sigma'+2, & z'\end{pmatrix} &= (-1)^{\rho+\rho'}\,\theta\begin{pmatrix}\rho, & \rho', & z\\ \sigma, & \sigma', & z'\end{pmatrix}\end{aligned}\right\},$$

where $\theta^+\begin{pmatrix}\rho, \rho', z\\ \sigma, \sigma', z'\end{pmatrix}$, $\theta^-\begin{pmatrix}\rho, \rho', z\\ \sigma, \sigma', z'\end{pmatrix}$, $\Theta^-\begin{pmatrix}\rho, \rho', z\\ \sigma, \sigma', z'\end{pmatrix}$, $\Theta^+\begin{pmatrix}\rho, \rho', z\\ \sigma, \sigma', z'\end{pmatrix}$ are derived from $\theta\begin{pmatrix}\rho, \rho', z\\ \sigma, \sigma', z'\end{pmatrix}$ by changing its typical coefficient $\phi(m-n, \sigma, \sigma')$ into $\phi(m-n, \sigma-1, \sigma')$, $\phi(m-n, \sigma, \sigma'-1)$, $\phi(m-n-1, \sigma, \sigma')$, $\phi(m-n+1, \sigma, \sigma')$, respectively, all these functions θ^+, θ^-, Θ^+, Θ^- being triply periodic. Also

$$\left.\begin{aligned}\theta\begin{pmatrix}\rho, & \rho', & z+\mu\\ \sigma, & \sigma', & z'\end{pmatrix} &= (-1)^\rho e^{-2\pi i z - \pi i \mu}\,\Theta^-\begin{pmatrix}\rho, & \rho', & z\\ \sigma, & \sigma', & z'\end{pmatrix}\\[2pt]\theta\begin{pmatrix}\rho, & \rho', & z\\ \sigma, & \sigma', & z'+\mu'\end{pmatrix} &= (-1)^{\rho'} e^{-2\pi i z' - \pi i \mu'}\,\Theta^+\begin{pmatrix}\rho, & \rho', & z\\ \sigma, & \sigma', & z'\end{pmatrix}\end{aligned}\right\}.$$

II. Let the coefficient in θ be $\psi(2m + \sigma - 2n - \sigma')$, where ψ is any even function of its argument except a constant or

$$p^{(2m+\sigma-2n-\sigma')^2},$$

always provided that the series converges. Then the sixteen functions $\theta(z, z')$ range themselves into two sets, the members of each set interchanging with one another for half-period increases of arguments, as in the first eight columns of the table (p. 254).

III. Let the coefficient in θ be a special case of the last, so chosen that

$$\psi(2m + \sigma - 2n - \sigma') = p^{(2m+\sigma-2n-\sigma')^2}$$
$$= e^{\tfrac{1}{4}\kappa\pi i(2m+\sigma-2n-\sigma')^2},$$

where there are limitations upon the real parts of $\mu + \kappa$, $\mu' + \kappa$, $\mu\mu' + \kappa(\mu + \mu')$ necessary to secure the convergence of the functions θ.

The sixteen functions are now quadruply periodic (being the double theta-functions): when we write

$$a_{11} = \mu + \kappa, \quad a_{12} = -\kappa, \quad a_{22} = \mu' + \kappa,$$

the four pairs of periods and pseudo-periods are

$$\begin{array}{cccccc} \text{for } z, & 1, & 0, & a_{11}, & a_{12} \\ z', & 0, & 1, & a_{12}, & a_{22} \end{array} \Bigg\}.$$

The three pairs of periods for the triple theta-functions are

$$\begin{array}{cccccc} \text{for } z, & 1, & 0, & (a_{11} + a_{12} =) \mu \\ z', & 0, & 1, & (a_{12} + a_{22} =) \mu' \end{array} \Bigg\}.$$

As already stated, the first four columns in the table give the laws of interchange for half-period increments when the coefficients in the triple theta-functions are quite general; the first eight columns give the laws of interchange for half-period increments when these general coefficients are limited so as to secure that the triple theta-functions are, each of them, either an odd function or an even function of its arguments; and now we add the result that the sixteen columns give the laws of interchange for half-period increments when the coefficients are further specialised so as to give rise to double theta-functions.

150. With the definitions just given for a_{11}, a_{12}, a_{22}, we write

$$\left. \begin{aligned} L &= \pi i z + \tfrac{1}{4}\pi i (\mu + \kappa) = \pi i z + \tfrac{1}{4}\pi i a_{11} \\ M &= \pi i z' + \tfrac{1}{4}\pi i (\mu' + \kappa) = \pi i z' + \tfrac{1}{4}\pi i a_{22} \\ N &= \pi i (z + z') + \tfrac{1}{4}\pi i (\mu + \mu') = \pi i (z + z') + \tfrac{1}{4}\pi i (a_{11} + 2a_{12} + a_{22}) \end{aligned} \right\};$$

and then the table is as on the next page.

151. Of the sixteen functions, whether they are the general properly triply periodic functions or the more special quadruply periodic functions, six are odd, viz. θ_7, θ_{11}, θ_5, θ_{10}, θ_{13}, θ_{14}; and the remaining ten are even.

The table enables us to deduce a number of irreducible zero-places for the functions, whether triply periodic or quadruply periodic, from the fact that the odd functions vanish at 0, 0. These zero-places are given, say for any function θ_0, by noting that

$$\theta_0 (z + \tfrac{1}{2}\mu + \tfrac{1}{2}, z' + \tfrac{1}{2}\mu') = \theta_7 (z, z'),$$

so that $z = \tfrac{1}{2}\mu + \tfrac{1}{2}$, $z' = \tfrac{1}{2}\mu'$ is a zero of $\theta_0 (z, z')$, and so for the others in turn. The whole set thus deducible is given in the succeeding table (p. 255): the first eight lines give the zeros when the functions are triply periodic and not quadruply periodic; the last eight lines give the further zeros when the functions are further specialised so as to become quadruply periodic.

254 TABLE OF RELATIONS [CH. VIII

	0	$\frac{1}{2}$	0	$\frac{1}{2}$	with factor e^{-N}				with factor e^{-L}				with factor e^{-M}			
	0	0	$\frac{1}{2}$	$\frac{1}{2}$	$\frac{1}{2}\mu$ $\frac{1}{2}\mu'$	$\frac{1}{2}\mu$ $\frac{1}{2}\mu'+\frac{1}{2}$	$\frac{1}{2}\mu$ $\frac{1}{2}\mu'+\frac{1}{2}$	$\frac{1}{2}\mu+\frac{1}{2}$ $\frac{1}{2}\mu'+\frac{1}{2}$	$\frac{1}{2}a_{11}$ $\frac{1}{2}a_{12}$	$\frac{1}{2}a_{11}+\frac{1}{2}$ $\frac{1}{2}a_{12}$	$\frac{1}{2}a_{11}$ $\frac{1}{2}a_{12}+\frac{1}{2}$	$\frac{1}{2}a_{11}+\frac{1}{2}$ $\frac{1}{2}a_{12}+\frac{1}{2}$	$\frac{1}{2}a_{12}$ $\frac{1}{2}a_{22}$	$\frac{1}{2}a_{12}+\frac{1}{2}$ $\frac{1}{2}a_{22}$	$\frac{1}{2}a_{12}$ $\frac{1}{2}a_{22}+\frac{1}{2}$	$\frac{1}{2}a_{12}+\frac{1}{2}$ $\frac{1}{2}a_{22}+\frac{1}{2}$
$z+$ $z'+$																
	θ_0	θ_4	θ_8	θ_{12}	θ_3	θ_7	θ_{11}	θ_{15}	θ_1	θ_5	θ_9	θ_{13}	θ_2	θ_6	θ_{10}	θ_{14}
	θ_1	$i\theta_5$	θ_9	$i\theta_{13}$	θ_2	$-i\theta_6$	θ_{10}	$-i\theta_{14}$	θ_0	θ_8	θ_8	θ_{15}	θ_3	$i\theta_7$	θ_{11}	$i\theta_{15}$
	θ_2	θ_6	$i\theta_{10}$	$i\theta_{14}$	θ_5	θ_5	$-i\theta_9$	$-i\theta_{13}$	θ_3	θ_7	$i\theta_{11}$	$i\theta_{15}$	$-$	$-i\theta_8$	$-i\theta_{12}$	θ_{13}
	θ_3	$i\theta_7$	$i\theta_{11}$	$-\theta_{15}$	θ_4	$-i\theta_4$	$-i\theta_8$	$-\theta_{12}$	θ_2	$i\theta_6$	$i\theta_{10}$	θ_{14}	θ_1	$-i\theta_5$	$-i\theta_9$	θ_{13}
	θ_4	θ_0	θ_{12}	θ_8	θ_7	θ_3	θ_{15}	θ_{11}	θ_5	θ_1	θ_{13}	θ_9	θ_6	θ_2	θ_{14}	θ_{10}
	θ_5	$i\theta_1$	θ_{13}	$i\theta_9$	$-\theta_6$	$i\theta_2$	$-\theta_{14}$	$i\theta_{10}$	$-\theta_4$	$i\theta_0$	$-\theta_{12}$	$i\theta_8$	$-\theta_7$	$i\theta_3$	$-\theta_{15}$	$i\theta_{11}$
	θ_6	θ_2	$i\theta_{14}$	$i\theta_{10}$	$-\theta_4$	$-\theta_0$	$-i\theta_{12}$	$-i\theta_8$	θ_7	θ_3	$i\theta_{15}$	$i\theta_{11}$	$-$	$-\theta_1$	$-i\theta_{13}$	θ_{11}
	θ_7	$i\theta_3$	$i\theta_{15}$	$-\theta_{11}$	θ_5	$-i\theta_1$	$-\theta_{13}$	$-\theta_9$	$-\theta_6$	$i\theta_2$	$-i\theta_{14}$	θ_{10}	θ_4	$i\theta_0$	$-i\theta_{12}$	θ_8
	θ_8	θ_{12}	θ_0	θ_4	θ_{11}	θ_{15}	θ_3	θ_7	θ_9	θ_{13}	θ_1	θ_5	θ_{10}	θ_{14}	θ_2	θ_6
	θ_9	$i\theta_{13}$	θ_1	$i\theta_5$	$-\theta_{10}$	$i\theta_{14}$	$-\theta_2$	$i\theta_6$	$-\theta_8$	$i\theta_{12}$	θ_0	$i\theta_4$	$-\theta_{11}$	$i\theta_{15}$	$-\theta_3$	$i\theta_7$
	θ_{10}	θ_{14}	$i\theta_2$	$i\theta_6$	$-\theta_8$	$-\theta_{12}$	$-i\theta_0$	$-i\theta_4$	θ_{11}	θ_{15}	$i\theta_3$	$i\theta_7$	$-\theta_9$	$-\theta_{13}$	$-i\theta_1$	$-i\theta_5$
	θ_{11}	$i\theta_{15}$	$i\theta_3$	$-\theta_7$	θ_9	$-i\theta_{13}$	$-\theta_1$	$-\theta_5$	$-\theta_{10}$	$i\theta_{14}$	$-i\theta_2$	θ_6	θ_8	$-i\theta_{12}$	$-i\theta_0$	θ_4
	θ_{12}	θ_8	θ_4	θ_0	θ_{15}	θ_{11}	θ_7	θ_3	θ_{13}	θ_9	θ_5	θ_1	θ_{14}	θ_{10}	θ_6	θ_2
	θ_{13}	$i\theta_9$	θ_5	$i\theta_1$	$-\theta_{14}$	$i\theta_{10}$	$-\theta_6$	$i\theta_2$	$-\theta_{12}$	$i\theta_8$	θ_4	$i\theta_0$	$-\theta_{15}$	$i\theta_{11}$	$-\theta_7$	$i\theta_3$
	θ_{14}	θ_{10}	$i\theta_6$	$i\theta_2$	$-\theta_{13}$	$-\theta_9$	$-i\theta_5$	$-i\theta_1$	θ_{15}	θ_{11}	$i\theta_7$	$i\theta_3$	$-\theta_{12}$	$-\theta_8$	$-i\theta_4$	$-i\theta_0$
	θ_{15}	$i\theta_{11}$	$i\theta_7$	$-\theta_3$	θ_{12}	$-i\theta_8$	$-\theta_4$	$-\theta_0$	$-\theta_{14}$	$i\theta_{10}$	$-i\theta_6$	θ_2	θ_{13}	$-i\theta_9$	$-i\theta_5$	θ_1

But it must be remembered that each such picked zero is, for a single function, only a place in a continuous aggregate of zero-places: for any pair of functions, any simultaneous picked zero (such as 0, 0 for θ_5 and θ_7) is an isolated simultaneous zero.

The table* of picked zeros is as follows:—

$z, z' =$	θ_0	θ_1	θ_2	θ_3	θ_4	θ_5	θ_6	θ_7	θ_8	θ_9	θ_{10}	θ_{11}	θ_{12}	θ_{13}	θ_{14}	θ_{15}
$0, 0$						×		×			×	×		×	×	
$\tfrac{1}{2}, 0$		×		×						×	×				×	×
$0, \tfrac{1}{2}$			×	×		×	×							×		×
$\tfrac{1}{2}, \tfrac{1}{2}$			×	×			×	×			×		×			
$\tfrac{1}{2}\mu, \tfrac{1}{2}\mu'$					×										×	×
$\tfrac{1}{2}\mu+\tfrac{1}{2}, \tfrac{1}{2}\mu'$	×		×								×	×		×	×	
$\tfrac{1}{2}\mu, \tfrac{1}{2}\mu'+\tfrac{1}{2}$	×	×				×	×						×		×	
$\tfrac{1}{2}\mu+\tfrac{1}{2}, \tfrac{1}{2}\mu'+\tfrac{1}{2}$		×	×		×	×			×		×					
$\tfrac{1}{2}a_{11}, \tfrac{1}{2}a_{12}$					×		×				×	×	×			×
$\tfrac{1}{2}a_{11}+\tfrac{1}{2}, \tfrac{1}{2}a_{12}$	×		×						×			×			×	×
$\tfrac{1}{2}a_{11}, \tfrac{1}{2}a_{12}+\tfrac{1}{2}$			×	×	×			×						×	×	
$\tfrac{1}{2}a_{11}+\tfrac{1}{2}, \tfrac{1}{2}a_{12}+\tfrac{1}{2}$	×			×		×	×	×		×						
$\tfrac{1}{2}a_{12}, \tfrac{1}{2}a_{22}$					×		×	×	×					×		×
$\tfrac{1}{2}a_{12}+\tfrac{1}{2}, \tfrac{1}{2}a_{22}$		×		×				×				×	×	×		
$\tfrac{1}{2}a_{12}, \tfrac{1}{2}a_{22}+\tfrac{1}{2}$	×	×			×		×							×		×
$\tfrac{1}{2}a_{12}+\tfrac{1}{2}, \tfrac{1}{2}a_{22}+\tfrac{1}{2}$	×		×	×					×		×					

Construction of functions that are strictly periodic.

152. The results of § 142 shew that each of the sixteen θ-functions is periodic in 1 and 0, save possibly as to sign; also in 0 and 1, save possibly as to sign; also in μ and μ', save as to the factor $\exp(-2\pi i z - 2\pi i z' - \pi i \mu - \pi i \mu')$ and save possibly as to sign. The actual periods (except for multiples of μ and

* Both the tables may be compared with the table given by Königsberger, *Crelle*, t. lxiv (1865), p. 23.

μ', when the variable exponential factor occurs) for the functions are as follows :—

$$1, 0\; ;\; 0, 1\; ;\quad \mu,\quad \mu'\; ;\quad \text{for } \theta_0 \text{ and } \theta_{12};$$
$$1, 0\; ;\; 0, 1\; ;\quad 2\mu,\; 2\mu'\; ;\quad \text{for } \theta_4 \text{ and } \theta_8\; ;$$
$$2, 0\; ;\; 0, 2\; ;\quad \mu,\quad \mu'\; ;\quad \text{for } \theta_3 \text{ and } \theta_{15};$$
$$2, 0\; ;\; 0, 2\; ;\quad 2\mu,\; 2\mu'\; ;\quad \text{for } \theta_7 \text{ and } \theta_{11};$$
$$2, 0\; ;\; 0, 1\; ;\quad \mu,\quad \mu'\; ;\quad \text{for } \theta_1 \text{ and } \theta_{13};$$
$$2, 0\; ;\; 0, 1\; ;\quad 2\mu,\; 2\mu'\; ;\quad \text{for } \theta_5 \text{ and } \theta_9\; ;$$
$$1, 0\; ;\; 0, 2\; ;\quad \mu,\quad \mu'\; ;\quad \text{for } \theta_2 \text{ and } \theta_{14};$$
$$1, 0\; ;\; 0, 2\; ;\quad 2\mu,\; 2\mu'\; ;\quad \text{for } \theta_6 \text{ and } \theta_{10}.$$

Hence the fifteen quotients of any fifteen of the functions by the remaining sixteenth function are actually triply periodic (save possibly as to sign) in $1, 0\; ;\; 0, 1\; ;\; \mu, \mu'$; the squares of these quotients are actually triply periodic in the three pairs of periods. And it may be noted that the eight quotients

$$\frac{\theta_0}{\theta_{12}},\; \frac{\theta_1}{\theta_{13}},\; \frac{\theta_2}{\theta_{14}},\; \frac{\theta_3}{\theta_{15}},\; \frac{\theta_4}{\theta_8},\; \frac{\theta_5}{\theta_9},\; \frac{\theta_6}{\theta_{10}},\; \frac{\theta_7}{\theta_{11}}$$

are actually triply periodic in $1, 0\; ;\; 0, 1\; ;\; \mu, \mu'$.

The analogy of the quadruply periodic functions which arise out of the double theta-functions suggests that, for the triply periodic functions, we should take the quotients

$$\theta_r \div \theta_{12},$$

where r has all the values $0, 1, \ldots, 15$ except $r = 12$. Triply periodic functions thus are secured without doubt: but it must at once be noted that the functions are tied as to their infinities. In the simplest case, when the θ-functions are regular for all finite values of the variables, the infinities of each of the fifteen quotients are the zeros of θ_{12} and are these alone. But such zeros are a continuous aggregate; and so the simultaneous poles of the fifteen quotients, taken in pairs anyhow, are not isolated points: the fifteen quotients are tied, through the common occurrence of θ_{12} in the denominator. The simultaneous zeros of any two of the fifteen quotients are isolated places, being the simultaneous zeros of the θ-functions which occur in their numerators: and these constitute the whole of the zeros simultaneously belonging to two quotients for finite values of the variables.

But, of course, the quotients indicated are, initially at any rate, not a potential aggregate of actually periodic functions. Thus, for any one of the θ-functions, it is clear that the quantities

$$\frac{\partial^{r+s} \log \theta}{\partial z^r \partial z'^s},$$

for integers r and s, such that $r + s \geqslant 2$, will provide periodic functions: and so for other possible derivatives and combinations.

Later (§ 161), we shall return to the "double" theta-functions which arise as a particular set of these "triple" theta-functions.

A property of uniform quadruply periodic functions in combination.

153. We proceed to consider the level places of two uniform quadruply periodic* functions $f(z, z')$ and $g(z, z')$, having four pairs of periods in the form

$$\begin{pmatrix} 1, & 0, & \lambda, & \mu \\ 0, & 1, & \lambda', & \mu' \end{pmatrix}.$$

Let α and β be two level values for f and g, so that

$$f(z, z') = \alpha, \quad g(z, z') = \beta.$$

If $z = a_1$, $z' = a_1'$ be a place where f and g acquire the values α and β respectively, they will acquire these respective values at the whole set of places

$$a_1 + p + r\lambda + s\mu, \quad a_1' + q + r\lambda' + s\mu',$$

for all integer values of p, q, r, s.

We have seen, in § 138, that, by taking an associated two-plane representation for the real variables x, y, x', y', we can choose a unique point-pair $Q_1 P_1$, where Q_1 lies in a parallelogram in the y, y' plane and P_1 in a square in the x, x' plane, such that the point-pair $Q_1 P_1$ may represent the whole foregoing set of values equivalent to a_1, a_1'. We shall say that the whole set of values is *expressible* by the point-pair $Q_1 P_1$.

Let $z = a_2$, $z' = a_2'$ be another place, not belonging to the set expressible by the point-pair $Q_1 P_1$, where f and g acquire the respective values α and β; and let the whole set of places, equivalent to a_2, a_2' by the addition of periods, be expressible by the point-pair $Q_2 P_2$.

And so on in succession, for places and sets of places equivalent to them, each new set containing no place belonging to any of the preceding sets. Each new set will be expressible by a point-pair, in the associated two-plane representation of the real variables x, y, x', y'. We thus obtain a succession of different point-pairs $Q_1 P_1, Q_2 P_2, \ldots$, expressing the succession of distinct sets of places where the functions f and g acquire the respective level values α and β. Each such set can be denoted by any one of the members of the set; and from the construction of the sets, each set contains finite places in the field of variation. Let these finite places be denoted by a_1, a_1'; a_2, a_2'; ..., in succession, corresponding to the point-pairs $Q_1 P_1, Q_2 P_2, \ldots$. We shall say that such a finite place z_m, z_m' is the *irreducible* level place for its set.

---

* An attempt to establish the property for triply periodic functions, similar to that which follows for quadruply periodic functions, did not meet with success.

If the number of point-pairs Q_1P_1, Q_2P_2, ..., which thus arise, is finite, then the number of irreducible level places z, z', giving level values α and β to the functions f and g, is finite.

If the number of point-pairs Q_1P_1, Q_2P_2, ..., which thus arise, is infinite, then within the finite y, y' parallelogram and the finite x, x' square, there must be at least one (and there may be more than one) limiting point-pair QP such that its immediate vicinity contains an infinite number of such point-pairs. We then, for all such point-pairs in that immediate vicinity, have an infinite number of finite places a, a', at which the functions f and g acquire the level values α and β respectively.

Now suppose that, for finite places in the field of variation, our functions f and g possess no essential singularities. On this hypothesis, we know (§ 121) that the level places are isolated, so that there cannot be an infinite number of those level places in the immediate vicinity of any one of them.

The second alternative must therefore be rejected; and so we infer the theorem:—

The number of irreducible level places, giving level values α and β to two independent free uniform quadruply periodic functions, is finite.

154. It has been established for a couple of independent uniform functions in general, and therefore for a couple of independent uniform quadruply periodic functions in particular, that the level places are isolated pair-places. Any such pair-place may be simple or multiple. Whether simple or multiple, it is isolated, provided the two functions are independent and free.

Further, if a, a' is a simple level place for two independent and free functions $f(z, z')$ and $g(z, z')$, such that
$$f(z, z') = \alpha, \quad g(z, z') = \beta,$$
so that it is an isolated level place of those functions for those values α and β, then there is one (and there is only one) simple level place in the immediate vicinity of a, a'—say at $a+b$, $a'+b'$, where $|b|$ and $|b'|$ are small—such that
$$f(z, z') = \alpha + \alpha', \quad g(z, z') = \beta + \beta',$$
where $|\alpha'|$ and $|\beta'|$ are sufficiently small, and
$$|\alpha + \alpha'| < |\alpha|, \quad |\beta + \beta'| < |\beta|.$$
For, by the theorems in Chapter IV and Chapter VII, if $z = a + b$, $z' = a' + b'$, then we can write
$$f(z, z') - \alpha = f(a+b, a'+b') - \alpha$$
$$= a_{10}b + a_{01}b' + ...,$$
$$g(z, z') - \beta = g(a+b, a'+b') - \beta$$
$$= c_{10}b + c_{01}b' + ...;$$

and therefore, as the level place a, a' is simple, the equations
$$\left. \begin{array}{l} a_{10}b + a_{01}b' + \ldots = \alpha' \\ c_{10}b + c_{01}b' + \ldots = \beta' \end{array} \right\},$$
for sufficiently small values of $|\alpha'|$ and $|\beta'|$, provide a single pair-value for b, b', where $|b|$ and $|b'|$ are small.

Similarly, from the theorems in §§ 113, 120—122, we infer that, when a, a' is a multiple level place of multiplicity M for two independent and free functions $f(z, z')$ and $g(z, z')$, such that
$$f(z, z') = \alpha, \quad g(z, z') = \beta,$$
so that it is an isolated level place of those functions of multiplicity M for those values, there are level pair-places (some perhaps simple, some perhaps multiple), in the immediate vicinity of a, a'—say at $a + b$, $a' + b'$ where $|b|$ and $|b'|$ are small,—of the same multiplicity M in additive aggregate for
$$f(z, z') = \alpha + \alpha', \quad g(z, z') = \beta + \beta',$$
where $|\alpha'|$ and $|\beta'|$ are sufficiently small, and
$$|\alpha + \alpha'| < |\alpha|, \quad |\beta + \beta'| < |\beta|.$$

155. Now consider the total finite number of irreducible level places such that the uniform quadruply periodic functions f and g acquire the values α and β. The propositions just quoted shew that we can proceed from these values of the two functions to other values having smaller moduli: to any aggregate of level places at or near any one place a, a' for the values α and β, there corresponds another aggregate of level places for the values $\alpha + \alpha'$ and $\beta + \beta'$, the corporate multiplicity of one aggregate being the same as the corporate multiplicity of the other. We can thus proceed from one pair of level values to another pair of level values for f and g—in the argument, we have chosen a succession with decreasing moduli—without, at any step, affecting the corporate multiplicity of the level places. Moreover, in this succession, it is necessary to have only a finite range for z, and only a finite range for z', because the ranges in the y, y' plane and in the x, x' plane in the two-plane representation described in § 138, giving the finite irreducible places z, z', of § 153, are finite. Hence we infer the theorem:—

The number of irreducible level places, at which two independent and free uniform quadruply periodic functions f and g, having no essential singularity for finite values of the variables, acquire finite values α and β, so that
$$f(z, z') = \alpha, \quad g(z, z') = \beta,$$
regard being paid to possible multiplicity of each such level place, is independent of the actual level values acquired by the functions. In particular, the number of level places is the same as the number of simultaneous zero places of two such functions, regard always being paid to possible multiplicity of occurrence at a level place or a zero place.

The property also holds when the level value for either of the functions or for both of the functions is a unique infinity so that the level place is a pole (an unessential singularity of the first kind) for either of the functions or for both of the functions, as the case may be; it follows at once by considering the reciprocal of the function or of the functions having the place for a pole. But care must always be exercised to make certain that the functions are free as well as independent: thus the theorem would not apply to the poles of functions, such as $\theta_0 \div \theta_{12}$ and $\theta_4 \div \theta_{12}$ of § 152, because the poles, so far from being isolated, are the continuous aggregates of zeros of the function θ_{12}.

But the unessential singularities (the unessential singularities of the second kind) of a single function are isolated; and when two functions are considered simultaneously, their unessential singularities are not necessarily (and are not usually) the same places. Hence the theorem does not apply to unessential singularities.

And the theorem does not apply to essential singularities.

If, then, we adopt a more comprehensive definition of level places and level values, the first including ordinary places and poles, and the second including zeros, finite values, and unique infinite values, we can say that *the number of irreducible level places of two independent and free uniform quadruply periodic functions, having no essential singularity for finite values of the variables, is independent of the actual level values, regard being paid to possible multiplicity.*

This integer, being the number of irreducible level places of the two functions when regard is paid to possible multiplicity, will, after Weierstrass[*], be called the *grade* of the pair of functions.

Algebraic relations between functions.

156. Now consider two uniform quadruply periodic functions $f(z, z')$ and $g(z, z')$—say f and g—which are independent and free; and let them be of grade n, so that there are n irreducible places giving level values α and β to f and g.

Let $h(z, z')$ be another uniform function, homoperiodic with f and g. At each of the n irreducible level places of f and g, the uniform function h has a single definite value; and therefore, at the aggregate of those places, there are n values of h in all. Hence there are n values of h corresponding to assigned values of f and g; and these n values arise solely from the values of f and g, without any intervention of the variables z and z' beyond their occurrence in f and g. Consequently, there is a relation between f, g, h,

---

[*] *Crelle*, t. lxxxix (1880), p. 7; *Ges. Werke*, t. ii, p. 132.

which is of degree n in h; the coefficients in this relation are functions of f and g alone.

Next, suppose that f and h, being uniform quadruply periodic functions of z and z', are independent and free; and let them be of grade m. Also suppose that g and h are independent and free; and let them be of grade l. Then an argument, similar to the argument just expounded, leads to the conclusion that the relation between f, g, h, already known to be of degree n in h, is of degree l in f and of degree m in g: it is an algebraic relation.

Of the n values of h, corresponding to assigned values of f and g, it can happen that several may coincide for some not completely general assignment of values. But if this coincidence occurs for completely general values of f and g, the values of h coincide in groups of equal numbers; and the number of values of h, corresponding to assigned values of f and g, is a factor of n. Hence we have the theorem[*]:—

I. *Between any three uniform functions, which are homoperiodic in the same four period-pairs and which taken in pairs are independent and free, there subsists an algebraic equation: the degree of this equation in each of the functions either is equal to the grade of the other two functions or is equal to some integral factor of that grade.*

It is assumed explicitly that the functions, in pairs, are independent and free; and the only level places that have been used for the functions are such as give finite level values to the functions. But it may happen that two functions, independent of one another, and free for all finite values (including zero), are tied as regards infinite values. Thus the quadruply periodic functions, which arise as the quotients by θ_{12} of the quadruple theta functions other than θ_{12}, cannot be estimated for grade by their infinities; their infinities are given by the zeros of θ_{12}, and (except for the irreducible isolated unessential singularities, limited in number) they are the same for all the quadruply periodic functions so framed. These functions therefore, while they are independent, are tied as regards their infinities.

The foregoing theorem is still true for these uniform functions: there is nothing to traverse the argument at any of its stages. But the effect of the tie, in connection with the infinities, is to simplify the form of the algebraic equation. We can suppose that the latter has been made rational and integral. The three functions f, g, h are infinite together and only together; and therefore the terms of the highest aggregate order in all the functions combined will, by themselves, give relations among the parts of f, g, h that govern their infinities.

[*] This theorem, and several of the theorems that follow, were enunciated by Weierstrass for $2n$-ply periodic uniform functions of n variables. The enunciations, in most instances, are not accompanied by proofs; they are to be found in his memoirs, *Berl. Monatsb.* (1869), pp. 853—857, *ib.* (1876), pp. 680—693, and *Crelle*, t. lxxxix (1880), pp. 1—8; see also his *Ges. Werke*, t. ii, pp. 45—48, 55—69, 125—133. See also Baker, *Multiply periodic functions*, ch. vii.

157. Among the functions related to any given uniform quadruply periodic function of two variables are its two first derivatives, which manifestly are homoperiodic with the function. Moreover, all the infinities of the original function are infinities (as to place, but in increased order) of the derivatives; and they provide all the infinities of these derivatives.

The foregoing theorem, when applied to a single function, leads to the result, practically a corollary:—

II. *Any uniform quadruply periodic function $f(z, z')$ and its first derivatives $\frac{\partial f}{\partial z}$ and $\frac{\partial f}{\partial z'}$ are connected by an algebraical equation. When the equation is made rational and integral, the aggregate of the terms of highest order gives relations among the constants of the infinities of f and its derivatives.*

Thus a quadruply periodic uniform function of two variables satisfies a partial differential equation of the first order, just as a doubly periodic uniform function of one variable satisfies an ordinary differential equation of the first order.

158. We return to homoperiodic functions. For purposes of reference among them, we select three uniform functions f, g, h, of the character prescribed in theorem I.

Now let $k(z, z')$—say k—be another uniform function, homoperiodic with f, g, h; and let it be untied with any of them. Then between f, g, k there subsists an algebraical equation, the degree of which in k is either n or is a factor of n: taking the degree as n, we can denote the equation by

$$A(f, g, k) = 0.$$

Also, between f, h, k there subsists an algebraical equation, the degree of which in k is either m or is a factor of m: taking the degree as m, we can denote the equation by

$$B(f, h, k) = 0.$$

Similarly, there is an algebraical equation

$$C(g, h, k) = 0,$$

which is of degree l in k; and there is the original algebraical equation

$$D(f, g, h) = 0,$$

which is of degree l in f, of degree m in g, and of degree n in h. These equations are necessarily consistent with one another; thus the k-eliminants of $A = 0$ and $B = 0$, of $B = 0$ and $C = 0$, of $C = 0$ and $A = 0$, all vanish in virtue of $D = 0$.

These k-eliminants can be formed by Sylvester's dialytic process, because all the equations are algebraic; and an added use of the process leads to another important result. The equations

$$k^r A (f, g, k) = 0, \text{ for } r = 0, 1, \ldots, m-2$$
$$k^s B (f, h, k) = 0, \quad \text{,,} \quad s = 0, 1, \ldots, n-2$$

are a set of $m + n - 2$ equations, linear and not homogeneous in the $m + n - 2$ quantities $k, k^2, \ldots, k^{m+n-2}$. When these are resolved for the $m + n - 2$ quantities, we have expressions for the various powers of k (in particular, for k itself) rational in the quantities f, g, h and reducible, by means of $D = 0$, so as to contain either f to no degree higher than $l - 1$, or g to no degree higher than $m - 1$, or h to no degree higher than $n - 1$. Paying no special regard to these degrees, but noting the assumption made as to the degree of the equation $A = 0$, we have the theorem:—

III. *When f and g are uniform functions, quadruply periodic in the same periods, and are of grade n, and when h is another uniform function, which is homoperiodic with f and g, and which takes n distinct values at the reduced point-pairs determined by given values of f and g; then any other uniform function, which is homoperiodic with f and g, can be expressed rationally in terms of $f, g,$ and h, provided every two of the four functions are independent and free, and provided also no one of the functions has an essential singularity for finite values of the variables.*

And, as before, we have a corollary to the theorem, as follows:—

IV. *When two uniform quadruply periodic functions $f(z, z')$ and $g(z, z')$ are independent and free, and when neither of them has an essential singularity for finite values of the variables, then $g(z, z')$ can be expressed rationally in terms of $f, \dfrac{\partial f}{\partial z}, \dfrac{\partial f}{\partial z'}$; and $f(z, z')$ can be expressed rationally in terms of $g, \dfrac{\partial g}{\partial z}, \dfrac{\partial g}{\partial z'}$.*

Note. But just as there was possible degeneration of degree in the equation $D(f, g, h) = 0$, so it might conceivably happen that, owing to the equation $D(f, g, h) = 0$, the actual expression for k might not be determinate. But this indeterminateness would not occur for every power of k; and so we should then only be able to infer that some power of k is rationally expressible in terms of f, g, h. Such cases occur when the fundamental periods of the functions considered are only commensurable with one another and are not exactly the same for all the functions. The exceptions may be wider than the exceptions of the same kind in the case of doubly periodic functions of one variable, though they will cover the generalisation of such apparent (but only apparent) exceptions to Liouville's well-known theorem which might imply that cn z and dn z are expressible* in the form

$$P + Q\frac{d}{dz}(\operatorname{sn} z),$$

where P and Q are rational functions of sn z.

159. Next, consider two uniform functions $f(z, z')$ and $g(z, z')$, homoperiodic in the same four pairs of periods; and, as usual, assume that they are independent and free, their grade being n, and that they have no essential singularities for finite values of the variables. Their Jacobian J, with respect to the independent variables, is

$$J = \frac{\partial f}{\partial z}\frac{\partial g}{\partial z'} - \frac{\partial g}{\partial z}\frac{\partial f}{\partial z'}$$
$$= \frac{\partial(f, g)}{\partial(z, z')}.$$

It is a uniform function, homoperiodic with f and g; consequently it satisfies an algebraical equation, which has rational functions of f and g for its coefficients, and the degree of which in J is either n or a factor of n. Moreover, as f and g are uniform, infinities of J can arise only through infinities of f or of g or of both; and no infinity of J can arise from finite values of f or of g, or from any integral relation between f and g satisfied by finite values of f and g. Hence, when the algebraic relation between J, f, g is completely freed from fractions, the coefficient of the highest power of J is a constant; and the degrees in f and g of the succeeding powers of J are limited. To indicate the limits, take the simplest forms of two extreme cases:

(i) when f and g are completely free as to infinities:
(ii) when they are completely tied as to infinities—in such a way as are e.g. the periodic functions indicated in § 152.

In the former case, consider the vicinity of a simple simultaneous pole of f and g; then we can take, in that vicinity,

$$f = \frac{U}{V}, \quad g = \frac{R}{S},$$

where V and S have a simple simultaneous zero at the place. Then

$$J = \frac{1}{V^2 S^2} T,$$

where T is a uniform function, regular, and usually not vanishing at the place. The place thus is an infinity of J, as is to be expected: manifestly it is of order 4. Hence in this case, the algebraic equation (taken to be of order n in J) must be such as to provide infinities of order 4 for J; hence the coefficient

---

* The explanation, of course, is that sn z, cn z, dn z do not possess the same fundamental periods.

of $J^{n-n'}$ is a polynomial in f and g of order not greater than $4n'$, while for some value or values of n', among $1, 2, \ldots, n$, it must be of order $4n'$.

In the latter case, we can take
$$f = \frac{U}{V}, \quad g = \frac{R}{V},$$
where the infinities of the functions (now tied) are given by $V = 0$; then
$$J = \frac{1}{V^3} W,$$
where W is a uniform function, regular, and usually not vanishing with V. The place thus is an infinity of J, as again is to be expected; manifestly it is of thrice the order for f and g. As in the preceding case, the coefficient of $J^{n-n'}$ is a polynomial in f and g of order not greater than $3n'$, while for some value or values of n', among $1, 2, \ldots, n$, it must be of order $3n'$.

Other orders of infinities belonging to f and g will lead to other degrees for the polynomial coefficients in the equation. In all instances, we have the theorem:—

V. *The Jacobian J of two uniform quadruply periodic functions f and g, which are independent and free, and which have no essential singularities for finite values of the variables, satisfies an algebraic equation; when this equation is of degree n, the coefficient of J^n is unity and the coefficient of $J^{n-n'}$ is a polynomial in f and g, of degree not greater than $4n'$, for $n' = 1, 2, \ldots, n$. Also, n is either equal to the grade of f and g, or is a factor of that grade.*

160. Combining this result with the earlier theorems I and III, we have the further theorem:—

VI. *When f and g are uniform functions, quadruply periodic in the same periods and of grade n, and when the algebraic equation satisfied by their Jacobian J is of degree n, any uniform function, which is homoperiodic with them, can be expressed rationally in terms of f, g, and J, provided no two of the functions are tied as to level values, and provided neither of the functions has an essential singularity for finite values of the variables.*

In particular, for such functions f and g, we have the relations
$$\frac{\partial f}{\partial z} = F_1(f, g, J), \quad \frac{\partial g}{\partial z} = G_1(f, g, J),$$
$$\frac{\partial f}{\partial z'} = F_2(f, g, J), \quad \frac{\partial g}{\partial z'} = G_2(f, g, J),$$
where F_1, F_2, G_1, G_2 are rational functions of the arguments. The algebraic relation
$$J = F_1 G_2 - F_2 G_1$$
must be satisfied in virtue of the algebraic equation between f, g, and J.

The quadruply periodic functions which arise out of the double theta-functions.

161. It is desirable to have some special illustrations of the foregoing general propositions relating to periodic functions of two variables.

Accordingly, we assume that the coefficients $\phi(m-n, \sigma, \sigma')$ of the triple theta-functions are so specialised as to yield the double theta-functions, periodic or pseudo-periodic in four pairs of periods, always limited so as to secure the convergence of the double series. Moreover, we shall assume that our functions have no essential singularity for finite values of the variables—an assumption which requires the theta-functions to be finite (as usual) over the whole field of variation given by these finite values. We thus have ten even functions, viz., θ_0, θ_1, θ_2, θ_3, θ_4, θ_6, θ_8, θ_9, θ_{12}, θ_{15}; and six odd functions, viz., θ_5, θ_7, θ_{10}, θ_{11}, θ_{13}, θ_{14}: all these being functions of z and z'.

When $z=0$ and $z'=0$, the six odd functions vanish. The ten even functions then acquire finite constant values which are denoted by c_0, c_1, c_2, c_3, c_4, c_6, c_8, c_9, c_{12}, c_{15} respectively.

The effects upon any function $\theta \begin{pmatrix} \rho, \rho', z \\ \sigma, \sigma', z' \end{pmatrix}$ of a period-increment in the various cases are given by the relations

$$\left. \begin{aligned} \theta \begin{pmatrix} \rho, \rho', z+1 \\ \sigma, \sigma', z' \end{pmatrix} &= (-1)^\sigma \theta \begin{pmatrix} \rho, \rho', z \\ \sigma, \sigma', z' \end{pmatrix} \\ \theta \begin{pmatrix} \rho, \rho', z \\ \sigma, \sigma', z'+1 \end{pmatrix} &= (-1)^{\sigma'} \theta \begin{pmatrix} \rho, \rho', z \\ \sigma, \sigma', z' \end{pmatrix} \\ \theta \begin{pmatrix} \rho, \rho', z+a_{11} \\ \sigma, \sigma', z'+a_{12} \end{pmatrix} &= (-1)^\rho e^{-2\pi i z - \pi i a_{11}} \theta \begin{pmatrix} \rho, \rho', z \\ \sigma, \sigma', z' \end{pmatrix} \\ \theta \begin{pmatrix} \rho, \rho', z+a_{12} \\ \sigma, \sigma', z'+a_{22} \end{pmatrix} &= (-1)^{\rho'} e^{-2\pi i z' - \pi i a_{22}} \theta \begin{pmatrix} \rho, \rho', z \\ \sigma, \sigma', z' \end{pmatrix} \end{aligned} \right\},$$

and by derivatives from these relations. The effects upon the sixteen functions, by way of interchanges consequent upon half-period increments of the arguments, are given in the full table on p. 254.

Among the even theta-functions, the simplest relations[*] are as follows:

$$\left. \begin{aligned} c_0^2 \theta_0^2 - c_{12}^2 \theta_{12}^2 &= c_1^2 \theta_1^2 + c_6^2 \theta_6^2 = c_2^2 \theta_2^2 + c_9^2 \theta_9^2 \\ c_0^2 \theta_0^2 - c_3^2 \theta_3^2 &= c_6^2 \theta_6^2 + c_8^2 \theta_8^2 = c_4^2 \theta_4^2 + c_9^2 \theta_9^2 \\ c_0^2 \theta_0^2 - c_{15}^2 \theta_{15}^2 &= c_2^2 \theta_2^2 + c_8^2 \theta_8^2 = c_1^2 \theta_1^2 + c_4^2 \theta_4^2 \end{aligned} \right\},$$

---

[*] These are taken from my memoir, *Phil. Trans.* (1882), pp. 783—862; they occur in many of the memoirs there quoted, and in others, relating to the subject, as well as in treatises such as those of Prym and Krause. Much algebraical discussion of the properties of the functions will be found in Brioschi's memoir, *Ann. di Mat.*, 2da Ser., t. xiv (1887), pp. 241—344, and *Opere Matematiche*, t. ii, pp. 345—454. Reference also may be made to Baker, *Abelian Functions*, ch. xi, and *Multiply Periodic Functions*, ch. ii, and notes, p. 327.

and others derived from these by linear combinations. The simplest relations among the constant values of the even functions when the arguments are made zero are the sets:

$$\left.\begin{array}{l}c_0^4 - c_{12}^4 = c_1^4 + c_6^4 = c_2^4 + c_9^4 \\ c_0^4 - c_3^4 = c_6^4 + c_8^4 = c_4^4 + c_9^4 \\ c_0^4 - c_{15}^4 = c_2^4 + c_8^4 = c_1^4 + c_4^4\end{array}\right\},$$

and others derived from them: as well as the sets of simple biquadratic relations,

$$\left.\begin{array}{l}c_0^2 c_{12}^2 = c_4^2 c_8^2 + c_3^2 c_{15}^2 \\ c_3^2 c_{12}^2 = c_6^2 c_9^2 + c_0^2 c_{15}^2 \\ c_0^2 c_3^2 = c_1^2 c_2^2 + c_{12}^2 c_{15}^2\end{array}\right\},$$

$$\left.\begin{array}{l}c_0^2 c_4^2 = c_2^2 c_6^2 + c_8^2 c_{12}^2 \\ c_1^2 c_4^2 = c_3^2 c_6^2 + c_9^2 c_{12}^2 \\ c_0^2 c_1^2 = c_2^2 c_3^2 + c_8^2 c_9^2\end{array}\right\},$$

$$\left.\begin{array}{l}c_0^2 c_8^2 = c_1^2 c_9^2 + c_4^2 c_{12}^2 \\ c_2^2 c_8^2 = c_3^2 c_9^2 + c_6^2 c_{12}^2 \\ c_0^2 c_2^2 = c_1^2 c_3^2 + c_4^2 c_6^2\end{array}\right\},$$

$$\left.\begin{array}{l}c_2^2 c_4^2 = c_0^2 c_6^2 + c_9^2 c_{15}^2 \\ c_3^2 c_4^2 = c_1^2 c_6^2 + c_8^2 c_{15}^2 \\ c_2^2 c_{12}^2 = c_6^2 c_8^2 + c_1^2 c_{15}^2\end{array}\right\},$$

$$\left.\begin{array}{l}c_1^2 c_8^2 = c_0^2 c_9^2 + c_6^2 c_{15}^2 \\ c_3^2 c_8^2 = c_2^2 c_9^2 + c_4^2 c_{15}^2 \\ c_1^2 c_{12}^2 = c_4^2 c_9^2 + c_2^2 c_{15}^2\end{array}\right\}.$$

Among the simplest relations, expressing the squares of the odd functions in terms of the even functions, are the set

$$\left.\begin{array}{l}c_{15}^2 \theta_5^2 = -c_2^2\ \theta_8^2 + c_3^2\ \theta_9^2 + c_6^2 \theta_{12}^2 \\ c_{15}^2 \theta_7^2 = -c_0^2\ \theta_8^2 + c_1^2\ \theta_9^2 + c_4^2 \theta_{12}^2 \\ c_0^2\ \theta_{10}^2 = c_8^2\ \theta_2^2 - c_3^2\ \theta_9^2 - c_6^2 \theta_{12}^2 \\ c_6^2\ \theta_{11}^2 = c_{12}^2 \theta_1^2 - c_{15}^2 \theta_2^2 - c_4^2 \theta_9^2 \\ c_0^2\ \theta_{13}^2 = c_{15}^2 \theta_2^2 + c_4^2\ \theta_9^2 - c_1^2 \theta_{12}^2 \\ c_3^2\ \theta_{14}^2 = c_{12}^2 \theta_1^2 - c_4^2\ \theta_9^2 - c_2^2 \theta_{15}^2\end{array}\right\},$$

as well as others derived from the relations, among the even theta-functions above given, by using the table on p. 254 for interchanges among all the functions for half-period increments.

Lastly, for the present purpose, it is sufficient to give the three relations

$$c_0{}^2 \theta_7{}^2 = c_2{}^2 \; \theta_5{}^2 + c_{12}{}^2 \; \theta_{11}{}^2 - c_9{}^2 \; \theta_{14}{}^2$$
$$c_0{}^2 \theta_{10}{}^2 = c_8{}^2 \; \theta_5{}^2 - c_6{}^2 \; \theta_{11}{}^2 + c_3{}^2 \; \theta_{14}{}^2,$$
$$c_0{}^2 \theta_{13}{}^2 = -c_{15}{}^2 \theta_5{}^2 + c_1{}^2 \; \theta_{11}{}^2 + c_4{}^2 \; \theta_{14}{}^2$$

connecting the squares of odd functions alone. They can be derived from the relations connecting the squares of the even functions alone, by using the same table of interchanges for half-period increments of the variables.

As regards the odd functions, we write

$$\theta_\mu = k_\mu z + k_\mu' z' + \ldots,$$

where the expressed terms are the terms of the first order, and μ has the values 5, 7, 10, 11, 13, 14; and we have

$$c_0 c_9 c_{12} k_5 = c_3 c_6 c_{15} k_{10} + c_1 c_4 c_8 \; k_{13}$$
$$c_2 c_9 c_{12} k_7 = c_1 c_4 c_{15} k_{10} + c_3 c_6 c_8 \; k_{13}$$
$$c_0 c_2 c_9 \; k_{11} = c_1 c_3 c_8 \; k_{10} + c_4 c_6 c_{15} k_{13}$$
$$c_0 c_2 c_{12} k_{14} = c_4 c_6 c_8 \; k_{10} - c_1 c_3 c_{15} k_{13}$$

with exactly the same relations when k' is substituted for k.

162. All the relations thus far given, connecting the theta-functions, and connecting the quotients of the theta-functions, are quadratic in form. In each relation, there are three such quotients. Every function involves two independent variables z and z'; and therefore it is to be expected that each of the functions is expressible algebraically in terms of two new independent variables. This expectation is justified by the detailed results and properties of the double theta-functions which give rise to the hyperelliptic functions of order two, being quadruply periodic functions; and the actual forms can be expressed as follows.

We take five constants a_1, a_2, a_3, a_4, a_5, unequal to one another; and we write

$$a_m - a_n = mn,$$

for all the five values of m and of n, avoiding equal values, avoiding also some other similar limitations that obviously are to be avoided. Two variables ζ and ζ' are introduced; and we write

$$\tau = \{(\zeta - a_1)(\zeta - a_2)(\zeta - a_3)(\zeta - a_4)(\zeta - a_5)\}^{\frac{1}{2}},$$
$$\tau' = \{(\zeta' - a_1)(\zeta' - a_2)(\zeta' - a_3)(\zeta' - a_4)(\zeta' - a_5)\}^{\frac{1}{2}},$$
$$P = \{(p - a_1)(p - a_2)(p - a_3)(p - a_4)(p - a_5)\}^{\frac{1}{2}}.$$

162] ORDER TWO 269

Two other variables u and u' are introduced, being defined by the equations

$$\left.\begin{array}{l}u=\tfrac{1}{2}\int_{a_1}^{\zeta}\dfrac{p-a_2}{P}\,dp+\tfrac{1}{2}\int_{a_2}^{\zeta'}\dfrac{p-a_2}{P}\,dp\\[2pt]u'=\tfrac{1}{2}\int_{a_1}^{\zeta}\dfrac{p-a_1}{P}\,dp+\tfrac{1}{2}\int_{a_2}^{\zeta'}\dfrac{p-a_1}{P}\,dp\end{array}\right\}.$$

The variables ζ and ζ' are, in general, uniform quadruply periodic functions of u and u'; for sufficiently small values of u and u', we have

$$\left.\begin{array}{l}\zeta-a_1=\dfrac{13.14.15}{12}u^2+\ldots\\[4pt]\zeta'-a_2=\dfrac{23.24.25}{21}u'^2+\ldots\end{array}\right\},$$

where the unexpressed terms are of even orders (beginning with the order 4) in u and u' combined.

The fifteen quadruply periodic functions of z and z', arising from the quotients of the double theta-functions, are algebraically expressible as follows:—

$$\left.\begin{array}{l}\theta_{13}\div\theta_{12}=(12.13.14.15)^{-\frac{1}{4}}p_1\\\theta_{10}\div\theta_{12}=(21.23.24.25)^{-\frac{1}{4}}p_2\\\theta_{9}\div\theta_{12}=(-31.32.34.35)^{-\frac{1}{4}}p_3\\\theta_{2}\div\theta_{12}=(-41.42.43.45)^{-\frac{1}{4}}p_4\\\theta_{0}\div\theta_{12}=(51.52.53.54)^{-\frac{1}{4}}p_5\\\theta_{11}\div\theta_{12}=(13.14.15.23.24.25)^{-\frac{1}{4}}p_{12}\\\theta_{8}\div\theta_{12}=(12.14.15.32.34.35)^{-\frac{1}{4}}p_{13}\\\theta_{3}\div\theta_{12}=(12.13.15.42.43.45)^{-\frac{1}{4}}p_{14}\\\theta_{1}\div\theta_{12}=(-12.13.14.52.53.54)^{-\frac{1}{4}}p_{15}\\\theta_{15}\div\theta_{12}=(21.24.25.31.34.35)^{-\frac{1}{4}}p_{23}\\\theta_{4}\div\theta_{12}=(21.23.25.41.43.45)^{-\frac{1}{4}}p_{24}\\\theta_{6}\div\theta_{12}=(-21.23.24.51.53.54)^{-\frac{1}{4}}p_{25}\\\theta_{7}\div\theta_{12}=(31.32.35.41.42.45)^{-\frac{1}{4}}p_{34}\\\theta_{5}\div\theta_{12}=(31.32.34.51.52.54)^{-\frac{1}{4}}p_{35}\\\theta_{14}\div\theta_{12}=(41.42.43.51.52.53)^{-\frac{1}{4}}p_{45}\end{array}\right\},$$

where
$$p_r^2=(a_r-\zeta)(a_r-\zeta'),$$

for $r=1, 2, 3, 4, 5$; and

$$\frac{p_{rs}}{p_r p_s}=\left\{\frac{\tau}{(\zeta-a_r)(\zeta-a_s)}-\frac{\tau'}{(\zeta'-a_r)(\zeta'-a_s)}\right\}\frac{1}{\zeta'-\zeta},$$

for all the ten combinations of r and s from the set 1, 2, 3, 4, 5.

The constant values of the even theta-functions for zero values of the variables are related as follows:

$$\left.\begin{aligned}
c_0 \div c_{12} &= \left(\frac{51 \cdot 52}{53 \cdot 54}\right)^{\frac{1}{4}} \\
c_2 \div c_{12} &= \left(-\frac{41 \cdot 42}{43 \cdot 45}\right)^{\frac{1}{4}} \\
c_9 \div c_{12} &= \left(-\frac{31 \cdot 32}{34 \cdot 35}\right)^{\frac{1}{4}} \\
c_1 \div c_{12} &= \left(-\frac{52 \cdot 13 \cdot 14}{12 \cdot 53 \cdot 54}\right)^{\frac{1}{4}} \\
c_3 \div c_{12} &= \left(\frac{42 \cdot 13 \cdot 15}{12 \cdot 43 \cdot 45}\right)^{\frac{1}{4}} \\
c_4 \div c_{12} &= \left(\frac{41 \cdot 23 \cdot 25}{21 \cdot 43 \cdot 45}\right)^{\frac{1}{4}} \\
c_6 \div c_{12} &= \left(-\frac{51 \cdot 23 \cdot 24}{21 \cdot 53 \cdot 54}\right)^{\frac{1}{4}} \\
c_8 \div c_{12} &= \left(\frac{32 \cdot 14 \cdot 15}{12 \cdot 34 \cdot 35}\right)^{\frac{1}{4}} \\
c_{15} \div c_{12} &= \left(\frac{31 \cdot 24 \cdot 25}{21 \cdot 34 \cdot 35}\right)^{\frac{1}{4}}
\end{aligned}\right\}.$$

The lowest terms in the odd theta-functions are as follows:—

$$\left.\begin{aligned}
\frac{\theta_5}{\theta_{12}} &= \left(\frac{13 \cdot 15 \cdot 23 \cdot 25}{43 \cdot 45}\right)^{\frac{1}{4}} \left(u\frac{14}{12} - u'\frac{24}{12}\right) + \ldots \\
\frac{\theta_7}{\theta_{12}} &= \left(\frac{13 \cdot 14 \cdot 23 \cdot 24}{53 \cdot 54}\right)^{\frac{1}{4}} \left(u\frac{15}{12} - u'\frac{25}{12}\right) + \ldots \\
\frac{\theta_{10}}{\theta_{12}} &= \left(\frac{32 \cdot 42 \cdot 52}{12}\right)^{\frac{1}{4}} u' + \ldots \\
\frac{\theta_{11}}{\theta_{12}} &= (13 \cdot 14 \cdot 15 \cdot 23 \cdot 24 \cdot 25)^{\frac{1}{4}} \frac{u - u'}{12} + \ldots \\
\frac{\theta_{13}}{\theta_{12}} &= \left(\frac{31 \cdot 41 \cdot 51}{21}\right)^{\frac{1}{4}} u + \ldots \\
\frac{\theta_{14}}{\theta_{12}} &= \left(\frac{15 \cdot 14 \cdot 25 \cdot 24}{34 \cdot 35}\right)^{\frac{1}{4}} \left(u\frac{13}{12} - u'\frac{23}{12}\right) + \ldots
\end{aligned}\right\}.$$

The relations between the two variables u and u', and the two variables z and z', are

$$\left.\begin{aligned}
\frac{k_{10}}{c_{12}} z + \frac{k_{10}'}{c_{12}} z' &= \left(\frac{32 \cdot 42 \cdot 52}{12}\right)^{\frac{1}{4}} u' \\
\frac{k_{13}}{c_{12}} z + \frac{k_{13}'}{c_{12}} z' &= \left(\frac{31 \cdot 41 \cdot 51}{21}\right)^{\frac{1}{4}} u
\end{aligned}\right\}.$$

The quadruply periodic functions of z and z' are quadruply periodic functions of u and u': and conversely.

Finally, derivatives of any function, of the first order with regard to u and u', are linear combinations (with constant coefficients) of its derivatives of the first order with regard to z and z'.

Examples of the theorems in §§ 156—160.

163. Adequate illustrations of the first theorem, in § 156, are provided through the homogeneous relations among the theta-functions which have just been stated. Each of them, when divided throughout by the appropriate power of θ_{12}, gives a relation among strictly periodic functions. Many other such relations are given in the memoir by Brioschi already quoted (p. 266, note); and many can be deduced from the algebraical expressions for the functions p in terms of the variables ζ and ζ'. Among them, we select the following, as being of particular use in the succeeding investigation:—

$$\frac{p_r^2}{rs \cdot rt} + \frac{p_s^2}{sr \cdot st} + \frac{p_t^2}{tr \cdot ts} = 1,$$

where $rs = a_r - a_s$, and so on, and r, s, t are any three of the integers 1, 2, 3, 4, 5; also

$$p_r^2 + \frac{1}{st}(p_{rs}^2 - p_{rt}^2) = rl \cdot rm,$$

$$(st)\, p_r p_{rl} + (tr)\, p_s p_{sl} + (rs)\, p_t p_{tl} = 0,$$

where r, s, t, l, m are the integers 1, 2, 3, 4, 5, in any order. These examples will suffice for the present requirement.

164. We now proceed to give an example of theorem II, in § 157, by forming the partial differential equation of the first order which is satisfied by the uniform quadruply periodic function p_1.

From the values of u and u', expressed in terms of ζ and ζ' by means of definite integrals, we have the values of $\dfrac{\partial \zeta}{\partial u}, \dfrac{\partial \zeta'}{\partial u}, \dfrac{\partial \zeta}{\partial u'}, \dfrac{\partial \zeta'}{\partial u'}$. Using the expression for p_1^2 in terms of ζ and ζ', we find

$$\frac{2}{p_1}\frac{\partial p_1}{\partial u} = \frac{1}{\zeta - a_1}\frac{\partial \zeta}{\partial u} + \frac{1}{\zeta' - a_1}\frac{\partial \zeta'}{\partial u}$$

$$= \frac{1}{21 \cdot \zeta - \zeta'}\left\{\frac{2\tau}{\zeta - a_1}(\zeta' - a_1) - \frac{2\tau'}{\zeta' - a_1}(\zeta - a_1)\right\},$$

$$\frac{2}{p_1}\frac{\partial p_1}{\partial u'} = \frac{1}{21 \cdot \zeta - \zeta'}\left\{\frac{2\tau}{\zeta - a_1}(\zeta' - a_2) - \frac{2\tau'}{\zeta' - a_1}(\zeta - a_2)\right\};$$

and therefore

$$\frac{\tau}{\zeta - a_1} = (\zeta - a_2)\frac{1}{p_1}\frac{\partial p_1}{\partial u} + (\zeta - a_1)\frac{1}{p_1}\frac{\partial p_1}{\partial u'},$$

$$\frac{\tau'}{\zeta' - a_1} = (\zeta' - a_2)\frac{1}{p_1}\frac{\partial p_1}{\partial u} + (\zeta' - a_1)\frac{1}{p_1}\frac{\partial p_1}{\partial u'}.$$

Now, for the values $r = 3, 4, 5$ in particular, we have

$$\frac{p_{1r}}{p_1 p_r} = \frac{1}{\zeta' - \zeta}\left\{\frac{\tau}{(\zeta - a_1)(\zeta - a_r)} - \frac{\tau'}{(\zeta' - a_1)(\zeta' - a_r)}\right\},$$

so that

$$\frac{p_r}{p_1}p_{1r} = -(2r)\frac{1}{p_1}\frac{\partial p_1}{\partial u} - (1r)\frac{1}{p_1}\frac{\partial p_1}{\partial u'},$$

on substituting the foregoing values of τ and τ'. Thus, if we write

$$\frac{\partial p_1}{\partial u} = q_1, \quad \frac{\partial p_1}{\partial u'} = q_1',$$

we have

$$\left.\begin{aligned}\alpha &= -p_3 p_{13} = (23)\, q_1 + (13)\, q_1'\\ \beta &= -p_4 p_{14} = (24)\, q_1 + (14)\, q_1'\\ \gamma &= -p_5 p_{15} = (25)\, q_1 + (15)\, q_1'\end{aligned}\right\},$$

where α, β, γ are temporarily used to denote the combinations of q_1 and q_1'.

Again, from the values of the functions in terms of ζ and ζ', we have

$$p_1^2 + \frac{1}{34}(p_{13}^2 - p_{14}^2) = 12 \cdot 15,$$

$$p_1^2 + \frac{1}{54}(p_{15}^2 - p_{14}^2) = 12 \cdot 13,$$

and therefore

$$\frac{\alpha^2}{p_3^2} - \frac{\beta^2}{p_4^2} = 34(12 \cdot 15 - p_1^2) = C, \text{ say},$$

$$\frac{\gamma^2}{p_5^2} - \frac{\beta^2}{p_4^2} = 54(12 \cdot 13 - p_1^2) = A, \text{ say}.$$

Also

$$\frac{p_1^2}{13 \cdot 14} + \frac{p_3^2}{31 \cdot 34} + \frac{p_4^2}{41 \cdot 43} = 1,$$

so that

$$p_3^2 = 31 \cdot 34 + \frac{34}{14}p_1^2 + \frac{31}{41}p_4^2$$

$$= c + \frac{31}{41}p_4^2,$$

say; and similarly

$$p_5^2 = 51 \cdot 54 + \frac{54}{14}p_1^2 + \frac{51}{41}p_4^2$$

$$= a + \frac{51}{41}p_4^2,$$

say. Thus
$$\frac{\alpha^2}{c+\frac{31}{41}p_4^2} - \frac{\beta^2}{p_4^2} = C,$$

$$\frac{\gamma^2}{a+\frac{51}{41}p_4^2} - \frac{\beta^2}{p_4^2} = A.$$

These two quadratic equations satisfied by p_4^2 can be written
$$Cp_4^4 - (L - \beta^2 - Cc') p_4^2 + \beta^2 c' = 0,$$
$$Ap_4^4 - (N - \beta^2 - Aa') p_4^2 + \beta^2 a' = 0;$$
where
$$a' = a\frac{41}{51}, \quad c' = c\frac{41}{31}, \quad L = \alpha^2\frac{41}{31}, \quad N = \gamma^2\frac{41}{51}.$$

Eliminating p_4^2 between the two equations, we find
$$\{(L - \beta^2 - Cc') a' - (N - \beta^2 - Aa') c'\} \{(N - \beta^2 - Aa') C - (L - \beta^2 - Cc') A\}$$
$$= \beta^2 (Ac' - Ca')^2,$$

which is a form of the partial differential equation of the first order satisfied by p_1.

It is desirable that the equation should be simplified; the various reductions are mere exercises in algebra. We find
$$A - C = 53 (12 \cdot 14 - p_1^2),$$
so that
$$(A - C) a'c' = -\frac{34 \cdot 45 \cdot 53}{13 \cdot 15} (12 \cdot 14 - p_1^2)(13 \cdot 14 - p_1^2)(14 \cdot 15 - p_1^2);$$
also
$$a' - c' = \frac{14 \cdot 35}{13 \cdot 15} (13 \cdot 15 - p_1^2),$$
so that
$$(a' - c') AC = \frac{14 \cdot 34 \cdot 45 \cdot 53}{13 \cdot 15} (12 \cdot 13 - p_1^2)(12 \cdot 15 - p_1^2)(13 \cdot 15 - p_1^2).$$
And
$$Ca' - Ac' = \frac{34 \cdot 45 \cdot 53}{13 \cdot 15} (12 \cdot 13 \cdot 14 \cdot 15 - p_1^4).$$

As regards the parts involving derivatives, we have
$$(L - \beta^2) a' - (N - \beta^2) c'$$
$$= -\frac{14}{13 \cdot 15} \{54 (14 \cdot 15 - p_1^2) \alpha^2 + 35 (13 \cdot 15 - p_1^2) \beta^2 + 43 (13 \cdot 14 - p_1^2) \gamma^2\}$$
$$= -\frac{14 \cdot 34 \cdot 45 \cdot 53}{13 \cdot 15} \{12^2 q_1^2 - p_1^2 (q_1 + q_1')^2\},$$

F.

on substitution for α, β, γ; and, similarly,

$(N - \beta^2) C - (L - \beta^2) A$

$= \dfrac{41 \cdot 45}{31} (12 \cdot 13 - p_1^2) \alpha^2 + \dfrac{41 \cdot 53}{41} (12 \cdot 14 - p_1^2) \beta^2 + \dfrac{41 \cdot 34}{51} (12 \cdot 15 - p_1^2) \gamma^2$

$= - 12 \cdot 14 \cdot 34 \cdot 45 \cdot 53 \left\{ (q_1 + q_1')^2 - \dfrac{12}{13 \cdot 14 \cdot 15} p_1^2 q_1^2 \right\}.$

Hence the differential equation for p_1 takes the form

$$12^3 \cdot 13 \cdot 14^2 \cdot 15 \left(Q_1 + \dfrac{X_1}{12 \cdot 14^2} \right) \left(Q_2 + \dfrac{X_2}{12 \cdot 13 \cdot 15} \right)$$
$$= (24 \cdot q_1 + 14 \cdot q_1')^2 X_3^2,$$

where the various symbols in the equation (which manifestly is of the first order, and of the fourth degree, in the derivatives of p_1) have the values

$$\left. \begin{array}{l} Q_1 = q_1^2 - \dfrac{1}{12^2} p_1^2 (q_1 + q_1')^2 \\[6pt] Q_2 = (q_1 + q_1')^2 - \dfrac{12}{13 \cdot 14 \cdot 15} p_1^2 q_1^2 \end{array} \right\},$$

$$\left. \begin{array}{l} X_1 = (12 \cdot 14 - p_1^2)(13 \cdot 14 - p_1^2)(14 \cdot 15 - p_1^2) \\ X_2 = (12 \cdot 13 - p_1^2)(12 \cdot 15 - p_1^2)(13 \cdot 15 - p_1^2) \\ X_3 = 12 \cdot 13 \cdot 14 \cdot 15 - p_1^4 \end{array} \right\}.$$

The infinity of p_1 at any place being of order κ, that of q_1 at the place and that of q_1' at the place are $\kappa + 1$; from the terms of highest order in the infinities, as they occur in the differential equation, we have (as these orders)

$$8\kappa + 4, \quad 10\kappa + 2, \quad 12\kappa, \quad 10\kappa + 2,$$

which are the same when $\kappa = 1$: that is, any infinity of p_1 is simple. The result is to be expected because p_1 is a constant multiple of $\theta_{13} \theta_{12}^{-1}$: so that an infinity of p_1 is a zero of θ_{12}, that is, it is simple. The terms of highest order also provide relations among the constants connected with any such infinity: but these are not our present concern.

165. The partial differential equation of the first order for any other of the functions p can be constructed in the same manner; in particular, the equation satisfied by p_2 can be derived from the equation satisfied by p_1, through interchanging p_1 and p_2, q_1 and q_2', q_1' and q_2, a_1 and a_2, where

$$q_2 = \dfrac{\partial p_2}{\partial u}, \qquad q_2' = \dfrac{\partial p_2}{\partial u'}.$$

Note. Another proof can be framed, by noting the relations

$$\left. \begin{array}{l} c_2 c_3 \theta_1 \theta_0 + c_8 c_9 \theta_{10} \theta_{11} = c_0 c_1 \theta_2 \theta_3 \\ c_6^2 \theta_{10}^2 = c_{12}^2 \theta_0^2 - c_1^2 \theta_{13}^2 - c_0^2 \theta_{12}^2 \\ c_6^2 \theta_{11}^2 = c_{12}^2 \theta_1^2 - c_0^2 \theta_{13}^2 - c_1^2 \theta_{12}^2 \\ c_6^2 \theta_2^2 = c_4^2 \ \theta_0^2 - c_9^2 \theta_{13}^2 - c_8^2 \theta_{12}^2 \\ c_6^2 \theta_3^2 = c_4^2 \ \theta_1^2 - c_8^2 \theta_{13}^2 - c_9^2 \theta_{12}^2 \end{array} \right\}$$

among the theta-functions, by using the expressions for the constants c and the quotients of the theta-functions, and by observing that $\theta_1 \theta_0 \theta_{12}^{-2}$ is a constant multiple of the quantity denoted by γ and that $\theta_2 \theta_3 \theta_{12}^{-2}$ is a constant multiple of the quantity denoted by β.

A third proof can be framed by noting the fact that

$$\frac{P}{p-a_1} = (p-a_2)\frac{1}{p_1}\frac{\partial p_1}{\partial u} + (p-a_1)\frac{1}{p_1}\frac{\partial p_1}{\partial u'}$$

is satisfied by $p = \zeta$ and $p = \zeta'$, so that the quartic equation

$$(z-a_2)(z-a_3)(z-a_4)(z-a_5) - (z-a_1)\left\{(z-a_2)\frac{1}{p_1}\frac{\partial p_1}{\partial u} + (z-a_1)\frac{1}{p_1}\frac{\partial p_1}{\partial u'}\right\}^2 = 0$$

has ζ and ζ' for its roots. The analytical conditions for this property of the quartic equation ultimately lead to the partial differential equation of the first order satisfied by p_1.

166. The analysis in the preceding investigation leads to a simple illustration of theorems III and IV, in § 158. It must, however, be borne in mind that those theorems refer to functions that are homoperiodic.

Now the functions p_4 and p_1 are not homoperiodic: their periods are only commensurable. But the functions p_4^2 and p_1^2 are homoperiodic: and therefore by the theorem IV, we must have p_4^2 expressible rationally in terms of p_1^2 and its first derivatives, that is, expressible rationally in terms of p_1, q_1, q_1'.

The two quadratics that occur in the investigation give

$$-\frac{p_4^2}{\beta^2} = \frac{Ac' - A'c}{(N-\beta^2-Aa')C - (L-\beta^2-Cc')A},$$

or, with the preceding notation,

$$p_4^2 = \frac{(24q_1 + 14q_1')X_3}{12 \cdot 13 \cdot 14^2 \left(Q_2 + \dfrac{X_2}{12 \cdot 13 \cdot 15}\right)},$$

the required expression.

Also
$$-p_4 p_{14} = 24q_1 + 14q_1',$$

so that we can deduce at once a rational expression for p_{14}^2 in terms of p_1, q_1, q_1'. Expressions for p_3, p_5, p_{13}, p_{15} can be derived by interchange of the constants a_3, a_4, a_5; and expressions for the remaining functions can be derived by simultaneous interchanges of the variables u and u' and of the constants a_1 and a_2.

As an illustration of theorem V in § 159, consider the Jacobian of any two functions p_r, p_s: and let
$$r, s, l, m, n = 1, 2, 3, 4, 5,$$

in any order. We have

$$\frac{\partial(u, u')}{\partial(\zeta, \zeta')} = \frac{1}{4\tau\tau'}(\zeta - \zeta')(a_2 - a_1),$$

$$\frac{\partial(p_r, p_s)}{\partial(\zeta, \zeta')} = \frac{1}{4p_r p_s}(\zeta - \zeta')(a_s - a_r),$$

and therefore

$$J(p_r, p_s) = \frac{\partial(p_r, p_s)}{\partial(u, u')}$$

$$= \frac{sr}{21} p_l p_m p_n.$$

Consequently

$$\{J(p_r, p_s)\}^2 = \left(\frac{sr}{21}\right)^2 p_l^2 p_m^2 p_n^2$$

$$= \left(\frac{sr}{21}\right)^2 . lr . ls . mr . ms . nr . ns . P_{rs},$$

where

$$P_{rs} = \left(1 - \frac{p_r^2}{rl . rs} - \frac{p_s^2}{sl . sr}\right)\left(1 - \frac{p_r^2}{rm . rs} - \frac{p_s^2}{sm . sr}\right)\left(1 - \frac{p_r^2}{rn . rs} - \frac{p_s^2}{sn . sr}\right),$$

so that the square of the Jacobian of p_r and p_s is an even polynomial in r and s of joint degree six.

Similarly, we find

$$\{J(p_r, p_{rs})\}^2 = \frac{1}{12^2} p_{rt}^2 p_{rm}^2 p_{rn}^2$$

$$= \frac{1}{12^2}\{p_{rs}^2 + p_r^2 . st - rm . rn . st\}\{p_{rs}^2 + p_r^2 . sm - rn . rt . sm\}$$

$$\times \{p_{rs}^2 + p_r^2 . sn - rt . rm . sn\};$$

and so for other instances of Jacobians. So long as the Jacobians are formed from any two of the fifteen functions, the algebraical equation between two functions and their Jacobian is of even degree in the Jacobian. It is easy to verify that

$$\{J(p_{rm}, p_{rn})\}^2$$

is an even polynomial in p_{rm} and p_{rn} of degree six; and from general considerations (but without having constructed the respective equations) I infer that

$$J(p_r, p_{st}), \quad J(p_{rm}, p_{st})$$

each of them satisfy an equation, quartic in its own Jacobian and of the degree twelve in the term free from the Jacobian.

As a last illustration, consider a special case of theorem VI in § 160. The derivative of p_1 with respect to u, already denoted (§ 164) by q_1, is quadruply periodic. It is homoperiodic with p_1; but it is not homoperiodic with p_2, their periods being only commensurable. But q_1^2, p_1^2, p_2^2 are homoperiodic: and therefore, by the theorem, q_1^2 is rationally expressible in terms of p_1^2, p_2^2, and the Jacobian of p_1^2 and p_2^2; that is, q_1^2 is rationally expressible in terms of p_1, p_2, and $J(p_1, p_2)$. The actual expression can be obtained in a variety of ways, requiring mere algebra for the purpose. Proceeding from the relation

$$\frac{1}{p_1} q_1 = \frac{1}{21\,(\zeta - \zeta')} \left\{ \frac{\tau}{\zeta - a_1} (\zeta' - a_1) - \frac{\tau'}{\zeta' - a_1} (\zeta - a_1) \right\},$$

already obtained for q_1, we find ultimately the following result. Let $12, 1r, \ldots$ denote $a_1 - a_2$, $a_1 - a_r$, ... as usual; write

$$\Delta = (p_1^2 - p_2^2)^2 - 2 \cdot 12^2 (p_1^2 + p_2^2) + 12^4;$$

$$\kappa_r = p_2^2 - p_1^2 + 12\,(1r + 2r), \text{ for } r = 1, 2, 3, 4, 5;$$

and, for any quantity ξ, let

$$(\xi + \kappa_2)(\xi + \kappa_3)(\xi + \kappa_4)(\xi + \kappa_5)$$
$$= \xi^4 + S_1 \xi^3 + S_2 \xi^2 + S_3 \xi + S_4.$$

Then a rational expression for q_1^2 is

$$64 \cdot q_1^2 12^7 \cdot \Delta + 128 \cdot 12^7 p_1^3 p_2 J(p_1, p_2)$$
$$= (S_4 + S_2 \Delta + \Delta^2)(3\kappa_1 \Delta + \kappa_1^3) - (S_3 + S_1 \Delta)(3\kappa_1^2 \Delta + \Delta^2).$$

Other examples can easily be indicated: these will suffice for the present purpose.

INDEX

(The numbers refer to the pages.)

Abel's theorem partially extended to double integrals involving a couple of algebraic functions of two independent variables, 193–197.

Accidental singularity, 61; (*see* unessential singularity).

Algebraic functions in general, 61, 170 et seq.; rational functions, involving one algebraic variable, 171, and two algebraic variables, 173; integrals of, 178 et seq.

Algebraic relations between homoperiodic functions, 261 et seq.; illustrations of, from hyperelliptic functions, 265 et seq.

Analytic function, 59.

Analytical continuation, 60, 80.

Appell, 147, 235, 239.

Baker, H. F., 110, 131, 261, 266.

Berry, 170.

Borel, 77, 78, 126.

Boundaries of a region for certain fields of variation, and their frontier, 20, 24.

Brioschi, 266.

Bromwich, 72.

Burnside, W., 26, 58, 237.

Campbell, 42.

Canonical form of lineo-linear transformations, 26; leads to powers of the transformation, 28;
    of equations for quadratic frontier, 51;
    of rational functions which involve algebraic variables, 171, 173.

Castelnuovo, 170.

Cauchy, 4.

Cauchy's theorem as to the integral of a function of a single complex variable extended by Poincaré to functions of two complex variables, 13, 159.

Conformal representation with one variable extended to two variables, 18.

Continuation of regular functions, analytical, 80.

Continuity of a function, region of, 81, 82, 86.

Continuous function, 59.

Continuous groups, Lie's theory of, applied to determine invariants and covariants of quadratic frontiers, 40, 42.

Contour integrals, as used by Cousin, 131 et seq.

Cousin, 130, 147.

Dautheville, 80, 126.

Dependent variables, number of, 2; used for a kind of inversion, 4.

Divisibility (relative) of two regular functions, 112.

Domain, 57.

Dominant function, 71.

Double-integral expressions connected with coefficients in the expansion of regular functions, 64.

Double integral for real variables, application of theorem by Stokes on, 157.

Double integrals, defined for two complex variables, 154; Poincaré's extension of Cauchy's theorem for functions of a single variable, 159; residues of, with examples, 160 et seq.

Double integrals of rational functions involving two algebraic variables, 187; equivalent forms of, 189; conditions that they should be of the first kind, 190; Abel's theorem partially extended to, 193.

Double theta-functions, 249, 253 et seq.

Enriques, 170.

Equivalent functions, 134, 141.

Essential singularity, 61, 83, 119, 123; behaviour of a function at and near an, 77, 83; functions devoid of, 125.

INDEX

Field of variation, in general, 57; for periodic functions, with one pair of periods, 224; with two pairs of periods, 225; with three pairs of periods, 231; with four pairs of periods, 236, together with a modified two-plane representation of the variables, 237.

First kind of double integrals, conditions for, 190; extension of Abel's theorem to, 193.

First kind of single integrals of algebraic functions of two variables, 178; initial condition as to form of subject of integration, 180; equivalent forms of, 180, with the necessary relations, 185; do not exist for general equations, 187.

Four-dimensional space, used to represent two variables, 5; used by Poincaré in connection with double integrals, 153.

Free functions, 208; properties of two, 209–212.

Frontier of a region in certain fields of variation, 20, 24; its analytical expression, 21; invariantive, for lineo-linear transformations, 32; quadratic, 34.

Functions devoid of essential singularities, everywhere, 125; in the finite part of the field, 130 et seq.

Geometrical representation of two variables, Chapter I; in four-dimensional space, 5; by means of a line in ordinary space, 7; by means of two planes, one for each of the variables, 13.

Gordan, 25.

Grade of two uniform quadruply periodic functions, 260.

Hadamard, 126.
Hartogs, 62, 123, 131.
Hermite, 4, 131.
Hobson, 1.
Homoperiodic functions, algebraic relations between, 261 et seq.
Humbert, 170.
Hurwitz, 126.
Hyperelliptic functions of order two used to illustrate algebraic relations between homoperiodic functions, 265 et seq.

Independent functions, 208.
Infinitesimal periods excluded, 213–216.
Integral function, 60.
Integrals, of functions of two variables (Chapter VI); of algebraic functions, 178 et seq.

Invariant centres of lineo-linear transformations, 29.

Invariantive frontiers for lineo-linear transformations, 32; simplest forms of, 34, 37.

Invariants and covariants of quadratic frontiers, 39; invariants alone, 48.

Inversion, a kind of, 4.

Irreducible places of quadruply periodic functions, 257; any set expressible by a single place in an associated two-plane representation, 257; their number for level values of two functions is finite, 258, and is independent of those level values, 259.

Jacobi, 14, 26.

Jacobian of two homoperiodic functions, 264; used, in connection with the two functions, for the rational expression of other homoperiodic functions, 265; equation satisfied by, when they are hyperelliptic, 275.

Jordan, 26.

Königsberger, 255.
Krause, 266.
Kronecker, 4.

Laguerre, 126.
Larmor, 157.
Laurent's theorem extended to functions of two variables, 87–91.

Level places of two uniform functions (Chapter VII); must exist for assigned values of the functions, 203.

Level values of a regular function, 108; order of, 111.

Levi, E. E., 123.

Lie, 25, 40, 42.

Line in space used to represent two complex variables simultaneously, 7; limitations upon use of whole line, 11; by means of the points where it cuts two parallel planes, 12.

Lineo-linear transformations, Chapter II; canonical form of, 26; powers of, 28; invariant centres for, 29; invariantive frontiers for, 32; property of, when coefficients are real, 35; periodic, 52.

Lines, Volterra's functions of, 13.

Meromorphic function, 61.
Multiform function, 58.
Multiplicity, of a simultaneous zero of two uniform functions, 168; expressed as a double integral, 169; of a level value of two functions, as a double integral, 169.

INDEX

Nœther, 170.
Non-essential singularity, 61; (*see* unessential singularity).

Order of multiplicity, of a common zero of two uniform analytic functions, 205, 209; of level values of two uniform analytic functions, 212.
Order, of zero of a regular function, 111; of pole of uniform function, 119.
Ordinary place, 60.
Osgood, 62.

Pairs of periods for uniform functions of two variables (*see* period-pairs).
Periodic functions in two variables (Chapter VIII).
Periodic lineo-linear transformations, 19, 28, 52.
Period-pairs, if infinitesimal, are excluded, 213; may not be more than four for uniform function of two variables, 216–223; one, 224; two, 224, with the different cases; three, 226, with the different cases, and the general result, 231; four, 232, with the different cases, 235.
Picard, *Preface*, 5, 14, 26, 77, 78, 92, 152, 153, 156, 161, 169, 170, 178, 193, 197.
Picard's theorem, on functions that cannot acquire assigned values, extended to functions of two variables, 78.
Picard's theorem concerning single integrals of rational functions involving one algebraic variable extended to integrals of rational functions involving two algebraic variables, 180-187.
Poincaré, *Preface*, 1, 4, 5, 13, 26, 71, 126, 131, 153.
Poincaré's extension of Cauchy's theorem to double integrals, 159; with inferences, 160; extension to the residues of double integrals, 160, 161, with examples, 161 et seq.
Pole, 61, 85 (*see* unessential singularity); expression for uniform function in the vicinity of, 119; sequence and order of, 120.
Polynomial, when a regular function is a, 74; properties of, as regards singularities, 124.
Prym, 266.

Quadratic frontiers, 34; invariants and covariants of, 39; suggested canonical form for, 51.
Quadruply periodic functions, 253 et seq.; level places of two, 257; satisfy an algebraic partial differential equation of the first order, 262, with example, 273.

Rational, any uniform function entirely devoid of essential singularities must be, 126.
Rational function connected with algebraic equations in two independent variables, most general form of: (i) when there is one equation, 171; (ii) when there are two equations in two algebraic variables, 173; integrals of, 178 et seq.
Rational function, singularities of, 125.
Reducibility (relative) of two regular functions, 115.
Region of continuity of a function, 81; its boundary, 82, 86.
Regular functions, any uniform function having essential singularities only in the infinite part of the field is expressible as the quotient of two, 147.
Regular functions, 60; fundamental theorem relating to, 62; double integral expression for the coefficients in the expansion of, 64; one property of, 73; condition that it is a polynomial, 74; analytical continuation of, 80; level values of, 108; relative divisibility of, 112.
Relative, divisibility of two regular functions, 112; reducibility of functions, 115.
Riemann, 4, 16.
Riemann's definition of a function extended to two functions, 16.

Sauvage, 58.
Severi, 170.
Simart, *Preface*, 92, 152.
Simultaneous poles of two uniform analytic functions exist, 204; usually is an isolated place, 211.
Simultaneous unessential singularities of two uniform functions do not exist in general, 204.
Simultaneous zero, of two regular functions, must exist, 202; likewise for two uniform analytic functions, 203; usually is an isolated place, 207, 209, but there may be exceptions, 208.
Single integral, 152.
Single integrals of algebraic functions involving two algebraic variables, 178; equivalent forms of, 180, with necessary relations, 185; first kind do not exist for general equations, 187.
Singularities, 61, 82, 119; of a rational function, 125.
Stokes, 157.

Theta-functions, triple, 240 et seq.; even functions and odd functions, 248; double, 249, 253 et seq.

Tied functions, 208.

Transcendental function, 60.

Triple theta-functions, 240; effect on, caused by increments of periods, 242, by half-period increments, 250; two sets of, 251 et seq.

Triply periodic functions, 238.

Two functions, everywhere regular in the finite part of the field, must vanish at some common place, 202; likewise, when they are uniform and analytic, 203.

Two-plane representation of the real parts of the variables used for quadruply periodic functions, 237, 257.

Two-plane representation of two variables, 13; some properties of, 14; limitations of, 19.

Umbral symbols introduced for coefficients in homogeneous forms, 41.

Unessential singularity, 61, 83, 119; expression of uniform function in the vicinity of, 121; is an isolated place, 122.

Uniform analytic function must acquire an infinite value, 72, and a zero value, 76, and an assigned finite value, 76.

Uniform function, 58.

Uniform periodic functions (Chapter VIII).

Valentiner, 25.

Vicinity of a place, 58.

Vivanti, 12.

Volterra, 13.

Weierstrass, *Preface*, 4, 77, 80, 82–86, 92, 101, 105, 112, 122, 124, 141, 214, 260, 261.

Weierstrass's theorem on the behaviour of a uniform continuous analytic function in the vicinity of an ordinary place, 92; various cases of, 96, 97, 100; example of, 102; alternative method of proceeding in one case, 105.

Weierstrass's theorem on functions entirely devoid of essential singularities, 126; proof of, 126–129; on functions having essential singularities only in the infinite part of the field, 130, with Cousin's proof, 130 et seq.

Weierstrass's theorem on infinitesimal periods, 214.

Weierstrass's theorems on algebraic relations between homoperiodic functions, 261 et seq.; illustrated by hyperelliptic functions, 265 et seq.

Zeros (selected) of the theta-functions of two variables, 255.

Cambridge:
PRINTED BY JOHN CLAY, M.A.
AT THE UNIVERSITY PRESS

BY THE SAME AUTHOR

THEORY OF FUNCTIONS OF A COMPLEX VARIABLE

Second edition. Large Royal 8vo. 21s net

"Dr Forsyth has again undertaken a laborious task and executed it with his usual ability and success. Among the numerous branches of the already enormous, yet still rapidly growing science of Mathematics not the least interesting and not the least important is the Theory of Functions. To this the author devotes over six hundred large size pages; yet, with the end which he has in view, we cannot say there is a page too many." *Athenæum*

"The want of a treatise on this subject has too long caused a serious gap in our mathematical literature; and it may be at once said that Dr Forsyth's book supplies that want so completely that it is not likely to be felt again for a long time to come. Dr Forsyth has aimed at giving a complete introduction to the theory; and it may safely be said that, with his book as a guide, the task of the student who wishes to enable himself to follow its various recent developments will have lost half its difficulty." *Nature*

LECTURES ON THE DIFFERENTIAL GEOMETRY OF CURVES AND SURFACES

Large Royal 8vo. 21s net

"There are two well-known and excellent treatises on the subject, by Darboux and Bianchi respectively; but hitherto there has been nothing corresponding to them in English....The author's unrivalled power of dealing with complicated analysis is admirably illustrated by the section on differential invariants. It would be very difficult to improve upon this....On every one of these points Dr Forsyth writes with complete mastery, and gives a most valuable set of examples.... Dr Forsyth may be congratulated on producing a work of great interest and value, which is perhaps the best treatise that he has ever composed." *Nature*

"Le présent ouvrage vient donc combler une lacune....Les démonstrations de M. Forsyth sont présentées avec beaucoup de clarté et de précision. Selon la tradition, fort bonne, des auteurs anglais, le texte est accompagné de nombreux exemples et de problèmes....Il constitue un guide utile non seulement pour ceux qui veulent s'initier aux méthodes de la Géométrie infinitésimale, mais aussi pour tous ceux qui enseignent cette branche."
Revue Internationale de l'Enseignement Mathématique

THEORY OF DIFFERENTIAL EQUATIONS

Demy 8vo. In four parts

Part I. Exact Equations and Pfaff's Problem. 10s net
Part II. Ordinary Equations, not linear. In two volumes. 20s net
Part III. Ordinary Linear Equations. In one volume. 12s 6d net
Part IV. Partial Differential Equations. In two volumes. 25s net

"We have before us the two concluding volumes of Prof. Forsyth's monumental *Theory of Differential Equations*. The completion of so great a work is too important an event to be left unnoticed. No mathematical treatise on the same scale has appeared since Darboux completed his *Théorie Générale des Surfaces* in 1896. What Darboux' work is to the student of Differential Geometry, Prof. Forsyth's will be to the student of the pure theory of Differential Equations.... The carefulness and lucidity of his exposition remain unimpaired to the last page....If English mathematical research is to-day more vigorous and better directed than for many years past, it is largely to Prof. Forsyth that the credit is due." *Cambridge Review*

Cambridge University Press
Fetter Lane, London: C. F. Clay, Manager

SELECTION FROM THE GENERAL CATALOGUE OF BOOKS
PUBLISHED BY
THE CAMBRIDGE UNIVERSITY PRESS

The Theory of Functions of a Real Variable and the Theory of Fourier's Series. By E. W. Hobson, Sc.D., LL.D., F.R.S., Sadleirian Professor of Pure Mathematics, and Fellow of Christ's College, Cambridge. Royal 8vo. 21s net

The Integration of Functions of a Single Variable. By G. H. Hardy, M.A., F.R.S. Demy 8vo. 2s 6d net. Cambridge Tracts in Mathematics and Mathematical Physics.

A Course of Pure Mathematics. By G. H. Hardy, M.A., F.R.S., Fellow and Lecturer of Trinity College, Cambridge. Demy 8vo. 12s net

Principia Mathematica. By A. N. Whitehead, Sc.D., F.R.S., and the Hon. Bertrand Russell, M.A., F.R.S. Large Royal 8vo. Volume I. 25s net. Volume II. 30s net. Volume III. 21s net

Abel's Theorem and the Allied Theory, including the Theory of the Theta Functions. By H. F. Baker, Sc.D., F.R.S., Lowndean Professor of Astronomy and Geometry in the University of Cambridge. Royal 8vo. 25s net

An Introduction to the Theory of Multiply-Periodic Functions. By H. F. Baker, Sc.D., F.R.S. Royal 8vo. 12s 6d net

Theory of Groups of Finite Order. By W. Burnside, M.A., F.R.S., Honorary Fellow of Pembroke College, Cambridge. Second edition. Demy 8vo. 15s net

An Elementary Course of Infinitesimal Calculus. By Horace Lamb, LL.D., D.Sc., F.R.S., Professor of Mathematics in the Victoria University of Manchester. Second edition. Crown 8vo. 12s

Mathematical and Physical Papers. By Lord Kelvin, LL.D., F.R.S. Collected from different scientific periodicals. In six volumes. Demy 8vo. Vol. I. I—LXXIII, mainly 1841—53. 18s. Vol. II. LXXIV—XCI, mainly April 1853—Feb. 1856. 15s. Vol. III. Elasticity, Heat, Electro-Magnetism. 18s. Vol. IV. Hydrodynamics and general Dynamics. 18s. Vol. V. Thermodynamics, Cosmical and Geological Physics, Molecular and Crystalline Theory, Electrodynamics. 18s. Vol. VI. Voltaic Theory, Radioactivity, Electrions, Navigation and Tides, Miscellaneous. 10s

Mathematical and Physical Papers. By Sir George Gabriel Stokes, Bart., Sc.D., LL.D., Past Pres. R.S., etc. Reprinted from the Original Journals and Transactions, with brief Historical Notes and References. Demy 8vo. Vols. I, II, III, IV and V. 15s each

The Collected Mathematical Papers of James Joseph Sylvester, F.R.S., D.C.L., LL.D., Sc.D. Edited by H. F. Baker, Sc.D., F.R.S. Vol. I. 1837—1853. Vol. II. 1854—1873. Vol. III. 1870—1883. Vol. IV. 1882—1897. Royal 8vo. Buckram. 18s net each

Matrices and Determinoids. University of Calcutta Readership Lectures. By C. E. Cullis, M.A., Ph.D., Professor of Mathematics in the Presidency College, Calcutta. Volume I. Large Royal 8vo. 21s net

The Progress of Physics during 33 years (1875—1908). Four lectures delivered to the University of Calcutta during March 1908. By Arthur Schuster, F.R.S., Ph.D. Demy 8vo. With frontispiece. 3s 6d net

Outlines of the Theory of Electromagnetism. A series of lectures delivered before the Calcutta University. By Gilbert T. Walker, M.A., Sc.D., F.R.S. Demy 8vo. 3s net

Cambridge University Press
Fetter Lane, London: C. F. Clay, Manager